RUSSIAN CENTRAL ASIA
1867 - 1917

RUSSIAN AND

EAST EUROPEAN

STUDIES

RUSSIAN AND EAST EUROPEAN STUDIES

RUSSIAN
CENTRAL ASIA
1867-1917

A STUDY IN COLONIAL RULE

Richard A. Pierce

BERKELEY AND LOS ANGELES
UNIVERSITY OF CALIFORNIA PRESS | 1960

UNIVERSITY OF CALIFORNIA PRESS
BERKELEY AND LOS ANGELES, CALIFORNIA

CAMBRIDGE UNIVERSITY PRESS
LONDON, ENGLAND

PRINTED IN THE UNITED STATES OF AMERICA

PREFACE

RUSSIAN HISTORY still offers many comparatively neglected topics for investigation. One of the most interesting of these is the story of the expansion of Russia's Asian frontiers, and the colonization of the borderlands which have always played such an important role in her development. I hope that this survey of the half-century of Russian rule in Central Asia before 1917 may facilitate other more specialized studies of this area and period, which has much to offer the historian, sociologist, ethnologist, or economist.

Because this subject involves names and terminology in Russian and in a variety of Asiatic tongues, the problem of transliteration has been a thorny one. I have dealt with it by using a modified form of the Library of Congress system of Russian transliteration not only for Russian terms and names but also for those in Turkic and other languages, which I have used in their pre-1917 Russified forms. Although not satisfactory from a philological viewpoint, this method at least assures consistency, and follows the same form used in the bulk of the literature on the subject, which is in Russian. Dates in this work prior to February 1/14, 1918, are exclusively in the Old Style. To convert into New Style, add 12 days before 1900 and 13 days thereafter.

Research can never be self-sufficient, and this work has benefited from many types of aid. I wish to express a debt of gratitude first of all to the late Professor George V. Lantzeff, who aroused my interest in the history of the Russian frontier regions and in the subject of this book. Appreciation for their courtesy and coöperation is due the personnel of the various libraries where

I have sought the materials used in this study, particularly the University of California Library, the Hoover Library and Institute, the Library of Congress, the New York Public Library, the West German State Library at Marburg, the superb library of Russian materials at the University of Helsinki, the Turkological Institute of Istanbul, and others here and abroad. The quest was fruitful in many more ways than I had originally hoped.

A Fulbright fellowship to Germany in 1953–1954 was of great aid in my gathering of material. A grant from the Project for the Study of the History of the CPSU, of Columbia University, in 1956, enabled me to devote additional study to the origins of Bolshevism in Central Asia.

I am likewise grateful to Mr. G. C. Guins, Professor V. P. Timoshenko, Dr. S. N. Shendrikoff, the late General A. N. Vagin, and others who shared some of their personal experiences in Central Asia with me, thus helping me better to visualize and understand the bygone era with which this book is concerned. It is regrettable that those occupied with recent Russian history have made so little use of the valuable but ephemeral material to be found in the oral testimony of members of the Russian emigration.

I am indebted to the family of the late Senator Count K. K. Palen for allowing me to use his unpublished account of his inspection of the Turkestan administration in 1908–1909, the lively style and vivid description of which complements his lengthy and detailed official reports.

My deep appreciation is also extended to Professor V. A. Riasanovsky and Mrs. Olivia Price who painstakingly read the manuscript and made many helpful suggestions. Mr. Joel Walters has contributed much in the final editing of the book. To my wife, Vera Pierce, I am deeply grateful for the aid and encouragement which have meant so much in the completion of this task. To others who contributed to this undertaking in various ways I also extend my sincere thanks. However, the assessment and interpretation is my own and I am responsible for any errors of commission or omission.

RICHARD A. PIERCE

Kingston, Ontario

CONTENTS

Part Four: The Clash of Cultures

Part Five: Imperial Twilight

MAPS

I

THE IDEA that it is unethical for one people to control the destinies of another has come late in the development of the human social conscience, but it is increasing in force. Already this concept has caused the breakup of long-established systems, and has cast the very concepts of "empire," "colonies," and even "trusteeship" into the same disrepute accorded "imperialism," "colonialism," and "exploitation."

A large share of the responsibility for this change in attitudes can be ascribed to the doctrines of national self-determination fostered by the Union of Soviet Socialist Republics. Although most of its more than 175 different nationalities were brought forcibly under control by its forerunner, the Russian Empire, the USSR professes to have solved its nationality problem and has urged its own example upon the rest of the world.

Advocates of the Soviet solution to the nationality problem have given special publicity to the Soviet republics of Central Asia. The romantic past of these lands with their pathos of glory and long decline, their inhabitants' religious ties with the rest of the Moslem world, and their economic and cultural affinity with other underdeveloped regions have made Soviet accounts of the progress of these new states a potent propaganda weapon both at home and abroad.

An accurate appraisal of any historical era requires first of all a clear picture of what has gone before. Soviet accounts always paint the plans and achievements of the new order in Central Asia in glowing colors, but generally portray the old prerevolutionary regime in dismal hues. Until the late 1930's Soviet historical writing described the Russian conquest of Central Asian peoples as having resulted in a "double oppression"—"a national-colonial oppression, based on the bayonets of the Russian-military-feudal imperialism and the feudal oppression of the native upper classes." [1] "Tsarist" policy assertedly delayed these people's cultural growth, denied their children access to Russian schools, halted their national development, and in general led them toward poverty and extinction.

Accordingly, only in revolt was there hope of improving what was clearly an intolerable state of affairs. The uprisings of the toilers, striking back at the system of colonial oppression imposed upon them by "tsarism" and at the feudal oppression of their own upper classes, were therefore portrayed sympathetically as "national-liberation" movements. For many years such interpretations were standard doctrine, making the new regime stand out even more clearly against the darkness of the past. Then, during the late 1930's and World War II, the political wind changed. To promote internal solidarity it was found desirable to modify interpretations detrimental to the Russians. "Tsarism" continued to receive the blame for errors and retarded development, but instead of being an "evil," annexation to Russia was now found to have been a "lesser evil" than conquest by foreign powers or continuation of native rule. [2] In spite of "tsarism," association with Russia was seen to have accelerated bourgeois and capitalist relationships in Central Asia, while the Russian democratic intelligentsia were seen to have extended warm sympathy to the freedom-loving Central Asian peoples. The "common historical fate" of the Russians and the Central Asians thus became ever clearer. [3]

Meanwhile the Russian people, after having been extolled as "the first among the equal members of the Soviet family of peoples," [4] had become by 1945 "the leading people" of the USSR. [5] The "fraternal aid" extended in both past and present to the Central Asians and the other more backward, less numerous peoples of the USSR by the Russians, the "elder brother," began to be stressed. It was pointed out that "along with the tsarist generals and officials came Russian workers, scientists, doctors, agronomists, and teachers, who played a great cultural and revolutionary role in the life of the peoples of Middle Asia." [6] By 1951 Russian annexation was no longer even a "lesser evil" but a positive good.[7]

Uprisings, on the other hand, could no longer be pictured indiscriminately as "national-liberation" movements. Instead, a fine distinction was drawn between uprisings directed against Russians, which were invariably "reactionary," either fostered by feudal elements in native society or instigated and supported by foreign powers, and those directed solely against the native "exploiter" class, and therefore "progressive." [8]

Through the years the efforts of Soviet historians to thread their way through this ideological labyrinth and still keep faith with their personal convictions resulted in recurrent charges of adherence to "bourgeois-nationalism," "great-power chauvinism," "Pan-Islamism," "Pan-Turkism," "Pan-Iranianism," "cosmopolitanism," "nihilism," "the single stream theory," and various other specters of communist demonology, together with a succession of recantations, blasted careers, and revised editions. In February, 1954, apparently to clarify doubtful points and to end confusion in historical writing on Central Asia, an eight-day "scholarly session on the history of the peoples of Middle Asia and Kazakhstan" was held in Tashkent.[9] This conference purported to expose certain "pseudo-scientific nationalistic assertions" regarding patriarchal-feudal relationships among the nomadic peoples, and to reveal the "tremendous progressive significance" of Russian annexation on the development of the Kazakhs and Uzbeks, the "essentially reactionary" nature of the Pan-Islamic and Pan-Turkic movements, and the "revolutionary, popular-liberation nature" of the uprisings of 1916. It called for "a Marxist-Leninist periodization" of the history of the peoples of Central Asia.

Dicta laid down at the Tashkent conclave and confirmed a few weeks later at another conference held in Moscow [10] appear to have brought about comparative harmony. Taking the 1916 uprisings as an example, one later work states that "in the majority of the areas of Uzbekistan the uprising of 1916 was a popular-

liberation movement" (it is to be noted that the earlier term
national-liberation has been supplanted by *popular*-liberation);
another states that "in its fundamental character it was an antitsarist, anti-militarist, anti-feudal, popular-liberation uprising";
while yet another informs us that "in its character it was an anti-
colonial, popular-liberation uprising." [11] As for the Russian "annexation" of Central Asia (a more innocuous term which has supplanted earlier mention of "conquest") [12] we are informed by
various authors that it was "an historically progressive manifestation," "a deeply progressive manifestation," "of great progressive significance," "undoubtedly of progressive significance," "of
enormous progressive significance," and "of extraordinarily important objective-progressive significance." [13]

This, of course, is not history but catechism. With all due regard for the achievements of Soviet scholars in this realm, the
conflicts and inconsistencies in Soviet historiography regarding
Central Asia during the past several decades give ample ground
for doubt both as to the permanence and the validity of the equilibrium currently imposed by party theorists. In short, one may
question whether Soviet sources have given or are likely to give
an adequate picture of this period.

Nor can the gap be filled by the treatment given the Imperial
regime in Central Asia by most Western writers. The greater interest in the contemporary Soviet regime, and the rarity of much
of the older source material has led to neglect of the prerevolutionary period. What mention there has been of the subject in the
West has frequently displayed an afterglow of the prejudice
against the Imperial regime which prevailed abroad before 1917,
or has borrowed Soviet viewpoints.

With such evident defects in our knowledge of Central Asia
during the period in question, further study of it is necessary for
a clearer view of the present. Whatever the nature of this period,
it was the prologue to all that occurred after 1917. This study
will therefore undertake to give an impartial and objective survey
of the main features of the Imperial Russian regime in Central
Asia, and to present sufficient facts to make possible the determi-

nation of the nature and extent of the changes which took place there during that time.

Attention will be directed primarily to the period following the initial Russian conquests in the region, from the establishment of the Governor-Generalship of Turkestan in 1867 until the end of the Imperial regime in 1917. This period, spanning exactly half a century, gave ample scope for the Russian system of colonial rule to be applied and to display its characteristics. Central Asia thereby provided a laboratory, on the threshold of our own time, in which Imperial Russia could use the experience gained in Siberia and other borderlands in the course of several centuries. Better knowledge of what was undertaken there can add to our understanding of the colonial efforts of other powers during the nineteenth and early twentieth centuries. It will also provide background essential for correct evaluation of the aims, claims, and achievements of the present-day Soviet regime.

SOME ESSENTIAL GEOGRAPHIC BACKGROUND

The region which will concern us here is a largely homogeneous geographic, ethnic, and cultural unit extending eastward from the Caspian Sea and the lower Volga to the border of China, and northward from Iran and Afghanistan to Siberia. Today it comprises the Kazakh, Kirgiz, Uzbek, Turkmen, and Tadzhik Soviet Socialist Republics of the USSR.

There is no comprehensive term for this region in western usage. "Turan," "Turkestan," "Russian Turkestan," "Central Asia," and "Middle Asia" all have been used, but with various meanings. "Russian Central Asia" will be used here as the least ambiguous of the several alternatives.[14]

For clarity it will be well to describe this region in terms that will permit comparison with more familiar areas. Covering more than 1,500,000 square miles, it is about half the size of the United States and more than seven times the size of France. It occupies approximately the same range of latitude as the territory from Denmark to Algeria or from the southern tip of Alaska to southern California. Superimposed upon a map of North America it would be nearly equivalent in area to the United States west of the Mississippi, but in latitude a considerable part would lie north of the Canadian border.

Topographically, Russian Central Asia is generally lacking in outstanding features. Only the high mountain ranges of the Tien Shan to the east and the Pamir-Alai systems to the south relieve the prevailing monotony of prairie and desert. Lack of high barriers on the north has exposed the region to many invasions.

Most of Russian Central Asia forms a great basin, once the bed of an inland sea, of which today the Caspian Sea, the Aral Sea, Lake Balkhash, and many smaller lakes are all that remain. Most of the rivers of the region are fed by melting snow from the mountains fringing on the basin on the southeast. Many combine to make up the great Amu-Daria and Syr-Daria (the ancient Oxus and Jaxartes rivers of Alexander of Macedon's time). These emerge from the mountains and make their way across the desert plains until, wide and shallow and laden with yellow-brown sediment, they discharge into the Aral Sea. The Ili and several smaller streams flow into Lake Balkhash. Others, among them the Chu, the Talass, the Zeravshan, the Murgab, and the Tedzhen, are sucked dry by the hot sun or drained by irrigation and eventually dwindle and disappear into desert sands. This lack of outlets to the open seas has always hindered access of the Central Asiatic peoples to other lands.

Dry river beds throughout Central Asia testify to a moister climate and greater plant cover long ago. The snow fields and glaciers in the Tien Shan and the Pamirs, vestiges of the last ice age, have gradually diminished, with a consequent decrease in the amount of water supplied to rivers and lakes. Geographers still dispute whether the region is in the process of further desiccation, or whether the moisture supply has reached some sort of equilibrium subject only to cyclic variations. Only in the north is water relatively more abundant. There in the steppe, or prairie grasslands, rise the Tobol and the Irtysh, but these then flow toward the Arctic as part of the mighty Siberian river system. The grasslands of the north change into semidesert toward the south, and that in turn becomes desert, relieved occasionally by bands of vegetation in the river valleys. The greatest part of Russian Central Asia is desert. Even under modern conditions less than 3 per cent of the total land surface is arable.

Climatically, the region is governed by the continental conditions of the great Eurasian land mass of which it is a part. The lack of either natural barriers or the modifying effect of moisture expose it to the full extremes of summer and winter temperatures.

During the long winter, cold air from Siberia flows down unimpeded, and winters are cold and long. In the northernmost steppes, temperatures during January, the coldest month, may drop to as low as —60° Fahrenheit. In the semidesert region somewhat farther south, winter temperatures may drop to —40° F. in the west, and to —57° F. in the east. Strong northeast winds blow much of the time, often attaining blizzard force. Near large bodies of water the weather is somewhat warmer, though not significantly so. In the Volga delta, on the northeastern border of this region, the temperature has fallen to as low as —22° F., and the river has been frozen there for as long as 112 days.[15] In the delta of the Amu-Daria, —14° F. has been recorded.[16] Despite the cold, there is relatively little snow except where the wind forms drifts. There may be about twenty-five inches of snow in the north and between seven and eight inches in the semidesert region.

The spring is very short. Within a few days winter cold may be transformed to summer heat. During the summer, dry winds as hot as 104° F. sweep across the northern steppes toward the Volga.[17] In the desert regions to the south still higher temperatures prevail. At Kazalinsk, near the mouth of the Syr-Daria, the mean July temperature is 79° F., at Tashkent it is 82° F., and at Bairam-Ali, in the Kara-Kum desert south of the Amu-Daria, it is about 86° F. The maximum yet recorded at Kazalinsk was 108° F., and at Bairam-Ali, 114° F. July temperatures at Termez, on the Amu-Daria southeast of Bukhara, have reached the highest level recorded in Central Asia, 122° F.[18] The sun-drenched surface of the soil is, of course, even hotter than the atmosphere. At Repetek, in the Kara-Kum desert, a sand temperature of 174° F. was once recorded in July.[19] Throughout Russian Central Asia, precipitation is low and erratic, and has little modifying influence upon the climate.

Such conditions have discouraged most forms of plant and animal life. Plant growth is sparse except in the grasslands where the northern steppes border on Siberia, in the forests and meadows on the mountain slopes, and in the river valleys. The desert has only a meager covering of hardy perennials, such as sagebrush and scrub "forests" of saxaul. These are nevertheless of utmost importance in holding down the soil. The severe climate and the sharp seasonal variations in food and water supply have encouraged only the hardier breeds of camels, sheep, cattle, and other animal species.

The various peoples dwelling in the steppe and desert lands have practiced a pastoral economy since ancient times, each year moving with their flocks between lowland and highland, following the grass and the seasons. Dwellers in the river valleys learned to practice agriculture long before the Christian era. In order to exploit the fertile desert soil they developed or borrowed irrigation techniques. In the steppes, life went on almost unchanged from one century to another, but in the oases the requirements of more complex living conditions brought about a higher level of culture. The food supply assured by cultivation permitted a greater concentration of population than in the surrounding steppes. The tendency toward decentralization caused by the distances separating the scattered oases was overcome by the need for more elaborate centralized social organizations to provide for the construction of irrigation works, the apportionment of water, and defense against invasion.[20] Cities arose, states were formed, and the land became a tempting prize for conquerors.

THE ETHNIC PATTERN

The predominantly level terrain of Russian Central Asia has facilitated many invasions which have left as their heritage a complex mixture of races, languages, and cultures. Through many centuries the original predominantly Iranian stock in the region has been displaced by or has merged with various invading groups. Greeks (under Alexander), Persians, Arabs, various Turkic tribes, and the Mongols have, like the waters of the Central Asian rivers, flowed into the region, found no outlet, and remained. The region's inhabitants have had the enduring problem of absorbing these successive waves of invaders, and of adopting or rejecting their cultural innovations.

During the 1860's, at the outset of the period to be discussed here, the most numerous of the nomadic peoples of the region were the Kazakhs. Prior to the Russian census of 1897 there are no reliable figures, but it may be assumed that the total Kazakh population of 1867 was roughly 2,500,000.[21]

Pastoral nomads with a patriarchal form of society, the Kazakhs occupied the steppe region from Siberia as far south as the Syr-Daria. The Kazakhs are a Turkic people with an admixture of Mongoloid blood. Their ancestors were among the many Turkish tribes who were conquered by and who later became a predominant part of the hordes of Genghis Khan. When the Mongol Empire broke up in the fifteenth century, the stragglers in the steppe region formed new groupings, and came to be known as "Kazakhs," from a Turkic term meaning "fugitives" or "brigands."

Study of this region is complicated by the fact that the Kazakhs were long known to the Russians as "Kirgiz," actually the name of another nomad group. This originally came about through efforts to avoid confusion with the "Cossacks," people of predominately Slavic blood who settled on Russia's southern frontiers and in Siberia from approximately the fifteenth century. Both "Cossack" and "Kazakh" came from the same Turkish word, and had identical spelling in prerevolutionary Russia. To avoid further confusion, since the 1920's the mistermed "Kirgiz" have again been accorded their rightful name, but with a slight alteration in spelling and pronunciation ("Kazak" became "Kazakh"). The term "Kazakh" will be used here except where the original term of "Kirgiz" occurs in quoted material.

Like most of the natives of Central Asia the Kazakhs were Moslems of the Sunnite sect. However because of their way of life they were lax in many observances. They had no mosques, and their women were not secluded or veiled. Their worship included many survivals of their earlier shamanist religion, and

instead of governing themselves by the Shariat, Moslem religious
law, they followed an elaborate system of customary law, the
adat, with a judicial procedure which included testimony under
oath, a system of fines for wrongdoing, and group responsibility
for the expiation of the guilty party's deed. In case of failure to
obtain satisfaction the aggrieved party was entitled to seize compensation in kind. Retaliatory raids grew into blood feuds which
kept the steppe in constant turmoil.

The true Kirgiz, closely related to the Kazakhs in language,
ethnic composition, social organization, and economy, occupied
the mountain districts of the Ala-Tau and the vicinity of the great
fresh-water lake, Issyk-Kul. During the late 1860's the Kirgiz
probably numbered about 300,000. Before 1917 they were known
to the Russians as the "Kara-Kirgiz" or "Black" Kirgiz, to distinguish them from the mistermed Kazakhs.

The Turkmen, also numbering about 300,000 at the time of the
Russian conquest, inhabited the desert steppe region between the
Syr-Daria and the Caspian Sea. Like the Kazakhs and Kirgiz their
organization was primarily by family and clan. Most of the Turkmen carried on a pastoral economy, but some who were settled
in the Merv and Tedzhen oases also practiced agriculture.

The Uzbeks, the principal part of the settled population of
Russian Central Asia, probably amounted to about 3,500,000 in
the 1860's. They formed the khanates of Khiva and Kokand, and
the emirate of Bukhara. They were derived from an admixture of
the old Iranian settled population of the region, located mainly
in the valleys of the upper Syr-Daria (the district known as
Fergana in Alexander's time), the Zeravshan, and the Amu-Daria,
with various invading nomads of Turkic and Mongoloid stock.
The latest of such invaders, the Uzbeks, conquered the region in
the fifteenth century, settled, and mingled with the subjugated
population. Eventually they were to a large degree absorbed, but
their name was attached to the indigenous inhabitants of the
region. Formerly the older town-dwelling population of this region, supposedly closer to the Iranian stock, were termed "Sarts,"
while the villagers, supposedly more of whom were descendants
of the nomads, were called Uzbeks. Since 1917, however, the term

"Sart" has been considered derogatory, and townsmen and peasants alike have been called Uzbeks. The term Uzbek will be used here in the modern sense. The original term "Sart" will be used only when it occurs in quotations.

The Tadzhiks, a surviving Iranian group, occupied the valleys and mountain districts of the Pamir region. During the Russian conquest, about 100,000 of these came under Russian control and an approximately equal number remained within the emirate of Bukhara.

Besides these groups there were also a number of smaller ethnic groups in Russian Central Asia. The Turkic Kara-Kalpaks, totaling about 100,000 in the 1860's, inhabited the lower Amu-Daria region and the area immediately west of the Aral Sea. Late arrivals in the region were the Turkic Taranchi and the Chinese Moslem Dungans. Both groups, the Taranchi numbering about 50,000 and the Dungans about 15,000, migrated into Russian territory in the 1860's during disorders in western China (Chinese Turkestan). They settled in the mountains and oases south of Lake Balkhash. The Taranchi were a Moslem Turkic people descended from Kashgarians resettled in Kuldzha by the Chinese in the eighteenth century after the virtual extermination of the Dzhungars, a Mongol group who had inhabited that region. The Dungans were Chinese Moslems brought into the region by the Chinese government at the same time.[22] In addition, Persians, Arabs, Jews, Tatars, Indians, and members of other smaller groups were scattered throughout Central Asia.

BACKGROUND FOR CONQUEST

As late as the middle of the nineteenth century most of the peoples of Central Asia still followed their ancient living patterns, scarcely affected by modern influences. The Kazakhs, Kirgiz, Turkmen, and Kara-Kalpaks carried on their annual nomadic cycles, their raids, and their blood feuds. Family loyalties remained their main concern, and the clan their highest effective form of organization. The three so-called hordes of the Kazakhs (the Kazakh word is *orda* or *zhuz*) and the vague tribal forms of the Turkmen had only nominal significance. Some of the nomads

had come under the shadowy suzerainty of powerful neighbors—
Russia, China, the Central Asiatic khanates, or Persia—but these
exerted little influence except for occasional exaction of tribute.
Save for the introduced use of firearms, the way of life of the
nomads was still much the same as that of their ancestors a thousand years before.

The settled peoples of Central Asia had a more complex social
structure than the nomads, but they too remained backward. Inhabitants of the three main states of Khiva, Bukhara, and Kokand
and their dependencies carried on irrigated agriculture, handicrafts, and trade as in ancient times. Their great days, however,
were long past. Bactria and Fergana, Khoresm, and the empire
of Timur had risen, held their brief sway, and vanished, leaving
dead cities and empty canals to be covered by the desert sands,
or crumbling monuments which dwarfed the rude structures of
later times. The glories of the time when Central Asia was a highway for East-West trade and a center of wealth and civilization
lived on only in tradition, perhaps all the brighter in the telling
because of the oriental imagination. "Golden" Samarkand, Bukhara "the noble," and Merv "the Queen of the World" came
down to modern times as conglomerations of low flat-roofed
houses of mud and cobbles, clustered around the ruins of better
days.

Political power in the Central Asian states was of a feudal
nature similar to that of medieval Europe. Hereditary rulers had
nominal control, but the provincial beks (governors) were practically independent and carried on constant wars against their
neighbors or their sovereigns. The government was tyrannical and
oppressive and meted out cruel punishments. The clergy dominated thought, and illiteracy and superstition were widespread.

The economy of the settled population was based on agriculture, chiefly the growing of grain. Most of the land was worked
by peasants on shares, and many of the peasants were so heavily
in debt that they were in virtual serfdom. Unbelievers were en-
slaved.[23] Trade was poorly developed and sapped by heavy taxes.
Caravans were prey to the nomads. Almost constant warfare between the khanates or the bekdoms placed a heavy burden on

the inhabitants. Irrigation systems could not be repaired or expanded, flocks were driven off, and sown areas varied in extent depending on the ability of the inhabitants to defend them. Thus, though Central Asia had achieved a high level of prosperity in earlier times, by the middle of the nineteenth century the region was in a state of decay, isolated from the modern world, its population static, and its economy depressed. It was ripe for change, which in the nineteenth century usually came to backward lands through conquest by stronger, more advanced neighbors.

PART ONE

Conquest and Administration

II

THE RUSSIAN MOVEMENT into Central Asia in the nineteenth century was a late phase in an expansion already in progress over several centuries. The uniting of the Russian lands and the throwing off of the Mongol yoke were only the prelude to a succession of moves which gave Russia dominion over a number of other peoples. The Central Asian steppes and deserts, long a highway for westerly movements of Asiatic peoples, now became the scene of a reverse movement as Russia extended her influence toward the southeast.

The Russian advance in this region was begun for many reasons. Along the southern border of Siberia from the Urals to the Altai the Kazakhs had long been a source of difficulty. Turbulent by nature and impatient of control or restriction by any central authority, they were always ready to plunder villages, drive off livestock, and sell unlucky captives into slavery in Khiva, Bukhara, and other states to the south. They also hindered the development of trade, frequently raiding the caravans which essayed the long journey between Russia and the Central Asian khanates. The peasants and Cossack settlers along the frontier as well as native and Russian traders constantly asked the government for redress and protection against such depredations.

Another reason for the Russian advances was that the Kazakhs occupied rich lands, as attractive for Russian settlement as the lands of the Indians had been for settlers in the Americas. And beyond the Kazakh Steppe lay the fabled wealth of Turkestan,

Persia, and India, offering a vision of trade which had excited imaginations in Russia from early times.

By the early nineteenth century Russian statesmen and military men had also begun to feel concern regarding British commercial and political penetration in Central Asia. Their calls for decisive action to guarantee Russian trade and to raise Russian prestige among the Asian peoples, coupled with a tendency to use the region as a diplomatic lever by threatening to advance toward India in order to lessen British opposition to Russia at the Turkish Straits, caused alarm in Britain which clouded relations between the two empires for a century. Thus impelled by provocations, temptations, and apprehensions acceptable enough before a world opinion still uninhibited by questions of aggression or disregard for sovereign rights, Russia joined the rivalry for colonial acquisitions which dominated nineteenth century international politics.

The Kazakhs, numerous but disunited, courageous but ill-armed, were no match for their more advanced foes. Using a bag of tricks developed through long experience in border warfare—negotiation, bribery, blandishment, and patronage of the weak and subversion of the strong—the Russians moved ahead to new positions, set up defense lines and consolidated gains during times when they were occupied elsewhere, then moved on again when they were ready. It is no wonder that the succession of Russian acquisitions in this region appeared to some foreign observers as the result of a long-standing Grand Design.

THE ENVELOPMENT OF THE KAZAKH STEPPE

Toward the middle of the nineteenth century the process of expansion into the steppe moved toward a climax. General V. A. Perovskii's disastrous winter march against the khanate of Khiva in 1839, undertaken to settle scores with that slave-trading state and to counter the extension of British influence into Afghanistan, showed the need for advance bases. During the late 1840's, small forts were established in the steppe south of Orenburg—Turgai and Irgiz in 1845, and Raimsk, on the Aral Sea, in 1847. Insignificant in themselves, they were enough to establish control over the Kazakhs in the vicinity and to provide places to store supplies for further operations.

During the 1850's a double advance began which was eventually to take the form of a great pincer movement. On the west, Russian forces from Orenburg, led by Perovskii, made their way from Raimsk 450 miles up the Syr-Daria to take the Kokandian fort of Ak-Mechet (later Perovsk, and now Kzyl-Orda) in 1853. Soon other forts were established and two steamships, assembled on the spot after being brought from Europe, plied the river to supply them. Kokandian forces sent to oust the intruders were repulsed. Simultaneously with the advance from Orenburg came an advance of Russian forces from Semipalatinsk to the northeast. Between 1850 and 1854 the lands south of the Ili River were occupied. In 1854 the town of Vernyi (now Alma-Ata) was founded.

In 1854 the Russian government decided to connect these two southerly extensions of its power. The Crimean War (1854–1856) delayed conclusive action for a decade, but in 1864 the operation was finally begun. On May 1, 1864, Colonel M. G. Cherniaev set out from Vernyi with 2,600 men, and Colonel N. A. Verevkin came from Perovsk with a force of 1,600 to close the pincers. On June 4 Cherniaev's force stormed the important town of Aulie-Ata (now Dzhambul), and won it at a cost of only 3 men wounded, whereas the native garrison of about 1,500 men suffered 307 killed and 390 wounded. Superior discipline and modern arms prevailed with telling force against the medieval-style opposition.[1]

Verevkin had similar success. On June 12 he took the city of Turkestan (or Azret) with a loss of five men killed and twenty-four wounded. The two forces now joined under the command of Cherniaev to take Chimkent, and after a four-day siege stormed the citadel on September 22, 1864. Most of the native garrison of 10,000 men fled; the Russians lost two killed and seventeen wounded.[2] This action closed the gap between the two prongs of the advance, enclosing the Kazakh Steppe with a line of Russian forts.

For the invaders these operations could have been scarcely

more than tactical exercises. Lances, ancient flintlocks, and crude cannon were no match for the tight formations of the Russians, who were trained to stand in the open field under fire and mow down the enemy with a succession of volleys or to shatter his fortifications with well-aimed artillery and rocket fire until he could be overwhelmed with the enthusiastic *"Ura!"* and the cold steel of a bayonet charge. Had there been a Genghis Khan or a Timur to weld the Central Asians together into a disciplined host the story might have been different, but no such leader appeared.

The Russian government now sought to allay the alarm expressed by other powers, particularly England, over its advance. On November 21, 1864, Prince A. M. Gorchakov, the foreign minister, addressed to the powers his well-known circular note in which he justified the succession of conquests by citing Russia's need to protect her borders against lawless tribesmen. He stated the dilemma facing all great powers—the United States in America, France in Algeria, the Dutch in Indonesia, and England in India—of advancing until they could establish secure frontiers. He outlined the need for closing the gap between the two extensions of the Russian frontier line, and the need for the final extension to be based on fertile land suitable for colonization in order to counter strong states such as Kokand. But here, he said:

. . . we must halt, because on the one hand, any further extension of our rule meeting henceforth, not with unstable communities, like independent nomad tribes, but with more regularly constituted states, would exact considerable efforts and would draw us from annexation to annexation into infinite complications; while, on the other hand, having henceforth for neighbors such states, notwithstanding their backward condition and the instability of their political action, we can nevertheless be assured that to the common advantage regular relations will one day be substituted for the disorders which have hitherto paralysed the progress of those countries.[3]

Gorchakov was probably sincere, but he misjudged the khanates' capacity for stability and the extent to which the Russian government would be able to control its generals in the field. Cherniaev, now a major general, on September 27 pushed on southward to Tashkent, situated on the Chirchik River, a tributary of the Syr-Daria. This city, part of the khanate of Kokand, had nearly 100,000 inhabitants. Second in size only to the city of Kokand itself, it seemed well worth the taking. However, Cherniaev's small force of 1,500 proved unequal to the task. The walls of the city, surrounding it for twenty-four versts (about sixteen miles) kept off the assailants, and the Russian assault on October 4, 1864, was so vigorously repelled that after losing eighteen killed and sixty wounded Cherniaev was forced to order a retreat to Chimkent.

However, as Gorchakov had stated in his circular, "retreat is taken for weakness; the Asiatic peoples respect nothing but visible and palpable force. . . ." Encouraged by the Russian misadventure, a Kokandian force of at least 10,000 bypassed Chimkent and on December 4 attacked the Russian-held city of Turkestan. But even with an overwhelming numerical advantage, the natives again showed their military ineffectiveness. Trapping a small force of 112 Cossacks outside of the city, they spent 3 days in a vain attempt to dispose of them. The Cossacks, under *Esaul* (Captain) V. R. Serov, held the Kokandians off until the third day. Then, having lost fifty-seven of their number, and with no more food and water, the survivors staked all on a desperate charge through the enemy host and managed to reach their comrades within the city. When the natives learned of the approach of a Russian force to relieve the besieged, they abandoned further efforts and retired.[4]

The Russian government—if not its leaders in the field—now considered it advisable to pause and consolidate what had been won. The main centers for Russian administration in Central Asia had until then been farther north. The western part of the Kazakh Steppe, which had been organized in 1859 into the oblast (province) of the Orenburg Kirgiz, was administered from Orenburg, at the southern tip of the Urals. The eastern part of the steppe included the oblast of the Siberian Kirgiz (organized in 1854), administered from Omsk, and the oblast of Semipalatinsk (organized in 1854), administered from the city of Semipalatinsk on the Irtysh River. The oblast of Semipalatinsk was augmented in 1860 by Russian acquisition from China of the mountainous Trans-Naryn region south of Issyk-Kul. In addition to these units, the new territory extending from the Aral Sea to Issyk-Kul was organized early in 1865 as the oblast of Turkestan, to be under a military governor who would be in charge of both military and civil affairs and responsible to the governor-general of Orenburg. Cherniaev, now a general, was appointed to the post.

During the months that followed Cherniaev gained a reputation for pursuing a wise policy of noninterference in native affairs. Life in the conquered territory went on nearly as before, except that the tsar had replaced the khan of Kokand as the supreme authority and the region was governed by a Russian military governor instead of a native bek.[5] However, this tolerant rule apparently stemmed less from policy than from Cherniaev's preoccupation with further military activity. The temptation to go on to new conquests and additional glory, seeking decorations and promotions, was strong. The dilemma of the conqueror outlined by Gorchakov, wherein each successive advance only brought the need of further advances to secure what had already been taken, provided sufficient excuse for action.

THE HUMBLING OF BUKHARA

An excuse for a further Russian advance soon came in the person of a new enemy, arisen to take the place of the chastened khan of Kokand. The emir of Bukhara, Seid Muzaffar Eddin, seeking to forestall the intrusion of a powerful new force into Central Asian politics, and seeing his chance to profit from the weakness of a rival, prepared to occupy some Kokandian territory. Hearing rumors of a concentration of Bukharan forces which might indicate a plan to seize Tashkent, only fifteen miles from Russian-held territory, Cherniaev hastened to get there first. On April 29, 1865, he defeated a force of 7,000 Kokandians at Fort Niaz-bek which, located near the Chirchik River, was the key to the irrigation system of Tashkent. After taking this stronghold at a cost of only seven men wounded, Cherniaev then continued his advance.[6] In a battle before Tashkent on May 9, 1865, the Kokandian general, Alim Kul, was mortally wounded in defense of the city and about 300 of his followers were slain. The Russian force had ten men wounded.[7]

Some of the inhabitants of Tashkent now requested the emir of Bukhara to come to their aid and to take the city under his protection. On June 9 a small Bukharan force entered the city and took control of its defense. Unwilling to permit this development, Cherniaev mopped up the remaining resistance in the vicinity and prepared to attack the city. The taking of Tashkent would belie the Russian government's protestations that it intended to go no farther. Cherniaev accordingly was sent instructions not to take the city. By this time, however, he was too deeply enmeshed in the affair. Retreat would have meant a serious loss both of Russian prestige and of an opportunity for personal glory. Sensing the content of the instructions, Cherniaev left them unopened and with only 1,950 men and 12 guns against 30,000 natives with 63 guns began the attack.

The assault on the city walls began on June 14, 1865. Entry was gained through a point which reconnaissance had determined to be weakest. The defenders fought furiously but ineffectually; a series of Russian feints had led the native commanders to disperse their forces around the entire vast circumference of the walls, leaving few to deal with a thrust in any one spot. The citadel was taken by storm, and the rest of the city fell after street fighting. By June 17 it was all over. The native garrison fled or melted into the mass of the inhabitants. The native losses were heavy, whereas the Russians lost only twenty-five killed and eighty-nine wounded.[8]

The emir of Bukhara now chose to enter the contest, but instead of attacking the Russians he took advantage of the weakness of his traditional rival and marched on the khanate of Kokand. The demoralized Kokandians gave little resistance, and the emir occupied the main cities of Khodzhent and Kokand. Khudoiar Khan, the ruler of Kokand, acknowledged the sovereignty of the emir over his erstwhile domain and was appointed by the emir as his viceroy.

All through the autumn of 1865 relations between the emir of Bukhara and the Russians remained critical. Negotiations proved fruitless. Cherniaev ordered the arrest of Bukharan merchants on Russian soil, and the Bukharans detained a Russian embassy.

After demanding the return of the envoys and an end to the emir's artful vacillation, Cherniaev again resorted to arms. Undertaking a winter campaign, in January, 1866, he led his troops against Dzhizak, a Bukharan fortress and trading center northeast of Samarkand. Dzhizak was the key to power over the entire Zeravshan River valley, in which lay the chief population centers of the emirate. This move was a blunder, however. The severe weather conditions exhausted his troops and forced him to order a retreat in February without reaching his objective.

This abortive attempt would have been enough to unseat most commanders, but even before the news reached St. Petersburg Cherniaev's spectacular but unpredictable leadership had aroused disapproval, and on February 8, 1866, an order was issued for his recall. He received the news from his successor, General D. I. Romanovskii, upon the latter's arrival to take over command. Cherniaev returned to St. Petersburg ostensibly in disgrace and was retired on a meager pension, but soon his salary was restored,[9] he received honors and decorations, and his policies in Central Asia were continued.

Romanovskii waited until the following spring and then continued Cherniaev's program by again invading Bukhara. On May 8, 1866, at Irdzhar, on the road to Samarkand, Romanovskii led a force of 3,600 men against an army of the emir comprising about 5,000 regular Bukharan troops and 35,000 Kazakhs. The Bukharans had the advantage of entrenched positions, but as usual were incapable of defending themselves. The Russians routed them with a loss of only 1 killed and 11 wounded; the natives left over 1,000 on the battlefield.[10] Instead of moving on to Samarkand, Romanovskii then determined to drive a wedge between Kokand and Bukhara, and moved up the Syr-Daria into Kokandian territory. On May 14 the Kokandian fort of Nau fell without resistance. On May 24 the city of Khodzhent, after artillery bombardment, was taken by storm. In this action the Russians lost 5 killed, 6 missing, and 122 wounded. The Kokandian defenders lost 2,500 in killed alone.[11]

This changed the situation completely. Convinced of the futility of further resistance, Khudoiar Khan came to terms. He acknowledged himself a vassal of the tsar, agreed to the Russian conquests, consented to let Russians trade throughout his territories, and undertook the payment of an indemnity which would provide reimbursement for the expense involved in his own defeat.[12]

There were indications that the emir of Bukhara was also disposed to make peace, but he took no definite steps. The Russian government, on the other hand, was determined to put the emir in a position which would leave no room for doubt as to his future conduct. The Amu-Daria, not the Syr, was now seen as the logical southern boundary of Russian authority. The domination of Bukhara was seen as a necessity to forestall any English advance, to secure what had already been won, and to develop Russian trade in neighboring regions of Central Asia. Plans were again put forth for the seizure of Dzhizak. There was no middle way, asserted one of the officers of the General Staff in a memorandum to General Romanovskii in July, 1866; it was necessary ". . . either to take possession of the Central Asiatic khanates, or else to put the khans in such a position that they would not dare to take a step without the agreement of Russia. . . ."[13]

In August, 1866, General N. A. Kryzhanovskii, the governor-general of Orenburg, arrived in Turkestan, assumed command, and prepared a new campaign. He led his troops first against the fortress of Ura-Tiube, which he captured on October 2, 1866. The Russians lost 17 killed and had 103 wounded. The natives lost at least 2,000 killed.[14]

A few days later, on October 18, 1866, Kryzhanovskii took Dzhizak. There the struggle caused Russian casualties of 6 killed and 92 wounded, while the natives lost at least 6,000 killed, and 2,000 taken prisoner.[15] On November 1, 1866, having distinguished himself and achieved the desired objectives, Kryzhanovskii returned to Orenburg.

There was now a lull until the spring of 1867, when the Russian leaders again yielded to the temptation to go on. The water supply of Dzhizak was controlled by the Bukharan fort of Iany-Kurgan, so on May 25, 1867, Lieutenant Colonel A. K. Abramov took this too. In Russia, in the meantime, major changes in administration and organization of the conquered territories were in preparation. On July 11, 1867, an Imperial decree declared the formation of a new unit, the Governor-Generalship of Turkestan. General K. P. Von Kaufman, previously governor-general of the Northwest Region, a part of Russia's share of Poland, was appointed to the new post.

Von Kaufman arrived in Tashkent early in November, 1867. He engaged at once in the complicated task of organizing the administration along lines desired in St. Petersburg, and at the same time endeavored to bring the emir of Bukhara to terms. The emir, however, though with seemingly no alternative against his powerful foe, balked at capitulation. He played for time by promising to negotiate, while his forces raided Iany-Kurgan, Dzhizak, and other Russian positions.

In April, 1868, Von Kaufman received news that the emir was gathering his forces at Samarkand with the evident intention of invading Russian-held territory. Von Kaufman thereupon marched into Bukharan territory, routed the Bukharans, and on May 2 took Samarkand. The Russian losses in the operation were two killed and thirty-one wounded. Leaving a garrison of 700 men behind in Samarkand under Major Shtempel, Von Kaufman then led 3,500 men in search of the main Bukharan force, along the way taking the towns of Urgut (May 14) and Katta-Kurgan (May 18). Soon afterward, on June 2, Von Kaufman's army came to grips with the Bukharans on the Zerbulak heights, near Katta-Kurgan in the decisive battle of the campaign. The Bukharans, although occupying excellent positions with over 6,000 infantry, 15,000 cavalry, and 14 light cannon, were put to flight with heavy losses. The Russians suffered only 38 wounded.[16]

In the meantime on June 1, 1868, the garrison left behind in the citadel at Samarkand was attacked by 15,000 of the city's inhabitants, by a Kazakh–Bukharan force of 15,000, and by up to 25,000 men from the nearby Bukharan mountain province of Shakhrisiabs. Faced by such overwhelming odds, the 700 Russians in the garrison had a difficult time. During the ensuing siege, 49 of the defenders were killed and 172 wounded, provisions and ammunition ran short, and the garrison was nearly exhausted when Von Kaufman's relieving army arrived a week later, on June 8.[17]

The defeat at Zerbulak finally obliged the emir of Bukhara to submit to the Russians on their terms. In a treaty concluded on June 18, 1868, Bukhara ceded Samarkand, Katta-Kurgan, and adjacent territory to Russia and agreed to pay an indemnity. As in the case of Kokand, Russian subjects were accorded free access to Bukhara and trade within its boundaries, while only an insignificant tax was to be levied on imported Russian goods.

The emir asked for permission to abdicate and make a pilgrimage to Mecca, but Russian policy opposed this. It was deemed important for Russia to have in Bukhara a ruler who had learned to recognize Russian supremacy and who had lost all taste for further hostilities. The Russians therefore not only confirmed the emir as ruler in Bukhara, but even assisted him in the suppression of an uprising against his authority led by his eldest son. Abramov, by now a major general, led a force from Katta-Kurgan to meet the rebels, and defeated them at Karshi on October 21–23, 1868. Though nominally independent the emir was thereafter an obedient vassal of Russia, which gained the advantage of having the populous emirate completely under her control, without the need of spending money on its policing and administration, and also avoided the danger, at that time acute, of further arousing England by such a major annexation in the direction of India.

The lands taken from the emirate of Bukhara, including Samarkand, were formed on June 27, 1868, into the Zeravshan *okrug* (district), over which Abramov was appointed *nachal'nik* (commandant). The district was occupied at first only on a temporary basis; the final decision as to its annexation came only several years later.[18]

The pacification of the region was not completed until 1870. The beks of the two Bukharan mountain provinces of Shakhrisiabs and Kitab had aided in the rebellion in Bukhara in October, 1868, and had given the fugitive rebels shelter. In August, 1870, Abramov led his troops into the mountain country on a punitive expedition. In spite of difficult terrain they took the towns of Shakhr and Kitab, drove out the rebel beks, Dzhura-Bek and Baba-Bek, and invited the emir to resume the government of this portion of his territory.[19]

THE OCCUPATION OF KULDZHA

In 1871 further military action brought yet another substantial addition to Russia's Central Asian realm, this time east of Lake Balkhash. Previously, in 1862 a rebellion had broken out in Dzhungaria and spread to the Ili valley, where in 1864 the Dungans and Taranchi united to throw off Chinese rule. The Russian consulate in Kuldzha and a Russian factory in Chuguchak were destroyed, commerce ceased, refugees poured into the Russian territory of Semirechie, and there were continual disturbances on the frontier. The rebels then quarreled between themselves. Taranchi victory in the contest in 1867 forced additional thousands of Dungans to cross the Russian frontier.

In the meantime Yakub Beg, a Kokandian general who had led the defense of Ak-Mechet on the lower Syr-Daria against Perovskii in 1853, had raised a rebellion in Kashgar, ousted the Chinese, and carved out a khanate for himself (1867). This strong new native state threatened to upset the balance of power in Central Asia. Yakub Beg's friendly relations with England caused the Russians to fear that if he should spread his rule to Dzhungaria he might menace the adjoining oblast of Semirechie. This might also enable a major extension of British influence which could outflank Russian positions and ultimately even threaten the communication lines between European Russia and Siberia. In June, 1871, Von Kaufman therefore used his powers for independent action and ordered Major General Kolpakovskii, the military governor of Semirechie oblast, to avert any move of forces hostile to Russia by occupying the upper Ili valley, though this was nominally Chinese territory.[20]

The occupation of the Ili province, as it was known to the Chinese, or the Kuldzha district, as it became known to the Russians from the name of its chief city, was treated by Russia as a purely temporary affair as far as international opinion was concerned. The Chinese were assured that the occupation would last only until they could regain control over the rebel provinces in Kashgar and the rest of Dzhungaria. The Russians appear to have assumed that this would never occur, but in 1877 Yakub Beg was killed in battle with the Chinese, his realm crumbled, and the Chinese regained mastery over the region. After considerable diplomatic parleying, in which the evacuation of Kuldzha was employed as a useful lever to get concessions elsewhere, Russia finally relinquished control in 1883.

THE KHIVAN CAMPAIGN

The capitulation of Bukhara and Kokand left only the khanate of Khiva to be reckoned with of the three large Central Asian states which had opposed Russia's extension of her southern frontier. Khiva had a long history of affronts to Russia. Encouragement of Kazakhs in their robberies of caravans, exaction of tribute from natives who were nominally Russian subjects, incitement of the Kazakhs to revolt, harboring of fugitive Kazakh rebels, and the long-standing practice of buying and enslaving captive Russian subjects—all these made Khiva an outlaw state.

Immediately after the formation of the Governor-Generalship of Turkestan, Von Kaufman proposed to the khan of Khiva that the two states should live in peace and friendship on condition that all Russian subjects imprisoned in Khiva be liberated, that the Khivans cease interference in the affairs of Kazakhs living within the Russian border, and that commercial treaties be negotiated. These proposals only met with contemptuous replies from the Khivan officials and with further provocations. Accordingly, in 1870 Von Kaufman reported to St. Petersburg the necessity of military action and received permission to undertake it.

Russian public opinion required little persuasion as to the need for stronger measures. The memory of earlier defeats rankled—three half-legendary expeditions of the Ural Cossacks against Khiva in the early seventeenth century had been wiped out almost to a man; and the 3,500-man expedition of Prince Bekovich-Cherkasskii, though it had reached Khiva in 1717, had been massacred through treachery. Still more vividly in mind was the expedition of General Perovskii in 1839, which had started out from Orenburg with 5,000 men and a vast amount of supplies and transport, only to be beaten down by winter cold, so that scarcely a third of the original number made their way back. In view of the successes of Russia elsewhere in Central Asia, it was almost a patriotic duty to dispose at last of the legend of invulnerability which had grown up around Khiva.

There were also other, less evident, reasons that helped to bring about the Khivan expedition. In the judgment of one contemporary foreign observer, a popular war could serve to divert public attention from scandals in the administration of Turkestan and from its growing deficit, and to restore the somewhat tarnished prestige of General Von Kaufman. Another factor was the restlessness of the Russian army officers in Central Asia and their desire for a new campaign which would bring fresh opportunity for decorations and promotions.[21]

The chief difficulty offered by a campaign against Khiva lay in its remoteness. An oasis in the midst of a great desert, Khiva lay 600 miles from Tashkent, 930 miles from Orenburg, and 500 miles from Krasnovodsk. Distance and difficult terrain canceled most of the advantages which the Russians possessed in their disciplined forces and superior weapons. With these facts in mind, much attention was therefore devoted to planning. During the summers of 1871 and 1872 the part of the Kyzyl-Kum desert lying north of Bukhara was surveyed, and small detachments were sent from Kazalinsk to investigate the country on the way to Khiva. Other detachments were sent to explore south of the Emba River and southwest of Khiva in the region of the ancient former bed of the Amu-Daria.

The expedition was to be undertaken in the spring—the lesson of Perovskii's winter campaign was too fresh to be forgotten—and an advance from several directions was planned to give further assurance of success. The main column, under General N. N. Golovachev, was to advance from Tashkent; another column, under General Verevkin, was to march from Orenburg; Colonel V. I. Markozov was to approach from Krasnovodsk; and a fourth column, under Colonel N. P. Lomakin, was to come from

Fort Aleksandrovskii on the Mangyshlak peninsula. The entire expedition, amounting to 13,000 men and 62 guns, was to be under the command of General Von Kaufman, who was to accompany the Tashkent detachment.

The operation was probably hampered by its excessive size, too much planning, and too many eminent figures eager for promotions, decorations, and glory. The number of men involved was far in excess of anything required to deal with the poorly armed and badly organized antagonist. Figures like the youthful Grand Duke Nikolai Konstantinovich and Duke Eugene of Leuchtenberg, who had come from St. Petersburg especially to participate in the operation, lent it more color and dash than military worth. Von Kaufman, desirous of himself having the honor of capturing Khiva, issued strict orders that other detachments were neither to attack the city nor to negotiate with the Khan until his arrival.[22]

The Tashkent column got under way in March, 1873. It included 3,420 infantry, 1,150 cavalry, 20 guns, 2 mitrailleuses (breech-loading, multibarreled machine guns of that time), and 8 rocket launchers. Total personnel, including supply troops, numbered about 5,500 men. Over 10,000 camels were requisitioned from the natives for transport. At the outset the column was hampered by unseasonable snowstorms; the camels requisitioned from the Kazakhs proved to be poor and weak; and a large quantity of provisions were found to have spoiled in storage. Finally, at the last minute Von Kaufman replaced a feasible route to the Amu-Daria originally planned for the column with a shorter but little-known one.[23] Following the new route, the column ran short of water, lost all but 1,200 of its camels, and narrowly escaped total disaster before it reached the Amu-Daria on May 12, 1873. In the meantime, Markozov's column of about 2,200 men, proceeding from the south along the supposed ancient bed of the Amu-Daria, suffered so greatly from heat and lack of water that on April 22 they had to turn back toward their base. Sixty men died of sunstroke, nearly all of the others were ill, and the detachment's supplies including its artillery had to be abandoned in the desert.

Verevkin's column, numbering about 3,461 men, was perhaps the best prepared to encounter the difficulties of the route. His men suffered no privations, and after easy marches over well-explored terrain, arrived at Kungrad, near the mouth of the Amu-Daria, on May 8. The Mangyshlak column, under Colonel Lomakin, consisting of about 2,000 men, was likewise competently led and supplied. It arrived at Kungrad on May 12 without difficulty. Under Verevkin's command, both columns then proceeded up the Amu-Daria until on May 28 they reached the outskirts of Khiva.

At Khiva, virtually the only resistance was offered by Iomud Turkmen, vassals of the khan, but even these warriors could not hold out for long, and Verevkin's artillery soon had the city ready for storming. This was held off, however, until the rather anticlimactic arrival of Von Kaufman, leading the advance detachments of the Tashkent column, on May 29.[24] Once the desert was conquered, Russia's old antagonist proved of little consequence. During the entire campaign the combined Orenburg and Mangyshlak detachments lost 30 killed and 101 wounded; up to the capture of Khiva the Tashkent detachment lost but 1 killed and 4 wounded.[25]

It was now necessary to set up a stable regime in Khiva with which the Russian government could deal. The khan had fled, but was called back by Von Kaufman to rule henceforth with Russian guidance. The former chief counsellor of the khan, always hostile, was sent under guard to Kazalinsk and subsequently to Russia. Von Kaufman was magnanimous toward the populace, promising them the tsar's mercy if they would live quietly. The Russian soldiers were given strict orders, on pain of death, to take nothing from the inhabitants and to pay for everything they acquired at the bazaars.

The apprehensive Khivans had released all Russian slaves before the city's capture, but there were still nearly 30,000 Persians and a lesser number of other nationals held in bondage in the khanate. At Von Kaufman's order the khan issued a proclamation abolishing slavery in his realm. However, because the order was not followed up vigorously enough by the Russians, the emancipation was to a considerable degree ignored. A few hundred Persians were sent back to their homes, some perishing on the way at the hands of the Turkmen; but the status of the majority remained almost unchanged.[26]

Another problem was posed by the Turkmen of the Iomud tribe, living in the country around Khiva. The Iomuds had been the main element in the defense of the khanate; and as Von Kaufman considered it necessary to drive home the lesson of Russian supremacy in all quarters, in July, 1873, he proclaimed an indemnity of 300,000 rubles against this group. The conditions were so hard as to be impossible of fulfillment. The Iomuds were nomads who had only their flocks and herds and no ready cash nor even any central organization which could collect such a sum. No payments were forthcoming, so on July 7, even before the end of the prescribed period, Von Kaufman ordered General Golovachev to march into the Iomud country as far as Khazavat. Then, if the Iomuds still showed no signs of collecting the indemnity, or if they seemed to be assembling for hostile purposes or to leave the country, he was "to give over the settlements of the Iomuds and their families to complete destruction, and their herds and property to confiscation."[27]

Hearing that the Iomuds were in flight, Golovachev ordered a detachment in pursuit. The Russians overtook a great column of refugees moving through the desert, destroyed their carts and livestock, and drove the Turkmen into the Zaikesh River, where many drowned. At the same time all houses and food supplies of the Turkmen a mile on either side of the column were burned. Seeking vengeance for this slaughter and destruction, the Turkmen made several attacks on the Russians but were beaten off each time with heavy casualties.[28] At the end of July, after suffering great loss of life and property in the unequal contest, the Iomuds finally submitted and announced their readiness to pay. Von Kaufman, having carried out punitive measures to his own satisfaction, now permitted the Iomuds to pay half the indemnity in camels. The other half they paid in the only precious metals they had, the gold and silver ornaments of their women.[29]

In a treaty signed on August 12, 1873, Khiva submitted to

Russia and ceded its possessions on the right bank of the Amu-Daria. The Russians received the right of residence and tax-free trade in the khanate, and the khan was obliged to pay an indemnity of 2,200,000 rubles, payable over a twenty-year period.[30]

Because of the restlessness of the Iomud Turkmen and the distance of the new acquisitions from either Tashkent or Samarkand, the Russian military leaders felt that the territories ceded by Khiva could be united neither to the Syr-Daria oblast nor to the Zeravshan district. The region was therefore organized into the Amu-Daria military section (*voennyi otdel*) under a military administration.[31] Colonel N. A. Ivanov was put in command of the troops in the district and in charge of the administration, centered at Fort Petro-Aleksandrovskoe (now Turtkul') on the right bank of the Amu-Daria only twenty-five miles from Khiva. The inhabitants, numbering about 216,000, were chiefly nomadic Kazakhs, Kara-Kalpaks, and Turkmen, against whom Ivanov had to lead several punitive expeditions before all were inclined to submit to his authority.[32]

THE END OF KOKAND

By the end of 1873 the three largest states which had confronted the Russians in Central Asia—Kokand, Bukhara, and Khiva—had been reduced to vassalage, nominally independent, but actually within the Russian Empire. Of the three, Kokand was in the most unstable condition. Khudoiar Khan, the ruler, was unpopular because of his cruelties and exactions, and because of his connections with the Russians. When in July, 1875, an uprising broke out against him in the town of Uzgen he found no support. Led by one of his relatives, Pulat Khan (or Iskhak-Mulla-Khassan-Ogly), and by one of the local feudal landholders, Abdurakhman-avtobachi, the rebels advanced on the city of Kokand and on July 22 forced Khudoiar Khan to flee to the protection of the Russian army. In Kokand the rebels proclaimed Khudoiar's eldest son Nasr-Eddin the new khan.

In August the rebellion spread to former Kokandian possessions now held by Russia. Proclaiming a *gazavat*, or holy war, against the Russians, the rebels sent emissaries to arouse the inhabitants of Kuraminsk and Khodzhent uezds. On August 9 the rebels surrounded Khodzhent, besieged the Russian garrison in the citadel, and cut its communications with Tashkent. Von Kaufman acted quickly. He left Tashkent with his troops on August 12, relieved Khodzhent on the eighteenth, and then invaded Kokandian territory. On August 22 he attacked the main force of the rebels, an estimated 30,000 to 50,000 men occupying the fortress of Makhram, and routed them. The natives left 90 dead in the fortress, but Cossacks led by Colonel M. D. Skobelev pursued the fugitives along the banks of the Syr-Daria for several miles and killed over 1,000 more. The Russians lost only six killed and eight wounded in the entire action.[33]

On August 26 Kokand opened its gates to Von Kaufman. Abdurakhman-avtobachi and the remainder of his force fled to Margelan, but Von Kaufman pursued him and reached that city on September 8, whereupon Abdurakhman and 8,000 horsemen fled without a fight. Skobelev pursued and scattered the fugitives with a cavalry force, pushed on as far as Osh, which he took without resistance, and then returned to Margelan.[34]

For the moment the Russian efforts were successful. Andizhan and numerous towns and villages sent notice of their submission. On September 23, 1875, a peace treaty was concluded at Margelan with Nasr-Eddin Khan in which he promised to pay the Russians an indemnity of 3,000,000 rubles within six years, and to cede to Russia all the lands of Kokand on the right bank of the Syr-Daria, including the town of Namangan, to be known as the Namangan section. This annexation was made on Von Kaufman's own responsibility, under the broad military and diplomatic powers which he possessed. The tsar's authorization did not arrive until later.[35]

However, the pacification of the region was by no means as complete as had been supposed. Soon reports came that the entire eastern part of the khanate was still in rebellion. Andizhan went over to the rebels, and Abdurakhman-avtobachi, together with Pulat Khan, now a pretender to the throne, concentrated a new force there estimated to be between 60,000 and 70,000 men. A Russian force under Major General V. N. Trotskii was sent out to resubdue Andizhan. Trotskii besieged the city from September 30 to October 5 but then, avid for glory, attempted to storm it. The order proved premature; the inhabitants put up such resistance that Trotskii had to abandon the siege and return to Namangan. An official report stated that the Russians lost ten killed and seventy wounded, but private sources placed the loss at between four and five times as many.[36]

On October 16, in spite of the serious turn which affairs had taken, Von Kaufman left Namangan for St. Petersburg. He left in command Skobelev, who as a reward for his services in the campaign now held the rank of major general. The latter soon found ample opportunity for further glory. On October 23 he took a portion of his command to attack Tiura-Kurgan, a small fortified town eight miles west of Namangan, where he defeated one of the rebel bands, and razed the town in punishment for its inhabitants' share in the rebellion. On October 24, other bands took advantage of Skobelev's absence and entered Namangan, whose inhabitants immediately joined them in an attack on the small force of Russians in the yet unfinished citadel and on those in camp outside the town. These managed to defend themselves until Skobelev's force arrived on October 27. Placing sixteen guns in position outside Namangan, Skobelev then bombarded the portion of the town occupied by the rebel forces and stormed it. The natives fled, leaving 3,800 dead, according to Skobelev's possibly exaggerated report. The Russian loss was set down as six killed and thirty-two wounded. Most of the town was destroyed in the bombardment, and the Russian troops were quartered in the few houses that remained standing.[37]

His rear thus secured, Skobelev spent the next two months in a series of engagements in which he struck again and again at the enemy, ravaging the territory considered the center of the rebel population. On January 8, 1876, after a week-long bombardment, Andizhan fell. The Russians lost two killed and nine wounded in this action; the enemy loss was reported as "immense." [38] Other successes followed, and on January 20 Abdurakhman-avtobachi and several of the other rebel leaders negotiated personally with Skobelev and surrendered. Having placed themselves at the mercy of the tsar, they were pardoned. The Russians continued the pursuit of Pulat Khan.

During this time, Nasr-Eddin Khan had remained under Russian protection in Khodzhent. In January, 1876, he received a deputation from Kokand inviting him to return to the throne. He grasped at the chance eagerly and reached Kokand in February, dodging the forces of Pulat Khan on the way. Affairs had now gone too far for Russia to permit any restoration of Kokandian rule. Skobelev was therefore ordered to occupy Kokand. On February 19, 1876, the anniversary of his accession to the throne, the tsar signed an order for the annexation of Kokand to Russia as an oblast bearing the ancient name of Fergana. Skobelev was appointed the first military governor of the new territory.[39]

A few days later Pulat Khan was captured. Because of his crimes—he had killed twelve Russian prisoners, and had lately killed women and retainers of the families of Khudoiar Khan and Abdurakhman-avtobachi—he was hanged. Nasr-Eddin Khan and Abdurakhman-avtobachi, like Khudoiar Khan before them, were sent to Russia to live as pensioners of the government.[40]

TRANSCASPIA AND THE ROAD TO INDIA

While the Khivan campaign was under discussion, other operations were initiated south of the Amu-Daria in the Transcaspian region, the home of the warlike Turkmen. At the end of 1869, Russian forces from the Caucasus led by Colonel N. G. Stoletov landed on the south shore of the Caspian Sea at Krasnovodsk, the site of a Russian stronghold in the early eighteenth century. To avoid arousing England, Stoletov was given strict orders to avoid hostilities and to occupy himself with exploration, particularly of the road to Khiva. The occupied area was annexed to Russia as the Krasnovodsk prefecture (*pristavstvo*) of the oblast of Dagestan, a part of the Governor-Generalship of the Caucasus.

Mostly desert, a hot sandy wasteland removed from the main centers of Russian interest in Central Asia, Transcaspia offered little to justify the expense of military operations. Russian historians mention as excuses for penetration there the submission of this or that Turkmen tribe as far back as the seventeenth century, Turkmenian attacks on Russian fishermen along the Caspian shore, the need for a show of force against Khiva, and the need for control of the east shore of the Caspian as a support for the Russian army in the Caucasus. However, it is also probable that the Russian move into this region arose, in the words of the contemporary American observer Schuyler, simply from a desire "to give the large army stationed in the Caucasus something to do," [41] and to provide its officers with an opportunity to gain laurels in a field monopolized until then by the *"Turkestantsy"* of Von Kaufman's command.

In 1873, as already mentioned, Krasnovodsk became one of the several bases for the combined operation against Khiva. After the conclusion of the Khivan campaign the Mangyshlak area was made into a prefecture and combined with the Krasnovodsk prefecture to form the Transcaspian section. General Lomakin, who had led the Mangyshlak column in the Khivan operation, was appointed commandant of the section. Thus, nearly the entire east shore of the Caspian was administered from the Caucasus. Although the Russian government at first attempted only the control of the area adjacent to the Caspian and sought friendly relations with the Turkmen, peace was not to be had. The Russian annexations and reconnaissance aroused resentment and apprehension among the Turkmen. There were raids and skirmishes. Then followed annual punitive expeditions against the Turkmen and the establishment of advance bases. As usual, the establishment of one base demanded yet another to protect it.

In May, 1877, General Lomakin, with 1,800 men, took Kyzyl-Arvat, in the western part of the territory of the Akhal group of the Tekke Turkmen (sometimes known as the Akhal oasis, but actually consisting mainly of desert with the population centered around a few separate oases), adjacent to the Persian border and about 100 miles inland from the Caspian Sea. However, finding his supplies insufficient, after five days Lomakin ordered his troops back to their base.[42]

The Turkestantsy had watched with regret the rise of the new theater of operations, controlled from the Caucasus instead of

Tashkent. In 1878, however, a matter of far greater import intruded in Central Asian affairs. Britain's interference in the Russo-Turkish War (1876–1878) and her attitude at the Congress of Berlin caused Russia to undertake a diversionary action in the form of a threat against India. This show of force, though intended in St. Petersburg primarily as a bargaining weapon, raised hopes high in Turkestan. On orders from the capital, Von Kaufman fitted out 20,000 troops, the largest Russian force yet gathered in the region. The main body, under Von Kaufman, marched from Samarkand to Dzham, on the Bukharan frontier, ready to set out for Kabul and the Khyber Pass. Another column, under Abramov, was poised in Fergana ready to ascend the Alai and march on Kashmir. A third column, under Colonel Grotengel'm, advanced from Petro-Aleksandrovsk by way of Khiva to Chardzhui on the Amu-Daria, where it was to join forces with yet a fourth column under Lomakin, first in an advance on the Akhal Tekke oasis and then on Kelif. General Stoletov was sent to Kabul as ambassador in order to secure the coöperation of Afghanistan in the forthcoming offensive.

All was in readiness, and for a time the two nations stood close to war, but tensions then eased and on July 19 word arrived that peace had been reached in Berlin. With a few words in a telegram the war clouds dissipated and the main columns marched back to their garrisons.[43] Lomakin's force, however, was allowed to continue as far as its assigned objective, Chat, at the juncture of the Sumbar with the Atrek River, with the objective of establishing there a terminal point for a line of forts stretching from Chikishliar. Chat was occupied without resistance. The eager Lomakin then took it upon himself to advance farther, but he found supply problems and resistance too great and had to return to Chat. This then encouraged the Turkmen, who attacked Chat and Chikishliar and even threatened Krasnovodsk.

The resultant fall in Russian prestige was detrimental to Russian relations with Persia, particularly in view of the British successes in Afghanistan. Therefore in 1879 General I. D. Lazarev, commander of the First Army of the Caucasus, was ordered to lead another, stronger detachment against the Akhal Tekke.

Lomakin was second in command. Bypassing Kzyl-Arvat, Lazarev and Lomakin marched on the oasis of Geok-Tepe, about seventy-five miles farther on. Enroute, however, Lazarev suddenly contracted an infection and died on August 14. This put the command once more in the hands of Lomakin. Instead of waiting for further orders he grasped eagerly at the opportunity to vindicate himself and ordered his men on to finish the task.

Lomakin's force, amounting to about 3,500 men, reached the vicinity of Geok-Tepe on September 9, 1879. Nearly all of the population of Akhal, including women and children, a total of about 20,000 persons, took refuge behind the earth walls of a fortress on the hill of Dengil-Tepe and prepared to resist. Lomakin's men took the outer defense works without difficulty and poured artillery and rocket fire into the fort. The bombardment caused such loss of life among the defenders that noncombatants came streaming out, hoping to be allowed to escape. But this was contrary to Lomakin's plans; medals and promotions came in greatest abundance when a force closed with the enemy and inflicted total defeat. Lomakin relentlessly ordered the fugitives turned back and the bombardment continued. In all about 2,000 Tekkes were killed and 2,000 wounded up to this point.

Contemporary critics seem agreed that if the Russians had remained in place they could have caused the surrender or evacuation of the fort by bombardment alone, but after some additional fire Lomakin ordered the bombardment to cease and the infantry to take the fort by storm. The only hope of the ill-armed Turkmen had lain in coming to grips with the attackers at close quarters. When the Russians charged, the Turkmen saw their chance and poured forth. Their superior numbers prevailed and they drove the Russians back with heavy losses. Out of the 3,024 Russian troops engaged in the battle, nearly 200 were killed and more than 250 wounded,[44] the gravest loss yet experienced during the operations in Central Asia. Only with difficulty were the pursuing Tekkes beaten off and prevented from overwhelming the Russian artillery. The Russians retreated, and Lomakin was relieved of command.

Fearful that the defeat at Dengil-Tepe might undermine

Russian prestige throughout Central Asia, the government quickly planned another expedition. In May, 1880, preparations for the new attempt were put in the hands of General Skobelev, just back from a glorious role in the Russo-Turkish War. Skobelev calculated that he needed a force of 11,000 men, and this was provided, together with all the required artillery and supplies. After careful preparation, particularly with regard to supply, the expedition got under way in early November. Bases were established along the way. The army had already begun construction of a railroad from Krasnovodsk but this was not finished in time to be of any use and actually proved a hindrance to the expedition, drawing away much supply and personnel. Transport was accomplished with camels, 20,000 in all.[45]

Late in November, 1880, Skobelev's force, numbering by then about 7,100, after the detachment of those chosen to man the bases in the rear and to build the railroad, reached the Akhal-Tekke oasis. Again the Turkmen had retreated to their fortress at Geok-Tepe, concentrating almost the entire population of the oasis there. Skobelev's troops surrounded the fortress and began the siege.

Of the 20,000 to 25,000 native defenders only about 8,000 had firearms and the rest pikes and swords, but they resisted as stubbornly as in the preceding year. As before, their only hope lay in hand-to-hand combat, but Skobelev did not repeat Lomakin's error. He relentlessly continued the bombardment. The Turkmen made several fierce sorties but were beaten back. Russian sappers tunneled to the walls of the fortress and mined them. Finally, when all preparations were complete, on January 12, 1881, the Russians set off their mines, breached a section of the wall, and stormed the fortress. The blast demoralized the defenders. As the Russian troops penetrated the fort the natives streamed out of the gates on the other side in headlong flight. At Skobelev's orders the victors pursued them for eleven miles, cutting down the fugitives regardless of sex or age. Some 8,000 were killed in this way.

Inside the fortress were found the corpses of 6,500 persons and some thousands of living, chiefly women and children. The Russians killed all Turkmen males who had not succeeded in escaping from the fort, but spared about 5,000 women and children. They freed about 600 Persian slaves, who were easily recognized by the fetters on their legs.[46] In the storming of the fort the Russians lost 59 killed and 254 wounded. During the entire campaign of 1880–1881 they lost 290 killed and 833 wounded. Sickness, more deadly than Turkmen bullets, accounted for the death of 645 more.[47]

The taking of Geok-Tepe broke the Turkmen resistance and decided the fate of the rest of Transcaspia. A few days later, on January 18, 1881, a force led by Colonel A. N. Kuropatkin occupied Askhabad (now Ashkhabad) and then Kaakhka and other settlements. The Russian hold on the region was now firm. On May 6, 1881, Transcaspia was declared an oblast of the empire. In January, 1884, the region was augmented by the voluntary submission to Russia of the Tekke inhabiting the Merv oasis. The annexation of Kushka, taken from Afghanistan in March, 1885, provided the final accretion in the area, although it brought Russia and Great Britain perilously close to war.[48]

Yet another territorial extension came in 1895, incident to the Anglo-Russian settlement of the Afghan boundaries, when Russian claims to part of the Pamir region were upheld and another part was given over to the suzerainty of the emir of Bukhara.

THE SIGNIFICANCE OF THE RUSSIAN CONQUESTS

Acquisition of the Pamir region completed the Russian conquest and annexation in Central Asia. Faced by established powers with well-defined natural frontiers, and under the watchful eye of England, further Russian expansion was not possible. The Russians could be satisfied with their gains. During less than half a century after 1847, when they first took the offensive in the steppe, their nation had gained control over a region comparable in size to Western Europe, with resources which could add great wealth and power to the empire.

The cost in men, as we have seen, was relatively low. Maksheev, summing up, states that in all the campaigns in Central Asia during the 25 years from 1847 to 1873, the Russians lost less

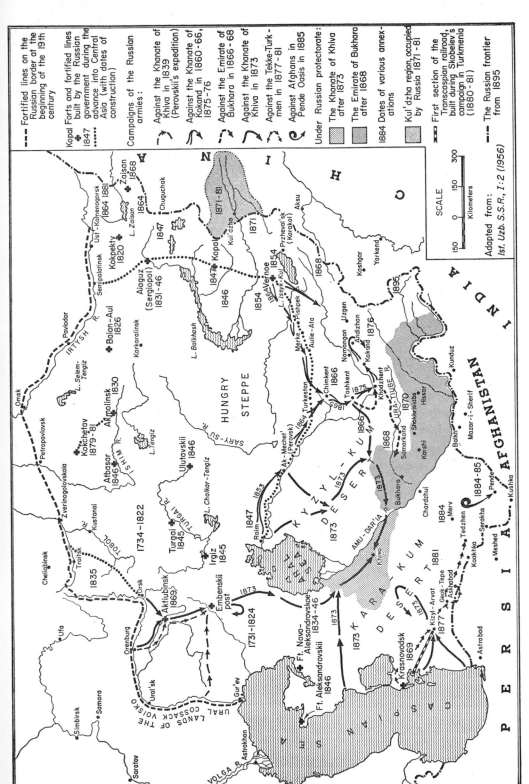

MAP 1. THE RUSSIAN CONQUESTS IN CENTRAL ASIA.

Adapted from:
Ist. Uzb. S.S.R., I:2 (1956)

Key:

- - - Fortified lines on the Russian border at the beginning of the 19th century
✚ Kopal Forts and fortified lines built by the Russian government during the advance into Central Asia (with dates of construction)

Campaigns of the Russian armies:

Against the Khanate of Khiva in 1839 (Perovskii's expedition)

Against the Khanate of Kokand in 1860–66, 1875–76

Against the Emirate of Bukhara in 1866–68

Against the Khanate of Khiva in 1873

Against the Tekke-Turkmen in 1877–81

Against Afghans in Pende Oasis in 1885

Under Russian protectorate:

The Khanate of Khiva after 1873

The Emirate of Bukhara after 1868

1884 Dates of various annexations

Kul'dzha region, occupied by Russia 1871–81

First section of the Transcaspian railroad, built during Skobelev's campaign in Turkmenia (1880–81)

- · - The Russian frontier from 1895

SCALE

150 0 150 300

Kilometers

than 400 men and a little over 1,600 wounded—only about 2,000 casualties in all.[49] Later losses no more than doubled this.

Supply, more than manpower, was the key to successful operations in Central Asia. It was mandatory for each force to carry enough provisions, ammunition, and especially water to see the troops through any given assignment. This required great numbers of transport animals, and these in turn created additional problems. Of the 10,000 camels employed in Von Kaufman's march to Khiva in 1873, or the 20,000 which Skobelev used in 1880–1881, many had to carry fodder. The length of the march, the choice of the season, and the location of water sources were factors of vital importance; miscalculations could mean disaster.

During the course of the conquest the Russians learned to master the supply and tactical problems confronting them. First of all, in the steppe, they learned to set up small advance bases. These posts were insignificant in themselves but were enough to ensure control of the surrounding nomad population. Later these posts facilitated the further advance of troops by securing the rear and aiding the transport of supplies.

The Russian tacticians soon learned that a small number of disciplined troops with modern weapons could withstand the charge of wild hordes of natives, undisciplined, uncoördinated, and poorly armed. As their forces grew, the Russians were able to rely more and more on offensive operations. When attacked in a fortified position they could sally forth and defeat the enemy in the open field. They learned to gain the enemy's fortresses and walled towns by use of comparatively few pieces of artillery which would soften up the enemy until the troops could charge and take the place by storm.

There were defeats, as Cherniaev's repulse from Tashkent in 1864, Trotskii's failure at Andizhan in 1875, and Lomakin's defeat at Geok-Tepe in 1879; there were discreditable episodes, as the slaughter of the Iomud Turkmen in 1873, the relentless bombardment of Geok-Tepe in 1879, and the pursuit and massacre of the Turkmen in their flight from Geok-Tepe in 1881. Yet, each setback was always followed by overwhelming victory that left no doubt on whose side the mastery lay; even bad faith and massacre helped to drive home the lesson of the invader's supremacy. As Skobelev himself expressed it: "I hold it as a principle that in Asia the duration of peace is in direct proportion to the slaughter you inflict upon the enemy. The harder you hit them the longer they will be quiet afterwards. My system is this: to strike hard, and keep on hitting till resistance is completely over; then at once to form ranks, cease slaughter, and be kind and humane to the prostrate enemy." [50]

The effectiveness of the Russian tactics was acknowledged by observers from other colonial lands. George Nathaniel Curzon, later Lord Curzon of Kedleston, the great exponent of British empire-building, gave grudging admiration to the decisive blows struck by the Russians in contrast with the less conclusive British method, "to strike gingerly a series of taps, rather than a downright blow; rigidly to prohibit all pillage or slaughter, and to abstain not less wholly from subsequent fraternisation." [51]

To counter the Russian advantages the native warriors had only their individual bravery and their natural allies of terrain, distance, and climate. After repeated demonstrations of their inability to stay the Russian advance by organized resistance, only mass revolt was left as a means of ousting the conquerors, and this was unlikely because of the hard facts of logistics, native disunity, and the force of Russian arms. The railroads, built from the 1880's on, clinched the matter by ensuring the swift passage of troops and supplies to any trouble spot.

The Russians were thus able to solve effectively the first great problem with which they were faced in Central Asia, the establishment of military supremacy. Their advance was made as certain as it was swift by their ability to profit from experience gained in coping with climate and terrain; the building of posts in strategic locations to facilitate control of conquered territory and supply of advancing forces; careful reconnaissance, resolute defense, and purposeful offensive action; and just treatment of the vanquished. The might exhibited in the Russian military operations, which planted the impression of absolute mastery in the minds of the Central Asians, laid the groundwork for subsequent rule.

III

RUSSIAN military advances into Central Asia were followed immediately by the extension of Imperial administration to the occupied territories. This phase of the conquest was less spectacular than the military operations, but equally vital. The successful consolidation and eventual exploitation of the Russian acquisitions depended on how well this administrative structure was built.

The need for extensive administrative reorganization in Central Asia was already apparent in the 1860's. Closing of the pincers formed by the thrusts southward from Orenburg and Siberia brought a vast area under the direct control of the Russian government. The Kazakh Steppe was no longer a borderland, but an interior region, ready for a form of government which would further economic development rather than purely military ends. The border now lay far to the south, in Turkestan. Nearly 1,400 miles lay between Orenburg and Tashkent, too great a distance for effective control over ambitious generals, for prompt action against the unruly native states, or for countering any threat that might arise in China or Afghanistan.

THE STEPPE COMMISSION

In 1865 the authorities in St. Petersburg formed the so-called Steppe Commission to inquire into the needs of Russia in the steppe regions of Central Asia. Headed by State Counsellor F. K. Giers, the four-man commission made a careful study over a two-year period of the ethnic, cultural, political, and economic characteristics of the region. The Commission's findings were embodied in drafts for two statutes for the administration of the steppe region and for the newly conquered regions in Turkestan.[1]

In March, 1867, Tsar Alexander authorized the formation of a special committee (*osobyi komitet*) under the chairmanship of the minister of war, to consider the Steppe Commission's recommendations and to reorganize Russia's Central Asian possessions.[2] On April 11, 1867, the special committee reported its findings. Largely on the basis of the Steppe Commission's recommendations, the special committee declared it necessary (1) to separate the oblast of Turkestan from the Governor-Generalship of Orenburg; (2) to establish a new unit, the Governor-Generalship of Turkestan, to include two oblasts, Semirechie and Syr-Daria; (3) to detach the southern part of the oblast of Semipalatinsk, until then under the Governor-Generalship of West Siberia, and join it administratively to the oblast of Semirechie; (4) to draft a statute for the administration of the region based on the general principles laid down by the committee; (5) to make the region a separate military district; (6) to unite the civil and military authority of the region in the governor-general; and (7) to leave all local affairs of the native population which were of a non-political nature in the hands of elected representatives of the natives themselves, to be administered according to local custom.[3]

General Kryzhanovskii, the governor-general of Orenburg, gave the only dissenting vote to these changes. Reluctant to see his own authority diminished, he protested that because of remoteness and different local conditions an independent administration in Turkestan would tend to depart from the interests and views of the Imperial government. He also protested that the Kazakhs, many of whom inhabited the Turkestan region as well as the steppes to the north, would be divided between different jurisdictions.[4] F. K. Giers, also serving on the special committee, protested that the interests of the Siberian frontier region were totally different from those of Turkestan and that combination of the two would make the area difficult to administer. The military authorities on the committee overruled Giers on the grounds that the change would provide a unified command in case of trouble with China.[5]

In the opinion of the majority of those serving on the committee, the military envelopment of the Kazakh Steppe had completely altered its position. No longer a borderland and a base of military operations, the Steppe was ready for peaceful development. The committee therefore recommended that a single statute be prepared for the uniform administration of the Steppe oblasts. The area concerned would comprise the oblast of the Orenburg Kirgiz, which the committee recommended be divided into the new oblasts of Orenburg and Turgai, the oblast of the Siberian Kirgiz, to be renamed the oblast of Akmolinsk, and the oblast of Semipalatinsk. The first two would remain under the governor-general of Orenburg, and the last two under the governor-general of West Siberia. To weaken native clan organization the oblasts were divided, as were the provinces of European Russia, into lesser units called *uezds*, similar to counties, and these in turn were subdivided into *volosts*, each containing several Kazakh *auls*, or family groups.

THE GOVERNOR-GENERALSHIP OF TURKESTAN

The special committee's recommendations were approved, and on July 11, 1867, Tsar Alexander II signed a decree ordering that a Governor-Generalship of Turkestan be established to include "the Turkestan oblast, the Tashkent district, the lands seized beyond the Syr-Daria in 1866, and the part of the Semipalatinsk oblast lying south of the Tarbagatai range."[6] On July 14, 1867, General K. P. Von Kaufman was appointed governor-general over the new territory. General G. A. Kolpakovskii was appointed military governor of Semirechie oblast, and General N. N. Golovachev was appointed military governor of Syr-Daria oblast.

The task of drafting a statute for the administration of the Turkestan region was given to the Committee of Ministers, but in view of the length of time required, the Committee asked and received the tsar's consent for the governor-general to administer the region under the draft statute already prepared by the Steppe Commission. He was to appoint as many officials within the statute's tables of organization as he considered necessary. On the basis of his experience with local conditions and within the framework of the special committee's recommendations, he was to revise the statute and eventually present it for approval and legislative enactment. Von Kaufman thus was given a virtually free hand in the organization of his new sphere of authority.

Because of the uncertainty of the Russian position in Central Asia at that time, Von Kaufman also received broad powers relating to foreign affairs. He was given plenipotentiary powers to wage war on the Central Asiatic states at his discretion, and to conduct negotiations and conclude agreements with their rulers.[7]

Arriving in Tashkent early in November, 1867, Von Kaufman at once set about the organization of the combined civil and military administration provided for in the provisional statute. The organization of the upper levels of the administration proceeded rapidly. By December 4, 1867, it was possible to open the Syr-Daria oblast administration, and on February 19, 1868, that of Semirechie oblast. In place of the earlier administrative subdivisions, the oblasts were divided into uezds as in European Russia.

The task of bringing the natives under the general scheme of the Russian administration was much greater. The Russians had only a vague idea of the native ethnic divisions and internal organization, and only rough estimates of their numbers. In December, 1867, Von Kaufman ordered the military governors of Semirechie and Syr-Daria oblasts to appoint commissions to work in the various uezds, there to conduct a census of the native population, to determine the boundaries of the volosts and smaller divisions, to organize the election of native officials to serve in the local government, and to begin the collection of taxes. The winter was considered the best time for the census, as during that season the nomadic population, needing fuel, fodder, and shelter, ceased all movement and took refuge in ravines and river bottom lands. Hidden by reeds and trees, they were more difficult to find than in the summer, but they were also more concentrated.

In spite of winter snows and the enormous area to be covered, the commissioners made their way about the region, seeking out the different groups of nomads and explaining the new order of things to them. As a guide, the commissioners had Von Kaufman's order given at the outset of their work. "Mere laws," Von Kaufman had stated, "will be of no use if the members of the commissions do not know how to acquire the esteem and trust of the natives regarding their intentions. Both can be obtained only by unimpeachable honesty, a patient and mild attitude . . . and a sincere wish, on the basis of the new laws, to improve their situation. I demand that the members of the commissions, understanding the importance of the task entrusted them, shall put their souls into it and work energetically and conscientiously." [8]

The commissioners registered each of the native *kibitkas* (native yurts, or dome-shaped felt dwellings, each constituting a household) as to the aul to which it belonged. The auls were grouped into volosts, or districts, and a number of these in turn constituted the various uezds. The commissions supervised the election of native officials and judges, and made it clear that the officials were to receive a set salary from tax funds instead of collecting random payments in the form of barley or sheep, as native leaders had done until then. They proclaimed an annual tax of three rubles on each kibitka. The changes, even the tax increase, were accepted without protest. A great many more natives were accounted for during the census than had been known of before. In Vernyi uezd, the figure of 10,943 kibitkas known before the census was increased by 12,815 which had been concealed previously. [9]

The organization of the settled native population presented greater difficulty because of the opposition of hostile elements, particularly the Moslem clergy and the former officials, and because of the extreme reluctance of the populace toward being counted in any sort of census. To accomplish the task, Von Kaufman appointed organizational commissions for the various towns. For Tashkent, he appointed an eleven-man commission headed by General A. K. Geins. Later four more Russians were added, and forty natives were invited to serve in a consultative capacity. As with the nomads, care was taken to explain to the town-dwellers the content and purpose of the changes contemplated. On January 1, 1868, Von Kaufman himself made a lengthy speech to a gathering of influential natives of Tashkent. He reminded them of the despotic rule of the khans; he explained why the Russians had come; he outlined the form that the new administration would take and the benefits that it would bring; but he warned sternly that the new regime must be obeyed. He concluded:

Mark my words, they bear weight because they are uttered by your leader, the representative of the Russian government in this land, which, as you know, is strong enough to carry them out, regardless of what your own wish may be. I warn you once again; your fate is in your hands. If you are concerned with your own interest, if you seek your own good, if you will help the government, then you will be happy. But if you desire something else, if you run counter to the government's views, then the authorities will begin to act sternly and forcibly. Wishing you well, I advise you to choose a loving, limitless devotion for your Great Sovereign, who never ceases to care for you. This love will guide your own conduct so that you may be worthy of that same love from our good "White Tsar." [10]

Proceeding in the spirit of such combined persuasion and coercion, the organizational commissions accomplished their work without incident. By the summer of 1868 administrative control was established over all of the native population of the Governor-Generalship of Turkestan.[11]

THE GOVERNOR-GENERALSHIP OF THE STEPPE

In the Kazakh Steppe the work of administrative reorganization began somewhat later than in Turkestan. On October 21, 1868, the tsar authorized the formation of the new oblasts of Ural'sk, Turgai, and Akmolinsk. The administration of these and of Semipalatinsk oblast, like that of Semirechie and Syr-Daria oblasts in Turkestan, was to be based on the recommendations of the Steppe Commission of 1865–1867.

The introduction of the statute had met with no resistance from the Kazakhs of Semirechie and Syr-Daria oblasts, most of whom had been under the rule of Kokand before and had in effect merely changed masters when the Russians came. There was also no opposition in the oblasts of Akmolinsk and Semipalatinsk, where similar administrative provisions had been imposed earlier under the "statute of the Siberian Kirgiz" of 1822. In Turgai and Ural'sk oblasts, however, the sultans confirmed in power by earlier Russian legislation resented giving up their authority to elected officials, and their people were unwilling to see the breakup of their traditional clan organization and judicial procedure coupled with closer supervision by Russian officials and higher taxes.[12]

The government realized the fundamental nature of the change, and in an attempt to prevent native unrest proclaimed that the new statute should be introduced at first only in its main points, with its remaining administrative, court, and tax provisions to follow gradually. Nevertheless, at the end of 1868, when an organizational commission began work in Ural'sk oblast it managed only to organize a few volosts near the Russian border defense lines and fortresses; when its members went farther into the steppe they met resistance and had to retire.[13] Native bands then began to raid the Russian outposts and to drive off the livestock of Cossack settlers and of natives friendly to the Russians. Soon the disorders had seized most of Ural'sk and had spread into part of neighboring Turgai oblast, where natives who had already accepted the new statute joined the rebels.

From January to June, 1869, the advantage lay with the natives. In several sharp skirmishes Russian detachments had to give way. However, by the end of spring the government was ready with countermeasures. Kryzhanovskii, the governor-general of Orenburg, sent detachments of infantry and of Ural'sk and Orenburg Cossacks into the steppe in such numbers that by November, 1869, the resistance was quelled. Many of the rebels were killed; others fled to Khiva.[14] Over 500 participants in the rebellion were tried in Russian military courts. Some were sentenced to death, but most of the death sentences were commuted to hard labor. The property of the rebels was confiscated, and fines were levied on the native clans as compensation for the Russian losses.[15] To ensure peace, the army built two new forts in the steppe, Aktiubinsk and Uil'sk, with the enthusiastic participation of some of the very Kazakhs who had taken part in the rebellion.[16]

In the following year, however, revolt broke out in a new quarter, this time in the Mangyshlak area, west of the Aral Sea, among the Kazakhs of the Adai clan. These tribesmen formed a strong group comprising about 14,000 households, who had had little contact with the Russians. There an attempt by Lieutenant Colonel Rukin, the commandant of the Mangyshlak area, to impose payment of the kibitka tax for both 1868 and 1869 and to enforce other provisions of the statute aroused the natives and they took up arms. Early in March, Rukin led a detachment consisting of two officers and forty Cossacks from Fort Aleksandrovskii into the steppe to force the natives to submit. Instead, on March 25, when nearly 100 versts from their base, Rukin and his men were surrounded by a large force of Kazakhs.[17] The Russians fought until their ammunition was gone, whereupon Rukin committed suicide and all of his men were killed or captured.[18] The Kazakhs then attacked parties of Russian fishermen on the Caspian shore and on April 5, several thousand strong, laid siege to Fort Aleksandrovskii. Only the timely arrival four days later of reinforcements, coming by sea from the Caucasus, saved the garrison from defeat.[19]

Punitive expeditions sent to the Mangyshlak area soon brought most of the rebels to terms. But others fled to Khivan territory or to the Ust-Urt desert, from which they made sorties against the Russians. This finally caused the Russian authorities to make certain modifications in the administration of the Kazakhs in the Mangyshlak area. Native judges were appointed, not elected; taxes were accepted in kind (that is, in livestock); and most of the participants in the uprising were pardoned.[20]

While the new administrative organization was being established in the Steppe, the Governor-Generalship of Turkestan was being further extended. The lands taken from the emirate of Bukhara in 1868 were formed into the Zeravshan okrug. This district was occupied at first merely on a temporary basis, and the final decision as to its annexation came only several years later.[21]

In drafting a statute for the Turkestan region in 1873, Von Kaufman proposed to combine the Zeravshan district with the Khodzhent uezd of Syr-Daria oblast to form a new oblast to be named after its chief city, Samarkand, but as the statute was not adopted the district remained as before.[22] However, some years later this proposal was embodied in the statute for the administration of Turkestan, adopted in 1886. On January 1, 1887, when the statute came into effect, the Zeravshan district became the oblast of Samarkand.

The conquest of Khiva, in 1873, resulted in the annexation of Khivan territory on the right bank of the Amu-Daria. The area was made a part of Syr-Daria oblast, but because of its distance from Tashkent, the unruly nature of its inhabitants, and the need to keep a watch on the khanate of Khiva, it was given a separate administration as the Amu-Daria military section (*voennyi otdel*).

Until 1875, it appears to have been the Russian government's intention to retain the khanate of Kokand in a nominally independent status similar to that of Khiva and Bukhara. However, the misrule of Khudoiar Khan was more than even his subjects could bear, and they rebelled. The subsequent anarchy and attacks on Russian territory caused the employment of Russian troops in the extended campaign previously described. At first only a part of the khanate was annexed as compensation, but when the impossibility of establishing any sort of order under native rule became evident, the remainder of the region was annexed. This was added to the Governor-Generalship of Turkestan as the oblast of Fergana.

REORGANIZATIONS

Thus far changes had all served to augment the Governor-Generalship of Turkestan. However, when Von Kaufman died in 1882 the authorities in St. Petersburg sought to reward General Cherniaev for past services by appointing him as successor. But to do this it was felt necessary to remove from the scene Cherniaev's senior in rank, General G. A. Kolpakovskii, the military governor of Semirechie oblast, who had served as acting governor-general since Von Kaufman was stricken in March, 1881.

As a result, a major reorganization occurred. Semirechie oblast was taken from the Governor-Generalship of Turkestan; Akmolinsk and Semipalatinsk oblasts were taken from the jurisdiction of the governor-general of West Siberia; and all three were made into the new Governor-Generalship of the Steppe, with Kolpakovskii at its head. Cherniaev was appointed governor-general of what remained of Turkestan, namely Syr-Daria and Fergana oblasts, and the Zeravshan district.

While these internal changes were taking place, further annexations were occurring in Transcaspia. The first of these was the establishment of Krasnovodsk in 1869. The taking of Geok-Tepe and Askhabad in 1881 made a large enough region to merit a separate administration, and it was constituted as Transcaspia oblast. Merv, annexed in 1884, and Kushka, in 1885, were later additions. In 1890, Transcaspia was separated from the jurisdiction of the governor-general of the Caucasus and made into a separate unit, directly subordinate to the Ministry of War. It was administered under its own "provisional statute for the government of the oblast of Transcaspia."

In 1895 the annexation of the Pamir region rounded out Russia's acquisitions in Central Asia and gave her holdings the external boundaries retained through the end of the Imperial regime in 1917 and up to the present day. Internally, however, the pattern was not yet complete. In 1898 another provincial reorganization of even greater magnitude than that of 1882 took place. The story of the behind-the-scenes shuffle at that time is told in the memoirs of a contemporary official in Tashkent. He relates how General A. N. Kuropatkin, who had served for some years as commandant of Transcaspia oblast (1890–1898) and was considered after the death of Skobelev to be the most promising Russian military figure of his day, enjoyed great trust from his immediate superior, Minister of War Vannovskii. According to the account,

In 1897 we began to hear rumors that Kuropatkin would soon be appointed head of the civil administration in the Caucasus. Such a great advance was entirely possible with the support of Vannovskii, who had great influence in St. Petersburg. These rumors began to take on such real significance that in Askhabad they were already congratulating A. N. Kuropatkin on such a splendid advancement. He did not confirm the rumors, but neither did he deny them. People waited day after day for the order which would appoint Kuropatkin to the Caucasus.

But, unexpectedly, the candidacy of General Kuropatkin did not go through. It was said that Vannovskii was furious at his failure, and wanting somehow to reward Kuropatkin, he decided to reorganize all the oblasts of Middle Asia, creating from them one great governor-generalship equal to the Caucasus, and to place Kuropatkin at its head. At a nod from Vannovskii, the Asiatic Section of the General Staff composed a report addressed to Tsar Nicholas II on the urgent necessity of uniting to the Turkestan region the oblasts of Semirechie . . . and Transcaspia. This report was at once confirmed by the Sovereign, and neither in the military, nor in the State Council did anyone suspect the great reform of our Middle Asian borderland which was being compounded. Kuropatkin was called to St. Petersburg, and work on the creation of a virtual viceroyalty in Middle Asia went on at full swing.

Suddenly, in the midst of these plans, came another development. It was announced that Vannovskii had given his resignation to the tsar, and had secured the appointment of Kuropatkin as minister of war in his place. The plan for the enlargement of the Governor-Generalship of Turkestan was retained, but General S. M. Dukhovskoi was appointed to fill the post originally designed for Kuropatkin.[23] With this bureaucratic revolution, Russian Central Asia achieved a territorial pattern which it retained until 1917.

In this final phase, the Governor-Generalship of Turkestan stood as follows. (The asterisks indicate oblast administrative centers. All but two uezds derive their names from the uezd centers.)

Oblasts	Uezds
Syr-Daria	Kazalinsk
	Perovsk
	Chimkent
	Aulie-Ata
	*Tashkent
	Amu-Daria section (center at Fort Petro-Aleksandrovskii)
Fergana	Kokand
	*Skobelev (called Novyi Margelan until 1909)
	Andizhan

	Namangan
	Osh
Samarkand	*Samarkand
	Katta-Kurgan
	Khodzhent
	Dzhizak (uezd center at Fort Kliuchev)
Semirechie	*Vernyi
	Kopal
	Lepsinsk
	Przhevalsk
	Pishpek
Transcaspia	Mangyshlak
	Krasnovodsk
	*Askhabad
	Tedzhen
	Merv

Tashkent served as the administrative center for both Syr-Daria oblast and the Governor-Generalship of Turkestan.

The Steppe oblasts, as finally constituted, consisted of the oblasts of Akmolinsk and Semipalatinsk, which made up the Governor-Generalship of the Steppe, and Ural'sk and Turgai, which were governed separately and were directly subordinate to the Ministry of the Interior. (The asterisks indicate oblast administrative centers; the names of the uezds and their administrative centers are identical.)

Oblasts	*Uezds*
Akmolinsk	*Omsk
	Petropavlovsk
	Kokchetav
	Akmolinsk
	Atbasar
Semipalatinsk	*Semipalatinsk
	Pavlodar
	Karkaralinsk
	Ust'-Kamenogorsk
	Zaisan
Ural'sk	*Ural'sk
	Lbishchensk
	Gur'ev
	Temirsk

Turgai	Aktiubinsk
	Kustanai
	Irgiz
	Turgai

Turgai oblast was governed from Orenburg. Omsk was the administrative center for both Akmolinsk oblast and the Governor-Generalship of the Steppe.

Two other large units in the region retained a separate status. The capitulation of the emir of Bukhara in 1868, and the khan of Khiva in 1873 was followed in each case by only partial annexation of their territory. After they promised to abolish slavery and certain cruel punishments, to grant trade concessions, and to relinquish the right to conduct relations with other countries, both rulers were permitted to retain almost complete independence in their internal affairs. They were subject only to the surveillance and occasional advice of a Russian political agent in Bukhara and of the commandant of the Amu-Daria section adjoining Khiva. All foreign affairs and trade relations with foreign countries had thereafter to be conducted through the governor-general of Turkestan and the minister of Foreign Affairs in St. Petersburg.

Reduced to such vassal status, both Khiva and Bukhara continued in nearly the same pattern as before. Slavery continued to be practiced, though in disguised form; criminals continued to be flogged to death, to be thrown from the Death Tower of Bukhara, to have their hands or feet cut off, or to be confined in noisome pits. The picturesque and colorful past lingered on at the cost of disease, squalor, ignorance, and despotism.

Sustained in power, the emir of Bukhara, Seid Muzaffar Eddin, proved adroit in maintaining and improving his position. He gave a flattering reception to all Russian officials who called on him and handed out decorations freely. By gaining friends in high places, he gradually improved his standing. Von Kaufman called him "Your Honor" (*vashe stepenstvo*), a title accorded to merchants and burghers, but his son, Seid Abdul Akhad (reigned 1885–1911), after his first visit to St. Petersburg was addressed first as "Illustrious," then "August," then "Serene Highness," then as "Excellency," then "High Excellency," and finally as "Majesty," which gave him a rank higher than a governor. When, during the Russo-Japanese War, the emir gave a torpedo boat to the Imperial Navy he was made a general in a Cossack Lifeguard Regiment, which in the eyes of the natives made him more important than the governor-general.[24]

After the revolution of 1905–1907 was suppressed the question of complete annexation of Bukhara began frequently to be raised in Russian military circles. One of the most active advocates of this was Lieutenant Colonel D. N. Logofet, geographer, expert on Bukhara, and one of the Black Hundreds in the Third Duma. As a result of Logofet's book *Strana bezpraviia* (Land of Injustice), the governor-general of Turkestan called a special conference on the Bukharan question on February 2, 1909. However, with regard to the reform of the administration the conference merely recommended that the political agent call the emir's attention to the injustice and oppression suffered by his people. The replacement of the 10,000-man Bukharan army with a Russian force was discussed but no conclusion was reached. In 1910 the Bukharan question was considered again, this time by the Council of Ministers. Prime Minister Stolypin declared that the emirate would be annexed sooner or later, but that because of external questions, particularly the attitude of England, the time was not ripe. The matter was scheduled to be discussed again in the autumn of 1914 by the Duma, but the outbreak of World War I caused the question to be tabled.[25]

MISTAKEN CONCEPTS

The course followed in the territorial organization of Russian Central Asia described above was a complicated story, but one which must be understood to clarify the other aspects of Russian rule in that region. Some interest can also be found in the story of what did *not* occur. The Soviet *History of the Kazakh SSR* published in 1943 declared that "all the Kazakh lands were divided intentionally between various administrative divisions with the aim of breaking up the unity of the Kazakh people, in order more easily to subdue them." [26] Another Soviet work, a history of the USSR used in university courses, describes in both its 1949 and 1954 editions the formation of the oblasts and governor-generalships of Central Asia and concludes that the territories of Uzbekistan, Tadzhikistan, Turkmenistan, Kirgiziia, and Kazakhstan were "torn asunder" between various administrative-territorial units.[27]

This idea has been accepted by various Western writers, who have asserted that the pattern of oblasts, governor-generalships, and native states in Russian Central Asia was the result of a deliberate policy of adjusting boundaries. Such "gerrymandering," as some have put it, borrowing a term from American political history, was done in order to divide nationalities and hinder the formation of any national political combination that might act against Russia.[28] The facts do not support these contentions. The statutes for the administration of the Steppe and of Turkestan did introduce uezds and volosts with the aim of weakening the clan organization of the Kazakhs.[29] However, there appears to be no indication of any intention of the Imperial government to separate the peoples of Central Asia in order to hinder the formation of any political combination, or to break up any existing national combination.

That even the Soviets have come around to this point of view is shown by the 1957 edition of the *History of the Kazakh SSR*, which omits reference to any deliberate divisive tactics except insofar as the territorial principle was introduced in order to weaken the clans. This is described as a progressive aim.[30] Another work, the *History of the Uzbek SSR*, even asserts that "in spite of the motley national composition of the population of the governor-generalship, it was grouped in oblasts so that in each oblast one nationality or another had a collective predominance and gave this oblast a definite national character." [31] The case for this assertion, however, is immediately weakened by the enumeration of exceptions.

Instead of relying on statements reflecting the ideological mode in the USSR regarding this question, it is worth while to look at the record. The difficulty of subdividing the region for administrative purposes already was seen clearly by Von Kaufman. As he wrote in his report of 1880 to Tsar Alexander II: "The division of the governor-generalship . . . should depend not so much on the external or temporary conditions determined by military-political situations of the past epoch of conquests and annexations, as by the requirements of civil organization of our occupied territories. With obvious advantage and convenience for internal administration, it can be based at the present time on ethnographic, territorial, cultural, administrative, economic, and financial conditions." [32]

Von Kaufman proposed that the Governor-Generalship of Turkestan, then comprising the three oblasts of Semirechie, Syr-Daria, and Fergana, along with the Zeravshan district, should be divided into two zones. The first was to be a northern zone made up of Semirechie oblast, five uezds of Syr-Daria oblast, and the Amu-Daria section. It consisted mainly of steppe land and was occupied primarily by the nomadic Kazakhs. This zone was estimated to contain about 15,550 square miles of territory with a population of 1,470,000 people, of whom only 135,000 were settled.

A second zone, to be formed in the south, would comprise only 3,870 square miles, but would have a dense population of 1,-550,000 people, of whom only 230,000 would be nomads. The population of this region, consisting of a mixture of Turkic tribes and Tadzhiks, was uniform in economy and social structure, in religion, and in history, for Tashkent, Kokand, and Samarkand had often been under one ruler. This region, Von Kaufman proposed, could be administered from Tashkent, which would not be more than 400–500 versts (275–350 miles) from all the uezd centers and from the borders, with great convenience for communications.

As another possibility, Von Kaufman suggested that the existing divisions of Semirechie and Syr-Daria oblasts be retained in large measure, but that a third oblast be made of the Zeravshan district (later Samarkand oblast), the Amu-Daria section, Fergana oblast, and the southern uezds of Syr-Daria oblast. Such an arrangement, he felt, would result in greater administrative efficiency and a saving in the salaries of officials. [33] Instead of any intention to divide nationalities or to hinder the formation of national political combinations, these proposals indicate an honest effort to solve a troublesome administrative problem.

Because of Von Kaufman's death, his proposals were never formally submitted, although they were published. Instead, still other ideas were put forth. In 1884 a commission under the chairmanship of Adjutant General Count N. P. Ignat'ev examined a project for a new statute for the administration of Turkestan. It also considered the rearrangement of oblasts. Various combinations were discussed. General Kuropatkin, a member of the commission, proposed that the Governor-Generalship of Turkestan should also include Turkmenia (i.e., Transcaspia). He proposed that the governor-generalship, thus augmented, should be reconstituted in three parts: (1) A Kazalinsk oblast, to include Aulie-Ata, Chimkent, Perovsk, Kazalinsk, and a part of the Orenburg Steppe. It would contain up to 350,000 square versts and would have a population of nearly 800,000. (2) An oblast with the settled population of Kuraminsk uezd (later Tashkent uezd) and Khodzhent uezds of Syr-Daria oblast, Fergana oblast, and the Zeravshan district, to be centered at either Tashkent, Novyi Margelan, or Samarkand. This division would have 180,000 square versts, and a population of 1,700,000. (3) A so-called Askhabad oblast comprising the population of Turkmenia.

Other members of the commission objected to Kuropatkin's proposal because it was not in accord with Imperial policy of the time regarding Bukhara and Khiva. It was felt that such a plan would end the independence of the two native states, evidently because it would mean surrounding them with one administrative unit (this, however, was done later in 1898 without appreciably altering the situation of the two states). In the end, virtually the only territorial change the Ignat'ev commission proposed—embodied in the draft of the "statute for the administration of the Turkestan Region" of 1886—was the formation of a separate "Zeravshan oblast" from the Zeravshan district, with the addition of Khodzhent uezd, to be taken from Syr-Daria oblast.[34]

The idea of a separate oblast in the Kazalinsk area, on grounds of the distinctive economic and geographical characteristics of the area around the Aral Sea and its isolation from other centers, continued to be discussed. In 1890 the Ministry of the Interior considered dividing the oblasts of Ural'sk and Turgai into four parts, two to be governed from Orenburg and two to be included in a new Kazalinsk oblast, but took no action. Among the evidence considered was the protest by a Kazakh delegation that such a division would separate clans closely related by blood and vitiate their religious customs and established traditions.[35] A few years later a Kazalinsk oblast was again proposed, this time to consist of Kazalinsk and Perovsk uezds and the Amu-Daria section,[36] but again no action was taken.

Although none of these proposals was adopted, one may see from them and from the actual course of events the variety of motives behind the territorial organization of Russian Central Asia. Economics, ethnic and geographic factors, personal ambition, and strategic considerations all played their part, but there is no indication of any deliberate "gerrymandering" to prevent the forming of national political combinations against the Russians. That such preventive measures were not taken was simply because they were not needed, as there had never been any national political combinations in the modern sense in Central Asia. Members of the individual ethnic groups were of course conscious of being "Kazakh" or "Uzbek" or "Turkmen" but these concepts played little or no part in the loose confederations of the nomads and the despotisms established over conglomerations of the settled peoples. The nearest thing to an over-all binding force was the Moslem religion, but as a uniting factor this was as vague as the concept of "Christendom" in the Europe of the Middle Ages. Such patriotism as existed was primarily local, and even that was dulled by class distinction and oppression. Kazakhstan, Turkmenistan, Uzbekistan, Tadzhikistan, and Kirgiziia were therefore at best still only "geographical expressions." Whatever the faults of the Imperial regime, its administrative divisions did not hinder the combination of the peoples of these units, for the simple reason that they could not hinder what had never yet existed. Consciousness of nationhood and aspiration toward political independence had to await the introduction and spread of European nationalist concepts.

IV

THE SETTING UP of a government for the newly conquered territories of Central Asia posed no easy task for the Russian military administrators. Intruders in a strange land, they had to gain the obedience and coöperation of an alien people, hostile or at best indifferent to their efforts. To this task, they could only apply what they had at hand, certainly not what some writers of a later era, sitting in *ex post facto* judgment, might have preferred them to apply. As Russians of the mid-nineteenth century they naturally brought with them some of the chronic inertia and backwardness of the social and economic order in which they had grown up. They brought a state order devised, at the outset of the preceding century, to direct the country toward modernization by means of parade ground discipline and rigid uniformity, accompanied by a tendency toward drastic solutions. They also brought some of the new liberalism which had appeared in Russia amid the sweeping reforms following the emancipation of the serfs in 1861.

But while other aspects of the Imperial system were undergoing major reforms, provincial administration had scarcely changed. The ruling groups were reluctant to loosen their iron grip on the country lest reform should turn into revolution. Therefore, with the exception of certain features in keeping with its frontier status, the same restrictive pattern of administration was applied to Central Asia as in the rest of the empire.

REGIONAL, OBLAST, AND UEZD ADMINISTRATION

As a borderland that required close supervision but was too large to form a single province, Russian Central Asia was divided initially between the three governor-generalships of Orenburg, West Siberia, and Turkestan. Each of these units, as the name indicates, was headed by a governor-general. Appointed by and immediately responsible to the tsar, the governor-general was in effect the tsar's personal agent, serving as "the chief guardian of the inviolability of the supreme law of the Autocracy, of the interests of the State, and of the exact fulfillment of the laws and decrees of the higher government in all parts of the administration of the region entrusted to him." [1] Possessing in addition a wide range of powers as a guardian of public morals and of the general welfare, and as a supervisor of the economy and of the administration within his area of jurisdiction, the governor-general served as one of the main Imperial functionaries.

The governor-general exerted his authority through an office staff (*kantseliariia*). This body, consisting of a number of secretaries and clerks with various specialties and headed by an office director (*upravliaiushchii kantseliarii*), was the nerve center of the regional administration. Through it flowed all the business between lower and higher echelons of the administration: it dealt with a multiplicity of matters relating to personnel, taxation, communications, the economy, the police, and many other things; and it supervised the activities of the lower administrative echelons. The various ministries of the central government also had representatives in the regional administration. Their local functions were subject to surveillance and coördination by the governor-general, but the ministerial officials were mainly responsible to St. Petersburg. The governor-general could convene a general meeting of various chief subordinates and ministerial representatives. This body could review problems and recommend action, but the governor-general could overrule its decisions if he saw fit.

A governor-generalship was composed of two or more provinces, known as gubernias in the older, longer-settled parts of the empire, and as oblasts in newer regions such as Central Asia. The gubernia or oblast administration resembled the administration of the governor-generalship, drawn on a smaller scale. Each province was headed by a governor, assisted in his duties by an assistant governor. The varied functions of the gubernia or oblast government were directed and coördinated through the administrative board (*gubernskoe* or *oblastnoe pravlenie*). Law enforcement, the execution of court sentences, public health measures, construction projects, communications, and taxation were all within its scope. This work was carried out through an office divided into several sections. Special problems were considered at a general meeting, comprised of the assistant governor and other leading officials, and presided over by the governor.[2]

The gubernia or oblast was subdivided into several uezds. Each of these was headed by an uezd commandant, aided by an assistant commandant. Administrative routine was carried out by an office staff. The uezds were divided into smaller districts (*uchastok*). Each of these was headed by a district pristav (the Russian term will be used here instead of "prefect," "bailiff," or "police officer," as it is sometimes translated) in charge of a small police and administrative force.

This was the basic organization for provincial administration in the borderlands of the empire, a simplified form of the provincial administration of European Russia. The same structure was introduced in Central Asia, but with an important modification: the command of the military forces and the control of the civil administration, usually in separate hands in other parts of the empire, were combined in a so-called military-civil administration headed by the governor-general. From the first, therefore, the military element dominated the scene.

ADMINISTRATIVE MALFUNCTION

In practice, the apparent symmetry and simplicity in the system of provincial administration introduced in Central Asia, with its highly centralized military-type chain of command and responsibility, proved illusory. The scandal and corruption which soon arose caused disgust and concern both on the spot and in European Russia. The artist and writer N. N. Karazin, who served in

Tashkent in the first years after the conquest, castigated the order of things there in his novel *Na dalekikh okrainakh* (In Distant Lands). The satirist M. E. Saltykov-Shchedrin used the personnel of Tashkent as prototypes in his biting satire on the Russian officialdom of his day, *Gospodá Tashkentsy* (The Tashkentians). Eugene Schuyler, secretary of the American Legation in St. Petersburg, who traveled extensively in Russian Central Asia in the 1870's, devoted much of his book *Turkistan* to a description of the corruption, inefficiency, and misrule in the new Russian possessions.

The causes of this malfunctioning lay first of all in the administrative mechanism itself. The effort to combine military and civil administration in order to provide a unified authority such as the natives were already accustomed to, and which would avoid inconsistency and conflicting orders, did not prove successful. "The chief evil," stated a Russian official in a report made in 1871, quoted at length by Schuyler, "consists in confusion of the military and administrative powers and the complete absence of any distinction between them." The superior military and civil authority was combined in the person of the governor-general, but in practice his administrative authority was delegated to his office director, and his military authority was vested in his chief of staff. The office director should have been confined to purely administrative affairs, but in reality he had the same prerogatives as the chief of staff. Officers of the lower echelons of the administration came to depend more on the office director in matters pertaining to the military forces than on the chief of staff.

In the oblasts the two powers were again united in the military governors, who were both administrative chiefs and troop commandants. Again, however, this united authority was more theoretical than actual, as there were constant disputes between the officials of the civil administration and the military commanders in the oblasts. In the uezds the military authority was vested in the officers in charge of the troops quartered there, and the administrative authority in the uezd commandants. However, the troop chiefs were often in doubt as to whether they should turn to the military commanders who were their nominal chiefs, or to the administrative authorities, whose influence often carried the most weight.[3] These divergencies of views at all levels caused continual antagonism between different branches of the administration, and these conflicts gave rise to factions, each the center of a group of career hunters eager for office and profit.

Although a certain amount of the difficulty with the Russian administrative mechanism in Central Asia may have been caused by faulty structure, a large share of the blame could be ascribed to the human factor involved. Like any other, the government of Russian Central Asia could only be as good as its personnel. In spite of whatever wisdom and foresight went into the drafting of statutes and the formation of policies, the final test lay in the performance of the men designated to apply the laws and carry out the policies.

Many of the officers in Turkestan were well fitted to undertake administrative tasks. Many had gained acquaintance with the region during campaigns. Coming from social groups loyal to the monarchy, instilled with devotion to sovereign and duty, recipients of some of the best educational background available in their day, their discipline and their capabilities made them the most reliable element on which the head of the empire could depend. Even so, there were never enough capable and honest administrators to fill the needs of the expanding governmental apparatus. The high qualities of the best of the Imperial officials in Central Asia were offset by lack of these qualities in others. The military administration of European Russia habitually rid itself of its worst officers by sending them to Turkestan. Others who had been penalized for irregularities sought transfers to Turkestan where they hoped to distinguish themselves and obtain promotions in the frequent campaigns. The army of the Turkestan region thus became "a refuge for the scum of military society." Such officers might do only slight damage in the mass of the army, but in Turkestan, where the troops were spread over a vast territory, and where the best officers were kept at the principal points, the scoundrels and wastrels could often nullify the work of the better men.

These qualitative differences were heightened by the distinction which soon arose between the officers serving in the administration and those still with the regular military forces. Discipline and morale suffered from the intrigue and wirepulling used to obtain transfers to the administrative posts. These practices were abetted by officials who made free use of the governor-general's power to appoint officers without consulting their chiefs. In addition, civil functionaries often received appointments to military posts as aides-de-camp, as ordnance officers, as chiefs of control, and sometimes as staff officers, which enabled them to interfere with the orders of the regular military personnel. Financial rewards were also disproportionate. The section chiefs of the office of the governor-general received greater salaries and perquisites than did generals. Simple copyists in the same office received more for having taken part in expeditions than did officers of merit who had undergone great hardships.[4] These conditions of low morale in the military service, the striving for advantage, the intrigue, and the frequently inferior personnel gave rise to a widespread corruption which soon earned a notoriety in Russia comparable to that of the contemporary carpet-baggers in the United States.

Governor-General Von Kaufman himself appears to have been scrupulously honest. His name was free of scandal during his lifetime and an investigation of his administration ordered soon after his death by his successor and political enemy Cherniaev could uncover no conclusive evidence of discreditable conduct. Far from enriching himself while in office, Von Kaufman was so low in funds at the time of his death that his widow had to borrow money in order to return to St. Petersburg.[5] However, his vanity, self-isolation, and excessive trust of subordinates frequently made him easy prey for the unscrupulous. The governor-general's office staff included some honest and capable officials, but there were others who were not so. Two of the office directors during Von Kaufman's time were eventually dismissed for incompetence or dishonest practices.[6]

On the oblast level, General Kolpakovskii, the military governor of Semirechie oblast, ran an honest and efficient organization, but General Golovachev, who served as military governor of Syr-

Daria oblast from 1867 to 1877 made the most of his position for his own gain. Golovachev, whom Von Kaufman esteemed as one of his ablest field commanders, was strictly a military general and had no interest in his administrative duties. "A fat, good-natured glutton, hospitable and terribly lazy," with a cheerful disregard for legality, Golovachev lived the life of a sybarite, surrounded by a group of incompetent and corrupt favorites who took bribes and made free with government funds.[7] Contemporaries termed his oblast administrative board a "cesspool."[8]

The various uezd administrations became equally notorious. In Kuraminsk uezd, which included the capital, Tashkent, the first commandant (1867–1872) was finally removed from his post for levying illegal taxes against the natives, misappropriating funds, and collusion. His successor (1872–1877) was eventually tried for embezzlement and misuse of authority and sent to Siberia. A third (1877–1880), "an honest man, but one who lived beyond his means," committed suicide.[9]

The situation of the uezd commandants was complicated by the great disparity between their incomes and the expenditures required of them. Except in the main cities, they were the chief personages in their districts. They had to play a leading role in local society, hold open house, and entertain all important travelers. During the Kokand campaign, for example, the governor-general and fifty staff officers stayed several weeks at the home of the commandant of Khodzhent uezd. His expenses for only one week of this mass visit exceeded his entire year's salary.

Most of the uezd commandants approached the problem of arrears by levying additional taxes on the natives, usually to a degree that not only covered normal expenses but enabled them to live in luxury. As long as this was done prudently and did not attract the attention of higher authorities the practice could be continued, although it might be an open secret. The commandant of Kuldzha uezd, Major Gerasimov, was considered one of the best officers in Turkestan, although it was generally known that for champagne alone he annually spent the equivalent of his entire salary.[10] Only when a commandant's abuses became particularly flagrant would he draw the attention of his superiors.

His career then usually ended in dismissal from the service or imprisonment. The commandant of Khodzhent uezd, Baron Nol'de, was finally tried and sentenced to eight years of hard labor in Siberia.[11]

MUNICIPAL ADMINISTRATION

When Von Kaufman chose Tashkent as his capital, he set about organizing its municipal administration to serve as a model for the other cities in Turkestan.[12] The setting up of effective machinery to govern the large urban concentrations of natives and the small Russian communities which were appearing alongside them offered many difficulties. First of all there was the task of coördinating Asiatic and European forms with as little friction and economic dislocation as possible, and secondly the establishment of orderly, efficient government in a frontier community. For personnel whose main experience lay in military affairs, in a day when techniques of organizing public administration were unknown, this presented a multitude of problems and pitfalls.

In its main features the administration of Tashkent followed the provisions for city government contained in the draft statute drawn up for the region by the Steppe Commission. At its head was to be a city commandant, aided by an assistant and an office staff. The city commandant was to direct a Russian police force drawn from the local garrison and to take over command of the native police force. Other city employees were to include a physician and a midwife, whose services offered the first modern medical facilities in the region.

Much improvising was required, however, in the details of administration. As early as June, 1866, General Romanovskii, the military governor of what was then the oblast of Turkestan, organized a "town committee" to look after town finances. At first, this committee's activity consisted only in giving out plots of land to the Russian inhabitants and receiving payments for these. Later, in 1869, the committee levied a tax on vehicles, which amounted exclusively to a tax on native carts, the only vehicles in Tashkent at that time. The receipts from this tax were spent for street cleaning, bridge building, tree planting, and other civic improvements. In 1868, General Golovachev, the military governor of Syr-Daria oblast, appointed another committee to supervise the distribution of irrigation water and the repair of ditches in the Russian part of the town. For this an irrigation tax was levied.

Both committees operated independently, uncontrolled by any central authority. No accounts were kept, and the tax money was spent at will by the city commandant, the committee members, the members of the oblast administrative board, and by the city police officials. Because of the blatant irregularities the better members of the committees resigned, and the populace protested at having to pay the taxes.

To improve matters, in 1870 General Golovachev concentrated all business affairs of the Russian part of the town under an economic administration (*khoziaistvennoe upravlenie*) headed by himself. This body was to define the city boundaries, draw up a plan for the city, lay out streets, allot homesites, accept payment for these, set aside sites for public buildings and parks, make a list of legal inhabitants of the city, levy taxes, make expenditures, manage irrigation, and take other steps necessary to the town's organization and further development.

To obtain funds the economic administration took over the taxes due the two previous committees and levied some of its own. Expenditures were made for the purchase of land for the city, for the maintenance of streets and bridges, irrigation systems, the bazaar, the city jail, and the cemetery, and for city lighting, sanitation, and the payment of salaries. However, no control was kept over these expenditures. The city commandant and the committee members merely took what was allegedly needed. This led not only to waste, but frequently to outright theft. Golovachev and many others profited by the ease with which accounts could be juggled or by the complete absence of accounts. Many officials acquired city land illegally.[13]

Means for eliminating the corruption and inefficiency in the Turkestan administration were not immediately available. The various ministries of the central government were represented in the regional administration, but their representatives were relatively ineffectual during the first years of Russian rule. The broad and ill-defined limits of the governor-general's authority frequently circumvented efforts of the ministries to exercise control over matters which they considered within their respective spheres. For the purpose of auditing accounts a regional control office opened in Tashkent in 1868. Most of its officials were Poles exiled for participation in the Polish uprising of 1863. Their work was precise and efficient, but they had no authority beyond their immediate task, and because of the chaotic state of most of the administration's finances, they were usually far behind current accounts.[14]

THE JUDICIARY

The judicial arm of the administration was unable to right matters, because it too was in a provisional, defective state. The modernized judicial system introduced in Russia in 1864 was withheld from border regions such as Central Asia until such time as they might have normal civil rule.

The lowest levels of the Russian judicial structure comprised the various rural courts of the peasants. These courts employed customary or unwritten law. The lowest judicial instance employing statutory or written law was that of the justice of the peace (*mirovoi sud'ia*). In European Russia these were elected by the zemstvo, the elective local administrative assembly, introduced in 1864. In Central Asia, however, the zemstvo was not introduced, and the justices of the peace were appointed by the military governors. Their districts usually comprised entire uezds.

Because of the sparse population and the lack of qualified personnel, the next higher judicial instance of European Russia, the sessions of the justices of the peace (*s'ezd mirovykh sudei*), was not introduced in Turkestan. Instead, Von Kaufman had the oblast administrative boards take over the functions of this court level. The military governors were given the right of cassation—the review of cases and perhaps the overruling of the decision of a lower court—over decisions of the oblast administrative boards.[15]

Elsewhere in the empire the prosecutor (*prokuror*) was directly responsible to the minister of justice, ensured proper procedure in the courts, and acted in criminal matters as public prosecutor. In Turkestan, however, Von Kaufman entrusted the functions of the prosecutor to the military governors. Von Kaufman also removed military governors, uezd commandants, and a number of lesser officials from the jurisdiction of the courts, believing it impolitic to subject the local administrative personnel to judicial action which might make the Russian government seem inconsistent or divided in authority before the natives.[16]

The next higher instance, the district court (*okruzhnyi sud*), consisting of a chairman and two members, normally examined matters beyond the competency of the justices of the peace as well as appeals from their decisions. Under Von Kaufman the function of this court, too, was vested in the oblast administrative board. A so-called Military-Judicial Commission, consisting of officers often unsuitable for military service because of alcoholism and other reasons, heard cases and handed down decisions.[17]

A method of bypassing the courts frequently resorted to in Turkestan was the practice of dealing with offenders "by administrative procedure." By this means an alleged political offender could simply be sent without trial to some distant town, there to live under police surveillance until the authorities might feel it possible to lift the restriction.

ADMINISTRATION OF RUSSIAN PEASANTS AND COSSACKS

The administration of Russian peasant communities in Central Asia followed the national system established after the freeing of the serfs in 1861. The basic unit was the village community (*sel'skoe obshchestvo*), formed by the inhabitants of each village (*selo*). Each community was administered by a village meeting (*sel'skii skhod*), including all the householders and headed by an elected elder (*starosta*). The elder acted as a judge in the trial of minor offenders.

Several villages constituted a volost. The volost was administered by a volost meeting (*volostnoi skhod*), consisting of one member from each ten householders in the village communities. An elected volost elder (*volostnoi starshina*) served as the executive official of the volost meeting and as chairman of the volost administrative board (*volostnoe pravlenie*), in which all of the village elders took part. The volost elder also had a judicial function and could mete out light sentences to minor offenders.[18]

The volost meeting likewise elected a chairman and members of a volost court, with jurisdiction over the inhabitants of the volost. Decisions of these courts could be appealed to the superior rural court (*verkhnii sel'skii sud*), which was made up of the chairmen of the volost courts of each uchastok of an uezd. The decisions of the Russian rural courts were not based on statutory law, but on customary law, derived from the ideas of right and wrong gained in the long experience of the people.

The administration of Cossack communities, as in the oblast of Semirechie, was similar in form to that of the non-Cossack Russian peasants, but differed slightly in nomenclature. Cossack villages were grouped into stanitsas instead of volosts, each headed by an elected ataman.

NATIVE ADMINISTRATION

The administration of the natives of Central Asia was reorganized by the Russians into levels roughly similar to those of the Russian rural population. As from time immemorial, the native peasants lived in villages (*kishlak*), each headed by an *aksakal* (literally "white beard") or elder, chosen by the community because of his age and wisdom. The Russians regularized the informal procedure which had existed before, and had the aksakal elected by the population for a three-year term and paid a fixed salary. He was charged with convening local meetings for the election of officials, making tax surveys of the village, and collecting taxes. In case of misconduct or incompetence the aksakal could be removed by the uezd commandant.

As among the Russian peasants, several native villages constituted a volost. Electors chosen in the villages on the basis of one for each fifty householders formed a volost meeting. This body, meeting at a time and place determined by the uezd commandant, elected a volost headman and judges (*kazi*). Successful candidates were confirmed by the uezd commandant.

The volost headman was charged with executing court decisions and government orders, keeping a list of inhabitants of the volost, and noting losses or accessions of population. In case of misconduct a volost headman could be removed by the military governor.

Two other local officials of considerable importance were charged with the maintenance of irrigation facilities and the allocation of water. The *mirab,* who performed this function on the village level, was elected by the village meeting. The *aryk aksakal* ("ditch elder"), who looked after trunk canals serving the several villages of a volost, was appointed by the military governor.

The organization pattern of the nomads was similar to that of the native peasants. The fundamental unit of the nomads was the kibitka, each of which was considered to constitute a family or household. Up to 200 kibitkas constituted an aul, and up to 2,000 kibitkas—or about ten auls—constituted a volost. In the eyes of the Russian administration the aul was equivalent to a village. The inhabitants of the auls chose electors, and these in turn met in a volost meeting to elect a volost headman.

The courts of the natives were so organized as to be roughly parallel to the Russian lower courts. Prior to the conquest, ecclesiastical judges called *kazis* presided over the courts of the settled natives of Turkestan. Their judicial procedure and decisions were based on Moslem written law, the Shariat. They were appointed by the khans or beks after an examination of their knowledge of the Shariat. They had no set district of jurisdiction; any native could turn to the kazi he trusted most.

By western standards, punishments in pre-Russian times were severe. Torture, the cutting off of hands or feet, and various more or less ingenious forms of the death penalty were employed. Confinement was in pits or dungeons, often for indefinite periods with little food and no sanitation. In theory the severest sentences were subject to confirmation by the bek, and the conduct of the kazi was subject to censure by other officials. In practice these slight judicial safeguards were more often disregarded.

Among the nomads, disputes and offenses had usually been

judged by elders of the clan or group, who received the title of *bii*. Although they were Moslems, the Kazakhs and other nomads did not use the Shariat, but employed instead the adat, an elaborate system of customary law developed through many centuries. While it was the Russian policy to preserve these native courts, considerable alteration resulted from the abolition of inhumane practices, and from efforts to regularize their procedure and bring the courts into conformity with the empire's basic judicial structure.

The chief Russian innovation was the election of judges. Both kazis and biis were elected for three-year terms and received regular salaries drawn from local tax funds.

The native courts were given jurisdiction over all criminal cases not concerned with the general order of the region, and over all civil matters not based on documents completed by or witnessed by Russian authorities and not involving Russians. Kazis could judge cases not involving more than 100 rubles. Cases involving more than that figure, and criminal cases not coming under the jurisdiction of the Russian courts were decided by a session of kazis or biis. The decision of this body was final. If both sides wished it and submitted a request in writing, a matter involving natives could be tried by a Russian court, although in practice this almost never occurred.

Punishments were left in the hands of the native courts, but were considerably modified. Corporal punishment and the death penalty were abolished in favor of light fines and short periods of confinement. For more serious cases, tried by the Russian courts, hard labor and exile to Siberia were meted out. Jails were built in the towns for the confinement of offenders.

The formal structure so carefully set up did not correspond with actual practice. The native administration, after a favorable beginning, quickly exhibited even more corruption and malpractice than the Russian administration. The elective system proved unsuccessful; bad or weak men were often chosen because they were able to secure Russian favor, and the buying of votes became standard practice. The elected members of the volost meetings and aul or village meetings had no voice in the management of affairs, and were never consulted by the Russians. All resolutions were drawn up by the uezd commandants or by the pristavs, and the native officials were ordered to put their seals to them, frequently without explanation.

Election was intended to lessen the influence of the kazis upon the people, but because of lack of surveillance by Russian authorities the kazis actually enjoyed more power under the new order than under the khans. Unrestrained by the traditional influence of other Moslem officials, the kazis relied less on the Shariat than on their own personal power. As a result, the native courts soon showed themselves to be partial and corrupt.[19]

Under these conditions, unscrupulous natives were quick to seize opportunities for personal advantage. The elections soon became battles royal between influential and wealthy natives, with victory going to whoever could buy the most votes. The winner's expenses were made up after election by exactions upon the populace.

Natives who fell into the hands of the Russian judicial authorities received no better treatment than in their own courts. Instead of having a normal trial, their cases were often disposed of by "administrative procedure." Either General Golovachev or Colonel Medinskii, the city commandant of Tashkent, could jail a native by verbal order without trial, and release him when it suited them. Medinskii frequently punished natives by flogging them with birch switches.[20]

Under such conditions the natives quickly lost any illusions they might have based on Russian promises. They had been used to tyranny under their khans and beks but it was a Moslem tyranny which they understood, imposed by men of their own race and beliefs. They knew nothing of the Russian system of government, and it was rarely explained. All that they could see was arbitrary action.[21]

ALTHOUGH the glaring defects in the Russian administration in Central Asia were evident, at first little could be done to improve the situation because of the obstacles Von Kaufman himself interposed. Loyal to those he considered to be his friends and supporters, trustful almost to the point of naïveté, he habitually overlooked all but the most insistent reports of wrongdoing. When evidence proving the guilt of one official was brought before him, Von Kaufman tore up the papers without reading them, saying "I know this person so well, and I believe him to be such an honest man, that I cannot think such things possible!" [1] Even when the guilt of a subordinate was inescapable, and he was tried and convicted, Von Kaufman preferred merely to transfer the offender to another post or send him out of the region instead of imposing a fine or imprisonment.

EARLY ATTEMPTS AT REFORM

Eventually, however, the realities of the situation became plain even to Von Kaufman, and in 1875 he ordered an investigation of several districts in which corruption was said to be most rampant. The powers given to the commission were limited; they were to abstain from questioning the natives and were to confine themselves chiefly to inspecting the books and accounts of the different administrations. Nevertheless they reported many cases of wrongdoing.[2] In 1877 one of the worst situations came to light in the capital itself. Von Kaufman discovered the nefarious activities of Golovachev and his henchmen and ordered him relieved, along with the assistant director of the governor-general's office and the local uezd commandant. Colonel Medinskii, city commandant of Tashkent, was also implicated but was merely transferred to another post.[3]

The defects in the government of Tashkent were now so obvious that Von Kaufman was spurred to introduce a modified version of the statute for city government adopted in Russia in 1870. The statute provided for a city Duma, elected from the populace by the direct vote of male property owners with a certain amount of wealth. Of seventy-two members (*glasnykh*) there were forty-eight Christians and twenty-four "non-Christians," or natives. This was the first and only body in the Russian administration on which natives could serve, but as the city's population ratio at that time consisted of about 20,000 Russians to 100,000 natives, this was hardly a step toward popular representation. This body voted on matters concerning taxation, city expenditures, and various other city affairs.

The city Duma elected an executive body, the city board (*gorodskaia uprava*). Of the six members of this body, four were to be Christian and two non-Christian. A mayor (*gorodskoi golova*), appointed by the governor-general, was placed at the head of activities of the city Duma and the city board. Most of the mayors in the first years were army colonels. These measures thus bestowed a certain degree of self-government upon the city. All decisions of the city officers, however, were still subject to the approval of the governor-general.

As a further supervisory measure, Von Kaufman appointed the Syr-Daria Oblast Board for City Affairs (*Syr-Dar'inskoe oblastnoe po gorodskim delam prisutstvie*). This body consisted of the military governor of Syr-Daria oblast, presiding, and the assistant military governor, the director of the governor-general's office, the head of the city treasury, the mayor, and the Tashkent justice of the peace.[4]

Efforts to regularize the administration of the Governor-Generalship of Turkestan as a whole involved the drafting of a statute for the government of the region to replace the provisional statute which was first used. Conforming with instructions given him at the time of his appointment in 1867, Von Kaufman compiled a statute and in 1871 presented it for approval, only to have it returned because of objections from the ministries in St. Petersburg to the limitations it set on the power of their representatives.

In 1873, Von Kaufman submitted another draft for a statute, but it fared no better than the first. The return of the work so irritated the general that he made little effort to prepare a new draft, preferring to govern by personal discretion on the basis of the broad powers given him by the tsar in 1867, within the framework of the unapproved draft statute of 1873.

Only in 1881, when the minister of war, citing the need to cut down expenses and increase revenue in the Turkestan administration, persuaded the tsar himself to order the drafting of a statute, did Von Kaufman recommence the task. Soon afterward, Von Kaufman fell mortally ill, and the statute was completed by General Kolpakovskii, the acting governor-general. A commission, to be under the chairmanship of General M. D. Skobelev, was then appointed to examine the draft, but Skobelev died in 1882 and the task was turned over to the new governor-general in Turkestan, General Cherniaev.[5]

THE GIERS INVESTIGATION (1882)

Under Cherniaev there was further delay in the drafting of a statute. Guided more by antipathy than by rectitude, the new governor-general requested that a commission be sent from St. Petersburg to investigate the records of the regime of his predecessor.

The request was granted. Privy Counsellor F. K. Giers, assisted by officials from the ministries of the Interior, Foreign Affairs, Finance, and Justice, was appointed to investigate the civil affairs of the Turkestan administration; Privy Counsellor Veretennikov, a member of the council of the St. Petersburg Military District, was appointed to investigate the military and economic administration of the region.[6] In instructions of October 20, 1882, the Giers commission was also enjoined to compose a new statute for the administration of Turkestan.[7]

Some contemporary observers called the Giers investigation a "court of posterity" trying the actions of Von Kaufman. Apparently motivated by wounded pride, Giers compared all acts of Von Kaufman's regime with the projected statute of 1867 which, as a member of the Steppe Commission, Giers had helped draw up, and with the "Code of Laws of the Russian Empire." Subjecting the records to careful scrutiny, Giers and his colleagues criticized projects which had been failures or too costly, and sought evidence of excess of official powers, misappropriation of funds, and corruption. They were especially critical of Von Kaufman's policies toward the judiciary, the abridgment of judicial power, and the concentration of judicial and administrative functions in the hands of the military governors and their oblast administrative boards.[8]

Cherniaev, in the meantime, tried to continue the rule of the region in the arbitrary manner of Von Kaufman, and thereby met his undoing. His abrupt handling of the ministerial representatives and especially of matters pertaining to the judiciary caused complaints and in February, 1884, after scarcely a year and a half in Tashkent, he was replaced by General N. O. Rosenbach.

THE IGNAT'EV COMMISSION (1884)

Rosenbach received his appointment in time to sit in on deliberations of a new commission convened in St. Petersburg under the chairmanship of Adjutant General Count N. P. Ignat'ev. It was charged with examining the draft statute of 1881 in connection with the findings of the Giers commission, and working out a new statute for the administration of Turkestan.

The new commission included ministerial representatives, the members of the Giers commission, and several officials from Turkestan, including General A. K. Abramov and General A. N. Kuropatkin. Ignat'ev's experience with Central Asia was limited to a mission to Khiva made several decades before; Rosenbach and most of the other members had never been there. Their lack of knowledge was partly compensated for by the practical experience of such men as Abramov and Kuropatkin.

As Ignat'ev stated in his opening address, he and his colleagues were to be governed by the need to put an end to the conditions revealed by the report of the Giers commission and by the need to cover the region's administrative expenses from local sources of income. The Turkestan region should be of use and advantage to Russia, he stated, and therefore the commission should consider every question from the point of view of state interests. It should create a simpler, more uniform, and more economical administration, without being carried away either by preconceived theories or exclusively local considerations.[9]

Among the matters taken up by the commission was the fundamental one of whether the existing "military-civil" form of government in the region should be continued or replaced by one permitting a wider appointment of civilian officials. Kuropatkin urged retention of the existing system. In Siberia, he stated, where Russians were more numerous than the natives, the introduction of Russian institutions had indeed been unduly delayed. In Turkestan, however, the Russian element was still insignificant, less than 1 per cent of the total population, and only a few years had passed since the region's annexation. Therefore, he maintained: "We must not deceive ourselves as to the complete peacefulness of the native population. It cannot be without enmity to us, as conquerors and unbelievers, and that which is advantageous to Russia will for a long time not be advantageous to Turkestan. To hasten to introduce general equality merely in a formal sense will be dangerous and disadvantageous."

Moreover, he added, the military action should not be considered entirely finished. Conditions might force the dispatch of a large part of the army beyond the borders of the Turkestan region. The slightest military setback could be regarded by the Asiatics as a final defeat, and could cause a popular uprising in the rear against which civilian officials would find it more difficult to maintain order than would a strong military authority. The disorders experienced by the French in Algeria, he pointed out, were a good example of the consequences that might arise from premature abolition of a military administration.

Giers, on the other hand, urged a broadening of civil authority in the region. He agreed that a strong authority was needed, but asserted that it should be enough to combine civil and military administration in the person of the governor-general, admitting civilians to other levels of the government.[10]

In the end, the Commission drafted a statute which comprised both points of view. The governor-general retained authority over both the civil and military administration in the region, and his subordinates retained their predominantly military character. The governor-general was given assistance in the form of a special consultative and administrative body, the Regional Council, consisting of the several military governors and the representatives of the various branches of the government. This council was to consider legislative questions, taxation, and other matters concerning the entire region. Although the questions before it were to be decided by majority vote, such decisions could be overridden by the governor-general.

For the first time, however, the region was given an independent judiciary similar to that already existing in the rest of the empire. Justices of the peace and district courts replaced the local courts which had been a part of the office of the governor-general and the oblast administrative boards.

THE TURKESTAN STATUTE

The draft of the Turkestan statute was finally approved by Tsar Alexander III on June 12, 1886, and it went into effect on January 1, 1887, as the "statute for the administration of the Turkestan region." No sooner was the new statute put into practice, however, than many found it unsatisfactory. In the words of one contemporary official: "An inescapable publication of explanatory circulars began; memoranda circulated in St. Petersburg of legislative changes, supplements, or revisions necessary for the application of the new statute; and the governor-general's council was clogged with work caused by the misunderstandings of the governors. In the end the original basic law for Turkestan, put together in some sort of garb from shreds, continued to apply. . . ." [11]

The main basis for criticism of the new statute was the governor-general's loss of authority. Although nominally he was still the center of the civil and military administration, a great deal had been taken from his control. The specialized branches of the government, which were under the representatives of the various national ministries, received more power.

The severest criticisms centered around the independent judiciary. General Baron A. B. Vrevskii, governor-general from 1889 to 1898, complained to the tsar that the separation of judicial functions from his office had resulted in a fall of the governor-general's authority and a lack of respect for the organs of administrative power. Vrevskii warned that the population of Fergana oblast was particularly restless, and that unless power was restored to the governor-general, disorders and uprisings could be feared (predictions which were, in fact, later borne out).[12]

Through the years, efforts continued to be made to reform the Turkestan administration. The matter was considered by a commission in 1894 [13] and again in 1898. At that date, however, new confusion was added by the joining of the oblasts of Semirechie and Transcaspia to the Governor-Generalship of Turkestan, with each remaining under its own statute.

THE ADMINISTRATION OF TRANSCASPIA OBLAST

Because of its separate development, Transcaspia's administration differed in several ways from that of the other oblasts of Russian Central Asia. It was headed, from its capital Askhabad, not by a military governor but by a commandant of equal rank and with similar duties, who was appointed by the tsar on recommendation of the minister of war. Besides his role as governor, the commandant was also in charge of the military forces in the oblast. There was no oblast administrative board in Transcaspia; the functions of this body were performed instead by the personal office staff of the oblast commandant.

Uezd administration in Transcaspia, including the administration of the towns and villages of the Russian settlers, was centered in the several uezd commandants, who were appointed from military ranks as in the other oblasts. Each commandant had an assistant and an administrative staff. As in the other oblasts, each uezd was divided into districts, each headed by a pristav. The Transcaspian natives, unlike those of Turkestan and the Steppe, were not allowed to elect their local officials. These were appointed instead by the uezd commandant, subject to confirmation by the oblast commandant.

Because of the location of Transcaspia, the commandant had certain duties with regard to external affairs. He was "to keep informed as to the state of affairs within foreign countries bordering on his territory," i.e., Persia and Afghanistan. He was "to preserve the inviolability of the frontiers against enemy attack and raiding bands of neighboring peoples." He was to have regular contact with the heads of territories adjacent to the Governor-Generalship of Turkestan, with the Russian minister at Teheran and, if necessary, with the Russian political agent at Bukhara and the Russian consul general at the important Persian border town of Meshed. However, he was to have no relations with the emir of Bukhara or the khan of Khiva except through the governor-general of Turkestan.[14]

This system of administration, in which broad powers were placed in the hands of the oblast commandant, was closely identified for many years with General A. N. Kuropatkin. From the time he was a young officer Kuropatkin had built his career in Transcaspia. When he became commandant of the oblast in 1890, he made full use of the powers given him and ran the oblast to suit himself in a manner reminiscent of Von Kaufman's regime in Tashkent. Unwilling to relinquish his powers, Kuropatkin postponed drafting a new statute for the oblast. Honest and industrious, he preferred to direct the administration on a patriarchal basis. When Kuropatkin left Transcaspia to become minister of war in 1898, the oblast became a part of the Governor-Generalship of Turkestan along with Semirechie oblast, until then a part of the Governor-Generalship of the Steppe.

MORE QUESTS FOR A STATUTE

The obvious inconsistency of having five provinces within the same administrative unit governed by three sets of laws caused repeated attempts not only to reform the administration of the three central oblasts of Syr-Daria, Fergana, and Samarkand, but to draft a statute under which Transcaspia and Semirechie oblasts could be administered as part of one unified government.

One of the first acts of General N. A. Ivanov when he took office as governor-general in 1901 was to appoint a commission to draw up a basic statute for the entire region. This commission worked with record speed and after eight or nine months issued a massive printed work, consisting of the new statute, explanatory notes, and a comparative index of all the articles of the Turkestan and Steppe statutes. Ivanov's regional council then spent three months reviewing the work, and in 1902 the completed project was presented to Minister of War Kuropatkin. In his hands the matter rested, and was forgotten.

A word from Kuropatkin, then at the zenith of his career, could have secured passage of the statute. However, in spite of his high office and many responsibilities, Kuropatkin had taken the unusual course of retaining direct control over the oblast where he had once been commandant, and of blocking any measures which would have changed the existing relationship of Transcaspia to the rest of Turkestan. Not only did his successors in the post of commandant report directly to him instead of to their nominal head, the governor-general of Turkestan, but Kuropatkin personally interfered even in such insignificant matters as the replacement of uezd commandants and pristavs. Only when Kuropatkin gave up his ministerial post at the outbreak of the Russo-Japanese war was the governor-general of Turkestan able to gain full control over the oblast.[15]

THE PALEN INVESTIGATION (1908)

The persistent reports of corruption in Turkestan, clashes between local authorities and the ministries in St. Petersburg, and the weakness shown by the local administration in coping with the revolutionary disturbances of 1905–1907 finally impelled the central government to undertake drastic remedial action. In 1908 the Governing Senate, one of the highest organs of the government, was ordered to conduct a complete investigation and to prosecute offenders. Senator Count K. K. Palen, famed for his ability and honesty, and known as the *"revizuiushchii senator"* (the inspecting senator) because of his energetic prosecution of corrupt officials, was chosen for the task. Given broad powers and a staff of twenty assistants, Palen spent over a year scrutinizing nearly every aspect of government and economic affairs in the region, including the regional, oblast, uezd, city, rural, and native administrations, as well as mining, agriculture, colonization, taxation, the police, prisons, courts, and state property. His commission's lengthy reports are the best single source concerning Turkestan in the pre-World War I period.

Palen made liberal use of his power to suspend and prosecute officials found to have been involved in indiscretions. In the first general housecleaning in the region's administrative history, scores of officials were arrested, tried, and convicted. General P. I. Mishchenko, governor-general for less than a year, was forced to resign his office because of the commission's criticisms and the arrest of some of his most trusted personnel.

Transcaspia oblast was hit hardest by the investigators. There Palen found the military element in almost complete control. While Kuropatkin was commandant he had dominated matters and had placed many of his old regimental comrades in good posts, but because of his frequent poor judgment many undesirables had attained responsible office.

Kuropatkin's honesty and untiring energy had sufficed to keep the Transcaspian administration on a straight path, but as soon as he became minister of war in 1898 the entire picture changed. For ten years there had been a rapid succession of oblast commandants, most of them with little interest in administration or the exercise of proper supervision and control. Affairs had been run mainly by the office director, a colonel who had served in the region for eighteen years. A tireless worker, he knew every man in the administration and his weaknesses. Every official in the oblast administration had been appointed by him. This man was the head of the evildoers in the province, but the remainder were no better. Among those mentioned by Palen were the assistant commandant, accused of extortion, bribery, falsification of official documents, and even of planning the murder of an unfavorable witness; the commandant of Askhabad uezd, "a gambler and a wastrel"; the police chief of Askhabad, accused of robbery and murder; and the director of the Askhabad Gymnasium, who gave diplomas for money. Palen suspended and brought charges against two-thirds of the officials in Transcaspia, and, after lengthy trials which continued long after his return to St. Petersburg, all were convicted.[16]

To right the administration of Turkestan, Palen felt that it was time for the military to give way to civilian elements. For Russians and settled natives he recommended introduction of the zemstvo. For the nomads, on the other hand, he felt that an abridgment of self-government was in order. To eliminate the abuses everywhere current in the election and practice of elders and volost headmen he advocated liquidation of the elective system and in its stead the appointment of native officials.[17]

The housecleaning of official personnel, and the commission's recommendations for changes in the administrative structure were widely discussed. A few saw in the proposed changes an opportunity to fulfill an obligation to "Russify" (*obrusit'*) the uncivilized peoples and to teach them self-government, but most of the Russians in Turkestan saw the proposals as a threat to their predominance in the administration while the Russian numerical inferiority was still so acute.[18]

In the end a familiar pattern was followed; after much discussion nothing was done. The reports of the Palen commission were printed in massive volumes and then, like the reports of many a previous commission, were forgotten. Radical measures, particularly of a liberal reform character, were not in style in the Russia of that day. The tendency of the conservative Imperial regime was to maintain the *status quo,* to use what was already at hand rather than to embark on new solutions. The prevailing mood of the regime was concisely summed up in 1912 by A. V. Krivoshein, the head of the Agricultural Administration, in a report made after a visit to Turkestan:

In Turkestan the formative period has not yet ended. It is not a special form of administration which is required for this period, but a strong administration, backed by means and energy. Only this can build a new Turkestan.

The introduction of general civil administration in place of the military, or, as proposed by Count Palen, the establishment of the zemstvo, are questions for the future and are of comparatively minor importance. Both reforms are useful, good, and beneficial, but only if there is a strong Russian population in the region.

Meanwhile, the actual Turkestan is an endless sea of natives. The Russian settlements and the new Russian "cities" within the old native cities are still only islands in this sea, although they are, thank God, firm bases for the further settlement of Russians. The Russian rural population, according to the latest statistics, amounts to only 4,775 in Transcaspia, 4,804 in Samarkand, 8,782 in Fergana and 40,234 in Syr-Daria, or from $1\frac{1}{3}$ to 6 per cent.

Under these conditions it is difficult to govern the land on general principles. When one has seen the universal predominance of the natives in Turkestan, one cannot but feel that this is still a Russian military camp, a temporary halting place during the victorious march of Russia into Central Asia. The Russian military might speaks a more comprehensible and impressive language to the subject mass of the natives than the civil administration. If . . . a governor in a frock coat is to replace the governor in epaulettes in each colony, this change is yet a long way off.

The military administration has not hindered the economic development of Turkestan so far, and will not do so in the future. The uezd commandants, the main working force in the local administration, are very well selected; the administration is in general well prepared for its immediate task. . . . The zemstvo is necessary *after* the establishment of a Russian Turkestan, but not *for* this establishment.[19]

This was the voice of the old order, vigorous, yet inflexibly conservative, setting forth the doctrine which was to prevail until the entire Imperial administrative structure was shattered.

It can be seen from the foregoing how the Russians, gaining control over a great area in Central Asia within a generation, used the opportunity to set up a government which would benefit from past experience and sum up what had been accomplished in Imperial statecraft. For Russian nationals that government was a mixture, first, of traditional authoritarian rule, a combination of military administration and a militarized civil administration ensuring the central government of control over the entire structure. On the other hand there were elements of the new liberalism which had appeared in 1861, applied reluctantly and with many safeguards to the judiciary and to municipal and rural government. For the natives, local self-government was retained, but this was less from any intention of preparing them for greater responsibility than it was from a laissez-faire principle which would enable greater ease in the administration.

The incessant adjusting of the government structure, the drafting and redrafting of statutes, resulted from an effort of the bureaucratic mind to reconcile the irreconcilable—to create honesty and efficiency in government by legislation, first bringing forth an ideal and then trying to live up to it. Although this combination of old and new was far from perfect, permeated as it was by corruption in both Russian and native officialdom, it provided an effective system for administering, peopling, and developing the region.

PART TWO

Colonization

VI

WITH RUSSIAN GARRISONS and administrative centers came urban
life in the European style, a new element in Central Asia. Wherever the troops stopped, Russian settlements arose, forming bases
for cultural and economic development. In the steppe, where
life was difficult and there was no urban tradition, settlements
were long mere outposts, usually consisting of a small fort, a
cluster of huts of Cossack or peasant settlers and of Uzbek or
Tatar traders, and a caravanserai.

Southward, cities were to be found, but of an Asiatic pattern,
crowded, noisome, and with narrow winding streets. A citadel,
a bazaar, a few Moslem mosques and schools, some crumbling
ruins, and hundreds or perhaps thousands of flat-roofed houses
of sun-dried brick—these were the cities of Turkestan, differing
from peasant villages in little but size.

For reasons of both health and defense, the Russians built
settlements of their own, of a European pattern, beside the native
cities. Tashkent was the prototype of these. It was already one
of the largest cities in Central Asia at the time of the conquest,
with a population of about 80,000. When it became the capital
of the Governor-Generalship of Turkestan it not only served as
the main center of the Russian population in the region, but
acquired many additional native inhabitants.

TASHKENT UNDER VON KAUFMAN

In November, 1867, when Von Kaufman arrived at Tashkent,
the Russian section of the capital still resembled a temporary

winter cantonment. Some earth huts within the walls of the citadel served as barracks and administration buildings; others nearby served as trading establishments and homes for the Russian civilian population. Ever mindful of Russian prestige in the eyes of the natives, Von Kaufman hastened to transform the settlement's appearance, to make it imply power and permanence. At his order an elaborate plan was drawn up for a European-style city with straight, broad avenues and imposing public buildings, which would contrast strikingly with the tortuous alleys and clay huts of the native city.

The rate at which the plans were executed astonished contemporary travelers, whose enthusiastic impressions after the weary journey through steppe and desert appear repeatedly in the abundant travel literature regarding this area. Visiting Tashkent in 1873, after only six years of Von Kaufman's regime, the American diplomat and authority on Russia, Eugene Schuyler, became almost lyrical:

As I sat on the porch in the bright moonlight, the first night of my arrival . . . , I could scarcely believe that I was in Central Asia, but seemed rather to be in one of the quiet little towns of Central New York. The broad dusty streets, shaded by double rows of trees; the sound of rippling water in every direction; the small white houses, set a little back from the streets, with trees and a palisade in front; the large square, full of turf and flowers, with a little church in the middle—all combined to give me this familiar impression.[1]

By daylight, however, Schuyler thought Tashkent more like

. . . one of the Western American towns—Denver, for instance, though lacking in the busy air which pervades that place, and with Sarts, in turbans and gowns, in place of Indians and miners. The conditions of the town are, indeed, much the same; it is built on the Steppe, and owes its green and fresh appearance to the canals, which bring streams of fresh water through every street. The sides of the streets are planted with poplars and willows, which in this country grow quickly and luxuriantly; a small stake driven into the ground soon becomes a fine tree; gardens spring up almost like magic; and I saw in the garden of a laboratory a peach tree bearing peaches the third year from the seed.

At the time of Schuyler's visit the Russian section of the city contained about 600 houses and had a population of about 3,000, exclusive of the garrison of 6,000 troops. It was growing rapidly: "New houses and streets are everywhere springing up . . . ," he wrote, but he found the growth to have an artificial quality: "The real, permanent population of the city is small, for trade is not great, manufactories do not exist, and, with the exception of the merchants, no one lives here who is not obliged to do so on account of his official duties. No one comes to Tashkent to remain, which distinguishes it from similar American towns, and most of these pretty houses have been built on money loaned by the Government."

Life in the new capital was governed by the climate and by the nature of the population. During the long summer, from May to September, everyone in Tashkent who could afford to do so went to live in summer residences in gardens in the suburbs, where they lived in small *dachas* (summer houses) or in Kazakh kibitkas. The usually critical Schuyler admitted:

Nothing can be more delightful than this; the heat does not penetrate through the thick elms and poplars; a freshness constantly exhales from the square pond and from the canals which water the garden, mixed with the perfume of roses and syringas. The *kibitka* is spacious and comfortable; and if to this is added a Bukharan pavilion-tent, with its embroidered and variegated walls, for a *salon,* the abode is charming. When at night the paper lanterns stand out against the dark green of the pomegranates, while the nightingale sings as the light shimmers over the still surface of the water, it is a scene taken bodily from the "Arabian Nights." [2]

Those forced to remain in town because of their duties in administrative offices and commercial establishments usually worked from 8 a.m. to 1 p.m., and then stayed in their homes until evening, when the heat lessened. Only then did the empty streets begin to take on life. During the evening the Russian population visited the native city, especially during the Moslem Lent (*uraza*). At that time the natives, after abstaining from food and drink all day, filled the bazaars, taverns, and teahouses or thronged the streets watching sideshows, jugglers, magicians, and dancing boys until dawn.

Colorful though such scenes were for the newcomer from Europe, as recreation they quickly palled for the average resident.

Only in the wintertime, when everyone was in town, was there more to do. Then the theaters of Russian Tashkent opened and social evenings, amateur theatricals, concerts, and meetings of various societies gave a semblance of European social life. But even this was permeated by an air of strict formality. As a garrison town and administrative center, Tashkent was characterized by a rigid class stratification based on rank and by a general dullness.

For many of the Russian residents, Tashkent was a place of exile. As Schuyler wrote, "nearly everyone who is there has either come there to avoid his creditors or been sent away to keep out of some scrape, or has come on account of increased pay or the shorter time of service necessary before receiving a pension, or in the hope of making a rapid fortune. . . ." [3]

This type of society, along with the remoteness from the homeland, the enervating climate, the few diversions, and the lenient public opinion had a corrosive effect on the morals of many residents. Prodigal living and the openhandedness of Russian hospitality consumed the moderate salaries of military and civilian personnel. Local custom demanded many servants for single men, and more if wives and children were present.

Drunkenness, an ancient curse in Russia, was all the worse in Central Asia. Franz Von Schwarz, a German doctor who spent fifteen years in Tashkent as an astronomer in the local observatory, ascribed this to the great heat and the dryness of the air. In his candid account he wrote that taverns lined entire streets in Tashkent, and that on holidays during the first years of the Russian occupation almost all of the Russian colony would be drunk. Excessive drinking was particularly widespread in the army. The troops received liquor as a part of their rations, and the heat and absence of reliable drinking water caused many to become alcoholics. Von Schwarz claims that Cherniaev's first assault on Tashkent failed because most of his force was drunk. He likewise mentions the "Battle of the Generals," long famous in Tashkent, in which in the early 1870's six Russian generals in uniform, among them the chief of staff and the chief of artillery, celebrated in a tavern. More in the tradition of one of the Western American towns cited by Schuyler, they roughed up the personnel and demolished the interior and the stock, so that each had to pay a large sum in damages.[4]

Such an atmosphere contributed in large degree to the widespread corruption in the administration. Bachelor officials and those who had left their families at home were drawn to the casino, where the small European society gathered. Wine, gifts to women, and gambling debts then led almost as a matter of course to falsification of accounts, extortion, and bribe-taking.

Fortunately for early Tashkent, the scoundrels, wastrels, and opportunists were counterbalanced by men sincerely interested in learning more about the country and in developing it. Schuyler, it is true, was unimpressed by this. Instead, he was struck

not only with the want of knowledge of the country, but with the lack of interest in it which was manifested, and it seemed to many difficult to understand how I could be interested in a country, and come so far to see it, which for them was the epitome of everything disagreeable. Of course there were exceptions to this, but I speak of the general impression. The number of Russians who know either Persian or Turki, or who care at all for the history, antiquities, or natural productions of the country, or who interest themselves in any way in the life of the people about them, is wonderfully small.[5]

However, Schuyler seems to have expected too much of a community which had been in existence for less than a decade. Von Kaufman himself, intent on transforming Tashkent from an outpost to an Imperial bulwark, took the initiative in providing a library, a museum, a newspaper for Russians and another for natives, a well-equipped astronomical observatory, and a meteorological station. To execute his plans he chose many officials who proved extremely able in the performance of their duties and who distinguished themselves by their contributions to knowledge. General N. I. Grodekov (1843–1913), on the General Staff of the Turkestan military district, and later Skobelev's chief of staff in Transcaspia in 1880–1881, General V. N. Trotskii (d. 1901), chief of staff of the Turkestan military district from 1873 to 1877 and military governor of Syr-Daria oblast from 1877 to 1883, General L. F. Kostenko (1841–1891), senior adjutant on the staff of

the Turkestan military district and chief of staff of Semirechie oblast, and Colonel A. P. Khoroshkin (d. 1875), who
represented Von Kaufman on various important missions, were
all outstanding historians, ethnographers, and explorers. Others
appointed by Von Kaufman included: Colonel N. A. Maev (1835–
1896), botanist, zoologist, and editor of the official newspaper
Turkestanskie Vedomosti from 1876 to 1892; A. L. Kun (1840–
1888), a naturalist, and chief inspector of schools (1876–1882);
N. P. Ostroumov (1846–1930), orientalist and historian, director
of the Turkestan Teachers' Seminary and the Tashkent Men's
Gynasium, and editor of the official newspaper for natives *Tuzemnaia Gazeta;* I. V. Mushketov (1850–1902), geologist, explorer, and mining official; V. F. Oshanin (1844–1917), naturalist,
explorer, and director of the Turkestan school of silk culture; Franz
Von Schwarz (d. 1903), director of the Tashkent observatory
from 1874 to 1890; and A. I. Vil'kins (1845–1892), zoologist,
explorer, and official in charge of various agricultural projects.
Unfortunately, however, for want of better mediums much of
their work was buried in obscure provincial journals or was published locally in limited editions.

Almost immediately after his arrival in 1867, Von Kaufman
saw to the founding of the Turkestan Public Library, designed
to collect all material written on the region. In the following
year Von Kaufman commissioned the bibliographer N. I. Mezhov
to start collecting what became one of the library's most noteworthy holdings, the *Turkestanskii Sbornik,* a 416-volume scrap-
book of newspaper and magazine articles on Central Asia. In
1872, Von Kaufman ordered the compiling of the formidable
Turkestanskii Al'bom, an album of six large volumes of more than
1,200 photographs concerning the history, archeology, ethnography, and industry of Turkestan.[6]

After Von Kaufman's death the library narrowly escaped destruction at the hands of his successor, Cherniaev. Hostile to
everything done by his predecessor, Cherniaev proclaimed the
library a waste of money and ordered it abolished, its literary
works sold at auction, and the remaining books distributed between the local schools, the Army General Staff, the military

hospital, and other public agencies. The intelligentsia of Tashkent, aroused by the threatened loss, protested vigorously and managed to delay the dispersal until Cherniaev's recall in 1884. General N. O. Rosenbach, the next governor-general, rescinded the order, and many of the books eventually found their way back to the library.[7]

Von Kaufman also saw to it that like other administrative centers of the Russian Empire, Tashkent was provided with an official government newspaper. *Turkestanskie Vedomosti* (Turkestan News), founded in 1870, printed governmental and administrative orders relating to Turkestan, and, during its forty-seven years of existence, published many valuable scientific articles concerning Turkestan. More influential than popular, however, its circulation during its first year of publication was only 100, and by 1906, 1,069.[8]

Besides *Turkestanskie Vedomosti*, Von Kaufman ordered the publication of the *Turkestanskaia Tuzemnaia Gazeta* (Turkestan Native Gazette), a small paper published in Uzbek with a Russian translation, designed "to acquaint native officials . . . with the orders of the local administration, and to spread among them useful information, especially history and geography." Though it used a "literary" language far removed from local speech, it was nevertheless for many years the only paper in the empire which was printed in a language of one of the Moslem peoples of Russia. N. P. Ostroumov, its editor from 1883 to 1917, compared the audience to which it was directed with the Russians of the beginning of the eighteenth century, who, except for those in court circles, were ignorant of happenings in the outside world until in 1702 Peter the Great decreed that newspapers should be made available. In 1906 the paper had 3,600 subscribers, but by 1909 the competition from the large number of privately published Turkish-Tatar newspapers which appeared after the 1905 revolution had reduced its circulation to half that figure.[9] Though naturally reflecting the viewpoint of the regime at all times, the newspaper was undoubtedly of great influence on the initial development of the native intelligentsia.

By 1882, near the end of Von Kaufman's fourteen-year ad-

ministration, Russian Tashkent was firmly established. The raw-
est elements of the earlier days had disappeared or mellowed;
there was still gambling and carousing, but the population, which
had reached 12,000, now included the families of many of the
military and civilian personnel, who exercised a stabilizing influence. Corruption in the government was characteristic, but at
least was not so obvious as earlier. On the other hand, the efforts
which had been made to study the region's inhabitants and
economic potential, and to provide means for the propagation of
knowledge, equalled or surpassed the efforts made in other colonial regions of that time. Von Kaufman's pride in the spacious
city he had built, and his regret at leaving so much still undone
is shown in lines written to a friend a few months before his
death: "If I should die as governor-general, please bury me . . .
[here] so that all may know that here is true Russian soil, in
which no Russian need be ashamed to lie." [10]

LATER DEVELOPMENT OF TASHKENT

By 1889, when Curzon visited Tashkent, the Russian section of
the city had grown to a population of 20,000, while the native
city contained 100,000. Together they covered an area the size
of Paris. But the two were distinctly separate, Curzon noted, far
more so than in the capitals of India—Bombay, Calcutta or
Madras—where the resident princes and noblemen and the native merchants mingled habitually in Anglo-Indian society and
took a prominent part in government or the management of
public institutions:

In Tashkent, on the other hand, several obstacles preclude a similar
amalgamation—the purely military character of the administration, the
dearth of any wealthy or capable men among the natives, and the recency
of the Russian conquest. I once remember reading the remark that "In
Russia the discipline of the camp is substituted for the order of the city;
martial law is the normal condition of life"; and of no Russian city that I
have seen did this strike me as more true than of Tashkent. Uniforms are
everywhere, parade-grounds and barracks abound, the extensive *entourage*
associated with a great administrative center is military and not civil in
character. It is hardly surprising that under such a system practical or far-
seeing projects for commercial and industrial development should not be
forthcoming; that the fiscal balance should be habitually on the wrong

side of the budget; or that Chauvinistic and aggressive ideas should prevail.[11]

But even with these convictions Curzon noticed a change from the adventurous policies of Von Kaufman and Cherniaev. The new governor-general, General N. O. Rosenbach, was primarily interested in the development of the country's resources. In five years the export of cotton from Tashkent had increased twenty-five fold; the city was becoming a center of Central Asian trade.[12]

These trends continued during subsequent decades. In 1877 the Russian section of the city covered only one square verst (approximately two-fifths of a square mile), by 1904 it covered twenty-five square versts, and by 1910, thirty square versts, an area equal to that of the native part of the city.[13] Out of a total population of 234,000 the Russian population numbered 47,500.[14] After the turn of the century, Tashkent became increasingly less isolated. The Orenburg-Tashkent Railway, completed in 1906, gave the city direct contact with European Russia. The development of commerce brought in people engaged in occupations unconnected with government service. A whole generation of Russian youth had grown up in Tashkent. A prosperous class of native merchants was beginning to take on European ways.

To the British specialist on Slavic Europe, Stephen Graham, who traveled in Turkestan in 1914, the European atmosphere of Russian Tashkent was unmistakable although, as always, the military element still predominated. He wrote:

The foundation of the society of new Tashkent is laid by the regiments quartered there, and the fine shops exist chiefly for the custom of officers and their wives. . . . The whole atmosphere is military, and there is an unusual smartness everywhere. Especially do you notice how well dressed the women are at the theatres and in the gardens, and the men accompanying them nearly all wear the sword. The middle-class Russian is out of sight, and the peasant labourer is rare. . . . There is, however, a dandy Armenian element; young hawkers and shoeblacks and barbers who appear in the evening in white collars and cheap serges, with combed locks under felt hats, with canes in their hands.

Tashkent has now many schools, from the important Corpus, the military college where officers' sons are educated, to the little native school where the Russian schoolmaster tries to give Russian to the Sart. . . .

There are six cinema shows at Tashkent, two theatres, an open-air theatre, a skating rink, and many small diversions. The native turns up in the cinema, and there are generally long lines of turbaned figures in the front of the theatre. At the real theatres it is necessarily those who know Russian who take the seats. At the open-air theatre they play *The Taming of the Shrew,* at the Coliseum the *Doll's House* and Artsibasheff's *Jealousy.* The town has two newspapers, and on the day on which I arrived I found that the leading article of the *Courier of Turkestan* was entitled "the State of Affairs in Ulster." All Europe seemed to have its eyes on our politics, and Europe extends now as far east as Tashkent, though it is of "Central Asia" that that city claims to be the capital.[15]

OTHER TOWNS

The other Russian towns of Turkestan underwent a similar development, though on a smaller scale than Tashkent. As the majority were built on open land adjoining the native towns, it was possible to avoid the monotony of construction and the inadequate streets characteristic not only of the native towns but of many of the older cities of Central Russia. Consequently, everywhere in the Turkestan region the Russian settlements were striking in their external appearance with straight, wide streets, lined with trees, often several rows, watered by aryks.[16]

Elsewhere in Syr-Daria oblast, small Russian settlements arose beside the towns of Turkestan, Chimkent, and Aulie-Ata. Kazalinsk and Perovsk, at first exclusively Russian, eventually acquired predominantly native populations. In 1897 there were only 2,610 Russians of 7,585 inhabitants in Kazalinsk, and only 742 Russians out of 5,508 people living in Perovsk. After the building of the Orenburg-Tashkent Railway, however, both towns nearly doubled in size, and the influx of railroad workers and other new settlers brought the number of Russians in both towns to about half the total population.

Samarkand was second to Tashkent in the size of its Russian settlement; in 1908 the city had a total of 11,654 Russians in a total population of 80,706. But the four other chief towns of Samarkand oblast, Khodzhent, Ura-Tiube, Dzhizak, and Katta-Kurgan, with a combined population of 84,138, had only 2,080 Russians between them.[17]

Only in Novyi Margelan (in 1907 renamed Skobelev and now called Fergana), in Fergana oblast, situated about twelve versts from Margelan in order to ensure better sanitation, was a large Russian center established which was not next to a native city. In 1911 this city had 11,000 inhabitants, including 7,000 Russians. The number of Russians in the other large cities of Fergana oblast—Kokand, Namangan, and Andizhan—was smaller, although the sections where they resided had a greater amount of trade and industry than Novyi Margelan.[18]

In Semirechie, only the ruins of former cities were to be seen when the Russians first came. The only town life was that which existed in the small settlements about the Kokandian fortresses. Pishpek (now Frunze), one of the largest of these, had about 1,000 households, but when the Kokandians fled the Kazakhs of the surrounding region razed the buildings. Vernyi, the administrative center of Semirechie oblast, rose around the Russian fort established in 1854 in a locality known to the natives as Almaty (now Alma-Ata), "father of apples," because of the wild fruit growing on the mountain slopes.

Subsequently, the considerable amount of colonization by Russian peasants was accompanied by the development in Semirechie of towns with large proportion of Russian inhabitants. In 1911 there were 26,000 Russians in Vernyi out of a total population of 35,000 (most of the remainder were Tatars and Uzbeks), Pishpek had 8,000 Russians out of a total of about 14,000 inhabitants, and Karakol (renamed Przheval'sk in 1888) had 6,000 Russians out of 15,000 inhabitants.[19]

Transcaspia oblast resembled Semirechie in its urban development, except that fewer Russians settled there. Askhabad, Merv, and Krasnovodsk were the only centers of any size. Askhabad, founded in 1881 as the oblast capital, grew with fair rapidity, stimulated by income brought by the Trans-Caspian Railroad. In 1897 the town had 19,426 inhabitants, and in 1911, 44,000, of whom 9,000 were Russians and the remainder mostly Persian and Caucasian immigrants.[20]

In the Steppe oblasts the Russian settlers were mainly peasants, residing, as always, in villages. Most of the towns of the region grew up around forts and declined or remained stationary in population after the military forces departed. As late as 1903 townspeople constituted only 8 per cent of the total inhabitants of the Steppe. The increase in settlement in the 1890's, and the construction of the Trans-Siberian Railroad brought a rapid increase in the population of several of the Steppe towns. Omsk grew from 37,000 in 1897 to 128,000 in 1910. In the same period Petropavlovsk grew from 18,000 to 43,000, Semipalatinsk from 26,000 to 34,000, and Kustanai from 14,000 to 25,000.[21]

A striking new element had appeared in Central Asia. The conquests of previous centuries had been made by peoples not fundamentally different from the indigenous inhabitants, and who could therefore readily be absorbed. Now the region had been conquered by an alien people whose absorption by the natives was out of the question, and who bore an advanced culture which instead threatened great changes in the native way of life.

VII

ALTHOUGH the urban communities that grew up beside the native cities became effective economic, cultural, and administrative centers, their establishment alone could not achieve the aims of Russian dominion in Central Asia. The immediate interests of military strategy, the long-term interests of state policy, and the consolidation of the newly conquered region all required colonization by a more representative cross section of Russian society, particularly by the preponderant peasant class. This posed many problems in the face of the limiting factors of physical environment, the low state of agricultural technology, and the backward social and political conditions peculiar to Russia, not to mention the prior claim by the natives to much of the best of the limited amount of arable land.

THE COSSACKS

The flow of Russian peasants into Central Asia was a late stage in a movement already several centuries old. Civil strife, invasion, and oppressive rule in European Russia had always weighed heaviest on the rural population, the mainstay of the country's economy. For most there was no escape, but from early times bolder spirits had fled to peripheral regions—to the Urals, to Siberia, and particularly to the great grasslands in the south and southeast. There, along the Don, the Kuban, the Volga, the Yaik (Ural), and other rivers they formed free communities, and as "Cossacks" took on many of the ways of their nomadic neighbors. As time went on the Cossacks in various districts merged into larger units called *voiskos*, or hosts, and seized some of the best steppe lands.

The Russian frontier was extensive, and many generations passed before the central government extended its control to the Cossack communities. When it did, the Cossacks became servants of the state. In return for service as militia and as border guards, the Cossacks in each voisko were given title to their vast lands and allowed to retain local autonomy.

In its day, this device served Russia well. Along the Central Asian border the Cossacks formed a living wall of devoted subjects of the tsar. The Ural Cossacks occupied lands from the Caspian Sea up the Ural River as far as the southern end of the Ural mountain range; from that point the territories of the Orenburg Cossacks extended past Cheliabinsk to the lands of the Siberian Cossacks. The latter occupied a fantastic strip 1,800 versts long (about 1,200 miles) and an average of 10 versts wide from the Urals as far eastward as Omsk, then southeastward along both sides of the Irtysh River to Ust'-Kamenogorsk. From there one branch extended eastward along the Bukhtarma River almost to the Chinese border, and another to Biisk, in the Altai Mountains.

These communities in turn spawned others. In the late 1840's, when Russia annexed some of the fertile lands of Semirechie, southeast of Lake Balkhash, the government used Siberian Cossacks to found settlements in the new lands. Men in the lower ranks were taken as volunteers or by lot, were settled with their families on parcels of land, and given several years of exemption from military service and taxation until they were firmly established. By 1867, 14 Cossack stanitsas and hamlets had been organized in Semirechie, with a population of between 12,000 and 15,000.[1] In spite of the fact that the area in which they were placed was somewhat larger than France, these settlements were of considerable strategic value, giving Russia a firm foothold within Central Asia and a buffer on her eastern flank against China.

To the west in the Orenburg Steppe, similar measures for colonization were undertaken, though on a smaller scale. In the

1840's, when several small forts were placed in the Steppe as part of a strategy to bring the Kazakhs under control, small settlements of Orenburg Cossacks were established near each fort to simplify the problem of supply. At this time, Russian policy in Central Asia was based mainly on military and political considerations; economic aims were limited to the encouragement of trade. As Von Kaufman stated in a report to the tsar in 1882:

> During the final subjugation of the Kirgiz Steppe the government did not have colonization aims in view. The occupation of the Semirechie and the Trans-Ili regions from one direction and the founding of the Syr-Daria forts on the other was impelled by the need to secure our border lines and to protect Kirgiz subjects from the attacks of hostile natives who had not submitted to Russia, and along with this the desire to guarantee the safety of our trade routes from Russian territory into Middle Asia and Western China.[2]

According to Von Kaufman, the government had resorted to the use of Cossack military colonies because "only military colonization could strengthen our power in the occupied steppe. . . . By the settlement of Cossacks in the steppe the Government acquired a disciplined military force ready for the defense of the region. At the same time the Cossack military settlements . . . occupied with agriculture and supplying provisions . . . could to some degree lessen government expenditures for support of a regular army in the steppe."[3]

After two decades there was no denying the flourishing condition of the Semirechie Cossack settlements, but Von Kaufman regarded this prosperity as due less to the efforts of the Cossacks themselves than to the extent and fertility of the lands bestowed upon them. Despite the fulfillment of the original aims, he and other military leaders in Central Asia could see numerous drawbacks to this type of colonization. In Semirechie, Von Kaufman recalled, each Cossack settler had received fifty-five rubles in cash and three years of rations for each member of his family, a considerable sum for those times. However, instead of helping settlers to become established, this aid had merely produced ". . . an abundance of the shiftless, homeless, and idle, happy to live off state means in the new region . . . always on the move from settlement to settlement, maintaining themselves by hunting, or by hiring themselves out to more industrious and thrifty Cossacks. . . ."[4]

Before the coming of the Cossacks, Von Kaufman asserted, almost all of the valleys and foothills of Semirechie oblast had been covered by virgin timber, particularly precious because of the rarity of such stands in Central Asia. Yet, only a few years after the establishment of the Cossack stanitsas, all of the natural forest growth in adjacent localities had become so depleted that by the end of the 1860's timber for building and fuel was to be found only in inaccessible ravines.[5]

Worse still, the establishment of the Semirechie stanitsas and the allotment of land to individual Cossacks had been "accompanied by systematic restriction of the nomads and complete neglect of their interests. . . ."[6] The Cossacks, Von Kaufman stated, had settled on some of the best winter pastures of the Kazakhs and had blocked routes which the natives had long been accustomed to use for seasonal migrations with their flocks. They had appropriated the tilled and irrigated land of Kazakhs who had taken up agriculture, and had disregarded Kazakh water rights. These injustices had caused numerous complaints and disputes, which had been difficult to settle because of the existence of two administrations in the region—one, the regimental administration of the Cossacks, and the other the oblast administration, then that of the oblast of Semipalatinsk.

The administrative reorganization undertaken in 1867 led to a more effective control over the Cossacks. In that year the oblast of Semirechie was organized and included in the newly formed Governor-Generalship of Turkestan. The Ninth and Tenth Regimental districts, located in Semirechie and settled in twenty-eight stanitsas, were detached from the Siberian Cossack voisko to form the separate Semirechie Cossack voisko. Von Kaufman, as governor-general, was given command over the voisko in both civil and military matters; the military governor of Semirechie oblast was given immediate command of the voisko. Control of the police and economic supervision was placed in the hands of the uezd commandants.[7]

This combination of military and civil authority, with jurisdiction over both Cossacks and Kazakhs, permitted closer supervision of both groups. Disputes between the two were thereafter decided by the uezd courts and by the oblast administrative board. Von Kaufman championed the rights of the natives by ordering that their herds be allowed free passage through unused Cossack lands, thereby ending the constant friction of previous years, though he saw permanent solution of the problem only through a general reorganization of agriculture throughout the region.[8]

Thus brought under firmer control, Cossack settlement in Semirechie achieved a degree of stability. However, in the opinion of Von Kaufman and others this type of colonization had outlived its usefulness, and the peopling of the new land should depend on another element, the Russian peasant.

PEASANT COLONIZATION

Unlike colonization by Cossacks, fostered by the government for specific aims, the movement of peasants to Siberia and Central Asia had always been subject to many hindrances. Under serfdom the peasants of European Russia had been prevented from moving to other regions because their departure from the land meant the loss of a valuable labor force. Only a few were able to emigrate surreptitiously, under great hardship; the majority who settled beyond the Urals came as exiled criminals.

This movement, then, was unlike any other in recent times. It was particularly unlike that which took place on the advancing frontier in the United States, for example, where settlers, often of moderate or even substantial means, had a wide choice of well-endowed, temperate regions. Instead it was a movement of the destitute, many in exile and some in flight, leaving their homeland by compulsion or in desperation to go to an inhospitable, all but unknown region, where there were but indifferent chances of wresting a living from a harsh environment.

During the 1840's a more liberal policy began to take form toward peasants from crown lands, but the serfs of private landholders were still bound to the soil. Even after the freeing of the serfs in 1861, high government officials remained reluctant to permit emigration, which they feared "might lead to the development of harmful mobility and vagabondage in rural society." Only a few liberals, who saw colonization as a means of improving the lot of the peasants, and some officials in the provinces of Asiatic Russia favored a change of policy.[9]

The first Russian peasant settlers in Semirechie oblast, some 242 families from the gubernia of Voronezh, arrived in Vernyi in 1868. Government plans for colonization were still incomplete, and no free lands were available, so some of the newcomers had to lease lands from Cossacks living around the town. In 1869 General Kolpakovskii, the military governor of Semirechie, worked out some temporary rules for colonization. Approved by Von Kaufman, these rules were applied in the establishment of two peasant settlements, Gavrilovskoe and Lugovoe, in the uezd of Kopal.[10]

One of the main goals in the plans for peasant settlement at that time was the colonization of the Issyk-Kul region along the Chinese border. Earlier attempts to establish Cossack settlements there had failed and had left the large uezds of Tokmak and Issyk-Kul without a permanent Russian population. It was therefore considered expedient to locate the new immigrants so that in combination with the Cossacks of Vernyi and other settlements to the north a network of settled places would be established at fairly regular intervals along the main lines of communication.

Surveys for the new settlements, to comprise thirty-four villages and forty-seven advance points, were begun in 1870, and the first two villages were established in the same year. Fifteen-year exemptions from taxation and military service were given to settlers in the villages and twenty-five-year exemptions to those in the advance points, where it was more difficult to get established. The land allotment for each male settler was first fixed at thirty desiatines, but was later reduced to seventeen desiatines. Even this much land proved ample with the irrigation and the abundant harvests which were possible.

By 1881 Von Kaufman was able to report that colonization in

Semirechie had succeeded far beyond his original hopes. During the period between 1868 and 1880, some 3,690 peasant families had arrived. Of these, 1,652 families, numbering 13,074 persons, formed 59 new settlements. The remainder, hoping to avoid taxes and other obligations in the regular peasant settlements, joined the Semirechie Cossack voisko, or leased Cossack lands. Thus, even the voisko was augmented by the new arrivals.[11]

In Syr-Daria oblast, Russian peasant colonization was much slower in getting started than in Semirechie. The first requests from peasants for permission to settle came in 1868, but several years elapsed before any immigration was permitted. The best lands in the oblast were already in use; the legal aspects of land ownership were not yet defined; the amount and location of free land suitable for agriculture was not yet determined; and there was doubt as to whether the natives were sufficiently pacified to risk forming Russian settlements in their midst.[12] In comparison with Semirechie, wrote Von Kaufman, the difficulty in Syr-Daria oblast was greater, "since besides the interests of the nomads it was necessary to pay attention to the rights of the native settled population." [13]

In 1873, following the provisional plan devised for Semirechie oblast in 1869, Von Kaufman worked out a master plan of colonization for the entire governor-generalship. This plan provided for settlements along the main post roads from Orenburg to Tashkent and from Tashkent through Vernyi to Semipalatinsk.[14] However, because of the difficulty of the journey from European Russia and the preoccupation with the Khivan and Kokand campaigns, it was not until 1876 that 197 people were finally settled in three localities of Aulie-Ata uezd.[15] Attempts were also made to form settlements of reservists—Russian soldiers discharged in Turkestan—but two calls to active duty, in 1878 and 1881, halted their attempts to farm and the greater part of them, some 1,200, eventually returned to European Russia.[16] Thus, in the first fifteen years little of note was accomplished in Syr-Daria oblast in the way of Russian peasant colonization.

In the eyes of Von Kaufman and other Russian leaders the colonization question was meanwhile rendered more urgent by movement of natives into desirable empty lands, taking advantage of the securer conditions under Russian rule. Uzbek peasants had begun to form small settlements in the Steppe uezds of Syr-Daria oblast and in the Tokmak and Issyk-Kul uezds of Semirechie oblast. Tatar traders were settling in considerable numbers in the towns bordering the Steppe, and some lived among the Kazakhs and moved about with them on their migrations. Zealous Moslems, the Tatars frequently worked as missionaries and teachers as well.

Von Kaufman looked with concern upon these shifts in the native population. If the Kazakhs, previously mere nominal devotees of Islam, could be stiffened in their religious fervor by the Tatars, they might resist Russian rule more stubbornly. If the Uzbeks, on the other hand, continued to move into the Steppe they might eventually absorb the Kazakhs culturally, just as they had already absorbed many other nomadic peoples, and certainly they would occupy lands otherwise open to Russian settlers.[17] "I consider it necessary and timely," wrote Von Kaufman, "to take more proper and active measures regarding the widely developing spread of settlement of the Sarts beyond the surveillance of the government, threatening to occupy soon all the best free places where our Russian settlement could be particularly useful."[18] The Kazakhs were clearly looked upon as a people slated for closer ties with Russia, and the Kazakh Steppe as a place reserved for Russian colonization.

VIEWS OF THE IGNAT'EV COMMISSION

The problems of colonization in Central Asia received further consideration by the Ignat'ev commission at its meeting in St. Petersburg in 1884 to review a projected statute for the administration of the Turkestan region. The record of the commission's deliberations, originally classified as "Secret," gives a revealing picture of official opinion which influenced subsequent legislation.

General A. N. Kuropatkin, a member of the commission, was a particularly strong advocate of colonization. In his opinion Russian colonization in Asia was a historic movement, the rapid growth of which was both necessary and desirable. Failure of the government to aid and regulate colonization would not stop this movement, but would slow its growth. In 200 years, he pointed out, Russia had achieved a population in Siberia of only 5,000,000. If she increased the Russian element in Siberia and Central Asia as slowly in the future, she would be able neither to struggle with invaders (he foresaw the threat of an invasion by the Chinese) nor to utilize all the advantages from her vast Asian possessions. But if the government organized colonization correctly, in 60 or 70 years Russia, with a population which by that time would have doubled to reach the figure of 200,000,000, would firmly hold her Siberian and Central Asian possessions by means of 25 to 30 million Russians.[19]

In order to achieve successful colonization in Turkestan, Kuropatkin stated, it would be necessary to assign the settlers all free lands in the region and to "crowd" the Kazakhs somewhat, especially along the post roads and in other places which were of strategic importance. It would also be necessary to permit and encourage the settlers to acquire land from both the nomadic and settled native population.[20]

Ignat'ev concurred. "At the present time," he wrote in his explanatory notes to the new statute, summing up the opinions of the commission, "our authority in Turkestan depends almost exclusively on military strength and special administrative powers. This authority has no other support, and this constitutes a weak side of our administration. In the neighboring oblast of Semirechie, on the other hand, thanks to the development of Russian settlement, our rule rests partly on a Russian population, an imposing force which is gradually giving the oblast a Russian character."

There was need, he continued, to hasten Russian colonization in the region before native Moslems took all of the available land:

At the present time the region is fully tranquil; the native population understands very well the advantage of such a situation compared with the former, and hastens to make use of the favorable conditions for the development of its material welfare, striving to seize for cultivation all lands having any sort of irrigation. Not only Uzbeks and Sarts, accustomed to agriculture, but also the Kirgiz [Kazakhs], little inclined toward it, have yielded to the general tendency and have begun to sow a considerable area and to enlarge their area of irrigation. If this continues over several decades, it can easily happen that in Turkestan there will remain hardly a spot free and suitable for Russian settlers which will not be occupied by Moslems.[21]

For these reasons the commission included in its draft statute general rules for the organization of Russian settlement in Turkestan, together with a detailed commentary. Settlement, the commission decided, should be limited to inhabitants of the empire who were of the Christian faith. This was explained as being necessary "in order to prevent an influx of Tatars and Jews, the first because they would strengthen the Moslem element and consequently would be entirely unsuitable to the aims of the Government, and the second because of their natural inclinations, which could exert a harmful and corrupting influence on the economic life and morals of the population."

"Russian settlement," the draft of the statute stated, "will be organized without constraint upon the native population." This remark, according to the accompanying commentary, "is considered necessary mainly for the protection of the nomadic population, which because of the extent of stock-herding needs places for pasturage, for gathering hay, and for driving herds from the winter camp to the summer pastures. This rule in relation to the settled population means that Russian settlement can be organized adjacent to the settled native population, under condition of leaving the native population that amount of water which it actually needs for *complete* irrigation of its fields." [22]

The governor-general of Turkestan would determine the location of settlements and the amount of individual land allotments. The commentary stated that the first locality for settlement should probably be the area adjacent to Semirechie oblast, where in fact several Russian settlements had already become established in preceding years. This would ensure that "the Kirgiz will not succeed in occupying all places suitable for agriculture. After that . . . the Russian population which might come from Orenburg to Kazalinsk could settle along the Syr-Daria from that point. The organization of Russian settlements along the Syr-Daria, without, of course, crowding the Kirgiz, presents no particular difficulties, as the Syr-Daria is a mighty source for irrigation."

Allotments for settlers should not exceed three desiatines of irrigated land per person because "thanks to the excellent climate, land which is well irrigated gives an abundant harvest." Settlers were to receive no financial aid from the treasury, but during the first five years they were to enjoy tax exemption. Settlers were to form separate rural communities so that they would be able to develop independently without mixing with the communities of the natives or being under the control of the local native administration.

Russian settlers on state land were to receive their land with full rights of use and of disposition by sale or bequest. However, during the first ten years the individual would be able to transfer ownership of the land only after constructing a farmstead and after receipt of the permission of the oblast administrative board. "This condition is considered necessary," the commission's report stated, "in order to protect the settlers from exploitation by strong kulaks who might appear in their midst." For every settlement of over 100 households, the state would provide a church and a school.

The commission also considered creating a separate Cossack voisko for Turkestan. Privy Counselor F. K. Giers, a member of the commission, asserted that the colonization question could be solved only by recourse to the historic method of settlement by means of Cossacks. However, Ignat'ev cautioned that although history showed the great use derived by the state from Cossack colonization, their use in Turkestan would require too much land, "for the Cossacks utilize great portions." The government would have to construct great irrigation projects to provide such quantities of land. The Cossacks were unaccustomed to carry on an intensive agriculture, the only kind advantageous in Central Asia. Moreover, they would pay no taxes for the state lands granted them, so the treasury would lose a considerable income.[23]

In the end, most of the Commission's recommendations regarding colonization were omitted from the final version of the statute, which eventually became law in 1886. The reason for the omissions is not clear, but it appears likely that the decision may have been to leave colonization to the discretion of the governor-general. Section 270 of the statute even stipulated that "state lands occupied by nomads will be reserved permanently for the common use of the nomads in accordance with custom and the laws of this statute."

ILLEGAL COLONIZATION IN THE KAZAKH STEPPE

In the Kazakh Steppe and Semirechie, in the meantime, the movement of settlers was beginning to assume major proportions. Colonization of Semirechie oblast was favored by the natural conditions of the region and the fact that Cossack settlements had already paved the way, but in the virgin lands of the Steppe oblasts to the west of Semirechie, peasant colonization had at first not even been foreseen. The Steppe region in the 1870's was in fact much like the Great Plains region of the United States during the same period. Settlers avoided the region at first in preference to lands of easier access or of greater promise. Natural conditions and the agricultural techniques of the time limited colonization to the northern rim of the Steppe during the first years. Only gradually did the settlers move southward.

As in the Governor-Generalship of Turkestan, the colonization of the Steppe was at first directed toward administrative ends. With future post stations in mind, the government tried to locate settlements at regular intervals along the post roads without regard to the quality of the soil, the water supply, or the presence of wood for construction. After several years of bad harvests in such places, some of the peasants turned to cattle raising, but disease and insufficient water curbed even this, so that many had to move elsewhere.[24]

In spite of the government's efforts to limit colonization and to direct it into desired channels, the 1880's saw a constant increase of unauthorized (*samovol'nyi*) immigration into the steppe. First came *khodoks* (land scouts), who leased suitable small tracts from the Kazakhs, and then came the settlers. They lived at first on separate farmsteads, in earth huts similar to those of the Kazakhs around them. They usually paid for the use of the land they occupied, and worked a certain number of desiatines for the benefit of the native owners. Later, as they became more securely established, they built wooden cottages and began to form villages. Gradually they invited in other settlers. If the Kazakhs protested they would be given additional payment, but generally they did not become aware of the situation until the peasants were firmly established. Finally, when the settlers felt they were numerous enough they would request the provincial officials to divide the land into individual allotments and to give their villages legal status.[25]

As a result of this rapid and unplanned settlement, the Kazakhs began to find their customary routes between winter and summer pasture blocked by the grainfields of the peasants, and to find access denied to the river bottoms where they had sheltered their flocks against winter storms.

Although anxious to organize and settle the impoverished Russian peasants, some of the provincial officials wished to keep the colonization movement within bounds and to prevent settlement in places where it could cause hardship to the Kazakhs. In 1886, General Kolpakovskii, the governor-general of the Steppe, cautioned against too rapid settlement because the Kazakhs themselves did not have enough land. He pointed out that the Kazakhs of Tobolsk gubernia were already renting meadows from Cossacks and peasants, and that in some parts of the Steppe which were not well suited for agriculture the Russian peasants were themselves turning to stock raising, thereby competing with the Kazakhs in their own traditional economy. He requested authority to resettle some of the Russian peasants on better allotments, and to have further settlement in the Steppe dependent on renting from the Kazakhs, with legislative regulation of relations between owners and tenants.[26] Kolpakovskii actually tried in several instances to have the peasants moved forcibly from unauthorized places of settlement, but such orders proved almost impossible to execute.[27]

THE RESETTLEMENT ACT (1889)

During the 1880's, government approval of settlement had been reserved mainly for peasants in overpopulated areas, without provision being made for peasants from other regions who also desired to emigrate. In 1889, however, a new decree removed many of the shortcomings of the previous system. The new law opened emigration to peasants from any district provided the ministries of the Interior and of State Domains considered that there was sufficient need and that there was free land available. Settlers received tax exemptions and state aid in their new locations. Resettlement without permission was strictly forbidden, and violators were to be compelled to return to their place of origin, although this threat was never put into effect.[28]

In practice, the new law still hindered the colonization movement because of its emphasis on bureaucratic control, but in spirit it represented a major change in government policy from restraint to protection and aid, and it paved the way for more liberal legislation. Nevertheless, although intended to foster peasant colonization in Asiatic Russia, the resettlement law of 1889 only legalized what was already well under way. Impelled by population pressure and shortages of land and food, the number of emigrants continued to grow, regardless of legal sanction. The disastrous famine of 1890–1891 brought new thousands and taxed the local administrative apparatus in the outlying regions as never before.

The situation in Akmolinsk oblast was typical of what was occurring throughout the northern part of the Kazakh Steppe. At the beginning of 1889 there were 8,352 peasant settlers in the oblast. During the year, 3,398 more arrived. In 1890, an estimated 9,000 arrived. It was said that

> . . . settlers literally inundated all the Cossack and peasant settlements. Whole crowds of them roamed aimlessly about . . . spending their last means, seeking any kind of work . . . in such numbers that the situation became impossible. Lured by the letters of relatives about the abundance of the steppe lands, as if they were freely given out for settlement, and deceived in their bright hopes, in place of which they have met only want, the spirits of the newly arrived naturally fall, and their helplessness makes a depressing sight.[29]

During the second half of the year, an estimated 15,000 persons in the oblast were hungry, ragged, and without shelter. As fast as the oblast authorities prepared new lands for settlement new colonists arrived. Undernourished and crowded in damp sod huts, the new settlers were plagued by scurvy and typhus during the winter. The governor of Akmolinsk was forced to appeal for public subscriptions for food, medical aid, and loans for the purchase of grain. Private committees tried to care for the colonists in cities along their route eastward. In 1891, the government tried to impose a two-year ban on settlement in Akmolinsk oblast in order to give officials time to organize the settlers who had already arrived and to find unoccupied tracts for new ones, but in vain.[30]

THE SIBERIAN RAILROAD COMMITTEE

Having found it impossible to stem the tide, many officials began to be attracted to the idea of using the rush of colonists for government ends. The change was expressed in a series of measures centered around the project for the construction of the Trans-Siberian Railroad. On December 10, 1892, a special body known as the Siberian Railroad Committee (*Komitet Sibirskoi zheleznoi dorogi*), composed of eminent government figures and headed by the future Nicholas II, was formed to direct construction of the 5,000-mile link with the Pacific. Besides its main objective the committee was assigned the task of managing colonization "to settle and animate" the region through which the railroad would pass. An initial fund of 14,000,000 rubles was appropriated to further the committee's work in this field.[31]

Colonization had now ranged from bare toleration to open encouragement. The Siberian Railroad Committee sponsored legislation which clarified the status of unauthorized settlers and legalized their holdings. The peasants of European Russia were informed of the location of lands suitable for settlement, how to acquire them, and how to obtain government aid in connection with transportation and initial establishment. Reduced fares and other assistance were granted to the khodoks sent out by villages to seek proper places for settlement.[32] Surveying parties were sent out to find and delimit new lands for settlement.[33]

With this encouragement the movement of settlers accelerated. The town of Kustanai, founded in 1885 in the northern part of

Turgai oblast near the sources of the river Tobol, grew with such "American rapidity," to use the words of a contemporary, that by 1896 it already had 16,000 inhabitants. Caravans of settlers quickly occupied the 13,000 desiatines (about 35,100 acres, or about 55 square miles) set aside for settlement in the vicinity of the town, and then spread around it until they took possession of 40,000 desiatines. Others, finding no room near Kustanai, founded settlements to the west on the river Aiat, or as far as the Ubagan River, over fifty miles to the east, and in a "disorderly, insubordinate wave" inundated Kokchetav uezd in Akmolinsk oblast.

Thus, the steppe was filling in, and the virgin lands were being taken. The older belt of settlement in the north was now matched by another farther south. One observer wrote in 1898:

> Until recent times, the so-called Cossack lines existed—the Orenburg Line, on the northern border of Turgai oblast, and the Gor'koi Line, to the north of Akmolinsk oblast—established as early as the first half of the eighteenth century as a barrier between the Russian settlers and the Kirgiz nomad population. Now, one can say, it exists no more. Or, if you wish, it still exists . . . but as a barrier, or as a border or "line" dividing two worlds, it is already no more. In its place there is a new line, not a Cossack line but a peasant line. In places it has not yet succeeded in filling densely, but in four or five years it will be filled uninterruptedly. Based on other aims, the peasant line differs from the Cossack line; it is not so even; it is not such a narrow strip, and it has perpetual tendencies to spread out and from side to side, and to fill in the gaps separating it from the Cossack line. And, of course, the time when both lines actually will merge is not far off.[34]

THE SHCHERBINA EXPEDITION

The Kazakhs, nominal owners of the steppe by right of century-long possession, had meanwhile continued to exist on whatever free land was still to be found within the settled area and farther south. As the peasant influx continued and good land became more scarce the question arose of whether the natives might not after all be in possession of more land than was necessary for their use.

Various attempts had been made to calculate the amount of land not needed by the Kazakhs and hence available for Russian settlement. A study made in Akmolinsk oblast under General Kolpakovskii concluded that out of a total of 49,916,687 desiatines in the oblast it would be possible, "without crowding the Kirgiz," to set aside 2,421,506 desiatines for settlement. At 15 desiatines each, this would be enough for 161,432 families. A later study under Kolpakovskii's successor, Baron Taube, brought a higher figure. Again "without crowding the Kirgiz," it was asserted that there were 5,500,000 desiatines of free land in the oblast, or enough for nearly 400,000 individual allotments. In 1893 a still higher figure emerged from a study made by the Imperial Geographic Society, by which it was calculated that although about 20,000,000 desiatines in the oblast must be considered as either unsuitable for agriculture or already farmed or needed by the Kazakhs, some 27,000,000 desiatines was free for settlement.[35]

To settle the matter once and for all, in 1895, at the behest of the Siberian Railroad Committee the Ministry of Agriculture and State Property dispatched a large-scale expedition to the Steppe to study the land question. The expedition, a biological, economic, and statistical survey headed by the statistician F. A. Shcherbina, had as its stated purpose the ascertainment of lands in the oblasts of Turgai, Akmolinsk, and Semipalatinsk which could be assigned to Russian settlers without loss to the Kazakh stock-raising economy. It was also to attempt the prediction of future changes and developments in the Kazakh economy.[36]

Operating until 1903, the Shcherbina expedition investigated eight uezds in the northern parts of the assigned oblasts, but refrained from study of the remaining ten uezds in the south which were regarded as unsuitable for cultivation. The expedition found that the Kazakhs were changing rapidly from a nomadic to a settled existence. As explained by Shcherbina:

. . . strips of plowland, corn fields, and large areas sown to grain already form inviolable borders on the Steppe before which the nomad stock-breeder must halt with his herds, a boundary not to be crossed, a historically necessary symbol of change from one form of economy to another. . . . Replacing the nomad with his eternally wandering herds there has arisen here a half-settled form of life, and occupation with the land. And where the plow has cut into the bosom of the earth pastoralism has already started to break up and an agricultural way of life has begun.[37]

The "historically necessary" phenomenon of Russian colonization had therefore exerted a direct effect on many of the Kazakhs by forcing them to give up their traditional economy and take up agriculture. Of still greater importance in the opinion of Shcherbina and other officials was the fact that when the Kazakhs settled they used less land. This transition had assumed such proportions that large additional amounts of steppe land could be freed for colonization. The net conclusion derived from the expedition's data was that the 106,000 Kazakh households in the eight uezds studied would require 17,000,000 desiatines of land, leaving as "surplus" a total of 18,000,000 desiatines (or, at 2.7 acres per desiatine, an area of nearly 70,000 square miles, which if all in one place would form a square of over 250 miles in each direction). With this information as a basis the government made up a "fund" of the lands deemed surplus, from which tracts considered suitable for agriculture could be allotted to settlers.[38]

THE RESETTLEMENT ADMINISTRATION

To ease the burden on the Siberian Railroad Committee, on December 2, 1896, a new body known as the Resettlement Administration (*Pereselencheskoe upravlenie*), was formed within the Ministry of the Interior to manage resettlement affairs. This agency was charged with preparation of laws and administrative acts pertaining to resettlement, publicizing new locations, supervising the establishment of settlers, and managing credits for resettlement assigned to the Ministry of the Interior.[39]

Colonization had by then assumed the nature of a panacea for the problems besetting Russia. The agrarian distress and discontent in European Russia which was causing the peasants to move from the overcrowded regions to the more sparsely populated areas of Asiatic Russia was in itself a threat to the established order of things, but experience had shown that this movement could not be stopped. The idea of encouraging it therefore found greater and greater support in various quarters. Government officials favored colonization as a safety valve against revolutionary disturbances which might arise from agrarian discontent. Conservatives began to favor colonization as a means of strengthening Russia's hold on her borderlands by establishing loyal elements there who would further the interests of the empire. Certain revolutionary elements favored colonization because it reflected the fundamental desire of the peasantry for more land. Finally, many residents of the pioneer communities of Asiatic Russia desired to develop what had already been begun, to fill in the empty spaces that existed on every hand, and to render more secure the position of the Russian population in regions such as Central Asia which had a considerable native, non-Russian majority.

How closely liberalism and strong nationalism could be mixed in consideration of the colonization question is evident in the writings of O. A. Shkapskii, a liberally inclined Tashkent lawyer and authority on resettlement matters. Using ideas sometimes curiously similar to present-day Soviet themes even down to the phraseology, Shkapskii advocated preparing the steppe for colonization by means of great government-sponsored irrigation projects, foreseeing in such means the possibility of changing the desert climate and even to the extent of planting forests on the shifting sands.

Shkapskii considered the growing impoverishment of the nomads to be due in large part to the severe natural conditions of their habitat and oppression by their tribal aristocracy; he believed settlement to be the answer to their problems. If the natives lived and worked alongside Russian peasants they would be drawn closer to the Russians, and this would facilitate "the spread of our European civilization among them," [40] and their entry upon "the path of cultural and civil development." The Russian people, "the elder brother of all the peoples inhabiting the country," should help them along this path, but "as a loving and not as an oppressive brother." He favored setting aside "surplus" nomad lands for Russian peasants and even proposed legislation to permit the settlement of peasants on unused lands in Cossack holdings.[41]

A new resettlement law, enacted on June 6, 1904, gave still further encouragement to colonization in Central Asia and other parts of Asiatic Russia, replacing the system which had been in operation since 1889, and setting the pattern for colonization for the next decade. The new law permitted would-be settlers to emigrate on their own volition, without special permission from the government.

In the same year, having in effect ushered in the new period of colonization by its work, the Siberian Railroad Committee disbanded.[42] The preparation of allotments, establishment of settlers in new locations, and all other colonization matters were placed under the Resettlement Administration. When in 1905 the Ministry of Agriculture and State Property was reorganized as the Main Administration of Land Organization and Agriculture, the Resettlement Administration was transferred to the jurisdiction of the latter body from the Ministry of the Interior.[43]

At the same time the Resettlement Administration itself underwent a major reorganization. The parts of Asiatic Russia suitable for colonization were divided into twelve large resettlement districts (*pereselencheskii raion*). Five of these were located in Central Asia: in the Steppe, the districts of Turgai-Ural'sk, Akmolinsk, and Semipalatinsk; and in Turkestan, the districts of Semirechie and of Syr-Daria (the latter including the Syr-Daria, Fergana, and Samarkand oblasts). Each of these districts was in turn divided into subdistricts (*podraion*). Officials of the resettlement districts had broad powers, independent of the local authorities, for selecting and preparing new allotments for settlement, and aiding colonists in transit and in getting established.[44]

Although these administrative changes were of undoubted benefit to the colonists, they left the welfare of the natives in a secondary position. During the 13-year period from 1893 to 1905, in which the 18,000,000 desiatine land "fund" was established, some 400,000 Russian peasants settled in the Steppe on approximately 3,800,000 desiatines of land. However, although less than a third of the total land fund was thereby utilized, and in spite of professed intentions of taking only land not needed for the Kazakh economy, it soon became apparent that serious injustice was being done. Repeated complaints from the natives, and frequent articles in the Russian press expressing fears for the ruin of the native economy were without avail.

Measures at least to slow the influx might have been in order, but in the official view

. . . life and reality dictated otherwise. The nomadic way of life of the Kirgiz, under the influence of changing economic conditions brought by Russian settlement in the Kirgiz Steppe, pointed the way increasingly toward a transition to a settled existence. This in its turn naturally lowered the existing average needs of the Kirgiz for lands, because in an agricultural economy the average amount of land needed is significantly less than that needed for nomadic stock breeding. Moreover, there has been increasing evidence of unprofitableness and *uneconomic utilization under a nomadic economy of those lands which nature itself has foreordained for the raising of grain.*[45]

New studies conducted by the Resettlement Administration confirmed the earlier conclusions of the Shcherbina expedition as to the changes taking place in the Kazakh economy. As one of many examples, in 1901 a survey of Arakaraginsk volost, in Kustanai uezd (Turgai oblast) revealed that 72.3 per cent of the Kazakhs there were raising grain, using an average of 3.3 desiatines of land per household. Four years later, in 1905, the percentage of the Kazakhs in the same volost who were growing grain had risen to 94.4 per cent, and the sowed land to an average of 8 desiatines per household.

For government officials, the significant feature of this process was that it provided more surplus land. According to their calculations, four head of livestock, which could scarcely support one person for a year, required 20.5 desiatines of land, but one desiatine of the same land could produce 100 poods (3,600 pounds) of grain. Consequently, the previous norms, varying from 150 to 550 desiatines, were considered superfluous, and new norms of 55 to 350 desiatines per native household were set.[46]

This reduction of Kazakh holdings opened great new areas for settlement and even reopened regions previously closed to further settlement, as Kustanai and Kokchetav uezds, in Turgai oblast. Between 1906 and 1912 the new norms made possible the freeing of 12,000,000 desiatines of land in the Steppe, and settlement of nearly 1,500,000 colonists.[47]

COLONIZATION IN TURKESTAN

The Steppe oblasts and Semirechie were the main centers of Russian peasant colonization in Central Asia. The other oblasts—

Syr-Daria, Transcaspia, Samarkand, and Fergana—were already heavily populated in most sections where soil conditions and water supply made it possible to practice agriculture. Nearly all of the remaining area required irrigation and was closed to colonists by section 270 of the Turkestan statute.

In Syr-Daria oblast, colonization took its first spurt forward under General N. I. Grodekov, military governor from 1883 to 1892. At the beginning of this period there were only two Russian settlements in the oblast, both in the vicinity of Tashkent. Mindful of the numerical inferiority of the Russians, Grodekov appealed in European Russia for settlers, secured funds to aid them on their journey to Turkestan and during their first years of settlement, and sometimes himself went out to search for suitable land.[48] His efforts were particularly successful during the famine years of 1891 and 1892. In two years he established 18,000 peasants in Tashkent and Chimkent uezds,[49] principally Volga Germans and members of various Russian schismatic sects, such as Molokans, Baptists, and Khlysty. Several small irrigation works were undertaken to help provide additional land for their settlement.[50]

In Transcaspia oblast, colonization began in 1889. As in Syr-Daria oblast, Germans and Molokans were prominent among the settlers. By 1896 there were 10 settlements, and by 1909 there were 27, with a population of 5,000, although this was but a negligible proportion of the oblast's total population at that time of 290,000.[51]

In Fergana oblast, the first Russian village, Pokrovskii, was founded in 1893 on unirrigated land in Osh uezd. The settlers there were later given irrigated land at nearby Kurshab, abandoned by the native owners when the dam at the head of the aryk was destroyed by a flood. The dam was rebuilt by the oblast government. In 1901 and 1903, four other villages were established in the same uezd, but Pokrovskii remained the only Russian settlement of any size. In Namangan uezd, several small Russian settlements were established, the inhabitants of which were occupied exclusively with grain growing. In Andizhan uezd, three Russian peasant villages were established between 1897 and 1901,

and several others in later years. In Margelan uezd, the village
of Russkoe Selo was founded on the land of several native villages whose inhabitants, involved in the Andizhan revolt of
1898, had had their land confiscated by the Russian government
as a punishment. As Russkoe Selo was in an irrigated area, the
Russians planted most of their land in cotton. In Samarkand
oblast, as late as 1909 only one Russian village had been established.[52]

THE CONTINUED INFLUX INTO THE STEPPE

The administrative difficulties which hindered the settlement of
Russian peasants in Turkestan were absent in the Kazakh Steppe,
but settlers came in such numbers that there were never enough
facilities for their care. As always, the most numerous element,
the unauthorized settlers, who came without government sanction or previous arrangement for land, were worst off. Mainly
from the southern gubernias of European Russia, where the land
shortage was most acute, these settlers were usually poverty-
stricken at the outset, and destitute of physical and material resources at the end of the long journey. The heart-breaking rigor
of the journey afoot over thousands of versts is graphically presented in the contemporary painting by S. Ivanov, "The Death of
a Settler," portraying a dead migrant laid out with pathetic care
on the open steppe, his wife prostrate with grief, their little girl
sitting quietly by, her face darkened by the pitiless sun, their
few possessions strewn about the small wagon.

Even after the construction of the Trans-Siberian Railroad the
trip was still difficult, as all transportation facilities remained
overtaxed by the mounting tide of settlers. Because there were
not enough coaches, the migrants traveled in boxcars, of the type
provided for troops. Crowded for days in these cars with little or
no heating or sanitary facilities, and with inadequate food, many
of the migrants fell ill. The stations along the way had scant
facilities for their care, so many died of sickness and starvation.

After going as far toward their destinations by rail as they could,
the colonists had to set out on the long journey from the railroad
to their place of settlement. For those seeking land in Central

Asia, this was usually from Omsk via river boat on the Irtysh to Semipalatinsk, and then several hundred miles to the south by horse or on foot. Even those who came later by way of the Orenburg-Tashkent Railroad had to cover another several hundred miles before reaching places where they could settle.[53]

After the settlers received land allotments their situations were still difficult. The bare expanse of the Kazakh Steppe gave no possibility of living off the country. Most of the immigrants had to dwell in hastily erected clay huts. Many suffered from malnutrition or were stricken by typhus, malaria, and other diseases. There was an especially high mortality among children.[54]

When the revolutionary disturbances of 1905–1907 were quelled, the government again turned its attention to colonization. Driving relentlessly to stamp out all threats of revolt, P. A. Stolypin, the new prime minister, strove simultaneously to correct the underlying causes of discontent, attempting to hold back the tide of change until he could instill new energy into the mighty though faltering Imperial system. Seeing the agrarian problem as one of major importance, Stolypin attacked it with characteristic determination. Adopting plans already urged by his more liberal predecessor Count Witte, and in accord with a movement toward land partition already begun by the peasants themselves, he sponsored laws permitting the division and distribution of communal lands, thereby completing the emancipation of the peasants from serfdom. The government-operated peasant land bank helped peasants to purchase additional land. Government agencies embarked on a broad program of securing better land utilization by introducing new methods of plant and animal husbandry. But these measures, aimed at more equitable and productive use of the already insufficient land in European Russia, were at best only palliatives. Stolypin's hope for the alleviation of the agrarian problem lay in the colonization of Asiatic Russia through an expanded resettlement program. "We propose a modest but a true path," he told critics of his land program in the Duma, "the opponents of the state would take the way of radicalism, the way of release from the historic past of Russia, release from its cultural traditions. They would have a great up-heaval; we would have a great Russia." [55]

Under Stolypin's new program, the Resettlement Administration became one of the most flourishing agencies of the government. Its expenditures for the aid of settlement in Asiatic Russia rose from 4,500,000 rubles in 1906 to 13,000,000 rubles in 1907.[56] The agency flooded Russia with printed propaganda explaining the advantages of resettlement in the new regions. Rail fares for colonists were reduced; baggage and domestic animals were carried at nominal fees. Shelters for colonists were built at the larger stations along the route eastward. At their new locations, settlers received liberal government loans and five-year exemptions from taxes and military service. State-operated stores were established in many localities to enable settlers to buy needed supplies and farm equipment.[57]

Thus encouraged, and spurred by the mounting population pressure, the number of colonists moving across the Urals into Asiatic Russia rose to record heights. After a temporary drop to less than 50,000 a year during 1904 and 1905 because of the Russo-Japanese War, the number rose to 216,700 in 1906 and 577,000 in 1907.[58] It soon became clear to Stolypin and other advocates of resettlement, however, that there was a land shortage in Asiatic Russia just as in European Russia. Whereas in 1907 the prime minister calculated that a land "fund" of 57,000,000 desiatines would be required to meet the needs of peasants emigrating to Asiatic Russia, he had to admit that the government had only 10,000,000 desiatines which could be devoted to their use.[59]

As it seemed impossible and even undesirable to stop the movement of peasants out of European Russia, the only alternative was somehow to find more land. In Central Asia the Shcherbina Expedition, which had marked for settlement a "surplus" of 18,000,000 desiatines of land, had investigated only eight uezds in the northern parts of Turgai, Akmolinsk, and Semipalatinsk oblasts. Now, however, it was proposed that the extensive but less arable southern portions be investigated as well.

The unremitting pressure of colonists and diminishing amounts of free land posed an insoluble problem for the officials charged with resettlement operations in the field. It was often rendered even more difficult by the quality of the officials themselves. Many of the Resettlement Administration personnel, from the chiefs down to the statisticians, agronomists, and surveyors, came directly from the organization's central offices in St. Petersburg, and were unfamiliar either with field work or with the localities to which they were assigned. Empowered to act independently from the governor-generals and military governors, under pressure from their superiors and from the impatient immigrants, they often seized as "surplus" whatever land lay most convenient, even plowed and irrigated tracts belonging to the natives. They also gave out lands haphazardly, without preliminary surveying or adequate inspection to determine their potentialities. As a result, not only was injustice repeatedly done the natives, but many allotments proved useless and the peasants who settled on them were ruined.[60]

In 1908, these practices finally became the object of a governmental inquiry during Senator Count K. K. Palen's sweeping investigation of the Turkestan administration and economy. Because of his revelations of waste, corruption, and careerism a number of officials were tried and sentenced to imprisonment for the theft of government funds.

Palen reported that little additional land could be taken for colonization without depriving the natives of their livelihood and arousing their resistance. He therefore urged the abandonment of the policy of using Turkestan as a dumping ground for the surplus rural population of central Russia. Instead, he proposed the colonization of the region in a slower, more dependable fashion by attracting private enterprise and by freeing Russians residing in the region from previous restrictions on buying and selling land. This would permit them to compete with the natives in normal economic processes, and in his opinion would work to the benefit of both.[61]

Palen's recommendations brought bitter criticism from the advocates of colonization. "There seems to be some sort of hatred for the Russian settler," opined a writer in *Okrainy Rossii* (Russian Borderlands), a right-wing publication extolling colonization. There was no danger in bringing in additional settlers, on the contrary, "it should be several millions. Then the Turkestan border region would be forever firmly bound to Russia, and the native population would become accustomed to and acquainted with the Russian population and would become truly devoted to Russia." [62]

A report more to the liking of colonization enthusiasts appeared a few months later, following a tour of Western Siberia and the Kazakh Steppe made in August, 1910, by Stolypin and A. V. Krivoshein, the head of the Main Administration of Land Organization and Agriculture, the latter like his chief an advocate of an expanded resettlement program. In a memorial addressed to the State Duma and the State Council, they stressed the necessity of resettlement as "a natural process," the task of which was not to be "the transplanting (*vyselenie*) of toiling masses from the Motherland, but the colonization (*zaselenie*) of the borderlands," and a change of emphasis in resettlement from the quantitative to the qualitative. Instead of giving out great unsurveyed expanses of land at one time for hundreds of settlers, gathered from all over Russia, they urged the allotment to individual peasants of small, carefully subdivided tracts, with roads and a guaranteed water supply and simultaneous improvement of the general cultural conditions of settlement. [63] They saw the problem of getting more land for settlement in the Kazakh Steppe as depending on improvements and careful use of land. They advocated dry-farming, deep well-drilling, and soil improvement, as means which would permit the settlement of many acres in the Steppe that were previously considered unsuitable for agriculture. [64]

As an example of how colonization could increase the national wealth, the report cited the Kulundinsk Steppe, a region of over 900,000 desiatines lying east of Pavlodar. Formerly this area had provided pasture for the herds of only 1,089 Kazakh families. Later, 745,000 desiatines of this land were declared surplus to the needs of the natives and were turned into allotments for

settlers. The soil was second-rate, and there was a shortage of
water, but the area was quickly settled. In two years, 200 settlements were established. These were populated by 55,000 settlers,
chiefly Ukrainians and German Mennonites. The village of Slavgorod, founded on empty steppe only two years before, was already a thriving town. "In the previously lifeless steppe the pulse
of Russian life begins to beat," the report stated.[65]

As for the Kazakhs, Stolypin and Krivoshein asserted that
"resettlement will crowd them, but will not deprive them. Losing
millions of desiatines, they will be reimbursed by the fact that
their remaining land for the first time will acquire a market
value; in the steppe prices will be put on hay, plowland, wheat,
and livestock." However, their report cautioned, "only those
groups of Kirgiz [Kazakhs] who are already fully ready for settlement can and should be settled." [66]

In order to hasten Kazakh settlement, the report urged a change
in the existing system of native local self-government, in this
respect agreeing with the conclusion reached in the report of
the Palen commission of the previous year. The volost headmen
and judges, elected by means of bribery and vote purchase,
assertedly tried in various ways to hinder the trend of their poorer
brethren toward settlement. The report advocated abolition of
the privileges of the native leaders, and a change to the "more
responsible" system of administration under which the Russian
peasants were governed, that is, the system of land commandants installed to curb the power of the Zemstvo. This, they asserted, would protect the interests of the majority of the Kazakhs
and prevent hindrance to the development of Russian dominion in
the steppe.[67]

"A broad flow of Russian settlers into the steppe," the report
concluded, "will be to the advantage of the settlers, the Kirgiz,
the steppe, and the Russian state." [68] Thus, by 1910 resettlement
(or colonization, if one preferred) had become a virtual ideology
in certain segments of the Russian government and of Russian
public opinion, a panacea which could at once cure and
strengthen. But no amount of optimism could eliminate the fact
that there was not enough land. The best had been taken, leav-

ing only marginal land or land which had to be taken from the natives as "surplus."

INCREASED COLONIZATION IN TURKESTAN

During the rush to colonize the Kazakh Steppe, one large part of Russian Central Asia had remained relatively untouched. Both in the Steppe oblasts and in Semirechie the Steppe statute of 1891 had allowed lands allegedly superfluous to the needs of the nomads to be taken for peasant settlement, but, typical of the lack of legislative uniformity in the codes governing Central Asia, the oblasts of Syr-Daria, Fergana, and Samarkand contained no such device. The troublesome section 270 of the "statute for the government of the Turkestan region" still barred the lands of the nomads of Turkestan to Russian peasant colonists except on a very limited scale, as in areas newly won from the desert by irrigation.

Pressure for a change in the colonization status of Turkestan mounted, however, until finally, on December 19, 1910, the statute was amended so that all lands in Samarkand, Syr-Daria, and Fergana oblasts which the governor-general determined to be in excess of the needs of the nomad population on the basis of "natural-historical, economic, and statistical investigation," were to be placed under the control of the Main Administration of Land Organization and Agriculture and, "with the interests of the nomadic population guaranteed," were to be formed into allotments for settlement.[69]

These few words freed vast areas for settlement, but even with the lip service paid to the rights of the natives the step taken so easily by the authorities in St. Petersburg posed a real problem to the local authorities charged with carrying out the provision. On June 19, 1910, General A. V. Samsonov, the newly appointed governor-general of Turkestan, appealed to all local administrative officials and officials of the Resettlement Administration to coöperate in the work ahead. He stated that "as a first condition for the correct development of resettlement in the region, the Kirgiz population must be well informed concerning the forthcoming measures of the government. Every Kirgiz must understand that he is going to be crowded a little, but that the question of the seizure of his surplus lands is going to be accurately decided by the government." [70]

In spite of such intentions, however, the work of resettlement in the newly opened central oblasts of Turkestan proceeded in a familiar pattern. Native peasants already occupied most of the lands in any way suited for agriculture without major efforts at reclamation. The Resettlement Administration, nevertheless, took all it could, causing the commandant of Chimkent uezd to report to the military governor of Syr-Daria oblast that its officials were marking out allotments for settlers with complete disregard for the irrigated lands and even the habitations of the natives, and likewise were staking out "lands unirrigated and up to now uninhabited because of the impossibility of making a living on them." Not only would there be a tremendous waste of money on untillable land, he warned, but there would be bloodshed if the plan for resettlement of the Kazakhs in that area and their replacement by Russian peasants was put into effect.[71]

The difficulty of finding land for Russian settlements in Turkestan, the insignificant number of Russian settlers, and Russia's need for greater self-sufficiency in cotton impelled further efforts toward colonization in the region. After a visit to Turkestan in the spring of 1912, Krivoshein set forth vast new plans of combined political and economic significance. He recommended irrigation projects which would reclaim 3,000,000 desiatines of unused land, the establishment of 300,000 Russian peasant farms, and the immigration of 1,500,000 Russian settlers. He also proposed laws to restrict natives to the land they then occupied, uniform regional legislation to govern the use of water, state credits for settlers, and additional transportation facilities to further his program.[72] However, the outbreak in 1914 of World War I prevented any attempt to put Krivoshein's far-reaching plans into effect.

NET RESULTS OF THE MIGRATION

War abruptly halted the movement of colonists who for forty years had poured across the Urals in one of the major population shifts of recent generations. Like similar phenomena in the contemporary United States and other parts of the globe, the movement had radically altered the ethnic composition and way of life of the areas affected.

In the Steppe oblasts and in Semirechie, the influx of colonists nearly tipped the ethnic balance in favor of the newcomers. In 1911, 40 per cent (1,544,000) of the total population of the four Steppe oblasts of Ural'sk, Turgai, Akmolinsk, and Semipalatinsk (approximately 3,834,000) were settlers from European Russia. Naturally, however, the proportion between Russians and natives varied from one area to another. In some regions scarcely a Russian was to be seen, but in others they were predominant. In Akmolinsk oblast in 1911 the Russians formed 58 per cent of the total population.[73]

The influx, as has been indicated, also caused radical changes in the economy and society of the native inhabitants of the Steppe. In 1911 only 281,795 of the Russian population of the four above-mentioned oblasts was urban as against 1,261,720 which was rural. This meant the appropriation of the best lands and the dispossession of the nomads or their transformation into settled population, with much impoverishment and social dislocation as a consequence.

The balance was much different in the Governor-Generalship of Turkestan, however. There, out of a total population of 6,493,000 in 1911, only 407,000 or a mere 6 per cent, were Russians. Even of this number, 177,374 represented urban population, leaving only slightly more than half (229,233) as rural population. If the oblast of Semirechie, with its Russian population of 204,307, or 17 per cent of the total population, was excluded, the balance for the remaining oblasts of Turkestan was overwhelmingly in favor of the natives. Out of a total population of 5,291,152 in 1911, the Russian population of Syr-Daria, Fergana, Samarkand, and Transcaspia oblasts numbered only 202,290.[74] Most of this was to be found in Tashkent and other cities; only a minute percentage was engaged in agriculture. How much Krivoshein's ambitious program would have changed this ratio was never decided.

A spontaneous movement, sparked by economic necessity, in disregard of all restraints, had caused an almost constantly increasing flow of colonists. They poured into Siberia and the Kazakh Steppe to take up the best land that could be farmed with existing techniques, until in the end the government undertook active sponsorship of the movement. Finally, proponents of the monarchy assigned the Kazakh Steppe and Turkestan a major role in plans to ease the agrarian problem in European Russia and to populate the borderlands with a strong loyal element. By 1914 control of the region had been wrested from the natives, and the effectiveness of the Russian settlers as a stay to revolution was all too soon to be put to the test.

PART THREE

Economic Development

INFLUENCED by other cultural and geographic factors, the indigenous economy of Central Asia differed in many ways from that of Russia. If the region was to be integrated successfully with the rest of the empire these differences had to be eliminated or at least minimized.

NATIVE LAND TENURE

One of the main problems facing the Russians in Central Asia was the native system of land ownership. Although well established on the basis of law and custom, this system was so different from that known in Russia that readjustment was mandatory.

Among the nomads, land tenure was determined by family organization and by the conditions of their stock-raising economy. The nomad group, comprising numerous households governed on a patriarchal basis, moved about as a unit and held grazing lands in common. The extent of a group's pastures depended on its ability to seize land and to maintain its position against other groups. The boundaries of the summer grazing lands (*dzhailau*) of the various groups were only vaguely defined. They shifted with variations in rainfall and with the waxing and waning of tribal strength. The winter camp (*kstau*) was in a more definite location. Only around the winter camps did there exist what was in effect the private ownership of land. There the poor and the aged, who did not migrate with the herds, grew a small amount of grain on tilled plots or gathered hay on meadows (*kol*).[1]

The settled population inhabiting the irrigated oases of Turkestan had a more complex system of land ownership. The principles of land utilization there were already ancient when the Arabs conquered the region at the beginning of the eighth century A.D. The conquerors merely regularized and defined these principles more accurately on the basis of the Shariat, establishing forms which prevailed down to the nineteenth century.

As in other regions governed by the Shariat, there was a theoretical absence of private ownership of land. The emir or khan, regarded as the viceroy or deputy of the caliph, was recognized as having supreme control over all lands. Land used by the population was considered a part of the state holdings, loaned out in perpetuity.[2] Land in this system fell into four general categories.

(1) The public domain (*miriie*), comprising lands at the immediate disposal of the state (i.e., of the emir or khan). This included the sovereign's personal land (*zamin-i-podshohi*), which consisted of cultivated land, orchards, and palace grounds; uncultivated or waste land (*zamin-i-mavot*); and lands whose owners had died without leaving an heir.

(2) Proprietary (*miul'k*) lands, held in hereditary ownership by the proprietors settled on them. Lands in this category were of several types: (a) tax-free land, held by means of a special charter given by a head of the state, (b) lands retained by the indigenous population at the time of the Arab conquest on condition of payment of a tax (*kheradzh*), theoretically a tenth (but more often amounting to a seventh or even a half) of the harvest, and (c) lands originally divided among the Arab conquerors of the region as spoils, but also held on condition of payment to the treasury of one-tenth of the harvest. Miul'k lands were at the complete disposition of the owner and could therefore be sold, given away, bequeathed, or set aside to be held in trust for charitable purposes. However, if the owner died without heirs the land reverted to the government. Whenever these lands were leased or rented, a native variety of dependency emerged on them similar to the system of feudal obligations characteristic of medieval Europe, with special services given in return for the use of the land.

(3) *Amliak* land, previously unirrigated and unoccupied land (i.e., *zamin-i-mavot*), reclaimed from the desert and becoming, under the Shariat, the property of whoever irrigated and planted it. This land was utilized in perpetuity in return for a tax, larger than the kheradzh because, by decisions of native jurists, the kheradzh represented payment for irrigation water, while the tax on the amliak land represented payment for both water and land. Unlike miul'k land, the amliak land could not be transferred to another owner, or turned into a *vakf* or trust. Native jurists differed as to the absolute tenure of these lands. Some held that they belonged to the state, and that the holders of the lands were only tenants of the state and therefore were unable to sell their lands without permission. Others said that these lands, too, were miul'k, that is, the property of the persons residing on them, and that they were the property of the state only in the sense that the taxes from them went to the sovereign's treasury, unlike other taxes, which went to the treasury of the bek.[3]

(4) Vakf lands, given by private individuals or by the sovereign, to be held in trust by the Church or state, with their incomes devoted to religious purposes, such as maintenance of a medressa or mosque, or to charity. In Central Asia there were four types of vakfs, two of them the so-called normal, or legal types, found in all Moslem countries, and two of them derived from custom, and peculiar to Central Asia. They were:

(a) Pure vakfs, free from all taxes and obligations and managed by the emir or khan.

(b) Conditional vakfs, in which the vakf right was limited to a specified share of the profits gained from it, set by the state when it approved the conferring of the vakf.

(c) Vakfs in which the property was not actually transferred to the use of an institution, but remained in the hands of the founder of the vakf and after his death was transferred to his heirs. Establishment of these so-called hereditary vakfs made property inalienable. It remained in the hands of the original owner and his heirs, as if it were transformed into family property. The aim of the establishment of this type of vakf was the guarantee of property to posterity, whereas according to the Shariat a person working these lands had no right of inheritance.

(d) Finally, there were also fictional vakfs, founded by land-owners who sought to guarantee themselves from confiscations and to avoid government taxes and obligations. In this case the landholder entered into an agreement with some religious-educational institution, which for a specific sum agreed to be the holder of the vakf, allowing the "bestower" to retain the right to actually own the "donated" property.[4]

Abuses concerning the vakfs were common. The state had no control over the exact disposition of vakf income, often appropriated by the Moslem clergy, as executors of the vakf, for their own use. The clergy usually had complete control of the conditional vakfs and all their revenue, and only a portion of the revenues due the state were actually paid to it. The khans and provincial administrators were powerless to take action in such cases because of the power of the clergy. Even if action could have been taken the lack of clarity, doubtful validity, and sometimes the total lack of documents rendered impossible any exact accounting of the income from vakf lands.[5]

NATIVE WATER LAW

Land tenure in Central Asia was closely associated with the question of water rights. Because of the region's aridity, irrigation was of prime importance. Life itself depended on the available water supply and how it was apportioned.

The regulation of water rights and irrigation facilities followed ancient custom and the Shariat. The distribution and sale of water, the cleaning of ditches, and various servitudes were defined by custom. On the other hand, the extension of aryks through the land of various owners was regulated by the Shariat, which unlike customary law connected the right to water with the right to land. Whereas all unirrigated and uncultivated land was considered subject to the supreme authority of the government, any irrigated and cultivated section of land belonged to whoever had made the improvements upon it. This ownership, however, did not extend to the water supply which made the cultivation of the land possible. It only conveyed the right to an equitable share of the water among the various properties, a right which could not be enhanced by purchase or profited from by sale.

This, in turn, created special forms of economic and personal dependency for most of the population. Irrigation projects required a tremendous expenditure of labor and could only be conducted by the sovereign or powerful individuals able to hire, or more often, to draft the necessary working force. The supervision of canal maintenance and the disposition of water required election or appointment of suitable personnel. A *mirab* looked after apportionment of water in each village, and an *aryk aksakal* ("ditch elder") had the same duty in a number of villages served by one main canal or aryk. Religious law and custom notwithstanding, many of these traded in water, taking bribes for diverting an unequal share to the land of the wealthy and exacting payment in money or labor from the poor.

THE NATIVE TAX SYSTEM

The native system of land tenure and water rights formed the basis of a complex structure of taxes, duties, and obligations. As the economy was primarily agricultural, the greatest burden lay upon land. Owners of miul'k land paid the kheradzh tax. This was of two kinds: the proportional tax (*mekasim*) on grain lands, determined annually by a sampling of the harvest, amounting to as much as half of the harvest, paid in kind; and the fixed tax (*mudazer*) levied on lands of fixed dimensions for which the harvest could not be readily determined, as on gardens, orchards, and meadows. This was usually called the *tanap* tax, after the unit of land measurement of the same name, one tanap corresponding to about one-sixth of a Russian desiatine, or about a half acre. Owners of amliak or reclaimed land paid a somewhat higher tax than did the owners of miul'k land.

There were many other taxes besides those on land. For the upkeep of the irrigation system the people paid the *koshnyi* (or *koshpul*) and *miraban* taxes, and performed a labor service (*mardvaliat*) or *corvée*. Handicrafts, trade, and capital were taxed by the *ziaket,* a tax of one-fortieth of the worth of all cattle, manufactures, trade turnover, and money capital on hand.

A bazaar tax was paid by landholders, stock raisers, craftsmen, entrepreneurs, and traders on the value of their products or wares sold in the bazaars. A tax of 7 per cent or more was levied on wool, cordage, felt, tea, clothing, silk, muslin, cotton goods, leather goods, paints and oils, books, fur, fruits and confections, woodenware, charcoal, and salt products. Other items taxed included grain, silk, silkworm cocoons, cotton, sesame oil, cottonseed, sheep, horses, camels, cattle, hay, wood, clover, straw, melons, and grapes. There was even a tax on fighting cocks and quails. Carters paid a special tax, as did the operators of ferries. Upon the division of an inheritance, an inheritance tax in the form of a percentage of all property or capital was paid to the khan. Property without heirs (*lukat*) was appropriated by the khan.[6]

Most taxes were levied on individuals, but some were imposed on groups. Entrepreneurs, craftsmen, and traders, organized in several dozen guilds (*kasaba*), paid taxes through their guild elders.[7]

Besides taxes, the state treasury received revenue from customs duties and from a number of monopolies. In Kokand the khan owned the majority of shop locations in the great bazaars of the khanate. A high rent was exacted for their use, and trading outside them was forbidden. He also owned factories and mills, and he had a monopoly on musical choruses, which he hired out to his subjects for special occasions. In Bukhara the emir had a monopoly on the hiring out of dancing boys.[8]

In addition to the heavy exactions of the central government, there were also local taxes levied by the beks. Besides the burden of the taxes themselves was the custom of collection by means of tax farmers—the *amliakdar* on amliak lands and the *serker* on other lands—who paid the khan or bek a set sum for the right to collect taxes. Such posts were diligently sought after, as those appointed to them usually retained at least half of all sums collected.

This tax system laid a heavy burden upon the country. Even

during relatively normal and peaceful years the multiplicity of taxes and the burden of the tax-farmer's exactions paralyzed the economy, stifled the enterprise of the productive classes, and held the mass of the people in poverty. In times of emergency, when the authorities resorted to forced requisitions on private property, the load became far heavier. During the internecine strife between Bukhara and Kokand, and in the troubled years before the Russian conquest, these requisitions made it impossible for anyone to be secure in the possession of either property or money. The entire situation was anarchic and full of survivals from the past; local rule predominated, and the tradition of despotic, absolute rule offered no precedent for improvement.[9]

RUSSIAN REFORMS

Confronted with this confused and inequitable tax structure and complex pattern of property relationships, the Russian government had to take steps to bring these important features of native economic life into greater conformity with the system prevailing in the rest of the empire.

With regard to land tenure, the Russian government declared all lands in the annexed portions of Central Asia to be crown property. This step was in conformity with existing practice, in which basic title had rested in the person of the emir or khan; but the government then went further and, with the exception of land possessed by ecclesiastical institutions which received special consideration, recognized all land occupied by buildings and plantations as hereditary private property. This could be sold, bequeathed, or otherwise disposed of as the owner wished. By this means the land in the settled areas was transferred to those who worked it. In case of disputes the native courts were instructed to be governed not by traditional ownership but by the right of whoever used the land.[10]

This measure, more liberal than anything the government had dared to undertake in Russia with regard to the land worked by the serfs freed in 1861, disposed of the extensive landholdings of the khan of Kokand and of the emir of Bukhara within the annexed territory and, more important still, the land of the local

aristocracy. By conveying the land to those who had been working it as sharecroppers and leaseholders, making it their hereditary
property, the Russian government took a major stride toward
neutralizing the mass of the natives in the event of any rebellion
which the former privileged classes of the preconquest era might
seek to arouse. What the government undertook amounted to a
land and tax reform of revolutionary proportions; that contemporaries did not refer to it as such may have been because revolution was not then in style. It is unfortunate that Soviet historical
literature has not yet provided any detailed description of this
land reform, one of the most progressive steps taken by the
colonial regime. The measure also offers an interesting parallel
and is quite likely indirectly connected with similar measures
applied by Russia after the Polish uprising of 1863. Von Kaufman's experience with the land reform instituted in Russian
Poland during his service there as governor-general may well have
led to his support of a similar policy in Turkestan.

To avoid arousing native discontent, Russians in Turkestan
were forbidden to acquire land outside the city limits of the Russian settlements, except from special tracts. The government had
not yet become interested in large-scale colonization. The restriction remained in effect until the end of the 1880's. Permission to purchase such land was then granted, but with so many
restrictions that transactions remained very difficult.[11] Later, as
described previously, plans were laid for Russian colonists to acquire land through purchase.

Unoccupied lands adjacent to settled areas and lands occupied
by the nomads were declared to be state property. This was spe-
cifically stated in the statutes governing the Steppe and Turkestan; the population inhabiting these areas was accorded only
the right to use the land. Later the government declared much
of the Steppe lands "surplus" to native needs and allotted it to
Russian peasant settlers. Villages established on such land were
incorporated on the same legal bases as the villages in European
Russia, and the adjacent land was held in perpetuity by the
village residents. Kazakhs desiring to abandon their nomadic

life and practice agriculture could obtain official approval and
settle in villages in the same manner.

Although on paper the Russian reform gave official title to
landholders, it did not go so far in practice. As in Russia the
village was made the tax unit, and this actually eliminated many
of the private holdings already in existence. Insofar as the community held the land, however, the reform was far-reaching.
About 90 per cent of all irrigated land in Turkestan is said to
have become such "private" property by 1913,[12] although Count
Palen's inspection of 1909 established that in the oblasts of Fergana, Syr-Daria, and Samarkand only about 1 per cent of all the
land was truly privately owned.[13]

The question of taxation was laden with nearly as many difficulties as that of land tenure, but here too, Von Kaufman, acting
for the Russian government, undertook extensive reforms. For a
time several of the original taxes were retained, but in simplified
form. The kheradzh, or harvest tax, continued to be required of
the native settled population, but to the correct amount of one-
tenth of the harvest instead of the larger amounts exacted under
native rule. The tanap tax continued to be levied on land units.
Native traders paid the ziaket, levied on their trading capital. As
before, collections were made through native tax collectors.

The nomads had formerly paid tribute to the khans when
within their sphere of influence. In place of these random, unequal exactions the Kazakh population was now obliged to pay
a definite, uniform tax of two rubles and seventy-five kopecks
per kibitka or household. This tax was to be paid in a gross sum
by each volost, and apportioned by the members of the volost to
each kibitka-holder according to his ability to pay.[14] Other taxes
levied in the region under the native regimes were abolished.

Although now greatly simplified in comparison with the preceding system, even the new tax system soon required adjust-
ment. In areas where the Kazakh population was beginning to
settle and practice agriculture, some natives had to pay both the
land and the kibitka tax. The unvarying amount of the kheradzh,
always one-tenth of the gross yield, caused difficulty when crops

failed. Therefore, when Von Kaufman formed a commission to reorganize the native administration, one of its main tasks was to reform the tax structure. As a result of the commission's work a somewhat better system was adopted, based on occupation. The kibitka tax became payable only by nomads, the kheradzh and tanap by native peasants, and the ziaket by merchants.

This simplification adjusted many of the previous system's inequities, and was also more advantageous to the treasury. Difficulties of assessment and the abuses of the native tax collectors caused other troubles, however. Therefore, early in 1870, Von Kaufman replaced both the kheradzh and tanap taxes with a land tax (*pozemel'naia podat'*). The rate was based on the yield from the kheradzh and tanap collections of 1869, a good harvest year. The tax was payable by each volost in a gross sum, and as the apportionment within the volost was determined by the population itself, the native tax collectors were eliminated. The new system lowered the cost of tax collection, and gave considerable relief to the peasants.[15] The ziaket tax was abolished on January 1, 1875, by a decision of the Committee of Ministers (May 3, 1874).[16]

The vakf lands posed a more difficult tax problem. The institution reserved much valuable property, including caravanserais, bath houses, shops, and large tracts of arable land and pasture, in tax-free status. The government was thus deprived of revenue and the burden on other property was increased. As either confiscation or taxation risked arousing discontent among the natives, the Russian authorities were cautious in their approach to the matter.

A step toward solution of the vakf problem was made in the projected "statute for the government of the oblasts of Semirechie and Syr-Daria" of 1867. This recognized two types of vakf, the taxable and the tax-free, and required taxation of all new grants.[17] Under Von Kaufman's regime a few vakfs were confiscated for state use. When the Russians occupied the Zeravshan district, the Russian garrison at Samarkand commandeered several mosques within the citadel for use as military storehouses. Outside the city a medressa was converted into a temporary prison for natives, and another into a hospital. Vakf income was also used for restoration work on some of the city's ancient monuments.[18]

In most cases, however, the vakf lands and establishments were left undisturbed. "The question of the organization and administration of the vakf is so complex and little developed," said a State Council decision of 1886, "that this subject must be approached with great care. At the present time it can only be decreed that the Russian government will recognize the vakf lands and that they will be preserved in their present status." [19]

In line with this attitude, the "statute for the government of the Turkestan region" of 1886 provided for study and investigation of the vakf problem rather than its immediate disposition. The statute provided for a special temporary commission to examine the documents establishing the vakfs in order to determine the validity of the grants and the exact provisions of each. After this was done all matters pertaining to the vakfs were to come under the jurisdiction of the various administrative boards of the oblasts concerned. These were to approve the vakfs which were legally correct, provide for their administration, supervise expenditure of their incomes, and make periodic audits. New vakfs were to be established only in special cases, with permission of the governor-general.[20] In practice, however, not even the first step, examination of the documents establishing the vakfs, was ever completed, and large tracts of land remained in uncertain status until the end of the Imperial regime.

The question of water rights proved equally difficult of solution. After the conquest the Russian government reserved for itself the right to general supervision over all installations, but actually left the existing system of water rights in effect. This avoided any ill-advised dealing with the intricate problem which might arouse the natives, but at the same time did nothing toward elimination of the shortcomings and abuses characteristic of the native system.

As time passed, however, the need for better regulation of water distribution grew. Population increase, the expansion of sown areas, and the needs of Russian settlers complicated the distribution of water and made preservation of the old norms impossible. As a result the Russian government, through the Re-settlement Administration, examined existing native water law with a view to better regulation. Ownership, administration, settlement of disputes, and punishment for infractions all required careful investigation. Special surveys conducted by the government in Turkestan after 1905 yielded much data. Officials concluded that rights to water and land were inseparable in Turkestan, although land actually played the smaller role, and that it would be necessary for the state to assist in water allocation. A new and comprehensive law governing irrigation was worked out and presented to the Duma shortly before the outbreak of World War I. However, the war caused the measure to be tabled.

To sum up, the Imperial government tried to cope with three great problems of economic administration in Central Asia. A sweeping reform in land tenure abolished absentee ownership and tenantry, placing ownership in the hands of those who worked the land. This was of undoubted benefit to the native population although, as we shall see, the safeguards taken to preserve the gains proved inadequate during the later transformation of native agriculture. Taxation, a thorny problem anywhere, was cleared of the confusion which had characterized it under native rule, and was to a large degree eased. Water rights received careful but dilatory study, and measures for a regional solution to the problem of water allocation were finally prepared but never put into effect.

IX

THROUGHOUT the Central Asian steppes, the southern deserts, and on the eastern mountain slopes, animal husbandry formed the basis of the economy wherever agriculture could not be practiced readily under the existing conditions of native technology or political organization. The livestock of the various nomadic groups satisfied not only their main food, clothing, shelter, and transportation needs, but was a substantial source of products which could be traded for the foodstuffs and manufactured articles of settled peoples. Climatic and topographic factors prevented the steppe from being a Great Plains or an Argentine pampa as one of the world's great meat producers. Nevertheless, the region offered considerable potentialities as a source of meat and animal products for the rest of the empire.

Part of a great nomadic culture complex extending across all of Asia from northern China to the Near East, the livestock economies of the Kazakhs, Kirgiz, Kara-Kalpaks, and Turkmen all bore certain traits in common, and all felt the force of change under Russian rule. This account will deal mainly with the Kazakhs. The most numerous of the Central Asian nomads, and the most northerly, they were directly in the path of Russian expansion and experienced the forces of change more sharply than the other groups. As nomads, the Kazakhs were not aimless wanderers. In ordinary usage the term "nomad" is a misnomer. The aul, the patriarchal family group which was the basic economic unit of the Kazakhs, like its counterparts among other nomadic peoples, followed fixed cycles of migration, usually over the same general territory, year after year.

The annual cycle of the Kazakh economy was closely related to the four seasons. Migration began in the spring, when the cattle were driven to the early spring pastures (*koktau*), where melting snow and spring rains provided a few weeks of good grazing. Before the onset of summer heat, which renders these parts of the steppe parched and scarcely habitable, the herds were driven to summer pastures on open ranges, the *dzhailau*. Depending on the group's location, these might be on high mountain slopes, on the northern steppes, or on the shores of the Aral Sea. In the autumn began the movement back to winter pasture— places which would be the least exposed during the coldest months—in mountain foothills or in the southern deserts.[1]

The distances involved in these migrations varied according to the region. Some of the Kazakhs living in Syr-Daria oblast had to traverse as much as 600 miles, while others in more favored regions traveled as little as 50 miles.[2]

The conditions of their economy left the Kazakhs peculiarly subject to the caprices of nature. Unusually severe winters, occurring every ten or twelve years, offered great hazards to herding. A prolonged *buran,* or blizzard, could leave snow so deep that the cattle could not reach the grass beneath it. Dry winters with little snow could cause much of the grass to be killed by frost. A thaw was often followed by a sharp freeze resulting in *dzhut* (glazed frost or rime). The steppe would then be covered with a sheet of ice, and the livestock doomed to starve.

These disasters occurred every few years, now in one region and again in another. In the winter of 1879–1880, nearly half of the approximately 3,600,000 head of livestock in Turgai oblast died. In the same oblast, during the winter of 1891–1892, over a third of the livestock died. The greatest loss at that time was in horses, of which about 47 per cent died, followed by cattle, sheep and goats, 32 per cent, and by camels, 22 per cent. Such losses took from eight to ten years to make up. The increase might then be wiped out in one winter.

The plight of the Kazakhs of Lepsinsk uezd, Semirechie oblast, after the winter of 1896–1897 was typical of the chain of adverse circumstances which frequently reduced the Kazakhs to poverty. The winter was in general unfavorable. The Kazakhs dug trenches in the snow to enable their animals to reach the grass. About March 4–5 a thaw occurred, and on the night of March 7 it rained and the snow began to melt. Later in the same night there was a frost, and in the morning the whole steppe was covered with a thick layer of ice, through which it was difficult to reach the earth even with a shovel. Unable to reach their forage, the livestock began to fall by the thousands.

Later in the month, on March 28–29, a buran occurred which caused new losses. Already wet from rain and snow, the animals had no means to warm themselves when a light frost struck in the night, and more died. Later, when the snow melted somewhat, the survivors threw themselves so greedily on the pasture beneath the snow that many died from overfilling their stomachs. Only in auls near Lake Balkhash did this present no danger; there was no grass at all, as it had all been eaten by locusts the season before. Trying to save their cattle, the Kazakhs gave them grain, but it was impossible to obtain enough to enable more than part of the livestock to survive. To get money with which to buy grain the nomads sold what they could of karakul and wool from dead sheep, receiving only nominal prices. Merchants, acquiring grain at ten to fifteen kopecks per pood, sold it to the Kazakhs for sixty kopecks per pood.[3]

During the summer, drought was often a problem, making accustomed pastures useless. Anthrax, rinderpest, and other stock diseases were endemic on the steppe. Predators also took a high toll. In 1894, a normal year, wolves were estimated to have caused a loss in Turgai oblast alone of over 10,000 horses, 6,000 camels, 3,000 cattle, and 30,000 sheep and goats.[4]

In general, the herding economy of the Kazakhs had already begun to decline before the Russians conquered the steppe. During the eighteenth century the Kazakhs of the eastern part of the Steppe suffered disastrous defeats and subjugation at the hands of the Dzhungarian Kalmuks, while those in the lush grasslands of the north began to be crowded out by Russian colonists.

These factors limited the possibilities of finding new pastures during the periodic crises brought on by severe winters and drought. The various Kazakh groups therefore struggled for possession of the remaining available lands. The resulting intertribal strife and *baranta* (retaliatory raids by individuals whose grievances were not satisfied by recourse to Kazakh customary law) caused the gradual elimination of weaker groups. Those who lost out in this process became hired herdsmen or began to practice agriculture, though this was precarious because of the raids of hostile neighbors.

Increasing restriction of pasture lands caused a decline in horse raising and an increase in cattle, sheep, and goat herding. Herds of horses became the monopoly of the rich and powerful, while cattle, sheep, and goats became the mainstay of the poor and semisettled people. This tendency was further stimulated by the increasing demand for wool in Central Asian markets.[5]

The gradual extension of Russian rule over the Steppe in the first half of the nineteenth century ended intertribal strife and baranta. The resultant peaceful conditions, development of the caravan trade, and inclusion within the Russian internal market made animal husbandry more profitable. On the other hand, the new possibilities for development were nullified by the progressive restriction of pasture by Russian colonization, which limited accessions to the native herds. The loss of sheltered spots for refuge in inclement weather, and increasing limitations on the choice of pasture made the Kazakh economy more risky than ever during unfavorable years. More and more of the nomads were forced to dwell permanently in what had formerly served as their winter camps, and to occupy themselves with raising grain and hay.

The transition to a sedentary life afforded a certain security from severe winters and the loss of livestock, but brought no economic improvement for the majority of the Kazakhs. With the spread of agriculture the previous communal holding of property gave way to private property rights, and these developed to the benefit of the more well-to-do members of the Kazakh communities. Their power and the lack of any system within the community for periodically equalizing the use of land enabled them to secure substantial holdings to the detriment of their poorer neighbors. The local self-government introduced by the Russians only fortified these elements in their position. Elections were won by the candidates able to purchase the most votes. Once in office they recouped their campaign expenses by exactions from the losing side. This small well-to-do minority of natives continued to engage in stock raising and prospered, while the condition of the poorer class, forced to settle and work the land, worsened each year.

Although in general its policy was to encourage Kazakh settlement and thereby free more land for Russian peasants, the Russian government nevertheless took various measures on a local scale for the relief of Kazakh herdsmen in times of extremity. The oblast administrations often made loans to the Kazakhs to enable them to buy food and hay during severe winters, and seed during droughts. Experiments were also made to alleviate food shortages. In the spring of 1891 the Turgai Oblast Administrative Board ordered the purchase of fifty mowing machines in St. Petersburg for distribution among the Kazakhs of Burtinsk volost. Thanks to this equipment, the Kazakhs of the volost were able to mow enough feather grass (*kovyl*) to feed not only their own cattle but those of their nearest neighbors and relatives during the severe winter of 1891. To combat stock diseases the government attempted the quarantine of affected areas and the destruction of infected animals.[6] Though for the most part counteracted by the vast terrain, poor communications, and inadequate funds, these efforts on a larger scale might ultimately have helped to make the stock herding of the steppe a major asset to the Imperial economy and a source of increased profit to the natives.

Sheep, in both number and value, constituted the most important element in the economy of the nomadic stock breeders. They supplied mutton, the main meat of both nomads and settled natives, as well as milk, cheese, wool, and hides.[7] Each year large herds of sheep were sold in the markets of Khiva, Bukhara, Karategin, Kokand, and European Russia. The ability of the Kazakh sheep to withstand long migrations and to forage on the poorest *solonchak* (alkaline) steppes gave them the widest range of all the livestock. Their hardiness enabled them to survive in all but the most severe winters.

After 1900, fine-wooled (merino) sheep began to be raised east of the Urals, largely in the Kazakh Steppe. Sheep raisers in southern Russia and in the Caucasus leased additional land from the Kazakhs for this purpose. Karakul sheep were raised in Bukhara, Khiva, and Samarkand oblast and in the Pendinsk district of Transcaspia oblast. Each year about 500,000 of the valuable pelts were exported to European Russia, and from there many ultimately went to Western Europe and America.[8]

Horses were second in importance to sheep in the Kazakh economy. Like the other livestock of the nomads, the great herds of horses on the steppe were periodically cut down sharply by severe conditions, but usually recovered rapidly. About 50 per cent of the horses owned by the Kazakhs of the various Steppe oblasts were estimated to have died in the disastrous winter of 1891–1892, yet only three years later, in 1895, there were an estimated 4,000,000 horses, approximately the normal number.[9]

The so-called Kirgiz breed of horse—plain, shaggy, short-legged, and broad of chest—was the principal breed owned by the Kazakhs. Thought to be descended from the steeds of the Mongol conquerors, they had the great endurance necessary under rigorous steppe conditions. In the 1880's, when horse-raising began to decline in the regions of the Don Cossack voisko, the Caucasus, the Novorossiisk region, and elsewhere, the Russian government began to use Kazakh horses for cavalry remounts. The Main Administration of State Horse Breeding (*Glavnoe upravlenie gosudarstvennago konnozavodstva*) undertook a number of measures to encourage the improvement of horse breeding in parts of the Steppe closest to European Russia. Beginning in 1885, expositions of Kazakh horses were organized to show the nomads the advantages of breeding better horses. In order that the natives might have stallions of superior quality, the government opened several stud farms at points near Orenburg, Ural'sk, Orsk, Kustanai, and Turgai. To make it easier for the Kazakhs to use government studs and also to lessen state expenditures for these farms, studs were distributed annually among the most reliable Kazakh horse breeders, who were permitted to let the studs run with their herds for only the cost of their maintenance.[10]

Extensive purchases of horses for farm work in European Russia were also made on the Kazakh Steppe. In the spring of 1892 the government purchased over 9,000 horses in Turgai oblast for distribution among peasants in the famine-stricken regions of European Russia. The horses, all of the "Kirgiz" breed, proved of great merit. Losing their wildness in a few days, they quickly adapted themselves to farm work and surpassed the horses of the peasants in performance. In 1899 the government purchased 40,000 more for the same purpose.[11]

Besides the "Kirgiz" breed, found primarily in the Kazakh Steppe, there were also the horse breeds of Turkestan, to the south. These, the Tekke, Karabair, Gorno-Badakshan, and others, were all of the so-called "hot-blooded" types, with an Arabian admixture, always nervous and high-strung. In breeding these types for military use the government "cooled" their blood with the introduction of other strains.

The cattle of Russian Central Asia, also of a so-called "Kirgiz" breed, were found throughout the steppe and among the Kazakhs of Turkestan. The bulls, used for meat and for riding and pulling carts, weighed between 15 and 25 poods (540 to 900 pounds). Dressed weight averaged about 9 poods (288 pounds). The cows were even smaller, and gave little milk. Although hardy, the Kazakh cattle suffered even more than other animals from winter conditions, especially as their owners provided them with little care and no shelter in the winter.

In Turkestan, toward the end of his regime Von Kaufman had twelve head of cattle purchased in Holland and brought to Tashkent for the improvement of local breeds. But when Cherniaev succeeded Von Kaufman as governor-general, one of his many expressions of hostility toward his predecessor was an order for the immediate slaughter of the animals. He also destroyed sixteen cows of the local breed which had already been bred to the imported bulls, to avert allegedly harmful influence which might result from introduction of the new strain.[12]

Other breeds, subsequently brought into the region by the government and by settlers, gave greater promise for future development of cattle raising than did the indigenous variety.

Camels were also of great value to the Kazakhs and the other natives of Central Asia. Hardy, subsisting on the coarsest of fodder, and long-lived (15 to 20 years), they had many uses. Their main function was heavy transport. Great numbers were used in the Russian military expeditions—10,000, for example, in the Khivan expedition of 1873, and 20,000 in Skobelev's campaign against the Turkmen in 1880–1881. Before the completion of the Trans-Caspian Railroad, camel caravans bore cotton and other products from Central Asia to the nearest railheads in European Russia and brought back manufactured goods and military supplies. After the railroads were built, the numbers of camels in Russian Central Asia declined, but they continued to be important in the parts of the country without rail transport. The Kazakhs considered camel milk very tasty, and fermented it to make kumys (*chubat*). In the spring they gathered camel hair as the animals shed it, making felt for their kibitkas and for bags, boots, overcoats, and rope.[13] Both the single- and double-humped breeds of camel were used.

The total absence of any statistics before the conquest and the frequent unreliability of those compiled afterward make it difficult to assess the net effect of Russian rule upon Central Asian animal husbandry. It may be assumed that the peaceful conditions and the expanded market provided under the Russians resulted in an increase in the total number of livestock, but how much of an increase is impossible to judge. Statistics abound in the accounts of this region, but in the early years they were apt to be grossly inaccurate.[14] For the end of the Imperial period, a reasonably accurate approximation is provided by the following totals of the number of livestock in the Steppe oblasts and Turkestan for 1911, given in the official publication *Aziatskaia Rossiia:* [15]

Horses	5,313,804
Cattle	5,629,319
Sheep	28,524,219
Goats	2,868,350
	42,335,692

Considering the area involved, these figures indicate no particularly strong development in this field. What might have been achieved toward making the region a major meat producer had been ruled out by the continuing influx of Russian settlers, which in effect meant that grain was given preference over meat production, and the needs of the Russian peasant were given priority over those of the native herdsman.

There was undoubtedly considerable social dislocation among the nomadic cattle breeders during this transition because of the loss of pastures. Up to 1914 the trend toward native agricultural settlement continued unabated. In spite of this, the Resettlement Administration considered that the new trends were on the whole beneficial for the Kazakhs. Thanks to higher prices and new markets, the number of native livestock actually seems to have risen in many districts during later years. In 1913, the number of native-owned horses and cattle in Petropavlovsk uezd (Akmolinsk oblast) was double that of a few years before. In the Omsk and Kokchetav districts the number of native livestock had risen 52 and 68 per cent, respectively. In Atbasar uezd the number of cattle had risen 80 per cent.[16] However, where the Kazakhs were taking up agriculture there was a change in the composition of the herds. By 1911, the number of horses in such districts had fallen by 50 to 60 per cent, while the percentage of cattle had risen correspondingly.[17]

Thus, in spite of earlier difficulties, there was finally some prospect of improvement in the native position. By 1911, many of the wealthier Kazakhs were no longer living in sod huts but in wooden or stone houses, reverting to their traditional kibitkas only in the summer. They had begun to acquire harvest machinery and to improve their methods of raising cattle and of harvesting and storing hay. At the same time, the condition of poorer households had improved considerably over that of a few years before. In the Petropavlovsk area the percentage of households without livestock had fallen from 83 to 51, in the Kokchetav area from 75 to 49, and in the Omsk area from 67 to 55.

Another sign of improvement was to be seen in the high annual rate (2.3 per cent) of native population growth for the entire Steppe, which considerably exceeded the rate for all of Russia (less than 2 per cent). Between 1900 and 1912 the child mortality rate among the Kazakhs decreased sharply. During that period 25 per cent more children lived to the age of three years than previously.[18]

Much more data are needed on the number and composition of native herds and the condition of native society, but available facts appear to indicate that immediately prior to World War I the deterioration previously occurring in native society had halted. There was at least the possibility that as long as Russian settlements did not increase an equilibrium might be achieved which could bring about a sound economy in the Steppe and a simultaneous advance in the well-being of the natives.

X

WHILE the animal husbandry of Central Asia barely held its own under Russian rule, agriculture took a different course. The fabulous fertility of the areas under irrigation and the potentialities of the vast areas which might yet be reclaimed did as much to capture the imagination of the conquerors as did the promise of trade and mineral resources.

At the time of the conquest Central Asian agriculture was either on a subsistence basis or confined to the local market. Wheat, rice, and other cereals were the staple crops. Gardening played an important role; the region was famous for its melons, fruits, and vegetables. There were orchards wherever land was cultivated, and besides domestic fruit trees many species also grew wild. Lucerne (alfalfa) was grown for fodder.

Silk and cotton were virtually the only agricultural products exported. Silk culture, combining both agriculture and household industry, was introduced in Turkestan early in the Christian era, and could be found in one form or another on most native farms. The cultivation of cotton, brought from India by way of Persia, was even more ancient.

COTTON

Of all the crops of Central Asia, cotton was of most interest to the Russians. Even in the first half of the nineteenth century, before the conquest, raw cotton, yarn, and fabrics accounted for about two-thirds of the value of the goods which Russia imported from Central Asia.[1]

Until the Crimean War the United States was the main source of cotton for Russia's expanding textile industry, but in 1854, when the American supply was cut off, Russian textile manufacturers began to give serious attention to Central Asian cotton. Between 1840 and 1850 Russia imported a total of 100,000 poods of cotton (a pood being approximately 36 pounds) from Central Asia, but between 1850 and 1860 these imports rose to a total of 270,000 poods.[2]

During the 1860's Central Asian cotton growing received yet another impetus when Russia and the rest of the world experienced a cotton shortage as a result of the American Civil War. From 2,491,000 poods of cotton brought over her European boundaries in 1861, Russia's cotton imports from this quarter dwindled to 587,000 poods by 1863. At the same time, prices rose rapidly. In 1861 Turkestan cotton sold at Nizhnii Novgorod and Moscow for four to five rubles per pood, but by 1864 its price had risen to between twenty and twenty-three rubles. The rising prices greatly stimulated cotton cultivation throughout Turkestan. In 1861 Russia imported 152,000 poods of Asiatic cotton, and by 1864, 704,000 poods.[3]

In spite of this expansion, however, the cotton production of Central Asia was still hindered by defects in quality and method at the time of the Russian conquest. Only the inferior, short-staple variety (*Gossypium herbaceum* L.) was grown, and it was processed by hand. This type was suitable only for the production of the poorer sorts of yarn and textiles.

During the 1870's the idea arose of acclimating better varieties of cotton and of adopting processing methods based on the example of the greatest cotton producer of that day, the United States. By order of Governor-General Von Kaufman, two government representatives, M. I. Brodovskii and V. V. Samolevskii, were sent to Texas to study cotton growing. Superior types of American cotton were introduced for experiment, and American processing machinery was ordered.[4]

At first, the attempts to use American cotton were unsuccessful. Efforts centered around the sea-island variety (*Gossypium barbadense* L.), but this was unsuited to a dry climate. Then in the early 1880's the more suitable American upland variety (*Gossypium hirsutum* L.) was introduced. An experimental farm was established near Tashkent for demonstration of advanced methods of growing cotton, and American machinery was installed for processing it.[5] Excellent results were attained from the new variety of cotton, and the planted area increased rapidly: [6]

```
1883—several desiatines
1884—450 desiatines
1885—1,000    "
1886—12,000   "
1887—14,500   "
1888—68,000   "
```

The first shipment of upland cotton grown in Turkestan, about 100 poods, was made in 1884. It was sent from Moscow to American mills for ginning and returned to Russia.[7] Soon, however, the Russians mastered the processing techniques and with the simultaneous development of Turkestan's first rail connection with the outside world, the Trans-Caspian Railroad, shipments of Turkestan cotton accelerated. In 1888 they totaled 873,000 poods, in 1889, 1,470,000 poods, and in 1890, 2,673,000 poods.[8] Upland cotton was first planted extensively near Tashkent, located at latitude 41.30° N., but was later found to grow best south of the 38th parallel. Therefore it became centered in Fergana oblast and later spread to Samarkand, Bukhara, Khiva, and Transcaspia.

Up to the 1880's the natives of Transcaspia grew only a small amount of cotton. In 1884–1886 the Morozov firm, one of the largest Russian textile manufacturers, sent seeds of American cotton into Transcaspia oblast for distribution among the Tekke cotton growers of Ashkhabad uezd, but they accepted it reluctantly. The bolls of the American cotton did not open all at once like those of the Central Asiatic variety, but only gradually, thus lengthening the time of picking. The inattention of the natives caused much of it to fall from the bolls and be blown away. Later, however, the oblast administration brought Uzbeks from Samarkand to experiment with growing the cotton, distributed free seeds of the American variety, and permitted buyers to give cash advances to growers for future harvests, and the output increased. In 1890, 20,000 poods were harvested, and in 1893, 176,000 poods.[9]

In a few years, American upland cotton and improved methods of cultivation and processing transformed the Turkestan cotton industry. By 1902 the area planted to cotton amounted to 194,800 desiatines; by 1910 it had reached 328,700 desiatines; by 1911, 377,000 desiatines; and by 1913, 401,000 desiatines,[10] or nearly one-fifth of the total irrigated area of 2,105,000 desiatines of the oblasts of Syr-Daria, Samarkand, Fergana, and Transcaspia in that year.[11] Shipments increased with similar tempo. In 1901, 6,880,000 poods were shipped; in 1909, 10,771,000 poods; and in 1911, 13,181,000 poods,[12] or about half of Russia's cotton needs.[13] During the early twentieth century more than half of the total income from Turkestan's agricultural production came from cotton.[14] In Turkestan, as in the southern United States of that day, it could be said, "Cotton is king." [15]

As it became increasingly essential to the developing industry of Russia, cotton growing received every encouragement from the government. A tariff on imported cotton kept the market price at a level which was advantageous to growers. From 1879 to 1884 the tariff stood at 40–50 kopecks per pood; in 1887 this was increased to 1 ruble, then to 1 ruble 75 kopecks, and then to progressively higher figures until in 1903 the tariff reached the sum of 5 rubles 25 kopecks per pood. In addition, the government gave tax privileges to cotton growers, taxing cotton no higher than wheat and barley and less than rice. The cotton crop that could be grown on a given area was three to four times as valuable as a crop of grain, so the natives raised cotton to the exclusion of cereals.[16] Low freight rates on government-owned carriers facilitated shipment. In 1894, to diminish the cost of hauling cotton to fabricating centers and to eliminate middlemen, a single price was announced for the shipment of cotton from stations on the Trans-Caspian Railroad all the way to European Russia, including sea transport on the Caspian.[17]

These measures expanded the cotton-growing area in Central Asia, but only at the cost of other crops which were needed for food. The scarcity of these would normally have caused prices for them to rise until they matched cotton in advantage to the grower. To get around this fact and to increase cotton production still further, the Russian government either had to increase the area under cultivation in Central Asia or decrease the extent of the existing cultivated area devoted to other crops, particularly grain. The first course required difficult and costly irrigation projects; therefore the second was taken. In 1893 a cheap freight rate was set on wheat shipped from European Russia by way of the Caspian Sea and over the Trans-Caspian Railroad to Samarkand. As a result, the price of grain in Turkestan fell in ensuing years, causing more of the natives to turn to the raising of cotton. The process was also aided by a fall in Russia's grain exports during the early 1890's and a consequent surplus of cheap grain for the home market. The Orenburg-Tashkent Railroad, constructed in 1899–1905, provided another more direct means for the import of grain into Turkestan. Still another route, the Turkestan-Siberian Railroad, conceived as a means of supplying Turkestan with an abundance of cheap wheat from Semirechie and Western Siberia, was commenced just prior to World War I.

With concentration on cotton, it was naturally the native peasant who stood to gain or lose the most by the new order of things.[18] Most of the peasants were small holders. Plantations of from ⅕ to 5 desiatines (1 desiatine: 2.7 acres, therefore from about ½ to 13½ acres) accounted for over 90 per cent of all the cotton on the market. Under conditions of irrigated agriculture, demanding intensive effort and personal interest on the part of the grower, larger holdings proved impractical and native plantations of as much as 100 desiatines were rare. In the 1880's various Russian textile manufacturing concerns and private individuals began to acquire large holdings in Turkestan for growing cotton. However, after several years of crop failures caused by ignorance of irrigation techniques, the Moscow concerns liquidated their holdings and began to buy from the natives, giving seeds and cash advances to encourage additional sowing.[19]

Although the development of a large cash crop and the consequent gain in income might have promised a net benefit for the region, the increase in cotton growing and the accompanying change in the equilibrium of the Turkestan economy soon proved detrimental to the native growers. Previously subject only to local conditions and supplying a local market, they now became affected by a great number of external influences and a complex interrelation between local conditions and the world cotton market.

In spite of the Russian protective tariff, the price offered in Turkestan was affected directly by the relative abundance of cotton on the world market following a good or bad crop in the United States.[20] Moreover, although the return from cotton growing was higher than from other crops, costs were higher too, because this intensive type of farming required more hired labor. Wages rose and many native peasants were forced to seek loans. Moscow banks, competing to buy cotton, gave liberal advances in food or money through native buyers, local merchants, and money lenders. Not taking future events into account, the peasants took the money and planted more cotton, curtailing products of prime necessity, particularly grain. The prices of these products promptly rose, often to the advantage of the same persons who had furnished the money for cotton. Thus, just as in the American South, though profiting from cotton the population at the same time overpaid for foodstuffs, and their indebtedness mounted each year.[21]

The advances which promoted this indebtedness were of two types, the first involving money for a future harvest, either at a predetermined price or at the price prevailing when the cotton was sold, and the second involving pay for a definite amount of cotton regardless of the size of the plantation or the eventual harvest.[22] Usually a small advance was made when contracts were signed in January, and three larger installments were paid in March at seeding time, in June for irrigation and mulching, and in August when the picking began. Final settlement was made when the cotton was brought in, from October to January. Prior to World War I, these advances amounted to from 325,000,000 to 350,000,000 rubles annually.[23]

How the system of advances combined with other factors to heighten the risks of cotton growing may be seen from an example of one year in Fergana oblast, the most important cotton-producing region in Turkestan. A poor crop in 1911, brought about by insufficient water for irrigation and by spring frosts, low prices for raw cotton, and greater demand and consequently higher prices on grain and other foodstuffs, caused the area sown to cotton in Fergana oblast in the following year to be reduced by 10 to 20 per cent. Credit was also curtailed. Because there were many cases in which there was insufficient cotton to cover the money which had been advanced in 1911, and as the unpaid debts were payable in 1912, only about half the amount of money for cash advances was offered, and that at higher interest rates than in the preceding year.[24] Out of a total indebtedness of the Turkestan rural population in November, 1912, of 156,700,000 rubles, 80,000,000 rubles was borne by the inhabitants of Fergana oblast.[25]

Expansion of cotton growing was accompanied by an equally rapid growth of credit facilities for its financing. Up to 1889 there was only one branch of the state bank in Turkestan; by 1897 there were five branches. In 1898 the first branch of a commercial bank was established; in 1901 there were five, in 1903 there were nine, in 1910 there were twenty-eight, and by 1912 there were forty commercial bank branches and seven state bank branches. These did not loan money directly to growers, except to the few large landholders. Usually the money passed through several parties, each of whom increased the interest rate. The banks loaned money to cotton firms at about 6½ per cent interest; the firms loaned the money to middlemen for 8 or 9 per cent. These in turn loaned it to lesser middlemen, so that by the time the money eventually reached the native growers the interest rate often ranged from 40 to 60 per cent. Sometimes, when the money came through a local merchant, the grower was obligated to buy the merchant's wares for half the credit advanced, and these at high prices. With such exorbitant rates, the profits and most of the income of the peasant were taken, and his indebtedness increased year after year.[26]

When the peasants failed to meet their obligations their lands were sold for debt. Local magnates, the *bais*, could then purchase them cheaply. As a result a few individuals acquired ownership of hundreds and even thousands of desiatines, and accumulated fortunes totaling millions of rubles. Meanwhile the number of landless peasants grew. In 1912 the percentage of landless in Fergana oblast and in Askhabad uezd (Transcaspia oblast) reached 30 per cent. Some of these became sharecroppers (*chairiker*), perhaps on land formerly their own. Virtually en-serfed, they paid up to 80 per cent of their harvests to the land-owner. Others became mere day laborers (*mardiker*), hired only when they were needed the most.[27]

The government was aware of this situation and tried to ease the problem of credit. Some relief was promised by a program of local coöperative credit organizations, backed by the state bank in each oblast. These banks formed and financed credit corpora-tions, and these in turn sponsored coöperative credit societies in the various villages of Turkestan, lending money at low interest rates. Most of these were at a distance from the larger cities. Near the cities the native money lenders carried on a successful propa-ganda campaign in which they claimed that if the peasant could not pay his debt the coöperative societies would sell his land, but that they, the money lenders, would not. Where they were in operation, the credit societies were considered to be as well run as those for Russian peasants in European Russia. They were examined frequently on all levels by government inspectors. Their main defect was that the apparatus was overcentralized, causing money to be drained from local areas and to become centered in Moscow.[28]

Although a hopeful beginning had thus been made, up to World War I the government credit institutions were still far from exercising any appreciable influence on the economic problems which beset the native peasant. In 1910 there were 210 credit societies and 146 coöperative savings associations throughout Central Asia, with a membership of 80,500 and a balance of 1,264,000 rubles. The average loan was less than 100 rubles. Forty-one per cent of all loans were for the purchase of livestock, 33 per cent were for seed, and 8 per cent for the payment of wages. Wherever the credit societies operated, considerable sections of the local population made use of their facilities. However, these were primarily the more substantial groups; the poorer peasants were mainly dependent on private credit on usurious terms.[29]

OTHER CROPS

Although cotton became the dominant crop in the settled regions of Central Asia during the Russian period, other crops retained considerable importance and in most cases underwent various changes in growth and marketing.

Cereals grown in the region included wheat (the most important), rye, oats, barley, millet, sorghum, and rice. Most of the grains could be grown on *bogara,* the native term for unirrigated land. Only rice, the main ingredient of the favorite native dish, pilau, was an exception to this. As the water needed might otherwise be devoted to the raising of cotton, rice growing was confined to marshy ground requiring less irrigation than other types of land, and further expansion of the area sown to rice was discouraged. Because of the prevalence of malaria in rice-growing regions, the government forbade the growing of rice within 10 versts of towns.[30]

During the late 1860's the Dungans, Chinese Moslem immigrants, began growing rice in Semirechie oblast. Before their coming the inhabitants of the oblast imported rice from Syr-Daria oblast and Kuldzha, but through their efforts Semirechie became an exporter of rice to other regions. The Taranchi, another immigrant group, and some of the settled Kazakhs of Semirechie also took up rice growing.[31]

In the 1890's the Russian government began to experiment with the growth of Chinese "dry" rice, which required less water than other varieties. These experiments gave excellent results, and the population began to cultivate this type of rice.[32] In 1912, 110,000 acres of rice were grown in Turkestan.[33]

Fruit growing, like cotton production, advanced rapidly under Russian rule. The hot, virtually rainless summers of Semirechie oblast and the Syr- and Amu-Daria valleys are similar to those in the fruit-growing regions of Central California. The rich loess soils require only water to produce fruit which though small in

size is said to be unexcelled in taste. Babur, the Fergana prince-
ling who founded the Mogul dynasty, once conquered a city because he so esteemed the melons grown there.

Although several kinds of fruits and nuts had been grown in
Turkestan for local consumption for many centuries, and small
quantities had been sent abroad, even to medieval Europe, it
was not until the coming of the Russians that any large-scale export trade became possible. Transportation was the key factor.
The Trans-Caspian Railroad, completed in 1895, and extended
later, provided some impetus to fruit growing, but was too slow,
lacked necessary facilities for carrying perishables, and served
only a small part of the area potentially suited to the distribution
of the products. The completion of the Orenburg-Tashkent Railroad in 1906 made it possible to put Turkestan peaches, apricots,
pomegranates, cherries, eggplant, quinces, melons, and other produce on the market in European Russia. New foods appeared on
Russian menus. By 1914, shipments of fresh fruit from Turkestan
amounted to about 645,000 cwt. (5,786 tons) annually.[34]

By 1912 the Ministry of Public Works was planning to follow
the example of the United States and introduce refrigerator
cars to facilitate transportation of fresh fruit from Turkestan,[35]
but was prevented from doing so by World War I. To reduce loss
by spoilage, canning was undertaken, although even in the United
States at that time the method still required much technical improvement and better organization. Dried fruit was prepared in
traditional fashion by sun-drying, but as the product was fly-
blown, dusty, and of inferior quality, plans were made for the
introduction of oven-drying.[36]

Silk culture, though of ancient origin, was at a standstill in
Turkestan when Russia annexed the region. Crude, inefficient techniques were employed, such as hatching silkworm eggs by means
of body heat and unsanitary methods of handling the worms.
Measures for improvement were begun in 1871, when General
Von Kaufman established a school and experimental station for
silk production at Tashkent under the naturalist V. F. Oshanin.
After some years of successful operation the institution was closed
in 1883 by Von Kaufman's successor, Cherniaev.[37] Subsequently

silkworm rot threated the industry. It was saved only by timely government measures of inspection and quarantine. In 1886, under Governor-General Rosenbach, experimental stations where healthy cocoons could be obtained were established at Tashkent, Petro-Aleksandrovsk, Novyi Margelan, and Samarkand.[38]

By 1914, Turkestan produced about 100,000 poods of dry cocoons per year. This was much beyond the relatively insignificant production of South Russia, but less than half that of Transcaucasia, which in 1913 produced over 274,000 poods.[39] A part of the silk produced in Turkestan was exported in unreeled form, but the greater portion was processed locally, mainly in households, where it was made into cloth for local consumption as well as export.[40]

Besides developing traditional crops, the Russians introduced several new ones. The climate in Turkestan was ideal for growing grapes, but Moslem prohibitions against alcohol prevented the development of wine making. Von Kaufman, however, early envisaged wine as an export product and introduced French and Spanish varieties of vines. The experiments were successful and within a few years connoisseurs in Russia came to prize Central Asian brands.[41] In 1908 about 65,000 acres in Turkestan were planted to grapes, of which 87 per cent was controlled by Russians. In Samarkand, Russians operated the wine presses and cellars and natives supplied the grapes.[42]

Sugar beet growing and the production of beet sugar in Turkestan were proposed soon after the Russian conquest, but attempts to raise and process this crop in 1880 and again in 1887–1890 failed because of the inaccessibility of the region and lack of capital. However, in 1898 new attempts were made and in 1904 a sugar mill began operating successfully at Kaufmanskaia station, several miles out of Tashkent. The processing concern planted nearly a hundred desiatines to sugar beets annually, but a great deal more was produced on native holdings. In 1911 some 2,064 desiatines were planted to sugar beets.[43]

Another Russian innovation in Central Asia was the production of honey and beeswax. After introduction in Siberia from Orenburg in 1786,[44] beekeeping probably entered Central Asia with

Russian colonists from Siberia in the first half of the nineteenth century. By 1910 there were over 800,000 hives in Turkestan and the Steppe oblasts, out of a total of about 7,060,000 hives in the empire.[45]

It is safe to say that Central Asian agriculture underwent a considerable advance in nearly all fields during the period of Imperial rule. The greatest expansion was in cotton growing, which increased until Russia became a major producer, though far from the leader,[46] able to supply half the needs of her expanding industry. However, gains to the region from the development of this crop were lessened by the indebtedness and tenantry which the growers incurred through bad years, fluctuating prices, and other economic factors beyond their control, and by the region's dependence on other parts of the empire for its main food staple, wheat. Other agricultural production, including cereals, silk, and fruit, benefited from new methods and new markets. Innovations such as wine making and the production of honey and beet sugar also showed promise.

This growth and development was of course brought about primarily for the benefit of the occupying power, but it also contributed substantially to the material welfare of the natives. Through the experiments and planning which took place during the Imperial regime, Central Asian agriculture was placed on a firm foundation and the way was prepared for further development.

XI

THE ORDER AND STABILITY introduced by Russia made possible the first major public works undertaken in Central Asia in several centuries. These projects centered around the principal needs of the region—more irrigation, better communications, and improved transportation.

IRRIGATION

Irrigation techniques, essential to the practice of agriculture in such an arid land, were developed to a high degree by the natives of Turkestan long before the Christian era. Not only did the inhabitants excel in channeling water to desired locations and in properly applying it to the land, but, as previously described, they worked out an extensive body of law pertaining to the use of water and its distribution.

During alternating periods of peace and invasion the irrigated area of Turkestan spread and receded. Its greatest reduction occurred under the Mongols, who devastated the region in 1225. Under their sway, lasting until 1363, thriving districts reverted to desert. Timur (1369–1405) and his son Shah-Rukh tried to restore the ravaged land by having extensive canals dug and large areas reclaimed, but with the disintegration of their domain into small warring states, the irrigated area shrank again.

The Russian conquest, which brought peace to Turkestan, once again made it possible to devote attention to irrigation and reclamation, this time under alien auspices. Numerous articles in Russian scientific literature of the late 1860's and the 1870's not only

urged the improvement of existing irrigation systems, but the reclamation of the great wastes which had once been fertile oases or
which had never been cultivated before, in order to prepare for
Russian colonization.

One of the most obvious points at which to begin work was
the so-called Hungry Steppe southwest of Tashkent, where traces
of ancient irrigation canals seemed to assure that with modern
engineering techniques the region could again be cultivated. In
1869 surveys of the area were undertaken on the order of Governor-
General Von Kaufman, and an extensive canal-building project was
begun in 1874. In the manner traditional for such works in Central
Asia, thousands of natives were employed on the project without
pay. Much dirt was moved, but to no avail. The project proved to
be a great burden on the local population and full of engineering
difficulties. In 1879 it was finally abandoned.[1] The natives gave the
empty ditch the strongest pejorative at their command, calling it
tonguz-aryk, or "pig canal." [2] A project undertaken by Von Kaufman's successor, General Cherniaev, also failed, flooding 30,000
desiatines of land, so that there actually arose a problem of drain-
age rather than of irrigation.[3]

A member of the Russian royal family, the Grand Duke Nikolai
Konstantinovich, who lived in exile in Tashkent, finally constructed
the first successful canals in the Hungry Steppe. The Grand Duke's
first projects, known as the Bukhara-Aryk and the Khiva-Aryk,
were begun in 1886. They had only limited success, and the Khiva-
Aryk was later expanded to form the Emperor Nicholas I Canal,
completed in 1898. Constructed at a cost of 240,000 rubles, this
canal extended for some 83 versts and irrigated 12,000 desiatines
(about 50 square miles).[4] Several Russian villages were established
along this canal, inhabited chiefly by workers on the project and
their families.[5]

In 1900, the government began work on the most ambitious
project yet undertaken in the region, the Romanov Canal. The
new project included the existing Nicholas I Canal system and
was designed eventually to irrigate a total of 45,000 desiatines.
The canal was formally opened on October 20, 1913, at ceremonies
attended by Minister of War Sukhomlinov and Governor-General

Samsonov. The cost of the work, originally estimated at 2,500,000 rubles, had by then already mounted to 5,000,000 rubles, but it was then planned to expand the system to irrigate another 35,000 desiatines. This work was to be completed in 1917, but it was stopped by World War I.[6]

Irrigation projects were also undertaken in Transcaspia oblast. Ninety-five per cent desert, the oblast offered a virtually unlimited area for reclamation, although the supply of water from the Amu-Daria and the relatively small Murgab and Tedzhen sharply limited the possibilities.

The efforts in Transcaspia centered mainly around ancient Merv, where the Murgab River, flowing down from Afghanistan, fans out and disappears into the Kara-Kum desert. This area had been famed for its fertility in the days of antiquity, and had been irrigated long before the entry of the Arabs into Turkestan. In the twelfth century the irrigated area was greatly extended through construction of the Sultan-bent dam on the Murgab River by the Seljuk sultan, Sanjar. A half-century later, however, the dam was destroyed by the armies of Genghis Khan and the region reverted to desert. In the fifteenth century the region was restored to cultivation when the dam was rebuilt by Shah-Rukh, son of Timur, but again reverted to desert after 1786, when Emir Shah-Murad of Bukhara had the dam destroyed.

When Russia annexed the Merv oasis only a small area remained under cultivation. East of this area the region around the ancient city lay desolate; only ruins, covering 100 square versts, testified to the former dense population. The Russians were not long in seizing upon the idea of reclaiming the region. A Polish engineer, D. I. Poklevskii-Kozell, supported by Prince A. M. Dondukov-Korsakov, the commander in chief of the Caucasus, who then had jurisdiction over the Transcaspian region, interested authorities in St. Petersburg in rebuilding the Sultan-bent dam. Backers of the plan estimated that as much as several hundred thousand desiatines could be irrigated. The plan was approved, and on August 6, 1887, Emperor Alexander III, following Central Asian custom concerning ownership of reclaimed desert land, laid claim in an Imperial decree to "all uncultivated lands along the river Murgab which, by construction of the Sultan-bent dam, it will be possible to irrigate without loss to other lands already irrigated by the waters of this river. . . ." The zone to be reclaimed was given the name of the Murgab Imperial Domain.[7]

The first dam on the Murgab project, the Sultan-bent, was built by Poklevskii-Kozell by inexpensive native methods, and was completed in 1890. Soon afterward one of its spillways failed, and the dam burst. Another engineer, Andreev, recommenced the work, this time twenty versts downstream, where a second dam, the Hindu-Kush, was completed in 1895. This dam was built by more costly European methods, and featured the first reservoir built in Turkestan. Eventually the Sultan-bent dam was restored, and yet another, the Iolatan dam, was built.

By 1914 the Murgab Domain comprised about 104,000 desiatines, forming a triangle between the stations Bairam-Ali and Annenkov on the railroad east of Merv and the Sultan-bent dam on the Murgab River. About 25,000 desiatines of this were then under irrigation, half of which was devoted to cotton and half to cereals and such leguminous crops as peas and alfalfa.

Although the reclaimed area was considerable, it proved far less than the several hundred thousand desiatines originally hoped for, based on overoptimistic estimates of the amount of water available in the Murgab River. The project also had major technical shortcomings. Because the sources of the Murgab were in Afghan territory, it was necessary to build the reservoirs for impounding flood waters much farther down the river than good engineering practice would have dictated. For this reason, the waters picked up much silt before they were impounded.[8] Not only did the reservoirs begin silting at a rapid rate, but the irrigation ditches had been built improperly so that much land was rendered alkaline from overirrigation or transformed into marshes which led to malaria epidemics.[9]

Prior to World War I the Murgab Domain was peopled by about 11,000 natives and 4,000 Russians. The greater part of its lands were leased out to the natives; only 200 to 300 desiatines were farmed by Russians. Lease payments were made in kind, amounting to half the crop. Lessees were given irrigation water, seed, and bags for gathering cotton. In addition, the Domain ginned the cotton, furnished farm implements and gave loans when needed.[10]

Bairam-Ali, the administrative center of the Domain and the main processing and shipping center for cotton, was constructed as a model village, with paved streets, a thirty-bed hospital, a post and telegraph station, a telephone exchange, an auditorium, well-built electrically lit houses for the employees, a police station, and a church. In the center of the village a small "palace" was built for the tsar should he at any time visit the Domain.[11]

In addition to the Hungry Steppe and Murgab projects, various smaller projects were attempted on more modest means. General G. A. Kolpakovskii, military governor of Semirechie oblast from 1867 to 1882 and later governor-general of the Steppe, General N. I. Grodekov, military governor of Syr-Daria oblast from 1883 to 1893, his successor General N. I. Korol'kov (1893–1905), and General M. N. Annenkov, the builder of the Trans-Caspian Railroad, all tried to increase the cultivated area of Turkestan by improving existing irrigation works or building new ones.

The achievements of Russian engineers in the field of irrigation were of course far surpassed by the plans which were advanced at various times, and which for various reasons remained only on paper. Some were basically unsound, but others awaited only technological or material means for realization.

One of the oldest and most persistent ideas was that of diverting the Amu-Daria back to its former bed so that it would once again flow into the Caspian instead of the Aral Sea. Ever since Peter the Great dreamed of gaining a water route to the heart of Central Asia by this means the idea had cropped up repeatedly. To the nineteenth-century mind, growing accustomed to the realization of great designs and seeing good and evil as absolutes, the idea of the slave-owning Khivans holding the river from its rightful course to the Caspian, and therefore thwarting the advance of Western civilization, was abhorrent. Surveys of the Uzboi, the supposed old bed of the Amu, began to be made even before the Khivan campaign of 1873 and continued after it was over.

General A. M. Glukhovskoi, who explored the Uzboi between 1873 and 1883, drew up one of the most widely discussed plans for connecting the Amu with the Caspian. His object was to create a great oasis and to provide water transportation from the Volga to the frontiers of Badakshan. The plan survived criticism by a German savant who called it "the great Central Asian sea serpent." It was the basis of an exhibit in the Russian pavilion of the Columbian Exposition in 1893,[12] and may be regarded as the prototype of the so-called Main Turkmenian Canal project of a later day. This project, involving not only transportation and reclamation but also hydroelectric power production, was started with much fanfare in 1951, and then quietly abandoned in 1953, probably because of excessive expense and technical difficulties.

Early in the twentieth century several projects for a Transcaspian canal, to irrigate extensive areas of the eastern part of the Kara-Kum desert with waters of the Amu-Daria, attracted considerable attention in both official and scientific circles. One of these, worked out by I. P. Taburno, an engineer who helped plan the Trans-Caspian Railroad, comprised a grandiose 800-verst canal which would extend from Kelif, on the Amu-Daria near the Afghan border, across the desert to the Tedzhen and Murgab (Merv) oases, and then along the Trans-Caspian Railroad to a point well west of Askhabad. Designed to be self-liquidating, the scheme was to have irrigated over 1,000,000 desiatines, or 4,220 square miles.[13]

In 1909, Colonel Ermolaev, a military engineer, conceived a similarly ambitious plan for a great canal which would draw water from the Amu-Daria near Kyzl-Aian, carry it through the Kara-Kum, extend the Murgab and Tedzhen oases, and irrigate a total of nearly 600,000 desiatines. Ermolaev interested a group of Moscow capitalists in the project and they sent a large expedition to the Kara-Kum. The expedition found the steppe unsuitable. Ermolaev then turned to an English group and in 1910 received money for a new expedition to study the Kara-Kum and an adjoining part of the emirate of Bukhara. Ermolaev's new backers in turn lost interest, but in 1911 two other groups, one Russian and the other American, sent representatives to investigate the possibilities of the Kara-Kum. The Russian group favored a project similar to Ermolaev's, but proceeding from a higher point on the Amu-Daria and carrying more water. The American group, organized by John Hammond, a financier, sent two engineers, William McKee and Arthur Davis, to the region to make a preliminary survey. In the end, however, nothing further was done by either group.[14]

Meanwhile, attention shifted to Bukhara and the right bank of the Amu-Daria. Ermolaev obtained a ninety-nine-year lease from the emir of Bukhara permitting him to undertake an irrigation project using the water of the Kashka-Daria. He was to pay the emir a ruble a year for his rights and could utilize as much as he pleased of any new land put under cultivation. At the same time the emir gave a Captain A. G. Anan'ev a lease on similar terms for 100,000 desiatines in the Shirabad valley north of Termez, to be irrigated with waters from the Surkhan-Daria. Anan'ev received 30,000 rubles from the emir for his investigations and sought the estimated 12,000,000 rubles he would need for the project from foreign capital.[15]

All of these more or less speculative schemes were dwarfed by the proposals for regional development put forth in 1912 by A. V. Krivoshein. Combining economic and political aims, Krivoshein urged a vast colonization scheme which would make Russia self-sufficient in cotton, provide a safety valve for agrarian unrest, and achieve Russian ethnic dominance in Central Asia. This program, involving extensive irrigation works, would have made possible the farming of 3,000,000 desiatines of new land (about 12,500 square miles—an area nearly the size of the Netherlands) and the resettlement of 1,500,000 Russian peasants.[16] Only the outbreak of World War I prevented substantial efforts being made in this direction.

During half a century, only two major irrigation projects were brought to fruition in Russian Central Asia—one in the Hungry Steppe and the other on the Murgab. Neither of these fulfilled the original hopes of their designers or the great expectations of those who had foreseen vaster achievements encompassing the entire region. As a local writer lamented, describing the great development of irrigation in the Punjab under British rule, "In comparison with what the English engineers have done, our weak and largely unsuccessful attempts to irrigate a small area of land in Middle Asia appear positively pitiful and insignificant." [17] The time when engineering experience and technology and state means would be adequate to marshal the region's slender water resources for the tasks proposed by the planners was probably almost at hand, however, when World War I forced a prolonged postponement.

POST ROADS

The development of communication and transportation facilities played a major role in the consolidation of the Russian hold on Central Asia, and was as vital as irrigation in realizing the region's economic potentialities.

In ancient times, Central Asia had been a link between East and West, but political changes and shifting of the main trade routes left the region largely isolated. At the time of the Russian conquest the great expanses of desert and steppe between Turkestan and European Russia cut off the region almost as completely from the homeland as the remotest overseas dependencies of the other European powers. This was partly alleviated in 1869, when Turkestan was connected with the rest of the empire by telegraph,[18] but the pressing problem of transportation of mail, goods, and personnel remained.

To improve these conditions the government resorted to post roads, patterned on the system used elsewhere in the empire for many centuries. The first system of this type to be established in Central Asia was organized in 1864 by General Cherniaev, to connect the newly conquered towns of Aulie-Ata and Chimkent.

The maintenance of the post stations was entrusted to the biis of nearby Kazakh auls. The Kazakhs were charged with construction, lighting and heating, and operation, and were to keep three pairs of horses with three drivers at each station. For this the auls concerned received 360 rubles per year from the government. All travelers were obliged to pay fees amounting to 1½ kopecks per verst for each horse used. The fee was payable to the Russian authorities before the journey was undertaken, in order to guarantee payment to the postkeepers.

As early as 1866 there were 55 post houses, built at a cost of 75 rubles each, and 239 teams of horses in use on the post road from Chimkent through Fort No. 1 (Kazalinsk) to Orsk. This system, however, proved faulty and service quickly deteriorated. Facilities were inadequate; proper supervision was lacking; the Kazakhs were lax in supplying forage and horses had to be pastured the year around, often at a considerable distance from the stations; and travelers behaved arrogantly toward the postkeepers.

After Von Kaufman assumed office in November, 1867, measures were taken to improve the post service. Appropriations were increased, supervision was improved, and additional stations and horses were added. Mail service was also begun; ordinary mail was sent from Orsk to Tashkent four times per month; and a caravan of thirteen camels was provided to carry packages.

Several years passed, however, before this route could be developed fully. Uprisings and brigandage by Kazakhs caused frequent breaks in service. When disorders broke out in the Orenburg Steppe in 1868, the post on the Tashkent–Kazalinsk–Orenburg route was transferred to the Tashkent–Omsk route for several months. During this time the dispatch of mail from Kazalinsk to Orenburg, which took only six days by the direct route, took two and a half months by way of Omsk. The conquest of Khiva in 1873 brought peace to the Steppe and an end to such difficulties. Maintenance of the post routes was eventually relinquished by the state and given to private individuals on contract.[19]

As finally established, the post system operated with relative efficiency over a variety of routes until 1917. Descriptions of the system appear in nearly all accounts of travelers in the region. Stations were located at intervals of from fifteen to twenty miles. At each one, food, lodging, fodder, and fresh horses were obtainable, although the quality of the facilities varied. Some of the stations were in villages and towns; others were along the open road in the heart of the steppe. Those on the road usually consisted of two or three buildings and an enclosure for horses. At each station fresh horses would usually be available upon presentation by the traveler of his permit to hire post horses (*podorozhnaia*). If none were available he might have to wait for days at some isolated station before he could continue his journey. A special crown *po-*

dorozhnaia, granted couriers, military personnel, and government dignitaries, gave priority in use of the post facilities.

RAILROADS

The system of post roads in Central Asia was at best a half-way measure that could be utilized only for passengers and mail. The extent of the area and its isolation from Russia caused early consideration not only of more rapid communications with Europe, but of better means than the traditional camel caravans for transporting heavy goods to and from the region.

For a time the idea of an Aral "flotilla" which would ply the Syr- and Amu-Daria was put forth as a solution. Ships were introduced, but shoals and frequently shifting channels required small vessels of extremely shallow draft. Moreover, the fact that there was no outlet closer to European Russia than the land-locked Aral Sea limited their economic and military use.

The most obvious solution was rail transportation, then being extended rapidly throughout the globe. In 1871, Major General K. S. Beznosikov, assistant military governor of Semipalatinsk oblast, visualized a line reaching to the Indian border. He hoped that it would strengthen Russia's hand in international affairs, bridge the gap between East and West, and further the cause of peace by presenting England with the possibility of sending goods from India to Europe in only thirteen days. He obtained Von Kaufman's permission to undertake a survey, but no financial backing, and set out to investigate the feasibility of building a railroad from Orenburg to Tashkent. Although sixty years of age, and accompanied only by a Kazakh assistant, Beznosikov proceeded 6,000 versts on horseback and on foot, made surveys, and prepared a detailed map and description of the route. An ardent patriot, Beznosikov hoped to keep the work in Russian hands, but in 1873 Ferdinand de Lesseps, builder of the Suez Canal, approached the Russian government with a project based largely on Beznosikov's survey.

De Lesseps proposed a through railroad from Calais to Calcutta by way of Orenburg and Samarkand, tunneling through the Hindu Kush and going down the Kabul valley to Peshawar. He stressed the fact that of the 7,370 miles of the route a total of 5,100 miles had already been built, as far as Orenburg on one side and Peshawar on the other. To bridge the remaining 2,270 mile gap he proposed a "Grand Central Asiatic Railway Society," with Russia to build the 1,470 miles from Orenburg to Samarkand, and England the 800 miles from Samarkand to Peshawar.[20]

The Russian government appeared to favor the plan. De Lesseps formed a company in Paris to undertake the preliminary surveys. But to obtain the consent of England proved another matter. When a small party of engineers, led by de Lesseps' son Victor, went to India to reconnoiter they were refused permission to go beyond Khyber Pass, ostensibly because of the difficulties which might arise in Afghanistan. The party abandoned the idea of a route through Afghanistan in favor of a more easterly route from Tashkent to Kokand, Kashgar, Kashmir, and Lahore. Then, after their return to Europe, the scheme lost support and shortly de Lesseps turned his attention to the project for a canal across the Isthmus of Panama.[21]

In the meantime, however, the idea of a Central Asian railroad had taken strong hold on Russian public opinion. There were various proposals of possible routes. Prior to his death in 1876 the indefatigable Beznosikov, dissatisfied with the Orenburg route, covered another 12,000 versts in the course of investigating an alternative Ufa–Troitsk–Samarkand route.

The Russo-Turkish War diverted attention from railroads and nothing further was accomplished until 1879, when General Lomakin was making ready his expedition against the Akhal-Tekke Turkmen. At that time a railroad was proposed to expedite the passage of troops and supplies from the Caspian Sea as far as Kyzyl-Arvat, the first point on the wholly desert route where water was to be found, a distance of 145 miles from the Caspian. Lomakin's defeat accelerated the railroad project. The main difficulty, as in all Central Asian campaigns, had been the scarcity and loss of transport animals. Skobelev, given a free hand in the conduct of a campaign in 1880, was receptive to the idea of a railroad as a remedy for this problem.

An American engineer named Berry came forward with an offer

to build a line from the Caspian to Kyzyl-Arvat at his own expense. He proposed to sell the completed line to the Russian government or operate it on a franchise with a guaranteed annual profit. But the work was entrusted instead to General M. N. Annenkov, a Russian authority on military railroads, and his assistants Prince M. I. Khilkov (later minister of communications and a prominent figure in the building of the Trans-Siberian Railroad) and the engineer A. I. Iugovich.

Because of the difficulties supposedly facing the project, many viewed it skeptically. General Cherniaev wrote a series of articles to prove its infeasibility. In spite of such criticisms Annenkov and his colleagues went ahead with the work. Water shortage was overcome by distilling sea water from the Caspian and transporting it in large wooden vats over the completed portion of the railroad. The great sand dunes were checked by palisades, and where these failed, by constant work of teams of laborers. The line was not finished in time to be of use in Skobelev's campaign, but the 145 miles was completed in the relatively short time of 10 months. The road was opened to traffic on September 1, 1881. A few years later, because of disagreements with Great Britain following the Russian annexation of Merv (1884) and Kushka (1885), it was decided to extend the line 500 miles to the Amu-Daria. Annenkov was again put in charge.

The construction of the line was hailed by the Russian press as an engineering marvel and as a "miracle." However, more realistic foreign observers pointed out that except for the dearth of local material it was one of the easiest railroads ever built up to that time. The region was nearly flat, no tunnels were required, and there were only a few cuts through the sand dunes. Only three bridges of any size were required along the entire route—at the Tedzhen, Murgab, and Amu Rivers. The Russian labor involved was all military, and the native labor was cheap and abundant.[22]

On the other hand, there can be no doubt that the difficulties of supply and climate were considerable, requiring no little organizational ability. Two railroad battalions of 1,000 to 1,500 men each were employed on the work. The first, which had laid the rails to Kyzyl-Arvat in 1881, established headquarters there and operated the line. The second, especially recruited in 1885 from many regiments, laid the later stretches of the road. Native workmen, chiefly Turkmen, Persians, and Bukharans, performed the unskilled labor; at one time as many as 20,000 were employed. They constructed the earthworks, cuts, and embankments, and the soldiers placed and spiked down the rails.[23] Thanks to efficient organization of the work and supply of materials, the line was extended to the Amu-Daria in a year and a half. As much as four miles of track were laid in a day.[24] The capable Annenkov gained the nickname *"Energichestvo"* ("The Energetic," or, in freer translation, "The Human Dynamo") for his work on the project.[25]

In 1887, on Annenkov's proposal, it was decided to continue the line from the Amu-Daria to Samarkand. The chief obstacle was the river itself, with its broad and frequently shifting channel. A bridge was considered impossible and Annenkov was supplied with funds for a ferry at Chardzhui. However, at the urging of A. N. Rudnev, one of his engineers, Annenkov used the money for the construction of a temporary wooden bridge. A rickety structure, rude in appearance, nevertheless it was one of the marvels of the region in its day. Built entirely of wood brought from European Russia, it rested on more than three thousand piles, driven close together in the bed of the stream. Upwards of 800 sazhen in length (about 5,357 feet) over water, it was built in the record time of only 4 months and 13 days (August 23, 1887 to January 6, 1888), at a cost of but 46,000 rubles. Proponents of the project were justified by the durability of the bridge, in use almost fourteen years until it was supplanted by a steel structure, opened to traffic in June, 1901.[26]

The remainder of the 230-mile line was completed without great difficulty. Work began on July 1, 1887, and the first train arrived at Samarkand on May 15, 1888. This ended the work of Annenkov, who, during a total construction time of 4 years between 1880 and 1888, had directed the building of 900 miles of railroad, connecting the east shore of the Caspian with the heart of the Russian possessions in Turkestan.[27]

In 1894 the Trans-Caspian line was linked with the port of

Krasnovodsk, considered a more suitable terminal than Uzun-Ada, which had been used until that time. Between November 15, 1897, and December 4, 1898, a 200-mile branch line, the Murgab Railroad, was built between Merv and Kushka, on the Afghan border, for strategic purposes.

From Samarkand the railroad was next carried toward Tashkent and the Fergana valley. A. N. Rudnev, who had served under Annenkov, began the construction of the line in May, 1895. After his death the following year the work was continued by A. I. Ursati. The project was completed in 1898, and regular traffic to Andizhan began in 1899. An ornate bronze plaque embedded in the rock overlooking the railroad in the so-called Gate of Timur commemorated the project. Placed above two long inscriptions in Turko-Tatar honoring military campaigns at the time of Timur, the Russian inscription stated simply: "In 1895 Nicholas II ordered: 'There will be a railroad.' In 1898 it was accomplished." [28]

The Trans-Caspian Railroad opened up Central Asia economically. But in spite of the merit of the achievement, the line had many limitations. Chief among these was the necessity of transshipment of goods across the Caspian. Freight often took three or four months to reach Turkestan from Russia by this route.[29]

The obvious solution was a more direct line. Over the years several routes were discussed, but the one most in favor was that between Orenburg and Tashkent, already examined by Beznosikov in the 1870's. This finally became assured in 1898, when General A. N. Kuropatkin was appointed minister of war. He considered the line a strategic necessity, and used his office to promote it. In 1900 Tsar Nicholas II approved the plans, and work began from both sides of the 1,149 mile route. The road was completed in 1906.[30]

The Orenburg–Tashkent line gave a great stimulus to the transportation of goods, settlers, military forces, and matériel. But the need for yet another railroad between Turkestan and Siberia soon became apparent. Expansion of the cotton-growing area depended on an assured supply of cheap Siberian wheat with which to replace the food supply lost through diversion of land to cotton.[31]

In 1912, by Imperial order, a charter was granted to a Semirechie railroad company. The railroad was designed to further the economic development of Semirechie and to facilitate the colonization of some of the best lands in the empire; strategically it was directed toward what was considered to be the most dangerous spot in case difficulties should ever arise with China. This was the valley of the Ili River, the so-called "Dzhungarian Gate," which had always been the main route for nomadic peoples invading the west.[32] Construction of the Turkestan-Siberia Railroad began from opposite ends of the line in 1912 and 1913, but was abandoned because of World War I and the Revolution. The work was not resumed until 1927 and the line, now called the Turk-Sib, was completed in 1930.[33]

By 1914, still other Central Asian rail routes were under consideration. Particularly significant were plans for a South Siberian Railroad, to extend from Ural'sk to Akmolinsk and Pavlodar, and through the Altai Mountains to Minusinsk, finally to meet with the Trans-Siberian Railroad at Nizhneudinsk, with numerous connecting lines between the two main lines en route. Such a plan, only partly fulfilled even to this day, would have made available the full agricultural and industrial potential of the Kazakh Steppe.[34]

The public works constructed in Central Asia after the 1860's represented considerable achievements. Railroad building finally opened up the region, connected its products with external markets, and brought about modernization in many fields. The region was also bound more closely to the rest of the Russian Empire, regardless of the will of the Central Asiatic peoples. Less was achieved in irrigation, but much experience was gained in the projects which were completed; plans for their expansion would have enabled great numbers of Russians to colonize the region.

XII

AS EARLY AS the beginning of the sixteenth century the Russians were interested in the economic potential of Central Asia. There was a large Russian trading colony in Kazan at that time, and after the conquest of Kazan (1552) and Astrakhan (1556) both became important centers for the import of Central Asian cotton and silk fabrics, arms, jewelry, and spices. In 1558 the British merchant Anthony Jenkinson, under Russian auspices, visited Bukhara and Tashkent to investigate the possibility of setting up British trade with the East via Russia. Ivan Khokhlov visited Bukhara in 1620, Gorokhov and Gribov visited Bukhara and Khiva in 1642, Pazukhin was in Khiva, Bukhara, and Persia in 1669–1671, and Daudov and Kasimov went to Bukhara and Persia in 1675–1678, all with the idea of establishing direct trade relations.

MINING

Rumors of the abundance of gold in Central Asia caused Peter the Great to send large expeditions up the Irtysh (1714) and to Khiva (1716–1717). Copper ores were discovered in the Altai region in 1723 and smelters for their reduction were built by A. N. Demidov under state franchise at Kolyvan-Voskresenskii (1726), Barnaul (1739), and Shul'binsk (1744). In 1747, by ukase of the Empress Elizabeth, the crown took over the smelters, compensating the Demidov family by payment of a rent. In 1763, state-owned enterprises began lead and silver mining. In 1784, Philip Ridder opened rich lead and silver mines, later named after him, in the Altai on the Ul'ba river near Ust'-Kamenogorsk.

In 1834 a Russian merchant, Stepan Popov, penetrated far into what later became Akmolinsk oblast, and opened several lead and silver mines. He built the first smelter in the steppe in 1844. Granted exclusive title to his claims by the government, he at one time owned as much as 1,500 square kilometers of mining properties and made and lost several fortunes during a career that spanned half a century.[1]

In 1833 a Kazakh shepherd discovered coal at Karaganda, also in the Akmolinsk region. The site was sold in 1854 for 225 rubles to a Russian merchant, N. U. Ushakov, who began mining on a small scale. In 1864 the Riazanov family, of Ekaterinburg, already with extensive mining interests in the Enisei region, acquired an area of copper deposits twenty-two miles south of Karaganda, at Spasskii. They commenced mining operations and built a smelter, using Karaganda coal. When they discovered richer copper deposits at Iuspenskii, 70 miles farther south, they abandoned the Spasskii mine, but continued to use the smelter to process the ore extracted from the new mine.[2]

In the heart of the Kazakh Steppe the Dzhezkazgan copper deposits, among the richest in the world, were already noted in 1771 by Captain N. P. Rychkov, when he came by chance on old native workings. During the 1840's the merchant Ushakov purchased the deposits from local Kazakhs for 400 rubles; his heirs later sold the area to a British firm for 260,000 rubles. The new owners commenced shafting and construction of the Karsakpai copper smelter, but did not complete the project.[3]

Coal deposits were also discovered in Semipalatinsk oblast, particularly the rich field at Ekibastuz. About 1900 a company formed for working the mines built a railroad connecting Ekibastuz with the river Irtysh and commenced the manufacture of coke, for which it found a market among the metallurgical works of the Urals, and contracted to supply the Trans-Siberian Railroad.[4]

All of these early mining operations were carried on in a primitive, wasteful manner. Only ore from the richest deposits was taken. Hand labor, chiefly performed by Kazakhs, predominated, as manpower was cheaper than machines.

About the turn of the century, the development of mining began to quicken through the introduction of foreign capital. In 1896 a French firm took over the Zyrianovsk deposits of precious metals. In 1904 the Austrian Prince of Thurn and Taxis obtained a concession to exploit Altai deposits of gold and other precious metals. In the same year the firm of Spassky Copper Mine, Limited, was formed in London to operate the Karaganda–Spasskii–Uspenskii complex in Akmolinsk. The Russian–Asiatic Corporation, an American firm in which Herbert Hoover was prominent, formed two branches to exploit the Ridder deposits in the Altai and the Ekibastuz coal mines of Semipalatinsk.[5] In 1908 the Atbasar Copper Mining Company, an American firm, bought the copper mines at Dzhezkazgan.[6] Several foreign companies, including the powerful Nobel group, acquired rights to the Emba oilfields.[7]

In Turkestan, many mineral deposits were known long before the coming of the Russians, but primitive techniques limited their exploitation. Oil was already being extracted when the Russians came to the region. At Mai-Bulak (oil-spring), about twenty-five miles from Namangan, in Fergana, abundant springs of naphtha were worked by Kalmuks and Kirgiz, who prepared asphalt from it.[8] Other deposits were worked at Cheleken Island, forty miles south of Krasnovodsk and across the Caspian from the rich deposits at Baku. When a Russian surveying party approached the island in 1836 they smelled oil when still a half mile offshore. On the island oil oozed out of the ground in as many as three thousand places. The Turkmen collected it behind dams or drew it from crude wells. About 136,000 poods of oil were thus gathered annually and sold in Persia.[9]

Beginning in 1874, various Russian firms purchased the oil springs on Cheleken Island from the Turkmen and began production, but the limited market at that time and costs of transportation and refining restricted development. Early in the twentieth century, a greater world demand for oil aroused new interest in Cheleken. For a time a fever of speculation centered around the barren island as many firms, particularly the Nobel group, obtained rights and sold stock on the Moscow market. Then the bubble burst; many of the wells did not produce and costs froze out the owners of many that did. In the end only the Nobel firm was able to continue, but because of a world oil surplus it reduced production sharply.[10]

During construction of the Tashkent–Andizhan Railroad, oil was discovered at Chimion, in the Fergana valley. A small stock company was formed to exploit it, and although the Nobel interests tried to proclaim Fergana as a poor place for drilling, having then curtailed their own production at Baku, the company secured a contract with the railroad. They built a ten-kilometer pipeline and began supplying the railroad with oil which was so pure it did not require refining. However, they were dogged by labor troubles, and during a strike their main well was dynamited. Unable to meet their commitments, they finally had to go out of business. The oil interests at Baku then bought the field and thereafter produced only as much oil as was required by their franchise in order that the field would not compete with their main property.[11]

Production was similarly restricted at other Turkestan oil fields. As there were no refineries in Turkestan, crude oil extracted there had to be refined at Baku, across the Caspian Sea. Refined oil which cost twenty kopecks per pood at Baku cost forty-five to fifty kopecks per pood by the time it was transported back to Fergana, where the main industrial establishments of Central Asia were located.[12]

Coal was abundant in Turkestan, but had never been used by the natives as fuel. Instead they burned wood and dung, stripping the scanty tree cover of the region and depriving their fields of fertilizer. The Russians were aware of Turkestan's coal resources by 1866, even before the capture of Tashkent, when a Russian expedition discovered some strata of coal fifty miles from Chimkent. This field was worked for a time at government expense. In 1869, 1,608 tons were extracted, of which half was furnished to the vessels of the Aral flotilla. To save the vegetative cover in the neighborhood of Tashkent, an effort was made to accustom the natives to the use of coal. It was distributed to them free, but they could not be prevailed upon to use it to any extent. Decreased consumption, high transportation costs, and the low grade of the coal caused this field to be abandoned a few years later.[13]

By 1910 coal deposits were known in all the oblasts of Turkestan, but they were generally of low grade. In Khodzhent uezd

(Samarkand oblast) coal was mined at 14 pits, some 3,500,000 poods (38,500 tons) being extracted annually.[14]

The low production of coal, which was essential for the smelting of ores, and the lack of transportation facilities sharply limited the production of other minerals in Turkestan. Several small low-grade iron deposits were known but were not worked.[15] Copper deposits of great potential worth were exploited on a small scale, chiefly by foreign capital. Near Skobelev, in Fergana oblast, copper ore containing vanadium and the radioactive elements thorium and radium was extracted. Another vanadium deposit was found in the extreme west of Fergana oblast. These ores were sent to St. Petersburg and Riga for processing.[16]

Lead deposits were known in Transcaspia, Syr-Daria, and Semirechie oblasts. On the Kon-Kia River in the Kara-Tau Mountains, near the city of Turkestan, lead mines were worked by the natives for many years before the Russians came. They flourished during the Russian advance, when the Kokand government was making efforts to defend its sovereignty. Only the best and richest surface ore was taken, and the smelting left 31 per cent of the metal in the slag. After the Russian occupation the native owners sold the mines to a Russian merchant, who worked them for several years.

Gold, the aim of Peter the Great's Central Asian expeditions, was found in all the oblasts of Turkestan, and in Bukhara, but not in paying quantities. Manganese deposits were known on the Mangyshlak peninsula.[17]

Salt deposits were exploited near Khodzhent, on Cheleken Island, and at Kelif, south of Bukhara. There were many other salt lakes and springs in the region, but nevertheless salt had to be imported into Turkestan.[18] A salt deposit at Lake Urkach, in Turgai oblast, leased from the government by a Russian merchant, produced up to 2,000,000 poods a year for a time, but when the railroad from Samara to Cheliabinsk was built other deposits became accessible, and the Urkach production fell to about 200,000 poods per year.[19]

There were sulfur deposits in Transcaspia oblast northwest of Krasnovodsk and north of Askhabad, in Samarkand oblast, and in Fergana oblast south of Kokand. Those in Fergana had been exploited by the khans of Kokand in the making of gunpowder. None of these deposits were worked during the Imperial rule.[20]

FOREST EXPLOITATION

Although mostly semiarid, Russian Central Asia had timber in its mountainous areas and great stands of desert vegetation. These "forested" lands were retained by the state and managed by the Ministry of Agriculture. By 1910 there were 42,000,000 acres of such lands in Turkestan, although much of this bore only isolated clumps of trees. Of these lands 20,000,000 acres were managed directly by the Ministry of Agriculture; the remainder was leased to private concerns. Scientific methods of forestry were obligatory for the users of these lands, although strict enforcement of the rules by the handful of underpaid foresters was hardly possible.[21] Charcoal merchants would often burn off large areas of forested land in order to make their work easier; the livestock of the Kazakhs destroyed new growth; the use of wood for fuel in smelting operations (which might better have been performed with coal) caused whole tracts to be stripped; and the forests of Semirechie, the best in the region, suffered extensive damage at the hands of Cossack and peasant colonists.

The need for countermeasures to curb this destruction was seen from the beginning, but application was intermittent. In 1879, the assistant commandant of the Zeravshan district (later Samarkand oblast), General N. I. Korol'kov, forbade the cutting of timber or the burning of charcoal in the mountains of the district. Interested in forestry since earlier travels in western Europe, Korol'kov also carried on tree planting to protect irrigation works from spring floods, and attempted to establish the California sequoia in the higher mountains. Unfortunately the indifference of his successors nullified most of his work.[22] Other reforestation was practiced in the vital watersheds above Tashkent.[23]

Desert vegetation, though it might not have been considered among the forest reserves of more favored lands, was an important asset in Russian Central Asia. At first it was regarded only as fuel. Saxaul (*Haloxylon ammodendron*), a large shrub with an ironlike wood which burned like the best coal, was stripped from both sides of the Trans-Caspian Railroad when it was first built to provide fuel for the locomotives. After a few years, however, it was found that such vegetation was not merely useless growth, but that it played a vital role in controlling the shifting desert sands. By 1896, sand movement became so bad over one fifteen-mile stretch of track between Farab and Khodzha-Davlet that it had to be cleared by workmen with shovels.

Seeking a solution to this problem, the railroad administration engaged V. A. Paletskii, a specialist in forestry who had already gained distinction in the study of areas of spreading deserts west of the Volga. Paletskii, by careful study of the life cycles of desert plants, had discovered a whole sequence of stages in desert development. Where growth of a few particularly hardy types could be fostered, sufficient sand could be held in place to permit larger growth to commence. This in turn held down the sand still more, permitting even larger growth. Finally a stage was reached where large shrubs, especially saxaul, along with smaller varieties of the preceding stages, would hold the sands in place. Paletskii's recommendations were followed and within a few years the sand dunes were brought under control.[24]

PROCESSING AND MANUFACTURING

Other than the exploitation of natural resources, the industrial activity of Central Asia during the Imperial period was confined mainly to light industry devoted to the processing of agricultural products. The Steppe towns, particularly those along the Trans-Siberian Railroad, developed slaughterhouses, tanneries, tallow-rendering works, wool-washing plants, and soap plants in connection with the meat industry, and flour mills and distilleries based on the growing of grain. The rapid growth of these facilities gave old towns such as Omsk and Petropavlovsk a nearly constant boom during the two decades prior to 1914, although they accounted for less than 1 per cent of the total industrial output and working force of the Russian Empire.[25]

The situation in Turkestan was similar. About 85 per cent of the industrial activity there was connected with the initial processing of cotton or the production of cottonseed oil. A majority of these plants came to be owned by wealthy natives, although most of the larger ones were controlled by firms in European Russia. Out of 157 cotton-ginning plants operating in 1911, 109 were owned by local firms and 48 by Russian firms, although the average number of gins per plant was 7 for the Russian enterprises and 3.4 for the local ones. Flour mills, tanneries, and cocoon-drying plants made up the remainder of the processing industries in Turkestan.[26]

INDUSTRIAL LABOR

The working force in the Steppe in 1913 amounted to about 20,000 persons in the heavier industries, which comprised about 6,000 enterprises, most of them engaged in mining.[27] In Turkestan, the total industrial labor force in 1905–1908 was about 32,000, of whom 14,500 were employed in 552 industries and 29 mining enterprises, and about 15,000 on the Trans-Caspian and Orenburg-Tashkent Railroads. Most of Turkestan's industry was concentrated in Fergana oblast, which had 229 enterprises with 8,074 workers, or 40 per cent of all the industrial and mining enterprises of Turkestan and 49 per cent of the workers.[28]

Natives made up the majority of the workers in both the Steppe and in Turkestan. In the Steppe an average of about 60 to 70 per cent of the workers in all enterprises were natives, while in the mines the proportion reached 90 per cent. Most of these were poverty-stricken former nomads.[29] In Turkestan about 77 per cent of the industrial workers were natives, mainly from the poorer peasants and day laboring groups.[30] The remainder were mostly Russian workers, who performed the more skilled labor.

The working conditions for these groups were almost uniformly poor. In the Steppe there was a surplus of native labor, so pay was low and the working day was often fourteen to sixteen hours long. Because of the abundance of hand labor there was little mechanization or concern for living conditions.[31] In Turkestan a twelve-hour day prevailed, wages were low, and the work was seasonal.

The Russian workers were better paid than the natives and were generally employed the year around instead of seasonally, but were only relatively better off. Palen, in his inspection of Turkestan in 1908, found the railroad workers an unruly group, but admitted that they were faced with a difficult existence because of the extreme heat, monotonous work, and living conditions which left them nothing to think of but "cards, women, drink, and political extremism." [32]

TRADE

In its trade, monopolized by European Russia, Central Asia was in a largely secondary position as a producer of raw materials. As long as camels, carts, and horses formed the chief means of transportation, significant expansion of Central Asian trade was not possible, and only such portable items as silk, wool, hides, dried fruit, rice, and a relatively small amount of cotton could be sent from the region. In return Russia sent metal wares, tobacco, sugar, spirits, and cotton fabrics.[33]

When the Trans-Caspian, Trans-Siberian, and Orenburg-Tashkent Railroads were built this situation changed. The grain and cattle of the Steppe and the cotton, fruit, and other products of Turkestan rapidly became major export items. Thriving trade centers sprang up along the new arteries. Branches of large Russian and foreign firms appeared even in the smaller towns.

Away from the railroads, it is true, most of the trade in the great thinly populated expanses of the region continued to bear a primitive character, concentrated in small bazaars, with goods carried by cart and camel caravans. But the over-all effect of the railroads was an increase in demand and purchasing power. Salesmen penetrated to remote parts of the Steppe, so that "hundreds of versts from the railroads, in the felt yurt of the half-savage nomad, one could find the Singer sewing machine, the Tula samovar, and Kuznetsov chinaware." [34]

Although the trade between European Russia and Central Asia was demonstrably to the advantage of each, Central Asia nevertheless remained in the more dependent, less advantageous position. Like most colonies of that day, it was limited to being a producer of raw materials, which were partly processed and sent to

European Russia to be converted into final form, after which they were often sent back to Central Asia for sale as manufactured goods.

The reasons for this secondary role of Asiatic Russia with regard to European Russia were clearly set forth in an official publication in 1914:

> For the development of manufacturing a large amount of ready capital and sufficient cadres of technically prepared workers are needed. Capital long ago lost its local and even national character and is easily transferred to those countries where it can have the most advantageous investment, but one cannot say the same of the labor market. Culture of long duration and a considerable development of urban life is necessary in order to prepare in sufficient amount the workers needed for modern heavy manufacturing.
>
> Asiatic Russia lacks this. Capital can be moved to any Asiatic backwater, but it is impossible to find trained workers there. The result is a sort of vicious circle. For the development of manufacturing there must be a force of workers, but cadres of trained workers are created only with the development of manufacturing, and since the emergence from this circle comes about only gradually, the entire colony usually has to be a purveyor of raw material for the metropolis and a consumer of its manufactures.[35]

These then were the economic realities of the time which held back the region's development—insufficient capital, lack of a trained working force, and, finally, lack of suitable transportation with which to overcome the remoteness of the region and get its products to market. Capital was not lacking; there were merely more profitable places for its employment. The working force could be trained, and transportation facilities developed so as to make Central Asia a more attractive place for the introduction of capital, but this required time. To promote such development the Imperial government could use only the conventional devices of that day—a protective tariff, subsidies, monopoly, and, where private enterprise could not do the job, state ownership.

PART FOUR

The Clash of Cultures

XIII

JUST AS THE conquest of Central Asia was not to be accomplished by force of arms alone, neither were administrative and economic measures sufficient to consolidate what had been won. After achieving their military objectives the Russians were confronted by a second line of defense—the will of the natives to retain their traditional ways, their language, and their faith.

The Russians faced a problem common to every power which has extended its dominion at the expense of others—the problem of reconciling the overrun population to foreign domination. Multinational Russia had already faced this situation many times, and thanks to numerical predominance, relative cultural superiority, and relative absence of racism had frequently gone far toward cultural and ethnic amalgamation with the peoples she had engulfed.

However, there had always been great difficulties in assimilating Moslem populations. The annexation of Kazan, Astrakhan, the Crimea, the Caucasus regions, and finally of the Kazakh Steppe and Turkestan had each brought more Moslem subjects into the empire. The relatively high culture of the Moslem peoples, their militant traditions, their uncompromising attitudes where questions of faith were concerned, their numbers, and their ties with the rest of the Islamic world all worked against their ever wholly accepting infidel rule. Not only were they difficult to assimilate, but they had to be dealt with carefully lest their generally passive resistance flare into active opposition which could jeopardize large areas within and on the borders of the empire.

Over several centuries the Russian approach toward the Moslem population of the empire, with the notable exception of the Caucaus region, had been mainly one of tolerance. In the 1850's, however, a different trend had begun. A rise in Russian nationalism after the Crimean War brought a demand from many members of the Russian educated class for the assimilation of the tsar's non-Russian subjects in order to strengthen the empire. Adherents of this view sought to promote the "drawing closer" (*sblizhenie*) of other peoples to the Russians to win their sympathy and loyalty, to teach them the Russian language and other aspects of Great Russian culture, and if possible, in the case of non-Christians, to win them for Orthodox Christianity. "Russification" (*obrusenie* or *russifikatsiia*) became a policy and a goal.

In their pursuit of this endeavor the Russians came up against the second line of defense of the Moslems, their will to admit no change in their culture, particularly in its main fabric, the institutions of the Moslem religion. The Tatars of Kazan led the opposition. The most literate and energetic Moslems in the empire, they were also the most ardent in the practice and propagation of their faith. Much effort on the part of the Orthodox Church to convert them, and attempts by the Russian government to hold converts to their new faith and to punish apostates, merely added to the Tatar resolve. The Kazan Tatars furnished mullas for Moslems throughout the empire, and increased the solidarity and zeal of their coreligionists wherever they went.

The contest therefore centered at Kazan, and by the late 1860's was already well under way. The Russian Orthodox Church concentrated its efforts to propagate Orthodox Christianity and Russian ideals in the Kazan Ecclesiastical Academy. Within the Academy a section frankly called the Anti-Moslem Missionary Division (*protivo-musul'manskoe missionerskoe otdelenie*) trained missionaries for educational work among the Moslem peoples of Eastern Russia, the Caucasus, and Central Asia. An allied group, the Kazan Brotherhood of Saint Guriia, founded in 1867, began extensive work in translation of religious works into the languages of the non-Russian peoples of the empire.[1]

N. A. Il'minskii, a gifted orientalist with a combination of missionary zeal, ardent Russian nationalism, bigotry, and ultraconservatism, was a leading figure in these endeavors. Il'minskii regarded the contest for the loyalty of non-Russians, particularly those of Moslem faith, as essentially one between rival systems of education. As armament in this contest, he devised a program for instruction which became known as the "Il'minskii system." This consisted of elements of western-style education, "in the Russian spirit" with an Orthodox Christian background, imparted in the pupil's own language by native teachers. Where possible, Il'minskii's program included the use of the Cyrillic alphabet adapted for the use of the native tongues. He believed this would prepare the way for the student to learn Russian and would at the same time wean him from other, particularly Moslem influences. The instilling of Christian precepts in the student's mind by means of his own language would arouse in him a love for the Russian people, so that finally he would willingly occupy himself with the Russian language and seek a Russian education.[2]

RUSSIAN SCHOOLS IN THE KAZAKH STEPPE

Il'minskii's efforts encompassed all of the non-Orthodox peoples of Asiatic Russia, but he had a particular interest in the problems raised by Imperial expansion into Central Asia. From 1858 to 1861 he served on the Orenburg Border Commission, an administrative body headed by the orientalist and nationalist V. V. Grigor'ev. There Il'minskii learned the Kazakh language, observed the progress of Tatar influence among the Kazakhs, and absorbed Grigor'ev's convictions that if this threat could be overcome the Kazakhs could be won for Russia and Orthodoxy. Because of their primitive way of life and their situation, the Kazakhs had accepted Islam to an imperfect degree, and therefore appeared a vulnerable target and an attractive prize for Russian cultural penetration. It seemed that if the Kazakhs could be "drawn closer" to the Russians while receiving the rudiments of Western culture, aimed at developing "human understanding and Russian sympathies." [3] they might gradually be won from Islam. Ultimately the several million inhabitants of the great steppe region might become Russian in culture and point of view, and vastly strengthen the empire.

Russian schools for Kazakhs, designed to train interpreters, had

already been established at Orenburg and Omsk late in the
eighteenth century. At that time, however, the empire had few
facilities even for the education of Russians, and the Kazakh
schools suffered from inadequate funds, a lack of qualified personnel, and a general lack of understanding of the problem on the part
of the Russians. Under an appeasement policy adopted toward
Islam during the reign of Catherine II, and the erroneous idea
that Kazakhs and Tatars were essentially the same, the schools
at Orenburg and Omsk were organized on a purely Moslem pattern and were conducted in the Tatar language by Tatar mullas.
Accordingly, the Kazakh pupils in the schools were heavily indoc-
trinated with the principles of Islam and learned to esteem the
Tatar language and culture more than their own.

The Russian authorities eventually realized that such schools
were not in the Imperial interest and in the 1820's, by means of
special classes in the local Russian schools, began to provide the
Kazakhs with education which was on more of a Western pattern.
But these facilities were few, and fewer still were the Kazakhs who
were inclined to surmount the cultural and linguistic barriers necessary for attendance. Only with the founding of a military school
at Omsk (1813), later the Siberian Cadet Corps (from 1847), and
a military school at Orenburg (1825), later the Orenburg Cadet
Corps (from 1844), both with small classes for Kazakhs, a special
course in nursing and vaccination for Kazakhs at the Orenburg
military hospital (from 1844), and a seven-year school for the
preparation of interpreters in Orenburg in 1850 did education for
the natives begin to get on a firm footing.

In spite of these measures, Il'minskii, like Grigor'ev before him,
found that the Tatars monopolized administrative posts at Orenburg and everywhere acted as middlemen between Russians and
Kazakhs. He therefore strove to have schools established at which
the Kazakhs could be taught to read and write in their own language and trained so that they might be taken into the administration.

Although in the 1860's a few Kazakhs attended the Russian
schools at Orenburg and Omsk, the vast majority remained untouched by Western education. The meager budgets provided

for education in the Steppe oblasts in the statute of 1868 allowed little room for experiment. Because the initiative lay with the local authorities, subject to supervision by representatives of the Ministry of Education, uneven results were obtained in the various oblasts. The lead in native education was taken in Turgai oblast. Turgai had no large population centers, and in the earlier years of Russian settlement the peasant villages lay scattered among the large Kazakh population. These factors, and an enlightened attitude toward native education on the part of the oblast officials, resulted in more energetic steps being taken toward native education in Turgai than elsewhere.

Ibragim Altynsarin (1841–1889), a Kazakh who had been one of Il'minskii's pupils at Orenburg, served as the oblast inspector of schools from 1879 until his death in 1889 and showed particular initiative in the work of educating his countrymen. Through his efforts, supported by the Russian officials in the oblast, between 1879 and 1883 four central "two-class" schools (giving education through the grade-school level) were established in the towns of Turgai, Irgiz, Aktiubinsk, and Kustanai for the education of both Russian and Kazakh children. The Kazakhs were housed and boarded in *internats* (dormitories) at the schools; the Russian students lived with their families or with townspeople.

To solve the urgent need for teachers, in 1883 a Kazakh teachers' seminary was established at Troitsk. Kazakhs finishing the courses in the two-class Russian schools of Turgai and Ural'sk oblasts could continue in this school, after which they were obliged to teach in the elementary schools for Kazakhs for a six-year period.

In 1888, Altynsarin and other officials decided on an even more momentous step, and included an internat for ten Kazakh girls in a Russian girls' school opened at Irgiz the year before. The good appearance of the school and the careful supervision of the girls by the school authorities disposed the Kazakhs favorably toward the innovation, and additional facilities for ten more girls had to be provided to care for new applicants. The girls studied Russian and acquired a practical knowledge of sewing and housekeeping. Similar facilities were soon opened in Turgai and Kustanai.[4]

The impetus given education in Turgai oblast in Altynsarin's lifetime was continued through the support of his successor A. E. Alektorov, General Ia. F. Barabash, the military governor, and other officials of the oblast administration. "Aul schools" were established to give the children of nomads their first contact with learning. Patterned after the Russian elementary schools, they conformed nevertheless to the mobile way of life of the Kazakhs. Each school moved about with an aul during the summer migrations and settled with it in the winter camp, making it possible, in theory at least, to carry on instruction nearly the year around. The instruction was in Kazakh, but one of the main objectives besides teaching of the rudiments of reading, writing, and arithmetic was to impart a knowledge of Russian.[5] Il'minskii's teaching methods were employed, as well as special primers written by him.[6]

From the aul schools the pupils could advance to the one-class volost schools, or to the two-class "Russian-Kirgiz" schools, each class comprising two years of study. From there they could go to a Russian city school or to the Orenburg Kirgiz Teachers' School. After completing the course in the teachers' school the student could undertake to teach still others in the aul schools. Up to 1897, Turgai oblast had established 71 schools, with 2,000 students, of whom 52 were girls.[7]

Other oblasts were much slower in providing facilities for native education. In Ural'sk oblast in 1891 less than 500 Kazakh children were being educated in 10 Russian-Kirgiz schools.[8] Akmolinsk oblast at the same time provided only three Kazakh internats, at Omsk, Petropavlovsk, and Akmolinsk, the main population centers, and no other facilities.[9] Only in 1896 did the Akmolinsk oblast administration take serious steps to provide more schools, sending a commission to Turgai to study the system employed there.[10] In the 1890's various oblasts, including Semirechie and Semipalatinsk, both laggard in native education, began to provide agricultural schools for Kazakh and Kirgiz boys. This was intended to facilitate the settlement of the nomads.

Because of the great difficulties in efforts to educate the natives, the development in this field was slow. The lack of funds was a particularly severe hindrance. Turgai oblast led in appropriations, devoting about one-third of the annual oblast budget to education (in 1897, for example, 41,246 rubles),[11] but the sum was not high enough to support any sweeping program. Funds for the opening of new schools often had to be acquired through native donations.[12]

Conditions in the native schools were primitive, particularly in the aul schools. In the summer the schoolmaster went about with the nomads on their migrations and taught in a kibitka. Often the conditions of pasture during this time forced families to go to different areas, which might result in some of the pupils being as much as two or three hundred miles from the school. In the winter, school was usually held in one-room huts of earth or sun-dried brick, heated by a smoky stove burning dung. Windows were usually one or two narrow apertures covered with bladders in place of glass. Blizzards and severe cold frequently prevented the pupils from going to the school, though it might be only two or three miles away. During long periods of bad weather schools often had to close entirely. Rather than struggle against such odds many of the Kazakh teachers gave up their work as soon as possible and went to the nearest town.[13]

The higher school levels offered somewhat better facilities, but there was never enough money with which to meet educational needs, particularly for dormitories and stipends. Inevitably this reflected on the quality of the teaching. In 1895, for example, only 66 out of 135 teachers in Turgai oblast had special training.[14]

Even where funds were available, native suspicions sometimes had to be overcome before facilities could be established. The coincidence of the opening of the first aul schools in Akmolinsk and Semipalatinsk oblasts with the introduction of "land commandants" among the Russian peasants caused rumors to spread and proclamations in Tatar to be distributed among the Kazakhs. It was claimed that the Kazakhs were to be turned into peasants, bound to the soil and drafted for military service; that the teachers would be Russians or converted Kazakhs, under orders to prepare the Kazakhs for conversion to Christianity; and that when the Kazakhs had learned to speak, read, and write Russian they would be converted.[15] As a result of such rumors, no Kazakh would allow a school beneath his roof. To quell the suspicions it was necessary for the oblast administration to commission A. E. Alektorov, inspector of public schools in Turgai oblast and an authority on the Kazakhs, to go about Akmolinsk and Semipalatinsk oblasts and try to explain matters. Alektorov quoted Kazakh poetry written in support of education by his predecessor, Altynsarin; he compared the life of the educated man with that of the uneducated man; and he gave sample lessons showing the nature of the instruction. As a result of such explanation, ably and patiently given, Alektorov was able to allay the doubts of the natives and to secure their acquiescence in the opening of the schools.[16]

Another hindrance to Kazakh education arose from the rigid centralization of the empire's educational system, which led to efforts to standardize curricula regardless of local needs. When the heavy and impractical classical curriculum was adopted for Russian schools in 1868, for example, there was lengthy discussion in the State Council and in correspondence between Governor-General Kryzhanovskii of Orenburg and the minister of education as to whether the Kazakhs in the Orenburg men's high school should have to study the full curriculum. Happily, common sense prevailed and German, Church Slavic, Latin, and Greek were eventually eliminated as unnecessary to the Kazakhs. Nevertheless, Kazakh students who reached high school continued to have to study much other material unsuited to their way of life.[17]

Among contemporary Russians, opinions as to the efficacy of the education given the Kazakhs were sometimes diametrically opposed. Some were delighted at the ready assimilation by the Kazakh pupils of the principles of arithmetic, their ability to construct geometrical figures, to recite from *Boris Godunov* and other Russian literary masterpieces, and to give ready answers to questions about geography. It was believed that this knowledge, taken to the smoky yurts of their fathers, could somehow shed light on the customs and culture of their people.[18] Others pointed out, however, that most of the educated Kazakhs merely aimed to become officials, or to work in the uezd administration as translators, forgetting whatever else they had learned in agricultural school or the teachers' school; worse still, others merely returned to their native kibitka and their old nomadic life. One writer in *Sibirskii*

Vestnik in 1898 concluded after an indignant description of a former student at a technical school for Kazakhs:

> In other words, his way of life, in spite of his long stay in the big city while he was studying, is no different from that of the usual ignorant wild-Kirgiz. But you should meet this same technician in town: clad in a black frockcoat (bought by chance for seven rubles, probably while drunk) he drinks vodka, goes to the club, dances sometimes, speaks without stopping about elevated subjects, often of Dobroliubov, Pisarev, Dostoevskii, Goncharov, and of liberalism; in short, an observer would be agreeably impressed to note that there are such jewels among the Kirgiz. It would not enter his head, of course, that this jewel does not eat with a Russian knife, that his children do not learn Russian, and that his wife is slovenly. This technician is not the only example, but the general rule for the Kirgiz. . . .[19]

The truth, as always, could be better sought between the two extremes. Certainly not all that was imparted could be used under the conditions of steppe life, and certainly backsliders could be expected, as among any primitive people exposed to modern education. Nevertheless, the ability to produce cadres of native officials, even of minor levels, or an Altynsarin and other members of a small but growing intelligentsia, gave promise that the aims of the founders of the system might ultimately be fulfilled.

NATIVE EDUCATION IN TURKESTAN

In Turkestan, Russian education was established later and remained on a more modest scale longer than in the Steppe. Here the Russians met not a cultural vacuum as in the Steppe but a fully developed system of education which occupied a high position in the esteem of the people. The schools in this system were the strong points in the cultural defense lines of the settled natives. Here Moslem preachers and teachers, judges and arbitrators, usually the most learned and respected men in their communities held forth, schooling the rising generation in the ways of its elders.

The schools of Central Asia were of the same pattern as those in the rest of the Moslem world, consisting of two types, the primary schools (*mekteb*) and the higher schools (*medressa*). The mektebs were located mainly in mosques, and were supported by both private and public funds. Instruction was usually provided by the *imam,* or prior, of the mosque, or by the *azanchi* or *muezzin* who called the faithful to prayer. Their services were usually paid for by voluntary offerings from the relatives of the pupils, amounting, after the establishment of Russian rule, to about 50 to 100 rubles per year, depending on the wealth of the parish.

In two to five years the students in a mekteb were taught to read and write in Arabic, although usually without understanding what was read. They also learned how to write by copying original texts, studied the Koran, and received some training in religious ceremonies. Such knowledge had almost no practical value, and was so sketchy that the majority who finished study in the mekteb and returned to the occupations of their fathers quickly forgot even the rudiments of learning which they had received. For this reason, in spite of the considerable number of mektebs, the illiteracy rate of Central Asia was very high. Schools for girls were almost nonexistent.[20]

A few of the students finishing the course in the mekteb went on to the higher native school, the medressa. This was an independent, self-supporting institution, financed by the income from vakfs, property contributed by wealthy natives to be held in trust for the support of schools and other institutions. The medressa was managed by a *mutevali,* or steward. The school faculty was composed of *mudaris* (teachers) and the imam and muezzin in the mosque connected with each school. The students lived in individual cells and studied in auditoria in the open air or under awnings. The school faculty was paid and the students received small allowances from income derived from the vakf assigned to the medressa.[21]

The curriculum in a medressa consisted mainly of Arabic, philosophy, theology, and the Shariat. Other subjects included Persian, Turkish, logic, the rudiments of arithmetic and plane geometry, collections of legend and fable that passed for history, and a mass of confused and contradictory information concerning geography.

The length of time spent in a medressa varied. Some students, attracted by the easy living, security, and social standing of this form of occupation, remained until the end of their lives; others went on for advanced study to the medressas in Bukhara, considered to be the strongest bulwark of Islam and the source of the purest faith.

Anyone who completed the course offered by a medressa was considered to be an educated man, and was consequently eligible to become a teacher, or to hold a religious office. Before the Russian conquest graduates of the medressas monopolized the administrative posts in the native states. Because of this monopoly, the mutevalis of the medressas often achieved great influence. They were able to attract vakfs from rich patrons, and to persuade those patrons to help the students get advantageous and influential posts. Those who secured such posts in turn supported the interests of their benefactors. By this means the mutevalis were able to exert influence in many branches of the local administration to their consequent profit. If, in addition, they were able to create for themselves a reputation for holiness, a considerable crowd of devoted and obedient disciples usually grouped around them.

At the end of the nineteenth century there were about 6,300 native schools in Turkestan—about 400 of them medressas and the remainder mektebs—with about 75,000 students.[22] These were primary defense points of the native way of life in Turkestan. If the old ways were to change, if the natives were to be "drawn closer" to their conquerors, the Moslem schools had to be dealt with first.

RUSSIAN SCHOOLS IN TURKESTAN

Von Kaufman, the first governor-general of Turkestan, regarded the native schools as against Russian interests, but instead of making any direct move toward their abolition he followed the policy which he employed toward all Moslem institutions in the region: "This means—ignoring them. Without any sort of government protection, freed of all supervision and direction, deprived of all means for compelling parents to send children to it, the

Moslem school is in an entirely new position under Russian dominion, unfavorable for it, but extremely advantageous for us." [23]

Von Kaufman believed that the withdrawal of state support and the end of the former dominant position of the medressas in filling public office would eventually remove all basis for their existence, and would in effect either cause them to fall into disuse or to undergo drastic change "to bases more in agreement with the practical interests of the population." [24] He therefore refrained from interference with the native school system. However, beyond this laissez-faire attitude, his policy also led to active steps to help the process along by forestalling, on the one hand, the attempts of the Tatar-dominated Moslem Religious Administration at Ufa to extend its control over the Moslem institutions in Turkestan, and on the other by preventing all Russian Orthodox missionary activity in the region.[25] To avoid all possibility of arousing and consequently stiffening native opposition, he even forbade the establishment of an Orthodox bishopric in Tashkent. "We must introduce Christian civilization in Turkestan," he once wrote, "but we must not try to propound the Orthodox faith to the native population." [26]

Besides these negative measures, however, Von Kaufman was also keenly interested in building a Russian public school system in the region. Russian and native pupils would be educated together, subject to the same rules, without religious differentiation, with the aim of "making both Orthodox and Moslems into useful citizens of Russia." [27]

Mindful, as always, of possible adverse native reaction, Von Kaufman turned for advice to Il'minskii, as an authority on native education. The latter recommended a system of joint Russian and missionary education similar to the one used in teaching the Kazan Tatars. Von Kaufman rejected this plan and appointed a commission from his own staff to study the matter. However, because of preoccupations in other fields, particularly the troubles in Khiva and Kokand, little was done in the field of education in Turkestan until after 1876, when the Ministry of Education assumed control in the region through a chief inspector of schools.

Up to that time the region had been served by only ten Russian schools, all on the elementary level, and nearly all in Semirechie oblast. Only a handful of natives attended these schools.

Now began the organization of other schools to serve the growing Russian population and to fulfill the uncompleted plans for native education. Grade schools were established in the larger Russian communities, with internats for native students. In 1879 two high schools, one for boys and another for girls, were established in Tashkent together with a teachers' seminary.

The natives, however, continued to remain aloof from the educational advantages offered by the Russians. However weak the programs of their own schools, and however insignificant their results from a qualitative point of view, the population esteemed them because of their close connection with their faith. As for the Russian schools, the natives could see only that they included no study of native writing and no religious teaching. The advantages of learning to read and write the language of the infidel Russians gave no incentive to the natives to have their children attend.

The obvious solution was to include these items in the curriculum, but here those attempting to plan and promote native education came up against the general rules which had been passed in an effort to regulate Moslem education in the empire. According to rules issued on March 26, 1870, only the legal aspects of the Moslem faith could be studied in Russian schools for natives, and study of native languages had to begin with the use of the Russian alphabet.[28] It was not until 1884, under Governor-General Rosenbach, that a project for a network of one-class (i.e., providing instruction for the first four years) bilingual elementary schools for the joint education of Russian and native children was formed. The plan, a synthesis of the two types of education, was presented to Tsar Alexander III, who approved enabling legislation.[29]

On December 19, 1884, the first Russian elementary school for native children opened in Tashkent in the home of a wealthy Uzbek. V. P. Nalivkin, an orientalist, was appointed as instructor, and thirty-nine Uzbek boys made up the first enrollment. In 1885, three other such schools were opened, and in 1886, fourteen more.[30]

Considerable difficulties surrounded the opening of these first "Russian-native" schools. Nalivkin, a caustic critic of the conduct of Russian affairs in Turkestan, has described the situation:

> The rural population refused to give up their children to the New Russian schools. Even the officials of the native administration and the "honorable, influential" natives did not want to send them there. Part of the children (it was ordered that a certain number be obtained) were taken forcibly from the families of various small fry who were personally dependent on the volost headmen and village elders; another part were *hired* from among the poorest population.
>
> In Pskent the school opened in the presence of the governor. The children were gathered early in the morning, dressed as if for a holiday. The lips of some were pale and they were trembling from fear. Soon the boys turned, but the volost headman, fearing that the children would flee at the critical moment, had stationed *dzhigits* at the gate and doors. On the flat roofs of the houses near the school sat several hundred native women. The governor arrived and was immediately surrounded by a living wall of myrmidons. The latter had hardly succeeded in opening their mouths in order to begin their customary testimonials of faith in the devotion of the population, their gratitude, etc., when an unbelievable howl was raised from the roofs. The Sart women—mothers, sisters, grandmothers, and acquaintances of the future scholars in the Russian language—cried out as they would have done for the dead. The governor was perturbed, but the *dzhigits* quickly chased the foolish women away, and order was restored.[31]

The reluctance of the natives at having to entrust their children to the strange new institution and the necessity of actually paying the first students to attend were common phenomena in the first years of the Russian-native schools. So, too, was extortion by the native headmen, who taxed the population illegally to pay the pupil's stipends, and usually held back most of the money themselves.[32]

To overcome these initial handicaps the schools were conducted with as great a regard for native sensibilities as possible. Mullas were hired to teach the students Arabic writing and the principles of the Moslem faith; native visitors were given free access to the schools; and by the express order of the governor-general the instructors avoided any sort of punishment of the pupils or disrespect toward the native religion and customs.[33]

The effort spent on these new schools, however, was offset by the rigid, uninteresting methods of instruction. The so-called translation method was used, in which each phrase of the lesson was given in the native language, followed by an identical phrase in Russian, after which the word was written on the blackboard first in the native language, using the Russian transcription, and then in Russian. This method, following the Il'minskii system used in the schools of the Kazan region, was boring to teachers and pupils alike. The pupils learned Russian only mechanically, with no conversational knowledge; many who had been in school for six or seven years still could not speak or even understand Russian.

Only gradually, in the face of official inertia and conservative opposition, were new methods introduced. These were based on textbooks written by S. M. Gramenitskii, the inspector of schools for Syr-Daria oblast.[34] Thereafter the Russian-native schools began to enjoy greater success. Their growth in Syr-Daria oblast, for example, is shown by the following figures: [35]

	Number of schools	Number of students
1894	12	254
1900	23	722
1908	34	1,354
1911	54	2,658
1915	65	3,410

In the entire Turkestan region there were twenty-eight Russian-native schools by 1896, eighty-three in 1906, and eighty-nine in 1911.[36] If this was not impressive in absolute figures, it at least represented a considerable percentage gain.

During this time steps were also taken to improve the education of Russians in Turkestan, necessary in the words of one authority "to strengthen the Russian population so that it can successfully bear the cultural and economic struggle with the mass of the native population without losing its religious, national, and cultural characteristics, and also begin the cultural elevation of the native population." [37] In Tashkent a "real school (*real'noe uchilishche*, from the German *Realschule*, a secondary school teaching no classics) was established in 1894, a trade school in 1896, the Tashkent Cadet Corps in 1900, a "School of the Empress Mary" (a girls' boarding school) in 1901, a railroad technical school in 1904, and a number of elementary schools. As early as 1880, Von Kaufman had appointed a special commission to study the possibility of instituting compulsory elementary education for Russian children in Turkestan. Nothing came of it, but by 1912 the aim was almost realized through efforts to facilitate access to elementary schools. In that year approximately 95 per cent of an estimated 10,230 Russian children of school age in Syr-Daria oblast were receiving an elementary education. This figure, reflecting the special class composition of the Russian population of the oblast—mostly army officers, officials, business people, and their families—equaled or surpassed that of almost every other part of the empire at that time.[38]

Relatively few natives benefited from these facilities. Out of an estimated population for Syr-Daria oblast in 1912 of 1,876,000 natives and 134,500 permanent Russian inhabitants, about 8 per cent could be considered children of school age, or in other words, 150,110 native children and 10,760 Russian children. As of 1912, there were 130 elementary schools in the oblast, with 10,230 Russian children attending, and 56 Russian-native schools and internats at the Russian schools with a total of 3,033 native children. Thus, approximately 95 per cent of the Russian children and 2.02 per cent of the native children in the oblast were receiving a primary education in the Russian schools at that time.[39] At the higher levels of schooling the number of natives was even smaller. In 1896, 10 out of 327 students in the boys' high school in Tashkent, and 8 out of 377 students in the girls' high school were natives. Out of 415 students who completed their studies at the Tashkent Teachers' Seminary in the 25-year period from 1879 to 1904, there were only 65 natives (11 Uzbeks, Turkmen, and Tatars and 54 Kazakhs and Kirgiz).[40]

The other oblasts of the Governor-Generalship of Turkestan (excepting Semirechie oblast, which available statistics usually include in the Steppe) with much smaller Russian populations than Syr-Daria oblast, had correspondingly fewer educational facilities. Within the area now known as Turkmenistan (approximately the same as Transcaspia oblast) there were in 1914 an estimated 6,800 students out of a population of 472,500 (430,829 natives and 41,671 Russians and other nationalities), of whom 1,400 attended middle schools.[41] School facilities, mostly concentrated in Askhabad, included boys' and girls' high schools, a technical school, a railroad school, a three-class boys' elementary school, a three-class girls' school, and three parochial schools. There were also several schools for non-Russians, including a junior high school (*progimnaziia*) for Armenian girls organized by a local Armenian women's charitable society.[42]

Statistical information on the number of schools and pupils in the Kazakh Steppe, including Semirechie oblast, is even scantier than for Turkestan. In 1914 there were 2,011 schools of all kinds within the present bounds of Kazakhstan, which approximately equals the area of the former five Steppe oblasts, attended by a total of 105,200 students. Only 4,300 of these attended middle schools.[43] Only about one-third of the Russian children in the region received a primary education,[44] because of the difficulty of providing school facilities for a rural population spread over such a vast area. The same factor, complicated by linguistic and cultural differences, caused an even greater number of the natives to remain without schooling. Kazakhs constituted only 7.5 per cent of the total enrollment,[45] and most of these attended only the aul schools and Russian-native schools, which grew in number as follows: [46]

	Aul schools	Russian-native schools
1895	31	38
1905	135	128
1913	267	157

Students in the Steppe, including those from both the Russian and native populations, were mostly of the more prosperous families. Thus out of 360 students at the Vernyi gymnasium in 1913, 220 were children of the gentry class and officials, 40 were the children of prosperous Russian peasants or natives, 25 were the children of priests, and 13 the children of traders.[47] With due regard for the special characteristics of the region and its inhabitants, statistics on Russian educational efforts in the Kazakh Steppe and in Turkestan indicate that the Russians established facilities at least comparable to those in the rest of the empire, and that these facilities were undergoing a similar expansion.

The natives, as always, had equal right of access to the Russian schools, and a network of elementary schools was established in both Turkestan and the Steppe to enable them to make use of that right. However, the success of these facilities was slight. The education of a few hundred interpreters, minor officials, and traders was no revolution of the sort Il'minskii had in mind for transforming the Kazakhs into devoted Russified subjects of the tsar. Nor did it accomplish what Von Kaufman had envisaged for the Uzbeks, whose schools, through a policy of international neglect, he hoped would fall into disuse and either be supplanted by Russian schools or be transformed into institutions more in keeping with Russian aims of modernizing the native culture and outlook and "drawing closer" natives and Russians.

Definite accomplishments, on the other hand, were the introduction of new thought in a small segment of native society, the creation of a native intelligentsia, and the appearance of native schools of a reformed type. These changes, of great bearing on the native future, but hardly "in the Russian interest," will be discussed in a later chapter.

XIV

THOUGH tempered by caution and vacillation, and relatively ineffective, the Russian encroachments on the Central Asian way of life were clear enough in intent. Acquiescence in the Russian design of "drawing closer" would have meant eventual loss of ethnic and cultural identity for steppe- and oasis-dweller alike. On the other hand, the futility of physical resistance had been impressed repeatedly on the native mind by the crushing defeats inflicted upon the levies of the Central Asian states during the conquest. Though not extinguished, the spirit of opposition was at least lulled by fatalism and acceptance of material benefits during the occupation that followed. The peace which settled over the region caused the Russians satisfaction and astonished foreign visitors.

THE SPECTER OF NATIVE REVOLT

This tranquility led many observers, Russian and foreign alike, into believing that it reflected inner conditions as well, but behind the scenes there was less certainty. Throughout the period of Russian rule official documents refer again and again to the possibility of native uprising, and display uneasiness at the overwhelming numerical superiority of the natives to the scanty Russian garrisons and scattered peasant villages.

From the first, both the nomadic and settled populations of Central Asia were freed from any obligation for military service. The secret report by F. K. Giers after his investigation of the Turkestan administration in 1882, states clearly that this was because the government did not consider it safe to raise militant feelings in the natives and at the same time teach them European military organization and the use of modern arms. That a native army could be dangerous, the report recalled, was shown by the example of the Sepoy Mutiny in India in 1856. It was acknowledged that Russia had Moslem units from other parts of the empire, but assertedly even their loyalty would be doubtful in a war against other Moslems.

In the entire Turkestan region at that time, Giers wrote, there were only 30,000 Russian troops. The Moslem male population, on the other hand, numbered not less than 1,150,000. Taking even as few of these for military service as 5 per 1,000, he calculated, would yield 5,750 men annually, or 19.1 per cent of the strength of the entire Russian army in Turkestan. In 15 years, some 82,250 natives would have passed through the army, becoming accustomed to arms and military discipline. Among them would be several thousand noncommissioned officers, mostly literate, who if necessary could serve as officers and form a nucleus for the formation of units hostile to the Russians.[1]

The specter of native revolt was also present, as we have seen, in the deliberations of the Ignat'ev commission (1884) over the drafting of a statute for the administration of Turkestan. It was to appear repeatedly in the years to come. But regardless of the uneasiness of military men and civil officials, the chances were against the natives finding means for any rebellion. Not only were they virtually unarmed in the face of the Berdan rifles of the Russian detachments, but the terrain would not permit a rebel force to live off the land. More important still, the ethnic and cultural diversity of the peoples of the region, their diffused geographical distribution, and the feudal economic and political conditions under which they lived had never permitted the growth of other than a local patriotism. The traditional pattern of despotic rule in the region had accustomed them to rule by others.

The one uniting force to which all gave allegiance was Islam. More than a religion, it was a way of life. The traditions of earlier conquests, which lived on in the minds of its adherents, gave an equivalent of national pride. Violent overthrow of power, moreover, was part of the political pattern of the region.

The danger of a rebellion was least in the Steppe. The revolt in 1868 of defiant Kazakh sultans unwilling to submit to the new administrative organization was the last such episode of more than local significance. The precarious economy of the nomads, their impotence against modern arms, and the filling in of the steppe by Russian colonists rendered the danger of subsequent attempts increasingly slight.

Among the Uzbeks, however, the deeper religious feeling, the denser population, and the more advanced culture gave a greater possibility of outbreaks. Fergana oblast in particular was a focal point of resentment toward Russian rule. More isolated from outside influences than any other part of Turkestan, its inhabitants had developed a particularly intense feeling for Islam. Sufism, the creed of a semimonastic Islamic sect with an ascetic, pantheistic philosophy; the closely related dervishism, preached by fanatical sheikh-ishans; and mahdism, the belief in a coming savior, had numerous devotees. From the time of the Russian annexation small outbreaks occurred in Fergana almost annually, stirred up by adherents of these sects. Nearly all such cases involved some wandering dervish or mulla who proclaimed himself khan and, by force of his spurious rank and the incitement of religious feelings, gathered a handful of followers from among the ignorant peasantry or nomads and set out to win back Fergana from the unbelievers. The uprising in 1885 of Dervish-Khan-Tiuria, a former official in the Kokand khanate, affected Andizhan, Osh, and Margelan uezds, but it was quickly quelled by a Russian punitive expedition. None of these episodes appear to have caused the Russian authorities any particular concern. Most of the participants were quickly rounded up and ringleaders were sentenced to hard labor or hanged, if they had murdered some luckless volost headman.[2]

THE TASHKENT CHOLERA RIOT (1892)

Only in 1892 did a situation with more serious implications arise, this time in the regional capital itself. In June a cholera epidemic broke out in Tashkent. The death toll was particularly high in the crowded, unsanitary native section of the city. The city administration, headed by Colonel S. R. Putintsev, endeavored to enforce sanitary regulations which would help stem the epidemic, but paid little heed to native psychology and customs. The regulations required a medical inspection of all bodies, but because of the number of the dead and insufficient medical personnel the inspection was sometimes delayed for three or four days, with consequent decomposition of the bodies in the summer heat. A number of young Russians with no medical background were pressed into service as inspectors, but unfortunately they angered the natives by their disregard for the sanctity of the women's quarters in the houses they visited. Besides this, the twelve old cemeteries in the city were closed, and only one was provided in their place. This caused great difficulty in transporting the dead, which according to the Shariat had to be done by hand. The washing of the dead at the place of burial, also required by the Shariat, was usually impossible because of the decomposition which had occurred. To these factors were added rumors that the Russians were seeking to kill off the natives by purposely delaying the burials so that the cholera would spread.

Under such conditions only a spark was needed to arouse the populace to violence. On June 24 the threat of punishment for three secret burials caused a crowd to seek the head of the administration of the native city, Mohammed-Iakub Karymberdyev. Hearing that he was at the office of Colonel Putintsev, the city commandant, the mob took the unusual step of invading the Russian section to look for their man.

At the city administration building Putintsev met the mob and tried to turn them back, but was himself seized and beaten. The mob then tried to invade the building, but the rumor spread that Russian troops were coming and the natives began to flee, pursued by a small number of Russian civilians. In their panic many of the fugitives fell into the Ankhor-Aryk, a deep canal separating the Russian and native parts of the city, and at least eighty drowned.[3]

In the meantime the military governor of Syr-Daria oblast,

General N. I. Grodekov, heard of the outbreak and hurried to the scene. Although accompanied by less than a hundred troops, he quickly cleared the Russian city of stragglers and then led his small command into the native city. They drove the crowd before them, but the natives only dispersed into side streets and then collected behind the Russians, shouting abuse and throwing stones.

At the mosque of Dzham, Grodekov ordered one of his officers who had a good knowledge of Uzbek to warn the crowd to disperse or the troops would shoot. In spite of several warnings, however, the crowd did not obey. Several of the natives, baring their chests, cried in Russian: "Shoot!" and others shouted that the Russian rifles were loaded with blanks. The troops were then ordered to fire. After two volleys the crowd fled, leaving ten dead and several seriously wounded.

The episode at Tashkent shattered the confidence of many Russians and confirmed the fears of others regarding the degree of acceptance of Russian rule by the Turkestan natives. After an investigation, sixty natives were tried by a military court: twenty-five were acquitted, eight sentenced to hang, and the remainder to varying terms of imprisonment or exile. Governor-General Vrevskii later commuted the death sentences to imprisonment.[4]

Locally the disorders caused a shake-up among officials. Grodekov, although his decisive action probably prevented the disorders from assuming more serious proportions, was relieved as military governor and transferred to the Amur region. City Commandant Putintsev was replaced by a more "firm and energetic" officer. The native police were replaced by Russians or by natives from other districts.

On a regional level, Vrevskii pressed for changes in the Turkestan statute, blaming the outbreak on the introduction of civilian control in many parts of the administration, and the consequent fall in prestige of Russian military officials.[5] In the end, however, no changes were made and the majority of the Russian community settled back to its customary calm, typified by the confidence expressed by a writer in *Zakaspiiskoe Obozrenie,* a semiofficial newspaper published at Askhabad, in an article, "The Successes of Russian civilization in Middle Asia":

The Russian government has done everything so that the native will not regret the loss of his quasi-independent position of the past. He knows well that when made a subject of the White Tsar he becomes not only a citizen with full rights but also a privileged citizen of Russia, for he has no obligation for general military service. Guaranteed also the security of his life and property, and especially the inviolability of his religious beliefs, he thanks Allah and calls for blessings on the head of the Ak-Padishah and all the Russians.[6]

THE ANDIZHAN UPRISING (1898)

Just what blessings were called for was shown a few years later in the so-called Andizhan uprising of 1898, headed by a religious leader, Mohammed-Ali-Khalfa, or Dukchi-Ishan. According to evidence brought out at his trial, the leader of the uprising was born in Margelan uezd, Fergana oblast, then part of the khanate of Kokand, in 1856. His family was impoverished and he received no education. In 1874, at the age of eighteen, he became a follower of the Ishan Sultan-Khan, who lived in a village in Andizhan uezd. Sultan-Khan bore the title of Ishan as a leader of the Sufi sect. Mohammed-Ali became one of a number of disciples living on the bounty of Sultan-Khan, each giving in return an ample amount of work in his own specialty.[7]

In 1884, following the death of his benefactor, Mohammed-Ali made a pilgrimage to Mecca. He remained away for three years, spending the last year in the service of the Ishan Akhmet-Khan-Tiuria, at Samarkand. Akhmet-Khan died in 1887, and Mohammed-Ali took over his title, becoming known as the Ishan Madali (a contraction of Mohammed-Ali), or Dukchi-Ishan.

Returning to Fergana oblast, Mohammed-Ali settled at the village of Min-Tiube, in Margelan uezd. There he engaged in pious works, such as planting trees along the roads for the comfort of travelers. His piety attracted followers, from whose labor and contributions he began to grow wealthy. The fame of his holiness and charities spread and he became a power in his district. With contributions he built a guesthouse, barns and stables, and in 1889 a medressa and two mosques on his estate. He accumulated a library of religious books, although he could not read. Later, he built a high minaret. It was of clay, without a brick foundation, but in reply to the fears expressed by some of his followers the Ishan said it would be held up by his prayers. In 1897 the minaret fell, killing five men, but by this time the Ishan had gained such a hold on his followers that they did not question his judgment and quickly erected a new minaret.[8]

By 1898 the Ishan's influence had extended into the several uezds of Fergana oblast. His most ardent followers were of the older generation, men who had lived in the country before the Russians came. In many cases these men had occupied official positions, but had later been reduced to poverty and insignificance. Their grievances, combined with their religious feeling, made them willing followers of the Ishan, particularly when rumors began to spread in the spring of 1898 of his destined role as a liberator of his people.

All of this took place in a world far removed from that in which the Russian officials moved. None of the uezd commandants or district pristavs had any direct contact with the mass of the natives, and depended almost exclusively on the native interpreters in their offices and on the volost headmen for information. Vague rumors of an uprising reached some of the Russian officials through these sources, but were disregarded as having no more weight than dozens of previous reports in years past. The officials were unaware that in the volost elections held around Min-Tiube the people had replaced volost headmen friendly to the Russians with others who were partisans of the Ishan.[9]

Meanwhile, the Ishan and his disciples were planning an uprising which would seize the entire oblast of Fergana. They proposed simultaneous night attacks on the Russian barracks at Margelan, Osh, and Andizhan, seizure of those towns, and restoration of the former khanate of Kokand at Namangan, with the Ishan's fourteen-year-old nephew as khan. There seem to have been vague ideas that if all the people rose they could also seize Tashkent and Samarkand and drive the Russians from Turkestan.

The Ishan inspired his people with confidence in the success of the operation. They were ordered to dress in white garments to counter the invincibility supposedly conveyed by white head-gear and tunics. The Ishan promised to give his followers tooth-picks which if thrust in their *tiubeteikas* (skullcaps) or *chalmas* (flowing headdresses) would make them invulnerable to iron and bullets and cause the Russian guns to shoot water instead of bullets. He assured them that when he waved his right hand, all Russians on his right would fall, and that when he waved his left, all on his left would fall. On the night of May 17, they were told, a great white horse and a golden sword would be sent from Heaven to take the Ishan into battle. Rumors spread among the people that the Ishan would be aided by the Turkish sultan, the emir of Afghanistan, and even by the English, who, it was said, had already sent arms. These, however, were to be kept hidden in the mountains, as cudgels and the toothpicks would be enough against the Russians at first.

Particular hope was placed in aid from the sultan of Turkey, rumored to have just beaten the tsar in a war. (The war was the Greek-Turkish war of 1897, in which Russia had not participated, but the people thought that because the ruler of the Greeks was a Christian he must be the same as the Russian tsar.) As proof of the sultan's aid, the Ishan showed the populace an ornate document bearing the emblem of the sultan, and with the text written in gold. No one read it—it was enough that the Ishan had it.

On Sunday, May 17, 1898, before sundown, a crowd of the Ishan's devotees gathered in the two mosques on his estate. At about 7 p.m., following a religious service, cudgels were issued, banners were brought out, and the Ishan, clad in a green robe, appeared on a white horse. From the saddle, he cried "In the name of Almighty God—to the Holy War!" and at the head of the band rode out of the gate. In the street the crowd was joined by three other groups of followers—250 men mounted, and the rest on foot—600 in all. They were to be joined by several other detachments from villages along the way. At the same time other detachments set out toward the other points to be attacked—one group toward Osh, another toward Margelan. A third group was to hunt down and kill Russian foresters in the mountains, wipe out the Cossack command stationed at the village of Kara-kul', and then come to Andizhan.[10]

The Russians were oblivious of the impending danger. The plans had been in preparation for months and thousands of natives undoubtedly knew of the uprising, but the void that separated Russians from natives is illustrated by the fact that responsible officials received warning only on the morning of the day the attack was to occur. At that time Lieutenant Colonel Korytov, assistant commandant of Margelan uezd, Lieutenant Colonel Zaitsev, commandant of Osh uezd, and Enikeev, a Tatar who was the pristav of the Assake district of Margelan uezd were told of the planned uprising. In each case the information came from one of the former volost headmen who had been replaced by the Ishan's men. All three officials thought the reports either unfounded or based on minor brigandage. Zaitsev and Enikeev took security measures, but Korytov did nothing.

At about 2 p.m., Enikeev sent one messenger to Novyi Margelan with a report to the uezd commandant, Colonel Brianov, and a second to Andizhan. The messenger to Andizhan was waylaid and killed by the Ishan's adherents, but the first one got through. Brianov read the report and doubted its worth, but took it to the military governor, Lieutenant General Povalo-Shvyikov-skii. At the governor's house, an operetta was being rehearsed, part of it composed by the governor himself. The governor read the message, exclaimed impatiently: "It is all exaggerated; they are always making flies into elephants!" and took no further action.[11]

In the meantime, the Ishan and his troop were continuing toward Andizhan, picking up followers along the way. One group displayed the head of a Russian merchant who had fallen into their hands. Another group came upon a Russian salesman, pulled him from his horse, and hacked him to pieces. About four miles from Andizhan the Ishan and his force halted to pray, and were joined by 200 natives of Andizhan. Later they were also joined by part of the group which had been supposed to attack the Russian garrison at Margelan. News had come that the Russian garrison there was not all asleep, as expected, but was holding a dance, so could not be taken unawares. Therefore some of the force overtook the Ishan's party in order to take part in the Andizhan attack.

Two natives who had shops next to the Russian camp reported on the disposition of the Russian troops. The camp was occupied by the Fourth and Fifth Companies of the Twentieth Turkestan Line Battalion. On the basis of the information furnished by the two shopkeepers, it was assumed that the Fifth Company had gone seven miles from town for target practice, leaving only the Fourth Company, so the Ishan decided to concentrate on their barracks alone. Actually, the Fifth Company was in camp and its 111 men were in their barracks, but of the Fourth Company, only 52 were in camp.

The band advanced on the barracks. The buildings were of a low variety used for the summer, open from the roof halfway to the ground. The men inside were all sleeping with their heads next to the low wall. A dozing guard was killed, and then, with muffled cries of "Ur! Ur!" ("Kill! Kill!") the intruders dashed to the barracks wall. Some thrust their cudgels through the openings and began to belabor the sleeping soldiers. Others leaped inside and began to use their knives. If they had not cut and hacked so furiously even at the dead, it was asserted afterward, not a man of the fifty-two in the barracks might have survived.

As it was, a corporal serving as duty officer for the two companies, who was in the barracks at the time, managed to escape and make his way to the Fifth Company barracks, where he began to arouse the men. Back in the Fourth Company barracks, four shots rang out. A second lieutenant, sleeping in the infirmary because he lacked funds to rent a room in town, heard the commotion, drew his revolver from under his pillow, ran into the yard clad in his nightshirt and dashed to the other barracks, firing into a crowd of mounted natives on the way.

The Fifth Company men went forth at first with their guns and bayonets but with no ammunition, but soon thought better of attempting a hand-to-hand struggle and retreated to their barracks. A trunkful of guard ammunition was broken open and distributed, and the troops sallied forth again, firing on the natives.

The natives soon fled. The first shots had been a great shock to their morale, as they found that the guns of the Russians did not shoot water, and that their toothpicks could not save them from bullets. They left eighteen dead behind, as well as many of their cudgels and a green banner. In the Fourth Company barracks, twenty-two soldiers lay dead, and nineteen were badly wounded. The entire action had occurred in only fifteen minutes.[12]

In Novyi Margelan, Governor Povalo-Shvyikovskii belatedly received another warning of the advance on Andizhan at about 9 a.m., but he had just risen and delayed taking any action for another hour. At 10 a.m. he ordered a telegram of inquiry sent to Andizhan, but the rebels had cut the wire. The railroad telegraph still functioned, but no one thought of using it, and it was noon before the governor finally heard of the attack on the garrison. "This is serious!" he exclaimed, and at once set out for Andizhan with a small detachment of troops. In villages along the route taken by the Ishan and his force, the governor's men flogged all the natives in sight for not giving warning. In Andizhan some of the native wounded who had been captured were abused by a mob of local Russians. The governor did nothing to prevent this, and himself kicked some of the wounded.[13]

The Ishan was captured on the following day, May 19, 1898, and one by one most of his chiefs were taken. One still had the ornate scroll ostensibly sent by the sultan of Turkey. Translation revealed it to be only a testament of loyalty to the Ishan and his cause by several adherents, though perhaps even the illiterate Ishan had believed it to be authentic.[14]

The news of the Ishan's defeat spread quickly and discouraged any further native attempts at violence. Seeking to carry out their missions, but vague as to what they should do, the rebels who had not been a part of the group headed by the Ishan had accomplished little. Some murdered a Russian forester, others looted a Cossack camp of supplies, but that was all. The rumors of the prospective victories of the Ishan turned abruptly into equally exaggerated accounts of his defeat, and the flame of revolt burned out in disillusionment.[15]

Of about 2,000 active participants in the Andizhan uprising,

777 natives were arrested for complicity. Of these, 325 were later released for lack of evidence, and 25 were tried and acquitted. Of the remainder, nineteen were executed; the Ishan and five of his lieutenants were hanged on July 13, 1898, near the Fourth Company barracks at Andizhan. The rest were sentenced to various terms of hard labor and exile. The nature of the revolt was indicated by the age and station of those convicted. About three-fifths of the total number were elderly, and the religious element and former officialdom of the Kokand khanate predominated.[16]

Besides the punishment of the immediate participants in the uprising, more sweeping measures of a group nature were proposed. Count Palen states in his memoirs that General Kuropatkin, then minister of war, was particularly insistent that this be done. As Palen put it:

Kuropatkin came out with an Asiatic conception in the spirit of Tamerlane, wanting to clear of its native inhabitants a strip five kilometers wide from the Ishan's holdings all the way to Andizhan, thirty miles, and to settle Russians there so that all Asia could see how they punished those who rose against the White Tsar. He had the idea that not only the Ishan's village but all the villages he and his group went through and had adherents in, and which did not alarm the authorities, should be punished. The strip was in a densely populated, intensively cultivated area, the clearing of which would have affected several thousand innocent persons.[17]

In the end, however, local officials in Tashkent, Andizhan, and Margelan were able to have the order modified so that only the Ishan's village of Min-Tiube and the village near the barracks at Andizhan would have to be cleared. The inhabitants of Min-Tiube were resettled and a Russian village was established on the site. To finance the resettlement of natives and establishment of Russians, and to provide a compensation of 100,000 rubles for the families of Russian soldiers slain in the uprising, an indemnity of 1,000,000 rubles was imposed on the population of Fergana oblast, to be paid over a period of several years.[18]

Although the revolt was promptly put down, it left an indelible impression on Russians dwelling in Turkestan. The confidence of many in the security of the Russian hold on Central Asia was shaken; thenceforth neither declarations of loyalty by the native leaders nor the acquiescence of the native mass could restore it.

In his report on the Andizhan uprising the governor-general of Turkestan, General Dukhovskoi, concluded that in spite of the advantages which the natives of Central Asia might have derived from Russian rule, they were not reconciled to that rule and could not soon be expected to join the Russian population in feelings of loyalty to the sovereign and to the state.[19]

Why had the revolt occurred? Some observers gave credence to rumors of the presence of Turkish and Afghan *provocateurs* in the region before the revolt, but no concrete evidence of this was ever revealed. General M. A. Terent'ev, an authority on the history of Turkestan, with forty years of experience in the region, blamed the transfer of power from military to civilian administrators, lack of Russian surveillance over the Moslem religious leaders, lack of supervision over native elections, and lack of knowledge on the part of Russian officials of the local languages and customs.[20] His views underlined the failure of the Imperial system to establish identity with native society, or to reach down to the native village and family in order to establish control over the actions and thoughts of the people.

In spite of the arguments of Terent'ev and others, no appreciable change took place in the Russian administration. Nothing was forthcoming but talk of restoring a stronger military control, as in Von Kaufman's time, proposals for more control over the Moslem schools, and sporadic attempts in Tashkent to initiate a training program in the native languages for Russian officials.

As for the natives, although the Andizhan uprising testified that their attitude toward infidel rule had not been altered by the material benefits they had obtained, there were no new threats to Russian supremacy. The failure of the uprising drove home once again the inability of a backward people, virtually without arms, to wrest independence from a modern power able and determined to quell opposition. The uprising had been led by conservative elements, champions of the old ways, who had proclaimed the old issues. Only gradually did the realization arise among other native circles that there might be means of protest more suited to modern conditions, and leading ultimately to the desired ends of freedom and self-government of which they were becoming increasingly aware.

XV

DURING the first three decades following the Russian conquest, the steppes and oases of Central Asia had lain remote from the revolutionary circles, underground political parties, and extremist outrages in European Russia. The bomb blast which killed the "Tsar-Liberator," Alexander II, in 1881 had echoed even in Tashkent, where the news helped bring on Von Kaufman's fatal stroke, but in general the problems of European Russia had little immediate effect in the new territory. The region was too isolated; the conquerors and colonists were too occupied by the immediate tasks of exploitation and development; and neither the Russian peasantry nor the industrial proletariat, the main classes upon whom the revolutionists placed their hopes for support, were present in significant numbers.

Yet, by the end of the century the new forces had begun to operate. The ideas which fermented in the minds of the intelligentsia in European Russia worked also in Kustanai, Tashkent, and Askhabad. Many still clung to the ideology which wove Russian patriotism, the Orthodox faith, and devotion to the tsar into a fabric of rationalization for the Imperial regime. Others, however, were beginning to see the consequences of the nation's backwardness, the repression inherent in the traditional military and police rule, and the corruption and inefficiency in the administrative apparatus. New economic and political trends were hindered, but as literacy increased new ideas spread, and the slowness of change brought impatience and exasperation.

The extension of the Trans-Caspian Railroad to Tashkent in

1898 ended the isolation of the regional capital and other main centers, brought in the first sizable group of skilled workers, and provided a ready avenue for the spread of revolutionary ideas.

Turkestan and the Kazakh Steppe, like other outlying parts of the empire, were places of exile for "political undesirables" from European Russia. Revolutionary students and industrial workers were sometimes drafted and assigned to military units in Central Asia, "undesirable" soldiers were transferred there from units in other regions, and civilian exiles were domiciled in all of the main towns. Inevitably, these people transmitted their ideas to the land-hungry peasants, disgruntled soldiers and workers, and the frustrated members of the intelligentsia around them. The Russian government's effort to neutralize the revolutionary infection by transferring the carriers to remote, more tranquil regions only served to spread it throughout the empire.

THE RISE OF THE REVOLUTIONARY MOVEMENT

The first overt manifestations of social unrest in Russian Central Asia arose in the Steppe, in connection with the economic crisis of 1899–1903. During those years, just as elsewhere in the empire, workers at various widely separated points struck for higher wages and better working and living conditions. There were strikes at the Uspenskii copper mine, the Spasskii copper smelters, at the Ekibastuz and Karaganda coal mines, and at the Omsk railroad repair shops. In 1902, 800 railroad workers at the Mugodzhar station struck for two months' back pay. The strikes were all local in origin and spontaneous in nature, but the Russian revolutionists made the most of them as chances to display leadership and to gain support. On December 5, 1902, the governorgeneral of the Steppe reported "continuous underground activity by local agitators along the railroad, especially in the towns of Omsk, Petropavlovsk, and their vicinities." [1]

During the same period small revolutionary circles began to form in various towns in Turkestan. In 1902 the first of these gathered under the leadership of V. D. Korniushin, a carpenter from Kazan who had been exiled to Tashkent because of membership in a Social Democratic organization. He and a few kindred spirits held evening discussions in their rooms, or on holidays gathered out of town purportedly on fishing trips. Occasionally they received illegal literature from Social Democratic organizations in central Russia and Transcaucasia. Before long, two similar groups arose in the Tashkent railroad repair shops, and in 1903 Korniushin organized a circle among the students at the Tashkent trade school.[2] Few in number, and volatile and heterogeneous in composition, such groups must have seemed insignificant at that time, but their members were heirs of a hard purpose, already ruthlessly pursued for over a generation, of bringing down an empire and a way of life.

Not until after the outbreak of Russia's ill-starred conflict with Japan in January, 1904, did the minute revolutionary groups have an opportunity to strike at the Imperial regime. Then, with disillusionment added to the already existing economic distress and chronic social unrest, resentment focused more strongly than ever on the government and ruling class.

In Central Asia, partisan labels were still indistinct enough to enable adherents of the Socialist Revolutionary and Social Democratic movements to work together. In the spring of 1904 both joined in an attempt to organize a strike of workers in the Tashkent railroad repair shops for an eight-hour day and higher pay, but were thwarted by the police. Late in 1904 they combined in the so-called United Group of Social Democrats and Socialist Revolutionaries, and for a time worked jointly in organizing new circles and in preparing and distributing hectographed leaflets.[3] In Samarkand, the exiled Bolshevik M. V. Morozov led the formation of a Social Democratic group, and took over the editorship of the newspaper *Samarkand,* which with due regard for the censor became a legal voice for Bolshevik principles. In Askhabad, a former Kazan university student, Evgenii Kataev, formed what soon became the Askhabad committee of the Russian Social Democratic Labor Party (RSDLP), subordinate to the Baku committee of the same organization. Another Social Democratic group was formed among troops of the First Transcaspian Railroad Battalion at Askhabad, another among railroad battalion troops and repair shop workers at Kyzyl-Arvat, and lesser groups appeared at Krasnovodsk, Merv, and Kushka.[4] Some Socialist Revolutionaries participated in these organizations, and they may have had separate groups as well, but their characteristically loose organization and their eventual defeat have obscured their history.

Up to 1905 none of the revolutionary organizations were yet of significant size. The largest, those at Askhabad and Kyzyl-Arvat, had only a couple of dozen adherents; the weaker ones had only three or four. Contact with the center was sporadic, and news of ideological developments came haphazardly, chiefly by means of correspondence or clandestine literature passed from hand to hand or read in secret meetings.

The "bloody Sunday" demonstration and shootings in St. Petersburg on January 9, 1905, suddenly gave the revolutionary movement in Central Asia, as in the rest of the empire, new strength. Small strikes and demonstrations occurred in towns along the Trans-Siberian Railroad. On January 12, leftist intelli gentsia and workers attending banquets in Tashkent, Vernyi, Samarkand, and Kyzyl-Arvat to celebrate the founding of the University of Moscow took the opportunity to deliver speeches of protest.[5]

During February and March, strikes occurred among workers in the Tashkent, Chardzhui, Chernaevo, and Kyzyl-Arvat railroad repair shops, and in other enterprises. Workers' demonstrations became common. On July 4, 1905, at Askhabad, the funeral of L. L. Stabrovskii, a teacher associated with both the Socialist Revolutionaries and with the Social Democratic party who had died of tuberculosis in the local jail, was turned into a mass demonstration by assembled railroad workers and printing-plant employees. Shops along the procession's line of march closed for the day, and the leftist newspaper *Askhabad* printed a special edition in honor of the deceased. The demonstrators listened to antigovernment speeches alleging that Stabrovskii had died a victim of police brutality, bore red flags and wreaths with red ribbons, and broke windows in the city jail. On July 8 a requiem mass for Stabrovskii at Kyzyl-Arvat provided an excuse for a similar display.[6]

On July 16 the regional capital, Tashkent, saw its first workers' demonstration when several hundred men organized by the local Social Democrats paraded in protest against the proposed national assembly, the so-called "Bulygin Duma." On August 22 the Social Democrats of Kyzyl-Arvat organized another large demonstration in connection with the funeral of a Bolshevik named Morgunov, who had been killed while fabricating a bomb. About 1,500 persons took part in the procession, according to an official report.[7]

At the same time, disturbances began to arise in a far more vital quarter, among the troops of Turkestan, the bulwark of the Imperial regime. On May 24, soldiers of the Turkestan Sapper Battalion, stationed near Tashkent, rioted over the quality of the soup served at their evening meal. As punishment, fifty-six soldiers were given seven days confinement apiece. During succeeding months many similar disturbances took place. All were local in origin and trivial in nature, resulting from resentment at bad food or at rough handling by sergeants, but they indicated growing defiance toward authority. The mild punishments meted out to the offenders proved no deterrent.[8]

THE GENERAL STRIKE (OCTOBER, 1905)

So far, this was no revolution, but preparations were being made behind the scenes for activity on a broader scale. In March, 1905, the Social Democrats of Tashkent left the "Allied Group" which they had entered with the Socialist Revolutionaries the year before, and founded their own independent Tashkent group of the RSDLP. Tashkent became the *de facto* regional center for Social Democratic activity, though organizations in Samarkand, Askhabad, Kyzyl-Arvat, Chardzhui, Merv, Kazandzhik, and other towns retained considerable independence. Meanwhile, union organizing activity proceeded rapidly among railroad workers and employees, and among workers in printing plants and other enterprises in the towns.

In October, 1905, this organizational work bore fruit when the empire's one million railroad workers went on strike. They were joined October 14–16 by personnel of the Trans-Caspian, Orenburg-Tashkent, and Trans-Siberian Railroads. Traffic ceased and large parts of the lines came under the control of the strikers.

The Manifesto of October 17, 1905, granted reluctantly by Tsar Nicholas II to mollify popular discontent, merely brought forth additional demands throughout the empire. When news of the Manifesto reached Tashkent on October 18, demonstrations were organized. A crowd surged through the main streets of the Russian section closing schools and stores, and finally went to the city prison, demanding the release of political prisoners. At the prison the crowd was dispersed by Cossacks, but on October 19 a large meeting was held on the edge of town. A delegation was chosen to go to the prosecutor of the district court with new demands for the release of the prisoners.[9] The prosecutor refused, and the crowd, unappeased, gathered near the city Duma building at about 5 o'clock in the evening to hold another unauthorized meeting. Many were drunk, and there were large numbers of youths and curiosity seekers.

Hearing of the gathering, the assistant governor-general, General V. V. Sakharov, taking the place of Governor-General Teviashov who lay mortally ill in the official residence, ordered the military governor of Syr-Daria oblast, General I. I. Fedotov, to send troops to the city Duma. Fedotov came with two companies of Cossacks and gave the crowd a half hour to disperse, but they did not. After threatening force, still with no effect, he ordered the crowd dispersed. Someone then fired on the Cossacks with a revolver, and others threw stones, wounding several Cossacks and horses. Ordered to fire, the Cossacks sent two volleys into the crowd, killing three persons and wounding nineteen, most of whom were only curiosity seekers.[10]

This unparalleled event, of Russians shooting Russians, shocked the populace and spurred radical elements to fresh activity. Thousands attended the funeral of the slain, and on October 21, with permission of the acting governor-general, the city Duma met in extraordinary session to discuss the matter, holding the session in the town circus to accommodate the public. There, incited by a boisterous crowd of over 2,500 spectators, the Duma passed resolutions asking for the removal from office of the city commandant; the removal and trial of the military governor for his part in the shooting of the demonstrators; the removal of Cossacks from Tashkent and the abolition of military patrols; the replacement of the police by a popular militia to be under the control of the city Duma; the election of the mayor instead of his appointment by the military governor; universal, equal, direct, and secret elections to the city Duma; and the freeing of all political prisoners.[11]

In the week that followed, protest meetings took place in the circus almost daily, led by the Social Democrats and other left-wing elements. A Tashkent city revolutionary committee was elected, and the newspaper *Russkii Turkestan,* taken over by the Bolshevik M. V. Morozov, who moved to Tashkent from Samarkand at this time, was distributed free. It carried revolutionary proclamations and sensational news.[12]

Similar activities took place in the other strike-bound towns of Turkestan. In Askhabad crowds attended daily meetings in the municipal gardens and the circus. The schools closed, and students took part in rallies and went about the streets singing the "Marseillaise." They also demanded a change in the school management, an end to spying on students, and an end to condescension toward non-Russian students. On October 24, a group of Persians, marching with a portrait of the tsar, were fired on, reportedly by an Armenian. A pogrom against the Armenians by the large Persian element in the population was barely averted. General E. E. Usakovskii, the oblast commandant, took a conciliatory attitude toward all of these manifestations, promising the strikers that he would interfere only in case of violence.[13]

The ground seemed laid for further gains by the revolutionists, but after reaching this point they did not seem to know what to do. Daily meetings in Tashkent and Askhabad featured much oratory and voicing of revolutionary slogans, but no real program, and the power remained in the hands of the authorities. On October 26 the Tashkent City Duma modified its previous demands. Finally, at its sessions of November 7 and 14, it heeded warnings by the assistant governor-general and withdrew the demands entirely.[14] Meanwhile, the strike began to wane; it ended officially on October 27 and after sporadic demonstrations in Samarkand, Perovsk, Cherniaevo, Pishpek, and other towns finally ceased.

THE TASHKENT MUTINY (NOVEMBER, 1905)

The peace that followed the general strike was uneasy. Strike committees remained intact, the workers defiant. In Tashkent there was a feeling of insecurity because of the threat of new outbreaks of disorder, the excitement that remained among some elements of the population after their brief taste of libertarian license, rumors of an impending pogrom against the Jews, talk of unrest among the troops, and a rising crime rate.

Then, on November 15, new trouble broke out. The First Tashkent Reserve Battalion and several other units at the Tashkent citadel mutinied in their barracks and attempted to take over the fortress. They were opposed by loyal troops and finally disarmed and arrested on the following morning. Two of the mutineers were killed and twenty wounded; of the loyal forces, three were killed and eleven wounded.[15]

The causes of the mutiny remained obscure, but there were indications that both Social Democrats and Socialist Revolutionaries had taken part in the agitation which preceded it. Wherever the guilt may have lain, the occasion gave extremists a new opportunity to stir up the population. Wildly exaggerated reports of casualties among the mutineers, sent along the railroad telegraph, led to strikes and protest meetings. On November 16 another general strike was proclaimed.

GENERAL PRASOLOV'S "CRUSADE"

The reports of the Tashkent mutiny reverberated loudest at the remote fortress of Kushka, on the Afghan border, served by a branch rail line from Merv. Earlier in the month agitators had already started holding meetings of railroad employees regarding economic matters, and when the tie-up of railroad and post and telegraph facilities occurred on November 16 the meetings took on a political character. Fearing a rebellion among his troops, the commander of the 5,000-man garrison, Major General V. P. Pra-

solov, ordered several of the extremists jailed, but others harangued the populace and troops. The strikers intercepted Prasolov's reports to the oblast commandant at Askhabad and the
fortress commander found himself cut off from the world. On
November 18, in defiance of his orders, 200 of his men attended
a meeting of railroad workers at which a resolution was passed
demanding that all military commanders at the fortress be replaced by elected officers. Prasolov thereupon declared the fortress
in a state of siege and arrested the most active participants in the
meetings. Intent on restoring communications with the rest of
Turkestan, he then set out at the head of a task force on a "cru-
sade" to free the Trans-Caspian Railroad from the revolutionists.
Prasolov first went to Merv, where he arrested members of the
local strike committee, and then to Chardzhui, where he took
additional prisoners. By this time news of Prasolov's actions had
been telegraphed all over the empire by the strikers, and a new
general strike was threatened if he was not stopped. Prasolov had
turned back and was headed for Askhabad to arrest the central
strike committee of Transcaspia oblast when the Imperial government finally got word to him to return to his post.[16]

After November there was a lull in the revolutionary disturbances in Turkestan. Many strike leaders were jailed or in hiding,
and few heeded the call of the Moscow and St. Petersburg
Soviets and the All-Russian Union of Railroad Workers on December 6 for another strike. In Transcaspia, General Usakovskii,
the oblast commandant, was removed from office to be tried for
his inactivity in the November disorders. His more energetic
successor, General V. A. Kosagovskii, instituted a cleanup of
radical elements. Public meetings were forbidden, funerals and
requiem masses were allowed only with permission of the police,
and homes were searched for arms.[17] There were isolated outbreaks, such as the disorders in the Turkestan Pontoon Regiment
at Khodzhent on December 25–27, and there were demonstrations in towns throughout Turkestan on January 9, 1906, the
anniversary of "Bloody Sunday," but in general the government
was again in formal, although not firm control.

Soon, however, the revolutionaries received encouragement

from an unexpected quarter, with the arrival in Tashkent of a new governor-general, General D. I. Subotich. In an apparent effort to pacify the dissident elements, Subotich announced publicly that he condemned terroristic methods, but stood for the unconditional right of each citizen "to express, propagate, and struggle for the adoption of his views with all means permitted by an orderly civilized society." [18] Subotich's efforts at appeasement produced exactly the opposite of the effect he intended. The leftist legal press again became sensational and provocative, the underground press increased its activity, and fiery public meetings once more became common.

Hard times favored radical trends. In Tashkent there was already a surplus of workers, but new groups kept arriving from European Russia, hungry, ragged, and dependent on local charity. Wages fell for both Russians and natives.[19] In Askhabad members of a force of 700 laborers recruited for construction work in Kushka, but discharged after the disorders there, began arriving in a destitute condition.[20]

To add to the disquiet of the times, crime increased among the natives, with a wave of robberies, burglaries, and horse thefts. On January 25 a band of native robbers murdered Major General Dzhura-Bek, a leader of the native resistance against the Russians in the early days of the conquest, who after many years of service with the Russian army was living out his retirement near Tashkent. On February 2 a native convict named Namaz led a mass break of fifty inmates from the Samarkand oblast prison, and during the weeks that followed became an almost legendary figure, perpetrating one robbery after another and eluding all pursuit until he was killed on June 1, 1907.[21]

Aided by Subotich's tolerance, radical political elements were prompt to take advantage of the distress and unrest. As fast as the police arrested dissidents, they were out of jail again on bail; as fast as radical newspapers were closed, their names were changed and they reappeared. The revolutionary elements were able to make up for their lack of numbers by their audacity, persistence, singleness of purpose, and skillful use of legal safeguards provided by the very system they sought to destroy. The state, on the other hand, had an overwhelming preponderance of power at its disposal but was incredibly tolerant of arrant subversion. The independent judiciary frequently nullified the efforts of administrators to take forthright action toward radicals. Many officials were uncertain of the interpretation of the new laws regarding freedom of the press and of speech or hesitated to take action.

Among the revolutionists, party affiliations were still fluid at this time. The Socialist Revolutionaries, who appealed to both peasants and railroad workers, were the most numerous, but the RSDLP, although concentrating mainly on the workers and beginning to divide into Bolshevik and Menshevik wings, had greater discipline and more unified leadership.

At the end of February, 1906, several of the Social Democratic groups in the region met in the First Regional Conference of the Turkestan Organizations of the RSDLP. At the conference the local groups voted to unite into a Union of Turkestan Organizations of the RSDLP, headed by a "United Committee." This committee was to take the lead in coördinating work of the various organizations in the region in publishing, agitation, and propaganda and in communicating with the central institutions of the party. After the conference the Union of Turkestan Organizations officially entered the RSDLP, submitting thenceforth to the central organizations of the party, and sending delegations to the general party congresses and conferences. In April, 1906, three delegates from Turkestan, including two Bolsheviks and one Menshevik, attended the Fourth (Uniting) Congress of the party at Stockholm.

The lull in revolutionary manifestations in Turkestan in the spring of 1906 ended on May Day. Spurred on by appeals in clandestine leaflets, workers at various towns held one-day strikes and demonstrations. At Tashkent, 800 workers in the main railroad repair shops and at the railroad depot struck in defiance of police orders. The railroad management proclaimed that a fine would be levied on those who had left work. The workers protested, and on May 21 a crowd of them gathered in the office of the chief of the repair shops, the engineer N. O. Shpakovskii, asking that the fine be lifted. When Shpakovskii claimed that only the chief of the Middle Asian Railroad, General Ul'ianin, had authority to do this, a worker came up behind him and slipped a coal sack over his head. At this the crowd vanished in all directions.

The indignity became a byword. Ul'ianin demanded the name of the culprit, but although there were 800 witnesses he was not reported. On June 3, in accordance with telegraphed orders from the Ministry of Communications, all of the workers in the shop were discharged, but this too proved of no avail. When the government tried to recruit a new force only a handful of workers signed up and railroad troops brought from Chardzhui refused to work. This solidarity, combined with difficulties in other quarters, finally forced the government to abandon the principle at stake and on July 9 to reopen the repair shops and rehire all of the workers. The fine for participation in the May Day demonstrations was rescinded, and partial back pay was given.[22]

RENEWED STRIKES AND TROOP DISORDERS
(JUNE, 1906)

In June serious troop disorders flared up in Transcaspia. On June 13 the members of the Second Transcaspian Rifle Battalion took up arms in protest against the sentencing of three of their comrades to a disciplinary battalion. They gave their commander a thirty-five-point ultimatum for improvement of their service and living conditions, and when this was not met by June 15 they elected new officers from their own ranks. On the same day, troops of the First Transcaspian Railroad Battalion left their work at Askhabad station and met to formulate demands. On June 16, when two companies of the Third Transcaspian Rifle Battalion were sent to disarm the mutineers they fraternized instead, and soon the whole crowd marched on the railroad station singing revolutionary songs, crying "Kill the officers!" "Kill the vampires!" Other units encamped around Askhabad fell into a similar state of disorder. Only on June 18, when loyal troops were finally concentrated at Askhabad, did the rebellious troops lay down their arms. Over 500 soldiers were subsequently tried for participation in the mutinies.[23]

Two weeks later, fresh trouble broke out among troops at Tashkent. On July 3, 1906, eighteen men who had taken part in the troop mutiny of November, 1905, were taken to the Tashkent station under Cossack guard for transport to hard-labor camps in Siberia. A crowd, including many railroad workers, gathered on the station platform to demonstrate sympathy for the arrested men. Orators harangued the crowd concerning the "fighters for freedom," until the cry went up "Off with their chains!" When the prisoners claimed that they had not eaten for three days and would not board the train unless fed, the crowd protested until the commander of the guard detachment gave in and had the prisoners given food and tea on the station platform. The crowd then delayed the train by standing in the way and by throwing ties on the rails. They might have attempted to free the prisoners had not the Bolshevik editor, M. V. Morozov, urged them to desist and avoid retaliation by the troops. Accompanied by many last farewells, the train finally departed and the crowd dispersed.

In the meantime reports of the disturbance reached the soldiers of the Turkestan and Transcaspian Sapper Battalions, in camp about six kilometers away. The sappers grabbed their rifles and went at a run toward the station, determined to help liberate the prisoners, who were by then rolling toward Orenburg. When the sappers arrived they found not a mob but other troops, hastily summoned to the scene, deployed around the station. Some of the sappers opened fire, which was answered by the defending troops. After one sapper was killed and fifteen wounded, the others threw down their arms and fled back to their camp, where they surrendered.[24]

During the remainder of July there were disorders among troops at Chardzhui (July 11), at Novyi Margelan (July 15), at Krasnovodsk (July 16), and at Samarkand (July 25). At the same time meetings were held by radical groups in all the towns, at which agitators roused their listeners against the government. A congress of workers on the Trans-Caspian and Orenburg-Tashkent railroad lines, held in Tashkent in July, had a clearly revolutionary character; the railroad committee at Kyzyl-Arvat called itself a "Soviet of Workers' Deputies," and that at Perovsk was known as the "Perovsk Revolutionary Committee." [25] In addition, terrorists became increasingly active, so that no official, from the governor-general down to the ordinary policeman, could feel safe from a sudden onslaught by a bomb or pistol.

SUPPRESSION OF THE REVOLUTIONARY MOVEMENT

Gradually the government began to regain control. For excessive mildness in dealing with the disorders, General Subotich, the governor-general, and General Sakharov, his assistant, were both relieved of their duties, along with a shake-up in other posts.[26] Lieutenant General E. O. Matsievskii, appointed acting governor-general, hastened the arrest of key figures in the revolutionary movement and their banishment from the region in batches by administrative procedure, which avoided the use of the courts. In September, 1906, he asked for and obtained proclamation of a state of "extraordinary protection" throughout Fergana oblast and in a strip all along the Trans-Caspian Railroad, including the main towns from Krasnovodsk to Tashkent. This made it possible to sentence criminals within hours after their apprehension, even to the extent of the death penalty, and to employ strong measures to banish revolutionists and crush their organizations.[27]

Acting with this new vigor, the government was at last able to put down the revolutionary movement in the region, at least for the time being. Between October and December, 1906, most of the Social Democratic organizations in Turkestan were broken up, although the popular strength of the party was shown in the election of three Social Democratic deputies to the Second State Duma in elections held on January 27, 1907. Nevertheless, as an organized force the party had to cease its activity. The same fate befell the Socialist Revolutionaries. Some members of both parties formed small, independently operating cells designed to carry on terroristic activities. However, even this desperate recourse had no more than nuisance value for the revolutionary cause, and it merely increased the determination of officials to stamp out all revolutionary manifestations.

Attempts at revolution failed in Central Asia just as they did throughout the rest of the empire. The events in this region have been magnified in the many Soviet works describing the 1905–1907 period, but except for the period of the general strike of October, 1905, and the troop mutinies of June, 1906, the government retained control. The Imperial state was still too strong, the habit of regarding it as a part of the nature of things was too firmly ingrained in the popular mind, and the revolutionary groups were still too weak and inexperienced for any overthrow to be possible.

Nevertheless, the experience of 1905 and 1906 was of supreme importance as a dress rehearsal for what was to come only a decade later. Conservatism prevailed for a time, especially under Stolypin's premiership, but the revolutionaries could look forward to a time when national exhaustion, official vacillation, and popular discontent would again favor the ends of small but resolute dissident groups.

DURING the revolutionary years of 1905 and 1906 most of the
Central Asian natives remained apart from the events which were
threatening to shatter the Imperial edifice. The Russian political
crisis meant little to the illiterate native mass, accustomed to
accept its subject status with resignation, and no ishan arose to
try to profit from the Russian preoccupation by a call to a Holy
War.

To the small group of native intellectuals, however, the unsuccessful revolution brought a surge of new ideas more in keeping
with twentieth century realities and an opportunity for leadership. On the whole, the Russian empire-builders strove to bind
the Central Asians to Russia by cultural penetration in the face
of rigid conservative opposition, but some elements of native
society slowly assimilated new ideas and influences brought by
the conqueror. To a certain degree this was the *sblizhenie,* or
"drawing closer" which the Russians sought; but what the natives
were undergoing held greater significance as a general modernization of culture and outlook. In this process they drew closer
not only to the Russians but to the rest of the world.

Such modernization posed great difficulties. The Tatars and
certain other non-Russian peoples in the empire had developed
in this direction in the course of prolonged contact with Western
culture. The Central Asians, on the other hand, had to start almost
from the beginning, handicapped at the outset by their reluctance
to accept strange ways, and by the lack of facilities to aid in the
change.

The first natives affected by the new influences were members of the Kazakh aristocracy who found it advantageous to maintain the Russian favor. The Russians bought their support by giving them high military rank and subsidies in the form of salaries and pensions. They were also encouraged to have their sons educated in the Russian schools. Their sons, usually with the aid of stipends from the state, attended the various Cadet Corps schools, and later the Russian high schools which began to be established in the second half of the nineteenth century at Orenburg, Omsk, and other Steppe towns.

Compared with the total native population the number who made use of such facilities was very small. Those who did, already distinct from the mass of the population because of their noble birth, became increasingly isolated because of their education. They usually lacked acquaintance with the native culture and were often not proficient in their native tongue. Outstanding in this small group was the Sultan Chokan Chingisovich Valikhanov (1835–1865). He was a grandson of Ablai, the last khan of the Middle and Great Hordes of the Kazakhs. Valikhanov was educated in the Omsk Cadet Corps, learned Russian, German, French, Turkish, and Persian, wrote extensively in scientific journals, and distinguished himself in Russian service. He was one of the first to explore Kashgaria.[1] His nephew, the Sultan Gazi Bulatovich Vali-Khan (d. 1908), also trained in the Omsk Cadet Corps, aided in the subjugation of the Kirgiz tribes of Semirechie, served under General Cherniaev at the taking of the Kokandian fortress of Aulie-Ata, and was subsequently for over twenty years a colonel in the First Cossack Life Guard Regiment in St. Petersburg.[2]

A similar long service record was that of Sultan Mukhammed-zhan Baimukhammedov (d. 1896), great-grandson of Abul-Khair, the last khan of the Small Horde. Commissioned as an army officer with the rank of *cornet* (second lieutenant) in 1841, he eventually became a major general. He served under Cherniaev at the taking of Tashkent and for many years was an administrator of the Orenburg Kazakhs.

During the second half of the nineteenth century the gap between this group and the majority of the population began to be filled by a group of more modest rank. These, after education in the Russian public schools established in Central Asia, entered government service as interpreters, translators, and in other minor official capacities. Ibragim Altynsarin, previously mentioned in connection with his efforts toward native education, was a prime example of this group. Son of an elder of the Kipchak clan of the Middle Horde, grandson of an eminent *bii*, Altynsarin attended the Kazakh school at Orenburg between the years 1850 and 1857. He subsequently served the Russian administration as interpreter, teacher in the schools for natives, clerk in the Turgai uezd administration, uezd judge, assistant uezd commandant, and, from 1879 until his death, inspector of schools in Turgai oblast.

Another Kazakh, Tleu Seidalin, trained in the Orenburg Nepliuev Cadet Corps, became an assistant uezd commandant of Turgai uezd. Still another, Shagimarden Miriasovich Ibragimov, published a number of articles on Central Asian ethnography, and in 1891 was appointed to the post of Russian consul at Jidda. The "Kazakh Pushkin," Abai Kunanbaev (1845–1904), although born in a nomad tribe of Semipalatinsk oblast and educated in Moslem schools, secretly learned Russian and became friendly with several Russian political exiles. He also translated works of Pushkin, Lermontov, Krylov, and other writers into his native tongue.

Among the settled natives of Turkestan, similar individuals appeared who were willing to "draw closer" to the conquerors. However, in that region the process started later than in the Steppe and was hindered by the higher degree of advancement of the native culture, which gave its adherents more scope to resist the new ideas.

Many Uzbeks who were prominent at the time of the Russian conquest, even those who led in the resistance, were won to the Russian cause by preferential treatment. Dzhura-Bek (d. 1906) and Baba-Bek (d. 1898), both Bukharan provincial governors, were given high rank and permitted to serve in the Russian army. Both retired on pensions, Dzhura-Bek with the rank of major general and Baba-Bek as a colonel. Mirza Khakim, once a Kokandian ambassador, was decorated by the Russians and eventually given the rank of actual counsellor of state (*deistvitel'nyi statskii sovetnik*), a civil rank corresponding to that of major general. Mukhitdin (d. 1902), the son of the former chief judge (*kazi-kalian*) of Tashkent, served the Russians as judge in the native section of Tashkent. Two of his sons were educated in the Russian-native schools.[3]

Other natives, chiefly among the commercial classes, were quick to realize the advantages to be gained by association with the conquerors. Said-Azim, a wealthy Tashkent merchant who had learned Russian during trading expeditions to Orenburg and Troitsk before the conquest, assumed the role of interpreter and mediator between the Russians and the native population. He was treated well by Russian and native alike because each thought he enjoyed great influence with the other. Two of his sons served in the Tashkent City Duma, and in 1906 one was a candidate for the State Duma.[4]

These members of native society who drew closer to the conqueror were mostly of the wealthier classes. They had undergone greater exposure to Western ideas and had more reason to accept them. They profited from coöperation with the Russians and could thus afford to live in the Russian section of town, furnish their houses in European style, drive in carriages, and send their sons to Russian schools. A few visited European Russia and even Western Europe. Theirs was a gradual transition and a piecemeal one. They took what they pleased from Russian culture. One Uzbek merchant, described by Ostroumov, lived in the Russian section of Tashkent. Half of his house was built in the Russian style with windows opening on the street, but the other half, containing the women's quarters, was built in the native style with only a blank wall facing outward.[5]

Such individuals, bridging the gap between two cultures, were of course an insignificant minority in the total population, much smaller than similar minorities among Moslem peoples under Russian rule for a longer period. But the growing number of these in Central Asia showed that there too the elements of change could take hold. Therein lay the only hope the natives could have for attaining a more independent national existence. Modernization was essential for coping with the more advanced society which had achieved dominion over them. Paradoxically, however, in modernizing they lost some of the very elements of difference which had made foreign dominion seem so inimical in the first place. Their situation showed the paradox and dilemma of any people conquered by a more advanced society. They had to modernize, yet the only practical means to do so was to acquire for themselves the culture of the very people whom they opposed. Before they could lighten or throw off the burden of Russian rule they had first to accept the tutelage of the ruling power and become at least partially Russified.

Even Bukhara, the stronghold of conservatism, was not proof against new ideas. Akhmed Makhdum Donish (1827–1897) was a Bukharan statesman and poet who in consequence of official visits to St. Petersburg became a Russophile and advocate of reform. He attracted a small group of followers, who transmitted or developed his views.[6]

Central Asians receptive to new influences found kindred spirits among other Moslem peoples of the empire. During the second half of the nineteenth century a stirring began among all of these peoples, a distant reverberation of the contemporary nationalism of Europe, a restlessness at living under infidel rule, a growing awareness that while the rest of the world moved on, they had been standing still.

This restlessness took many forms, varying in strength and effectiveness from one region to another. For the Moslems of Russian Central Asia, by Western standards among the most conservative and backward of the entire Moslem world, these influences were importations rather than of native origin. Nevertheless, an advance made by one group became an advance for all; a protest measure on the Volga or in the Caucasus had repercussions in Central Asia. The process was slow because of geographical disunity and cultural backwardness, but it was accelerating.

The Volga and Crimean Tatars took the lead. Living close to the Russians for a long period they had absorbed more Western culture and generally had a higher living standard than other Moslems in the empire. Many gained considerable wealth from trade along the Volga and by acting as intermediaries in trade between Russia and Central Asia. They penetrated all parts of the Moslem world for purposes of trade and made pilgrimages to Mecca and to Constantinople. Thus many were able to contrast the Islamic and the Christian worlds, and to reflect on the need to ease the shortcomings of the first by what might be desirable in the second. Throughout the regions of Russia inhabited by Moslems, the Tartars carried not only an intensified Islamic faith, but convictions concerning the need for unity and reform.

DZHADIDISM

Prominent among the advocates of change was the remarkable Crimean Tatar, Ismail Bey Gaspirali (1851–1914), or, as known by the Russianized form of his name, Gasprinskii. Treading carefully to avoid trouble with the Russian censorship and political police, Gasprinskii became a leading advocate of Turko-Tatar unity and of modernization of the Moslem way of life. He urged Moslem school reform on the European model, a general Turkish literary language to be used in a national press among all the Turkic peoples of Russia, and, more noteworthy still, the emancipation of women. The term for the system of instruction which he devised for the Moslem schools, *usul' dzhadid,* or "new method," came to be applied to Gasprinskii's entire program, the adherents of which became known as *Dzhadids.* His newspaper *Terdzhiman* (The Translator), circulated widely among the Moslems of Russia, including those of Central Asia.[7]

Gasprinskii's practical program was welcomed in Central Asia by the handful of native thinkers who had already begun to entertain reformist views. In Tashkent the Imam Munevver Kari (1880–1933) opened in 1901 the first dzhadid school in Turkestan, organized a welfare society to send students to Constantinople and to Azerbaidzhan (this was soon forbidden by the authorities), and in 1902 wrote a textbook which became standard in dzhadid schools. He and Abdullah Avlani, Makhmud Khodzha Bekbudi, Akhmad Khodzha Vasli, and other reformers worked covertly against the influence of several native literary figures whom N. P. Ostroumov, editor of the *Turkestanskaia tuzemnaia gazeta,* had attracted as co-workers in an endeavor to create pro-Russian sympathies among the populace.[8] In 1903 Bekbudi opened a dzhadid school in Samarkand.[9]

The Russo-Japanese War and the revolution of 1905–1907 gave the native reform movement its first major impetus. It was the beginning of a time of change for the entire Moslem world. Nationalism and constitutionalism were on the march in Turkey, Persia, Egypt, and Morocco. The Moslem peoples were becoming aware that they could not keep their national individuality and preserve their cultural heritage without themselves marching with the rest of the world. Developments rising from this awareness transcended not only the reactionary Pan-Islamic movement but the chimerical goals of the Pan-Turk and Pan-Arab movements. The Central Asians shared in this cultural awakening and groping for nationhood.

THE MOSLEM CONGRESSES AND THE STATE DUMA

Between August 15 and 28, 1905, the first All-Russian Moslem Congress met illegally in Nizhnii Novgorod, convening on the steamer "Gustav Struve" on the river Oka. The Congress considered the main needs of the Moslems in the Russian Empire and organized a so-called Russian General Moslem Party (*Russkaia obshche-musul'manskaia partiia*). A second All-Russian Moslem Congress, meeting secretly in St. Petersburg on January 13–26, 1906, decided to work with the moderates in the Russian political parties then forming. It announced itself as representing a union of the Moslems of all Russia, organized at one central and sixteen regional points, and made plans for subsequent annual general congresses. In this organization, meeting as a self-appointed body of popular leaders to discuss national problems, can be seen a parallel to the Indian National Congress which had been meeting since 1885. If other events had worked out differently, the Russian body might ultimately have played a similar role.

The State Duma, promised in August, 1905, and given definite form in the October Manifesto, allotted the Moslems of Russia only thirty-six seats, far less than was proportionate to their number in the population. However, it provided them for the first time with a means of voicing their grievances to the entire country and of working toward their goals within the framework of the Imperial government. The elections to the First Duma took place in the spring of 1906. The election rules for Turkestan arrived too late for voting to take place there; in the Kazakh Steppe the limited franchise kept many natives from exercising the suffrage, but the elections generated wide interest. Speaking in the open air, often from horseback, candidates in the Steppe discussed land reform and urged the abolition of the Steppe governor-generalship and the establishment of self-government. In Turkestan influential Uzbeks jockeyed for power.

Five Russians and four Kazakhs were elected to the Duma from the Steppe oblasts. The Kazakhs included: for Ural'sk oblast —Alpyspai Kal'menovich Kalmenev, a jurist of the well-to-do native class; Turgai oblast—Akhmed Kurgambekovich Berem-zhanov, a justice of the peace; Akmolinsk oblast—Kulmanov, a mulla; and Semipalatinsk oblast—Alikhan Bukeikhanov, an agron-omist.[10]

The Duma met on May 10, 1906. Of the thirty-six Moslem deputies elected, only twenty-four arrived in St. Petersburg in time to take part in the sessions. Instead of adhering to any one party they formed a separate nonparty Moslem "fraction" led by the Baku deputy Topchibashev, who had been a leader in the two All-Russian Moslem Congresses. By thus acting as a group the members of the "fraction" were able to attract more attention to the problems of their constituents.[11]

The First Duma was dissolved on July 9, 1906, for being too radical. The Kazakh deputy Bukeikhanov arrived in St. Peters-burg on the same day. He followed the other deputies to Viborg, where he signed the manifesto protesting the dissolution. He later spent three months in jail in Semipalatinsk for having done so.[12]

Between August 16 and 21, 1906, the third All-Russian Moslem Congress met in Nizhnii Novgorod, this time with official authorization. The primary aim of the conclave was to work out a program for an All-Moslem party. The delegates formed the *Ittifak*, or Union of Moslems of Russia, with the program adopted in the congress of January, 1906. The party was to have an executive committee of fifteen members, with a permanent bureau of three members to be located in St. Petersburg. The congress also adopted a detailed program aimed at a complete transformation of the Moslem schools and their transfer from clerical to secular control. The new schools were to be managed by special uezd, gubernia, or oblast *medzhlises*, or councils, which were governed in turn by a higher council (*makhama islamiia*).[13]

The congress of August, 1906, marked the peak in the comparatively liberal conditions for the Moslems of Russia which followed the revolutionary disturbances of 1905. The coöperation of the Moslem "fraction" with the Kadets (Constitutional Democrats) in the Duma, and the liberal character of the Nizhnii Novgorod Congress made conservative circles in the government uneasy. The proposed party was refused official sanction, many Moslem newspapers were forced to discontinue, and some Moslem political leaders were prosecuted.

The Second Duma, which met on March 5, 1907, included thirty-one Moslem deputies. Of these four were from the Steppe and six from Turkestan. They were: for Ural'sk oblast, Bakhit-Dzhan Besalievich Karataev; Turgai oblast, Akhmet Kurgambekovich Beremzhanov (re-elected); Akmolinsk oblast, Shaimordan Koshchegulov; Semipalatinsk oblast, Khadzhi-Temir-Gali-Tiutevich Norokonev; Semirechie oblast, Mukhamedzhan Tynyshpaev; Tashkent, Abdu-Vakhit Kariev; Syr-Daria oblast, Tleuli Allabergnev; Fergana oblast, Salikhdzhan Mukhammed-zhanov; Transcaspia oblast, Makhdum-Kuli-Khan Nur-Berdyk-hanov; and Samarkand oblast, Tashpulat Abdukhalilov.[14] Three of the deputies—Karataev, Beremzhanov, and Tynyshpaev—had higher educations. Karataev, an examining magistrate, spoke eloquently before the Duma for a curtailment of seizures of Kazakh lands. Tynyshpaev, only twenty-seven and a communications engineer, was later prominent in the movements for native autonomy or independence after the revolution of October, 1917. The other deputies were educated in the native schools, and some of those from Turkestan could speak no Russian.

Already weakened as compared to the group in the First Duma, the Moslem "fraction" became even less effective when six of the more radical deputies left to form a Moslem Workers' Group, which voted with the *Trudoviks* (Group of Toil, a left-wing Russian peasant group) and the Socialist Revolutionaries.[15]

The dissolution of the Second Duma on June 16, 1907, was followed by a new electoral law which reduced the number of Moslem deputies to only ten, and entirely deprived Turkestan and the Kazakh Steppe of representation. The political expression of the natives of Central Asia was thereafter limited to what could be done by the now insignificant Moslem fraction made up of deputies from other regions of Russia. At the end of 1907, for example, conferences of liberal Kazakh intelligentsia in Kustanai, Troitsk, and other Steppe towns worked out demands regarding the needs of the Kazakh people. These were sent to the Moslem fraction for use in preparing a report for presentation to the Third Duma. The report included demands for cessation of peasant colonization in the Steppe, freedom of religious teaching, freedom to publish newspapers, and the right to elect deputies.[16] During the Fourth Duma the brilliant young Kazakh, Mustafa Chokaev (1890–1941), then studying law at the University of St. Petersburg, worked in the office of the Moslem fraction and sometimes aided the Moslem deputies in the preparation of their speeches.[17]

Once called forth, Moslem political activity in Russia did not die out. From 1905 onward, new ideas were placed before the people; the intelligentsia gained experience in political methods, and a flourishing Moslem press appeared. Having made some strides toward modernization and national self-determination in the course of the revolution of 1905–1906, the Moslems of Russia, including those of Central Asia, could anticipate further gains from new Imperial crises.

TOWARD CULTURAL REFORM

Although political opportunities were curtailed, there remained a broad field for development and reform in the cultural sphere of

Moslem life. The Dzhadids, propounders of the "new method" of Moslem education with which they hoped to bring about a Turko-Tatar and Islamic cultural revival, continued their efforts despite repression by the government and the opposition of the reactionary Moslem clergy. By 1908 there were ninety-two Dzhadid mektebs in Syr-Daria, Fergana, and Samarkand oblasts, including thirty-five in the cities of Tashkent, Samarkand, Kokand, and Andizhan. By 1912 the twelve mektebs in Tashkent had more than a thousand pupils.[18] Proceeding in the face of conservative opposition and with only private means, this was a considerable achievement, especially when compared to the rate of growth of the Russian-native schools.

Besides "pulling itself up by its bootstraps" with regard to education, the native intelligentsia was also developing and propagating its ideas by writing and publishing. At the end of 1905 the first Dzhadid newspaper *Urto Oziening umrguzorligi* (Middle Asian Observer) appeared in Tashkent. In the summer of 1906 Tatar nationalists published twenty numbers of *Tarakki* (Progress) before the paper was suspended by the authorities. In September, 1906, the paper *Khurshid* (Sun) edited by Munevver Kari, appeared, but was closed in November when the region was put under a state of "extraordinary protection."

In 1907, Abdulla Avlani, Bekbudi and other Dzhadids put out the first of 10 issues of *Shukhrat* (Glory); in 1908 *Azie* (Asia) and *Tudzhor* (Trader) appeared briefly; in 1912 the papers *Bukhoroi Sherif* (Bukhara the Noble) (153 issues) and *Turon* (Turan) (94 issues) appeared in Bukhara. In 1913–1915 the literary magazine *Oina* (Mirror) and in 1914 the newspaper *Samarkand* (45 issues), both edited by Bekbudi, appeared in Samarkand. In 1914, the newspaper *Sadoi-Fergana* (Voice of Fergana) (123 issues), appeared in Kokand; and in 1914–1915, *Sadoi-Turkiston* (Voice of Turkestan), edited by Ubaidulla Khodzha and Munevver Kari, appeared in Tashkent. In 1915, *Al-Islakh* (Reform), appeared in Tashkent; and in 1916, *Yurt* (The Homeland) appeared in Kokand.[19] Harried by the conservative Moslem clergy, the Russian censors, and lack of funds, most of these were ephemeral, but each contributed to the spread of new ideas.

In the Steppe, one issue of the newspaper *Kazakh* appeared in
Troitsk in the summer of 1907. In 1911, *Kazakhstan* (4 issues) appeared in Urda, and again in 1913 (14 issues), in Ural'sk. In
1913, *Ishim dalasy*, occupied with the land question, appeared
in Petropavlovsk. The editors of two other newspapers were skillful enough with regard to the censorship to continue for a longer
period. From 1911 to 1915 the newspaper *Ai-Kap* (88 issues),
edited by M. Seralin, appeared at Troitsk. It was devoted to literature and the awakening of national sentiments.[20] In 1912, Akhmed
Baitursunov, Miriakup Dulatov, Alikhan Bukeikhanov, and other
leaders of the Kazakh intelligentsia began publication in Orenburg of a second newspaper *Kazakh* which appeared until 1917.
It developed ideas earlier expressed by Dulatov in his collection
of poems *Uyan Kazakh!* (Awake, Kazakh!) written in 1906 after
the Russian defeat in the Far East, and published in 1910.
Dulatov compared an idealized past of the Kazakhs with the present, and advocated educational reform, the emancipation of
women, a Kazakh press, a halt to the seizure of Kazakh lands, and
a central religious administration.[21] The newspaper criticized the
native intelligentsia for having lost contact with the common
people and for having become preoccupied with office and rank,
and indicted the government for its Russification policies and the
displacement of Kazakhs by Russian colonists. It attacked conservative circles for Pan-Islamism; it urged military service for
the Kirgiz and Kazakhs, more schools, and the transition of the
nomads to a settled life.[22] Within the group, Bukeikhanov sought
to direct attention first to economic problems and to decide political problems along with Russian liberals, chiefly the Kadets,
whereas others sought to unite the Kazakhs with the other Turkic
peoples of Russia.[23] In 1916 this group formed the Alash-Orda
party (The Horde of Alash, taking the name of a legendary
Kazakh leader), which during the civil war following the revolution of October, 1917, constituted for a time an independent
Kazakh government.

Thus, following the turn of the century a cultural and political
awakening took place among the natives of Central Asia. Originally based upon concepts borrowed from the ruling people, the

Russians, by 1914 this movement had already veered away from the Russian goal of having the natives "draw closer" with a view toward eventual amalgamation, and its adherents were striving toward new goals of a nationalist character.

PART FIVE

Imperial Twilight

XVII

IN RUSSIAN CENTRAL ASIA, as in most of the world, the year 1914 marked the end of an era. Economic development, the spread of new ideas, and the revolutionary outbreaks of 1905 had all portended change, but the old order had continued. Now in the cataclysm of World War I the tempo of life was to be tremendously accelerated and many of the ideals and values of preceding decades were to be set aside or irrevocably modified.

At first little change was evident. The natives, like a number of other non-Russian peoples of the empire, were exempt from military service [1] and the mobilization affected only a small proportion of the Russian male population. Russians who had been born in Turkestan, or who had come there before the age of fifteen were also exempt, as were many who had come to the Steppe at the height of the colonization movement and received the six-year exemption from military service granted peasant colonists.

Among those called to service, however, was the governor-general of Turkestan, General of Cavalry A. V. Samsonov. Summoned while on sick leave in the Caucasus, Samsonov was given command of the hastily mobilized Russian Second Army and within a few weeks committed suicide after his troops suffered disastrous defeat at Tannenberg. General F. V. Martson became acting governor-general.

WAR PRISONERS AND REFUGEES

With the outbreak of war the movement of settlers from European Russia to Asiatic Russia declined sharply. In 1914, 336,339 persons crossed the Urals, including 241,814 colonists and 94,525 scouts, most of them before the outbreak of the war, but in 1915 only 28,185 made the journey, in 1916, 9,209, and in 1917, 4,820.[2] For the first time in decades the pressure of the landless and destitute on local administrations ceased, although resettlement officials continued to plan for a renewed flow of colonists.

Instead of colonists, large numbers of prisoners and refugees were transported to Central Asia. Following the Russian victories in Galicia in September, 1914, about 25,000 Austro-Hungarians were confined in camps at Cheliabinsk, Orenburg, Petropavlovsk, Ust'-Kamenogorsk, and other points on the northern edge of the Steppe. About 200,000 were sent to some twenty-five camps in Turkestan, chiefly at various places in Fergana oblast, but also at Perovsk, Troitsk, Katta-Kurgan, Samarkand, Askhabad, and Krasnovodsk.

Prisoners of Slavic extraction (Czechs, Slovaks, and others) enjoyed comparative freedom, but those of Germanic and Hungarian extraction were closely guarded. Part of the pattern of our time, appalling conditions reigned in the camps. Inefficiency, the theft of funds for the care of the prisoners, and callousness on the part of some Russian officials in charge of the camps resulted in hunger and epidemics among inmates. Nearly 40,000 prisoners died. Finally, at the urging of foreign Red Cross workers most of the survivors were sent to camps in Siberia (where thousands more died of typhus). By the autumn of 1917 only 38,000 remained in Turkestan.[3]

The Russians were apprehensive at having so many of the enemy present in their midst, but the prisoners presented no threat to the security of the region. Racked by hunger and sickness, sweltering in stockades on treeless steppe and desert, they were under strict guard and had little contact with either the Russian or native population. Escape was almost impossible because of the desert terrain and the unfamiliarity of the prisoners with the language of the natives. Kazakhs and Turkmen in the vicinities were paid bounties by camp commandants for the capture and return of fugitives.[4]

In 1915, thousands of refugees from the western part of the

empire, including many Poles and Belorussians, were brought from the zone of operations and placed in camps throughout Turkestan. The climate and inadequate facilities soon caused a death toll rivaling that of the war prisoners. During the following spring the government hastened to send 55,000 back to European Russia before the onset of the summer heat.[5]

ECONOMIC STRESS

The economic impact of the war was soon felt in Turkestan and the Steppe. At the beginning Russia's cotton imports virtually ceased and the country became dependent on its own production. To avoid a drastic rise, the government fixed the price of raw cotton at a level 50 per cent higher than that of 1913. However, nothing was done about the cost of grain, which kept rising until by 1916 it was nearly 400 per cent above that of 1913. The difference between prices for cotton and foodstuffs made many native peasants demand a supplementary payment from cotton merchants, but others fell into the hands of moneylenders and their properties were sold for debt. The cost of goods processed or manufactured in European Russia, such as sugar, clothing, shoes, and other necessities, rose 200–400 per cent, and there was widespread speculation.

Higher taxes and the requisitioning of goods for military use also contributed to the rise in living costs. From January 1, 1915, a 21 per cent supplementary war tax was levied on the natives of Turkestan in view of the fact that they were not obliged to give military service. The Kazakhs of Turkestan had to pay not only the usual tax of three rubles for local needs (*zemskii sbor*) and the kibitka tax of three rubles, but a war tax of three rubles and an additional kibitka tax of fifty kopecks. The government also requisitioned horses, camels, carts, yurts, and large quantities of commodities, all paid for at fixed prices which were usually far lower than those of the market. For example, a horse which would bring 150 to 200 rubles on the market would be purchased for 30 to 50 rubles by the government. Instead of the ten to twelve rubles paid for a sheep on the market, the government paid four to six rubles.[6]

Labor also was requisitioned. In some places in Semirechie, Kazakhs cut and gathered the hay and harvested grain for the families of Russians called to service. Men and transport were mobilized to carry loads of state property, such as requisitioned grain, to the railroads.[7]

Corrupt officials often failed to pay the natives the money allotted by the government for requisitioned goods and services. Meat, housing, and transport appropriated for the use of troops passing through a district were thus frequently a total loss to the owners. Yurts taken "temporarily" were usually never seen again or were returned broken or without felt.

Besides taxes, goods, and services, the government exacted considerable amounts of money from the natives in the form of "voluntary contributions" to further the war effort. In actuality, large sums were never reported, for such "contributions" became another excuse for local Russian and native officials to line their own pockets.[8]

TROUBLE AT KHIVA

In addition to the usual exploitation and corruption of Russian and native officials the war brought the average native additional hardship. In spite of these added inducements to discontent, however, and the consequent increased possibility of native outbreaks, war needs made necessary the transfer of part of the troops regularly stationed in Turkestan. Some units of Semirechie Cossacks served throughout the war on the Persian front, fighting the Turks.

The weakening of Russian armed strength furnished an opportunity for the settling of old scores within the khanate of Khiva. The Turkmen of the khanate had been restive for some years because of high taxes and infringement on their water rights. In 1913, under their leader Mukhammed-Kurban-Serdar-Dzhunaid-Khan, better known simply as Dzhunaid Khan, they had attacked Khiva but had been beaten off by the khan's troops and Russian artillery.[9] Seeing his opportunity during the Russian preoccupation in Europe, in the spring of 1915 Dzhunaid Khan again marshaled his forces. The khan of Khiva asked the Russian authorities of Tashkent for arms or Russian troops, but was told that he would have to get along without them. In June, 1915, Dzhunaid Khan attacked and defeated the Khivans, inflicting a loss of 600 men. The assistant military governor of Syr-Daria oblast, Major General Geppener, was thereupon dispatched to the scene with a small force, and on July 26 managed to get an agreement between the two sides in which the khan of Khiva agreed to lower the taxes on the Turkmen. However, the question of water rights remained unsolved.

Later in the year conditions became worse for the Turkmen of Khiva. Pasture was poor due to lack of rain, and at the end of January, 1916, they again took up arms. This time the Tashkent government sent a punitive expedition under the military governor of Syr-Daria oblast, Lieutenant General Galkin, who had orders to give the Turkmen "a severe lesson." Before his forces could arrive on the scene, however, the Turkmen had attacked Khiva and entered the city, blockading the Russian garrison there. Galkin forced the Turkmen to retreat into the desert, inflicted severe reprisals on the Turkmen communities, and confiscated over 1,000,000 rubles worth of Turkmen property as an indemnity. Dzhunaid Khan and many of his followers escaped to Persia, where they remained until after the revolution of February, 1917.[10]

Besides troop withdrawals, the government was compelled to take yet another risk regarding the region's security. In 1915 and 1916, as an emergency measure caused by the lack of small arms in the fighting forces, the Ministry of War called in thousands of rifles issued in former years to Russian peasant reservists and Cossacks in Turkestan. For the moment the urgent needs at the front far outweighed the danger of disturbances among the natives, but the measure left many Russian communities defenseless in case of need.[11]

MANPOWER SHORTAGE

Steady deterioration of the military situation caused scrutiny of the long-standing exemption of the natives from military service. By the autumn of 1915 the heavy losses suffered by the Russian army caused discussion in Petrograd of a call-up of natives,[12] but by early 1916 the question was laid aside [13] in favor of other types of service which would tap the manpower reserve within the non-Russian population of the empire. There were appeals in the Duma for more extensive use of this reserve, for employment of the *inorodtsy* (non-Russians) and *tuzemtsy* (natives) at least for labor in the rear of the military forces, if not for active service. This was demanded as a "blood price" to compensate for the fact that the Russians were doing the fighting, defending those who were not required to shed their blood in the struggle.[14]

By June, 1916, there seemed to be no other recourse. In that month it was reported in a conference of the Imperial General Staff that the need for replacements amounted to 500,000 per month, but that the reserves totaled only 1,175,000, or less than would be required in three months. In order to free Russian troops from noncombat duty, to provide an additional number for use at the front, it was thereupon decided to draw on the non-Russian populations.[15] On June 25, 1916, an Imperial ukase was promulgated ordering a special draft of the native male population of Turkestan, Siberia, and other areas for construction of defense works and communication lines in the rear of the fighting forces.[16]

XVIII

CONCEIVED in desperation and executed in haste, the Imperial decree of June 25, 1916, drafting non-Russians for labor in the rear of the fighting forces soon brought about the gravest situation Russia had faced in Central Asia since its conquest.

EXECUTING THE LABOR DRAFT

News of the draft decree was received in Tashkent on June 28 in a telegram from Prime Minister and Minister of the Interior Stürmer.[1] The Governor-Generalship of Turkestan was to fill a quota of 250,000 workers in the draft, or about 8 per cent of the estimated male population of nearly 3,500,000 (excluding Khiva and Bukhara of course, which because of their vassal status were not affected by the decree). General M. R. Erofeev, acting governor-general in the absence of General Martson, who had gone to Moscow on leave a few days before, at once summoned the leading civil and military officials of the region to Tashkent for a conference to consider ways and means of carrying out the order.

The officials attending the conference, held on July 2–3, had to consider the physical details of putting the draft into effect, the native reaction to such an unprecedented measure, and the effect of such a sweeping mobilization upon the region's economy.

The participants in the conference decided first of all that it would not be possible to call up the natives by age group, as was done in mobilization for military service. Not only were native births not registered, but any attempt at mobilization on such

a basis might cause alarm by leading the natives to think that
they were being taken as soldiers. Instead, it was decided merely
to establish quotas for each district and to have the individual
workers designated by their village elders and volost headmen,
just as labor had always been provided for repair of irrigation
facilities, road repair, and other public works.

At several collection centers in each oblast medical examina-
tions would be given to determine physical fitness, and workers
would be disinfected, deloused, and vaccinated. The workers
were to be organized in echelons of from 1,400 to 1,500 men, with
one man out of each 200 to serve as interpreter and elder. One
mulla was to be assigned to each echelon to take care of religious
needs.[2]

Coming as it did at the height of field work on the vital cotton
crop, the draft would be a blow to the regional economy, so instead of taking an equal percentage of the population of each
oblast, the conferees arranged a scale whereby areas with the
greatest cultivation of cotton would furnish a smaller proportion
of men. Oblasts with less important crops would have propor-
tionately larger quotas.[3]

Little heed was paid to possible native reaction to the labor
draft. The acting commandant of Transcaspia oblast observed
that because a Turkmen regiment was already serving with the
fighting forces and 10,000 natives had been engaged in construction work on the Caucasus front since earlier in the year, there
was little danger of any demonstration arising from the draft.
He suggested a proclamation that medals would be given to
especially brave workers in order to utilize "the inherent native
lust for marks of distinction."[4] To eliminate a potential source of
unrest the conference decided to exempt mullas, judges, and other
influential native leaders from the draft, as "the mood of the mass
depends on the so-called upper classes of the population. . . ."[5]

The conferees were apparently unaware that they were playing
with fire. The slight provision made for preparing the population for such a major policy change; the question of the effectiveness of having the selection made by local native officials, leaving
them either to bear the brunt of popular resentment or to use

the situation for their own personal advantage; and the exemption of influential natives, leaving the main part of the burden to be borne by the poor, all contributed to the inflammable situation.

REBELLION IN TURKESTAN

News of the draft spread among the natives before the official announcements could be made, and grew in the telling. On July 4, only two days after the conference at Tashkent, rumors that lists of workers were being prepared brought a crowd of demonstrators before police headquarters at Khodzhent, in Samarkand oblast. The crowd stoned a military guard detachment and the guard fired in retaliation, killing two natives and wounding thirty.[6]

This incident would have been a major sensation in the region a few years before, but it was now merely one among many similar occurrences. During the next several days the inhabitants of a number of volosts fell upon the volost administrative centers, destroying lists of workers in preparation and killing or putting to flight the volost headmen and other local native officials. These had long been hated for their corruption and their association with the Russian government.

In the city of Samarkand, General N. S. Lykoshin, the oblast military governor, one of the few Russian officials with a good knowledge of the Uzbek language and customs, managed to avert violence by explanations and promises. But in Tashkent agitation mounted until July 11, when thousands of natives assembled at police headquarters in the native section of Tashkent to prevent the making up of lists of workers. Police were stoned and beaten, and the windows of the police station were shattered. When the mob attempted to rush into the building the police opened fire. The mob retreated, but then settled down for a siege. It was finally put to flight only by fire from a company of Tashkent military school cadets and other forces hastily summoned to the scene. In the clashes during that day eleven native demonstrators were killed and fifteen wounded; one member of the punitive forces was killed and five were wounded.[7]

Almost simultaneously, disturbances flared up throughout Fergana oblast, always a center of unrest. Native officials in a number of volosts who tried to comply with the draft order were mobbed and had their houses burned. There were riots in all of the chief towns. On July 9 a crowd of 5,000 natives in Andizhan rejected attempts by native officials to explain the necessity of the draft. Urged on by mullas, they began to move toward the Russian section of the city, with the intention of destroying the lists of workers. At Gul'tepinskaia Square, on the edge of the Russian section they were met by police and Cossacks under Colonel I. A. Brzhezitskii, the uezd commandant. The crowd attacked and the troops opened fire, killing three and wounding twelve.[8] At Margelan, rioters seized control of the native city, killing several officials. Troops finally broke up the resistance and restored order in surrounding volosts, inflicting casualties of sixty-three killed and wounded.[9] On July 12, seventeen natives were killed at the kishlak of Shaarikhan.[10] At Namangan, on July 11, twelve natives were killed and thirty-eight wounded in a clash with a Russian force armed with machine guns.[11]

The widespread disturbances thus far described were spontaneous mob actions, unplanned and without a definite leadership, which flared up out of exasperation at the draft order. Most of them probably could have been averted by more careful explanation of the reasons for the draft, the nature of the service, and by greater tact and understanding on the part of Russian officials. In any event, the native mobs were quickly routed by a volley or two from the small detachments of troops on hand.

In Dzhizak uezd (Samarkand oblast), however, the disturbances reached more serious proportions. This was one of the most poverty-stricken and backward uezds in Turkestan. Its population supported itself mainly by sheep and goat herding and the grain raised by extended dry-farming methods. Isolation from outside influences caused the inhabitants to retain more survivals of old ways and to remain under the influence of the Moslem clergy to a greater extent than the people of other uezds. These factors, combined with the strain of wartime exactions and a recent crop failure, may well have caused even more resentment toward the draft and the Russians in general than was displayed in the more prosperous regions.[12]

On July 13, after news of the uprising in Tashkent, the religious leaders in Dzhizak incited the people. Led by an ishan, a great crowd made its way to the Russian section of the town to seize the draft lists. The uezd commandant, Colonel P. I. Rukin, the police chief, Captain P. D. Zotoglov, a native elder, an interpreter and two policemen rode out to meet the mob. They were seized and torn to pieces. Troops arrived and fired into the mob, which then turned back to the native section of town, leaving eleven dead and many wounded.[13] Aroused, and with insufficient troops to hold them in check, the natives destroyed the railroad station, tore down telephone lines, and set oil tanks on fire.

Outside of Dzhizak the village and aul populations throughout most of the uezd rose in revolt. The inhabitants of several districts elected beks, and one district elected a khan, who called for a gazavat to free Dzhizak from Russian rule. His supporters appealed to Bukhara and Afghanistan for aid. Both the nomadic and settled populace destroyed bridges, telegraph lines, and post stations. Tracks were torn up at many points along the sixty-five versts of railroad between Dzhizak and Obruchevka. Sixteen Russian railroad workers were killed. Volost administrative centers, where the lists of workers were made up, were destroyed.[14]

Fritz Willfort, an Austrian war prisoner who was confined at Dzhizak at the time of the revolt, describes the uprisings as having been a surprise to guards and prisoners alike. The prisoner-of-war barracks were situated between the new and old sections of Dzhizak. The rebels occupied most of the old section, and virtually besieged the Russian population of the new section. Willfort describes the alarm of the guards and the need for moving prisoners to a safer place each night, where they sweltered in close confinement. In the morning they were returned to their more spacious barracks for the day.

Willfort's view of the revolt was necessarily a limited one, but he gives details lacking in other accounts, and indicates excesses on both sides. He is vague on the actions of the natives, but mentions that near the city the body of a Russian youth was found, "frightfully mutilated, with his skin torn from his body in strips. The local forester and his children were slain; his wife taken into the mountains." [15] Other reports state that eighty-three Russians were killed in and around Dzhizak, twenty wounded, and seventy Russian women and children carried away as prisoners.[16]

The period of alarm in Dzhizak continued for several days. The Russians gained control only after arrival of punitive forces from Tashkent and Samarkand. The expedition, under the command of Colonel P. P. Ivanov (later notorious as General Ivanov-Rinov, minister of war under Kolchak in Siberia in 1918), comprised thirteen companies of infantry, six cannon, three sotnias of Cossacks, a company of sappers, and an armored train. This force was divided into five flying columns and sent out to meet and scatter the insurgents.

By July 17 the tide had turned. Telegraphic and railroad communications were restored. The would-be beks were captured or forced to flee. Some of the rebels, with Cossack columns in pursuit, fled to the hills, from whence they tried to return to their villages or to break through to Bukhara or Afghanistan.[17] Willfort describes how in a temperature of 58° Centigrade (137° F.) Russian patrols roamed the countryside, under orders from Petrograd to destroy all native villages for fifteen versts around Dzhizak. That night the sky was red with the light from the burning villages. On the next day, July 18, the patrols returned to Dzhizak exhibiting their plunder and many native captives, mostly women and children.

On July 20, in stifling heat, Willfort and other war prisoners were detailed to clean up the native section of Dzhizak, strewn with the remains of men and horses killed in the first days of the uprising. Later the native section of Dzhizak was set afire by incendiary grenades. From it great masses of booty were brought into the new section of town. What remained of the native city was leveled to the ground.

The Dzhizak events climaxed the uprisings in the settled areas of Turkestan. According to Willfort, a thousand natives were killed in the fighting around the town; [18] eighty-two participants were sentenced to hang, although many of the sentences were later commuted.[19]

Throughout the rest of July, however, the situation in the central oblasts of Turkestan remained critical. On July 18, at the urgent request of regional officials, the Imperial government proclaimed the entire region to be under martial law. Mass reprisals began: the administration took hostages, forbade public gatherings, required authorization by an uezd commandant before any native could use post, telegraph, or railroad facilities, and on July 21 required natives to bow before all Russian officers and officials.[20]

In spite of these measures, the attempts to gather native laborers proved fruitless. Between July 22 and 30 there were several new outbreaks, though of a lesser nature than before, in Tashkent and Samarkand uezds, and on July 29 a crowd of 600 Kara-Kalpaks at Chimbai, Amu-Daria section, killed the local police chief and his wife.[21] In Fergana oblast the hard-pressed military governor, General A. I. Gippius, exceeded his authority by proclaiming to the population that only volunteers would be taken for labor service. The agitation over the draft diminished as a result, but when only a few volunteers were forthcoming Gippius himself traveled about the oblast speaking before native gatherings. Finally at Namangan on July 23 he had the mullas assemble the people before a mosque and, donning the chalma (turban) and khalat (the flowing native robe) required in Moslem ritual, he read the parts of the Koran enjoining the people to serve the state, and ended by kissing the Book. Aghast at this lowering of the bars between conqueror and subject, Gippius' superiors called him first to Tashkent and then to Petrograd for explanations, and he was finally transferred to a reserve unit in the Caucasus.[22]

Meanwhile, seeking an experienced man to assume command in Turkestan, the government turned on July 21 to General A. N. Kuropatkin, then in command of the Russian armies on the Northern Front. At the same time, the question was raised in the State Duma of a temporary postponement of the mobilization of native workers in order to provide time to restore order in the region. The General Staff concurred, and on July 30, 1916, Tsar Nicholas II signed an order postponing the draft until September 15.[23]

Kuropatkin, who had begun his career in Central Asia, knew the region better than any other man in the High Command. Now at the end of his career—he was sixty-eight—and a personification of the old regime, he returned to the scene of his earlier campaigns and administration to try to restore order and Russian prestige. Arriving in Tashkent on August 8, 1916, Kuropatkin undertook a shake-up of personnel in order to correct some of the weaknesses and abuses which had helped cause the riots and rebellion of the month before. Within a week he relieved or confirmed the release from duty of the military governor of Syr-Daria oblast, Galkin (whom Kuropatkin had earlier described in his journal as "drunk every day"), the military governor of Fergana oblast, Gippius ("crazy"), several uezd commandants, and the chief of police of Tashkent.[24] But before Kuropatkin could proceed further in this housecleaning his attention was taken up by a new center of disturbance, this time among the Kazakhs and Kirgiz in the northern part of Syr-Daria oblast and in Semirechie oblast.

THE REBELLION IN SEMIRECHIE

The decree regarding the mobilization of native workers was proclaimed in Semirechie oblast on July 8, 1916. As in the oblasts farther south, there was a minimum of explanation of the reasons for the draft and how it would be put into effect. The authorities delayed explaining for several days the type of work which would be required, and then only stated by proclamation that the natives would be employed in digging trenches. This permitted rumors to spread among the Kazakhs and Kirgiz that trench diggers would be under enemy fire, and that those drafted would actually be taken as soldiers. After decades of exemption from military service, the natives were frightened by the sudden reversal of government policy. Near the border many of the young men resolved to run away to China before they would submit. The more sober heads in each volost counseled compliance with the draft in order to avoid trouble with the authorities, but few paid any heed. Volost headmen were defied when they attempted to draw up lists of workers.[25]

In this atmosphere of misunderstanding and alarm, violence quickly developed. Early in August several clashes occurred in Vernyi, Pishpek, and Przheval'sk uezds between natives and armed escorts of Russian officials attempting to hasten compliance with the mobilization order. Anticipating Russian reprisal, the natives of some of the affected areas fled to neighboring volosts, whose inhabitants, fearing Russian pursuit of the fugitives, fled in turn. Panic spread rapidly among natives in the well-populated areas along the Chu River and around Issyk-Kul. Many abandoned belongings, livestock, and even children and the aged in their flight.[26]

Where the disorders were greatest, the Russians likewise became panic-stricken. Where they were less acute many looked upon the situation as an opportunity to clear the area of nomads. Every native was seen as a potential enemy, his property eligible for seizure. When small army detachments sent along the road from Aulie-Ata to Pishpek caused further alarm among the Kazakhs, Russian peasants took the opportunity to drive off Kazakh livestock. Others went directly to the Kazakh auls and seized hides, felt, and anything else of value. Because of this many of the natives of the Chu and Merke districts fled to the district beyond the river Chu.[27]

Near Belovodsk, west of Pishpek, two Russians were killed by unknown assailants. Thereupon the local Russian colonists organized a *druzhina* (volunteer force) to put down what was alleged to be an uprising. They attacked the Kazakh auls in the Belovodsk area, plundering and shooting for several days. On August 13 the pristav of Belovodsk, Gribanovskii, lured 517 Kazakhs into Belovodsk for "negotiations," but instead locked them up and then departed, leaving them to be massacred by the Russian peasants. Later in the same day more than a hundred other natives were killed on the road while being taken under guard to Pishpek.[28]

A bloody sequence of panic and reprisal was now going on

over a wide area. The natives attacked post stations and isolated villages. At Novotroitsk, on the border between Aulie-Ata and Pishpek uezds, they killed forty Russian peasants, burned the buildings, and drove off the cattle. Another group ambushed a Russian transport detail in the Buam gorge near Rybach'e, on the west end of Issyk-Kul, killing 3 Russians and seizing 170 rifles and 40,000 cartridges. Emboldened by this success, they then attacked the village of Novorossiisk, situated in the valley of the Great Kebeb River northwest of Issyk-Kul. The peasants resisted in vain; some were killed and most of the village was burned. The nearby village of Samsonovsk fared the same. The Russian villages were hard to defend, as they were usually strung out for a mile or more along a single road instead of being concentrated, and as their inhabitants had given up most of their arms to the government.

In less than twenty-four hours all of the Kirgiz in the basin of the river Chu and around the north shore of Issyk-Kul had risen. They plundered and burned all the Russian settlements and post stations along the post road from Pishpek to Przheval'sk, on the north shore, and on the road from Rybach'e to Fort Naryn, southwest of the lake. They also burned bridges and destroyed telegraph lines. On August 13 between 4,000 and 5,000 Kirgiz attacked Tokmak and the nearby settlement of Pokrovka. They besieged Tokmak until August 21, when a troop of Cossacks and seventy infantrymen with machine guns arrived from Pishpek and forced the rebels to retreat to the mountains around the lake. The Kirgiz lost almost 300 men in the siege.[29]

In other areas around Issyk-Kul the uprising followed a similar course. On August 9 the Kirgiz destroyed the post stations and nearly all of the Russian settlements on the north and east shores of the lake. They also wiped out several villages and inflicted heavy losses on others on the south shore. The survivors of the raids and the inhabitants of villages where native attacks were anticipated, fled to larger, more defensible centers. Several of these villagers sought refuge at Teplokliuchensk; those living at the Issyk-Kul monastery went to Preobrazhenskoe. The entire population of Rybach'e crossed the lake on boats to Przheval'sk.[30]

Przheval'sk, the uezd center, was the main gathering point for refugees. Each day more peasants arrived and the tales of their losses and rumors of impending native attack kept the town in a high state of alarm. To defend the town, which now held 10,000 women and children, Colonel Ivanov, the uezd commandant (not the man who had put down the rebellion at Dzhizak), hastily organized a defense force of eight soldiers and nearly a thousand civilian men. These he armed with the only firearms available— fifty-five rifles, seventy-three hunting pieces, and three revolvers —supplemented with pikes, pitchforks, and staves.[31]

Official reports and testimony later given in court concerning these events paint an ugly picture of alarm, mistrust, mob violence, shirking of duty by those able to bear arms, and official incompetence. Enemies of Colonel Ivanov even spread rumors that he had sold the uezd to the Kirgiz for a million rubles.

Ivanov asserted in his reports that he did what he could to protect the natives from Russian vengeance. But the many cases of atrocities committed against natives indicate laxity on his or his subordinates' part. On August 11 a group of Dungans and Chinese from the volost of Mariinsk were brought into town. They were confined in a building under guard, but in the afternoon a few allegedly tried to escape and were shot down. This brought a mob of Russians to the scene who attacked the remaining prisoners with staves and pitchforks. Sixty of the prisoners were killed.[32]

"The next day," a Russian official reported later, "massacre and violence against the natives spread to the suburbs. The tale 'I killed so many Sarts or Dungans' was considered an honor; the teller became a hero. The massacre acquired a wholesale character when patrols reported that on the Mariinsk road no quarter was shown anyone." [33]

These occurrences had their match, however, on August 13, when Kirgiz attacked and burned the agricultural school near Przheval'sk, killing most of the school personnel, the students, and peasants from the village of Vysokoe who had taken refuge there and taking away the surviving young women and girls as captives.[34]

On August 15 a measure of calm was restored to Przheval'sk with the arrival of a company of volunteers from Dzharkent, dispatched by order of the military governor of Semirechie. Coming by way of Karkara this group brought along 500 Uzbek and Dungan traders from that town. When the detachment passed through the village of Teplokliuchensk they left the traders there. The villagers and refugees from other places killed all but twenty-one of these Moslems.[35]

The arrival of reinforcements made it possible to restore control over nearby areas. Sazonovka, beleaguered by the Kirgiz for six days, was relieved on August 16, and its inhabitants were taken to Preobrazhensk.[36] On the road, a band of Russian peasants and Cossacks fell upon a group of Uzbeks among the refugees and killed ninety, including women and children.[37]

During succeeding days, other small detachments of Cossacks and volunteers arrived in Przheval'sk and the Russian position became secure. Troops were sent out to find survivors of the native attacks. During their search they killed natives indiscriminately, and plundered and destroyed native property on a massive scale. On August 25 a detachment enroute to Pokrovskoe to collect refugees plundered and burned 800 native yurts. On August 26 another Russian detachment scattered a large allegedly hostile group of Kirgiz near Preobrazhensk, killed an estimated 800 natives, and drove off a great number of livestock. Much of the booty taken in such raids was confiscated from participants in the uprisings ostensibly to recompense Russian refugees for their losses, but much of it was taken wherever it was found and kept by the officers and soldiers who seized it.[38]

Further Kirgiz resistance now became impossible. By the end of August the Russian detachments, aided by reinforcements from Vernyi, routed the Kirgiz from the areas they had seized. The fugitives moved by the thousands into the mountains and then across the Chinese border, taking their prisoners with them, but having to abandon most of their livestock along the way because of lack of fodder. In China they suffered further losses from extortion by the Chinese authorities and raids by the Kalmyks, who made off with women and livestock.[39]

The carnage and turmoil displayed in Vernyi, Pishpek, and Przheval'sk uezds of Semirechie oblast were less evident in Kopal, Lepsinsk, and Dzharkent uezds, where there were fewer Russian settlers. In Kopal uezd there were no uprisings and no Russians lost their lives, although Cossacks killed forty Kazakhs at Kara-bulakskoe stanitsa, west of Kopal. In Lepsinsk uezd the abuses of native officials incident to the labor draft in one volost provoked a clash in which Russian troops killed a hundred Kazakhs, and arrested nearly a hundred more.[40]

THE ROLE OF KUROPATKIN

During the uprisings, Kuropatkin, in Tashkent, strove to send aid and to direct defense in a situation which, as General Follbaum, the military governor of Semirechie, wired Kuropatkin on August 10, "might suddenly take a turn which will ruin all Russian enterprise in Semirechie." [41]

To put down the uprisings, Kuropatkin sent troops into Semirechie from Andizhan by way of Fort Naryn, and from Chimkent along the post road to Pishpek and Tokmak. He had others brought by rail to Semipalatinsk and from there sent on foot to Sergiopol', Lepsinsk, and Vernyi.[42] Most of these troops were reservists and Cossacks on domestic duty, but two regiments of Cossacks and two machine gun detachments that had seen active service in the fighting forces were also sent into the region.[43] While these troops were on the way Kuropatkin wired Follbaum to organize a militia of all of the Russian population able to bear arms, to utilize the clan and tribal animosities of the natives during the struggle, and for the time being not to hinder their migration into China, but at the same time he ordered Follbaum to prevent "unnecessary and therefore harmful cruelty to those who do not resist, and under pain of death do not permit looting by our forces or by the Russian population." [44]

Following the campaign closely, Kuropatkin in his telegrams to Follbaum made frequent allusions to earlier events in the region, urging him to "Remember the example of Serov's Ural Cossack company, struggling with a horde of 10,000," and to "Keep in mind the example of Colonel Kolpakovskii's military activities fifty-two years ago. With much smaller forces than are at your disposal he went forth boldly to meet a great horde advancing on Vernyi and dealt it a decisive defeat in the Kastek Pass. The enemy was much better armed than the horde against which you now operate." [45] Again, on August 21, evidently in reply to new requests for reinforcements, Kuropatkin wired: "Together with the units you have formed, through the arrival of reinforcements . . . not counting the two Cossack regiments and horse batteries, you will have at your disposal 35 companies, 24 sotnias, 240 mounted scouts, 16 field-pieces, and 47 machine guns. Cherniaev, Romanovskii, Kaufman, and Skobelev conquered the oblasts of Syr-Daria, Samarkand, and Fergana with a smaller force." [46]

On August 20 Kuropatkin made a trip to Dzhizak "to calm the Russian population." After visiting the graves of the uezd commandant and the police chief killed there the month before, he assembled the leading natives and told them sternly: "All of you should be hanged, but we are sparing you so that you may be a warning for others. The place where Colonel Rukin was killed is to be enclosed for a radius of five versts. This will belong to the government. The people inhabiting this territory are to be evicted immediately." [47]

Back in Tashkent the next day, Kuropatkin addressed a native delegation. He recalled the Russian conquest, telling how after the struggle the natives and the Russians had worked together as brothers, and how under the protection of Russia the natives had in the course of fifty years peacefully developed and had achieved great prosperity. But he warned that the natives must know their place. He reminded his listeners:

The Russian Empire is great and powerful, but the main role in its formation, strengthening, and expansion is played by the Russians. One can hardly relate the sacrifices which they have borne in the course of 1,500 years in order to create Russia's greatness and might. To the Russians, contributing more than all others of toil and sacrifice for the creation of Russia must belong the foremost role in all corners of Russia. The many peoples inhabiting Russia are all children of one father, the Great Sovereign Emperor. All of these many peoples are children of one mother, Great Russia. But in this numerous family the Russians must be the elder brothers of all the rest. . . ."

In the war, he stated, the Russians had borne the main brunt of the struggle, but all of the peoples of Russia had to help achieve victory. The Russians had conquered Turkestan and had returned the land to the natives for peaceful toil; natives could not now be permitted to shed Russian blood on that land. Just as at Andizhan, eighteen years before, the government had taken the land where Russian blood had flowed, so it would do now, at Dzhizak and in Semirechie. Two roads lay before the natives, he concluded—to strengthen their bonds with Russia or to line up with her enemies. If they took the latter road their woe would be without limit, not only upon them but their children; if they proved worthy of the fifty years of friendship that Russia had given them, all could benefit by the flowering of the wealth of Turkestan.[48]

In general, however, Kuropatkin took pains to conciliate the natives. He formed local committees to provide better contact between the government and the natives. He lifted the restriction on native use of the post and telegraph and the railroads. He emphasized that the draft must be carried out, because it was ordered by the tsar, but admitted that it had been faultily executed at the start. He stressed that the living habits of the native laborers would be kept in mind, that they would receive good wages, and that their families would be cared for. He posed as the champion of the poorer class of natives by forbidding the taking of "volunteers" in the draft, as these had usually been coerced by the wealthier classes. Seeking the favor of the Tatars, in the hope that they in turn would influence the Uzbeks, he made General Abdulaziz Davletshin, a Russianized Tatar who had risen in the military service to post of assistant to the chief of the Asiatic Department of the General Staff, a member of his personal escort.[49] In a conversation with A. F. Kerensky, then a member of the State Duma, visiting Tashkent during an inspection tour of centers of the uprisings in Turkestan, Kuropatkin declared his desire to appease the Russian population by payment of compensation.[50]

In September, Kuropatkin began the first of several tours of the Turkestan region in order to reassure the population, to see that justice was done to both sides, to gain a first-hand knowledge of the situation, and to impress upon the people the fact that the Russian administration was concerned with their problems. At conferences along the way he inquired into the ideas of representatives of both the Russian and native populations regarding what he considered one of his most important tasks— revision of the Turkestan Statute of 1886.[51]

From September 4 to 13 Kuropatkin visited Samarkand and the main towns of Fergana. His diary indicates both an interest in current problems and also a considerable nostalgia for earlier times, especially the period of the Russian conquest, in which he had participated. At Kokand he met many old native leaders who recalled his entry into the city when it was taken by Russian forces forty years before, and who opined that he was now "sent by God to save them." They told him that they had been robbed by both the Russian and native administrations, that it was impossible to live, and they asked his protection.[52]

On September 18 a crowd of thousands of natives and Russians saw off at the station the first party of 1,000 native workers as they left Tashkent for European Russia. Students of the Russian-native schools were lined up with flags and portraits of the tsar and Kuropatkin, and the party was addressed by the assistant governor-general, General M. R. Erofeev, by the military governor of Syr-Daria oblast, General A. S. Madritov, by the chief of staff, General Sivers, and finally by Kuropatkin.[53] A second echelon of workers left Tashkent on September 28,[54] and on October 5 Kuropatkin published a plan for sending thirty-three echelons of workers between October 18 and November 18.[55]

THE REBELLION IN TRANSCASPIA

Between September 21 and 30 Kuropatkin made a tour of Transcaspia oblast. Because of its isolation from the rest of Turkestan and the different ethnic and cultural composition of its people, Transcaspia had experienced a somewhat different course of events in response to the labor draft than had the oblasts inhabited by the Uzbeks, Kazakhs, and Kirgiz. The Turkmen had received the proclamation of the draft quietly, though some had expressed dissatisfaction that they were to be taken as laborers like the Uzbeks, because they regarded pick and shovel work as unfit for warriors.[56] As members of the Tekke tribe were already serving in a volunteer regiment on active service, it was decided that the Turkmen should be used only for duty guarding prisoners, railroads, and forests.[57]

This concession appeased the majority of the Turkmen and the Tekke of Akhal and Merv, but the Iomuds, on the northern side of the oblast, refused to supply workers. In late August and early September a large number of Iomuds began to migrate over the border into Persia after clashes with Russian troops who were trying to make up the lists of men to be drafted as guards. "With them," Kuropatkin wrote, "there will be much trouble." [58] Two other Turkmen groups, the Sariks and Salars, prepared to move into Afghanistan.

Armed encounters with the Iomuds occurred through the latter part of September. Cossack patrols were fired on near Astrabad, and the Iomuds occupied the fortress of Ak-Kala, from which they were only dislodged with heavy losses after a two-hour bombardment by troops sent from Askhabad. Between September 25 and 29, the rebels destroyed four Russian settlements along the Giurgen River and drove off cattle from others in the same area.

Late in September, Kuropatkin noted that Iomuds from Persia were joining those of Transcaspia. Mentioning the skirmishing with Russian detachments, he wrote: "I sent reinforcements. Much blood will be shed, and the population awaits heavy punishment, but the government must insist that the sovereign's demands for workers be fulfilled; otherwise the prestige of our rule in Middle Asia will be shattered." [59]

On October 9, Kuropatkin began a tour of Semirechie oblast. M. Tynyshpaev, a Kazakh engineer and leader in the native intelligentsia, traveled with him as interpreter and gave him the native point of view regarding the revolt. During the tour, Russian colonists asked repeatedly for more land. Kuropatkin was unwilling to grant this as it would mean further dispossession of the natives, and he advised the colonists to use better methods of utilizing the land they already had. Arms were another persistent want, and he ordered their distribution, desiring that the settlers be protected against further native outbreaks. By so doing he was the unwitting cause of many excesses against the natives during 1917.

In Pishpek uezd, Kuropatkin heard of several instances of extortion from natives by Russian officials and began to hear frequent reports of Russian atrocities. At Belovodsk, where several hundred Kazakhs had been slaughtered by Russian settlers, he wrote:

At the entrance to the settlement . . . the widows of the murdered men stood on both sides of the road in Kirgiz mourning clothes, and as if at a command they raised a cry, asking me to return their men. Sokolinskii [M. A. Follbaum, the military governor of Semirechie, who, like certain other Russian officials of German extraction had adopted a Slavic name during the war] believes that this cruel punishment served a purpose, as it stopped the wavering Kirgiz of other volosts from joining the rebellion, for which they had made preparations. I strongly warned the population that anyone who now takes it into his head to plunder, whether Russian or Kirgiz, will be given over to court-martial and the gallows.[60]

At Pishpek, Tynyshpaev discovered and reported to Kuropatkin that a few hours before their arrival a Kazakh suspected of having taken part in the revolt had been stoned to death in the market place. Kuropatkin ordered the case investigated. It would be necessary severely to punish the Kazakhs who had taken part in the revolt, he wrote, but it would also be necessary sternly to put an end to such Russian mob law, otherwise "a proper way of life cannot be reëstablished." [61]

Continuing his tour into the devastated Issyk-Kul region, always "considering ways to set things right in Semirechie," Kuropatkin concluded that in the long run it was essential to reconcile both peoples—the Russians and the natives—wherever possible. But around Issyk-Kul, "wherever Russian blood has flowed," the land of the Kirgiz guilty of the outrages should be taken from them. In its place he thought the Kirgiz should be resettled in an all-Kirgiz uezd to be formed southwest of Issyk-Kul in the Naryn area, from which several Russian villages would in turn be transferred into the area vacated by the Kirgiz. Foreseeing the new home of the Kirgiz as a great horse farm where mounts for the Russian cavalry could be raised, he stated:

New fields of activity must . . . be opened for the Kirgiz. In the last forty years it has been tacitly agreed to wipe from the face of the earth this likeable, good-natured naïve tribe, still wild because of our fault. We have considered them unimportant, that their role was finished, that progress for them must be in the transfer to a settled existence. But it is not so. The Kirgiz are born cattle raisers and nomads. In this one must see their strength. A great area of land in Middle Asia is good only for cattle raising and a nomadic life. The Kirgiz is also a born cavalryman, and this also must be utilized.[62]

Typical of the paternalistic thinking of its originator, the plan's main drawback was the Naryn area's unsuitability for development. Of high elevation, it had little pasture and sowing area, no possibilities for irrigation, and was consequently incapable of supporting more than a sparse population.

For the Issyk-Kul region Kuropatkin declared a railroad essential, and foresaw the Russian settlers eventually shipping "millions of poods of grain and millions of poods of meat in refrigerator cars to European Russia." [63]

By this time virtually all of the disorders in the Turkestan governor-generalship had been put down except in Transcaspia. During October the Iomuds continued their attacks on Russian villages and small troop detachments. At the end of October the rebels appeared near Khodzha-Nefis on the Caspian coast, arousing the previously peaceful Turkmen of the maritime region. Along the Persian border they wrecked trains and destroyed telegraph lines. In November the Iomuds tried to destroy fisheries along the Caspian, but were beaten off by artillery on ships from the Ashur-Adinsk naval station.

The rebellion in Transcaspia was put down only in December, when Kuropatkin sent General Madritov to the scene with a large, well-equipped force which after several battles forced most of the rebels either to surrender or to flee to Persia. Madritov and his men made the most of their stay in the oblast through unrestrained plundering of the flocks and personal belongings of the natives.[64]

THE REBELLION IN THE KAZAKH STEPPE

Unrest and rebellion also spread through the vast reaches of the
Kazakh Steppe following proclamation of the labor draft. Like
the other peoples of Central Asia, the steppe dwellers looked
upon the sudden and wholesale draft with resentment and alarm.
Already sullenly hostile over the seizure of their lands and various
wartime requisitions, the natives felt that this new demand by
the government was too much. They had taken their long-standing exemption from military service for granted, but now they
became convinced that they were to be drafted as soldiers.

The attempts of the handful of Kazakh intellectuals in Orenburg, Omsk, and other Steppe towns to explain the decree and
to persuade their compatriots to comply were fruitless. The
editors of the newspaper *Kazakh,* published in Orenburg, had in
fact advocated military service for their compatriots several
months before the draft was announced,[65] ostensibly for patriotic
service but more probably as a means to give the provincial
steppe dwellers acquaintance with Western ways. Because of
the limited circulation of this organ, however, it had virtually no
influence among the mass of the Kazakhs.

As always, there were wild rumors. In Turgai oblast it was
said that Nicholas I, many years before, had written a document
on parchment freeing the Kazakhs from military service for all
time, that the mobilization plans were the work of the bais and
the volost headmen, and that the tsar knew nothing about it.[66]
In Semipalatinsk oblast there were rumors that not only were
the Kazakhs to be taken as soldiers but that they were to be
baptized as Christians.[67]

Volost headmen and aul elders were in a hopeless position for
they were under pressure from the government on the one hand
to take the necessary steps to make up the draft quota of 243,000
men which had been set for the four Steppe oblasts.[68] On the
other hand they were regarded as tools of the Russians by their
fellows. Attacks on volost headmen who tried to prepare the lists
of workers became frequent. In Turgai oblast many of the Kazakhs began to move southward into the semidesert regions. In

Semipalatinsk oblast they began to flee toward the Chinese border. Hay was left unharvested, and cattle remained uncared for. There were attacks on Russian settlers and thefts of live-stock.[69]

With few troops at hand, the Russian officials in the Steppe oblasts could do little to maintain order or enforce compliance with the draft decree. The postponement of the draft until September 15 apparently served only as a temporary easing of the crisis.[70]

The resistance was greatest in Turgai oblast. There the large Kipchak, Argyn, and Naiman groups settled their long-standing differences, and under tribal leaders who assumed the title of "khan" tried to present a united front against the mobilization. However, except for several clashes with punitive forces, even this combination did not take the offensive until October 23, when the united forces of the Argyn and the Kipchaks, amounting to about 15,000 men, laid siege to the town of Turgai. The town was defended by only a militia detachment of two or three hundred men and a Cossack sotnia with machine guns, but the Kazakhs, poorly armed, undisciplined, and under divided leadership, were unequal to the task. Abdulgafar Dzhambusynov, the elected "khan" of the Kipchaks, realized this and wanted to negotiate, but one of his lieutenants, Amangeldy Imanov, urged an attack. On November 5 the Kazakhs tried to take the town by storm, but were beaten off by the defenders. The Kazakhs menaced the town until November 16, when a Russian relief force arrived and drove them away.[71]

During the rest of November and throughout December Russian punitive forces pursued the rebel bands, experiencing as much difficulty from the season and the nature of the country as from the opposition of the elusive Kazakhs. One of the leaders of the resistance was Amangeldy Imanov, who has been made a folk hero in Soviet historical literature because he joined the Bolsheviks and became war commissar for Turgai oblast before he was captured and shot by anti-Bolshevik Kazakh forces on May 18, 1919.[72] By the end of the year most of the opposition had ceased and the region settled down to an uneasy peace, though some officials feared a resumption of hostilities in the following spring.[73]

The resistance to the draft in the other Steppe oblasts of Ural'sk, Akmolinsk, and Semipalatinsk was widely spread, but took the form of scattered incidents rather than any organized effort. In general, the pacification of the Steppe was less easily achieved than in the more restricted areas of Turkestan and the mountain valleys of Semirechie, but at the same time, again with the exception of Turgai, it was less acute. The Kazakhs of the Steppe had been in contact with the Russians for a longer time; they produced few leaders; and they were poorly armed and untrained in combat.[74] In addition they were hampered by the terrain, which could not support large concentrations of horsemen without external sources of supply. Russian villages already dotted the parts of the Steppe which had once been the best pasturage, and with surer means of supply the punitive expeditions of the Russians had greater advantages than their quarry.

THE SIGNIFICANCE OF THE REBELLIONS

By the end of December, 1916, the native uprisings had run their course. Considering the population and state of the economy of the region, the loss of life and property had been heavy. Kuropatkin stated the Russian civilian losses in the Governor-Generalship of Turkestan as 2,325 killed and 1,384 missing, or, assuming the death of all of the missing, a total of 3,709. Most of these losses were in Semirechie oblast. A total of twenty-four Russian officials and fifty-five native officials were killed. In military operations against the natives from July 13, 1916, to January 25, 1917, ninety-seven other Russians were killed, seventy-six were listed as missing, and eighty-six were wounded.[75] Most of the military losses were in Transcaspia oblast.[76]

Russian losses in the Steppe oblasts were on a much smaller scale. In Turgai oblast, where casualties were probably heaviest, forty-five of the Russian civilian population, and three Russian and six native officials were killed up to February 1, 1917.[77]

Russian property losses for the entire Turkestan region included about 9,000 farmsteads destroyed,[78] most of them in

Semirechie oblast. There are no published estimates of Russian property losses in the Steppe oblasts.

The natives suffered far greater loss of life and property than did the Russians, but such losses were almost incalculable even at the time they occurred. There are no reliable specific figures for casualties except in the case of the riots in Syr-Daria, Fergana, and Samarkand oblasts. There were considerable losses at Dzhizak (Samarkand oblast) and in Transcaspia oblast, but by far the greater number occurred in Semirechie. Some were killed in attacks on Russian settlements and in clashes with Russian troops and many more through reprisals by Russian settlers. However, most of the deaths were the result of hunger and exposure in the mountains and steppe lands and on the mass trek to China. According to one estimate, by January, 1917, the native population of Semirechie had fallen by about 275,000 from the estimated figure of January, 1915, or over 20 per cent.[79] In Pishpek and Przheval'sk uezds there were 62,340 Kirgiz and Kazakh households before the uprising, but in January, 1917, there remained only 20,365, indicating a loss of about 66 per cent.[80] Other writers, however, favor the figure of 300,000 for those who fled to China,[81] and a Soviet demographer has estimated an absolute loss of 1,230,000 persons in the population of Turkestan between 1914 and 1918, or 17 per cent, most of which he attributes to the disorders of 1916.[82] There are no published estimates of native casualties in the Steppe oblasts.

The official punishment meted out to the natives for participation in the riots and rebellions of 1916 was comparatively light. Kuropatkin wrote that 347 natives had been sentenced to death in Turkestan, but that because he believed that the real responsibility rested with the chiefs of the movement he had commuted the sentences of all but fifty-one. In addition, 168 were sentenced to hard labor, 228 to correctional labor detachments, and 129 to imprisonment. As further punishment of a group nature in the two main areas "where Russian blood was shed," Kuropatkin also planned confiscation of 2,000 desiatines of land in Dzhizak uezd (Samarkand oblast), and the mass transfer of the Kirgiz population from the Issyk-Kul area in Semirechie oblast to the Naryn

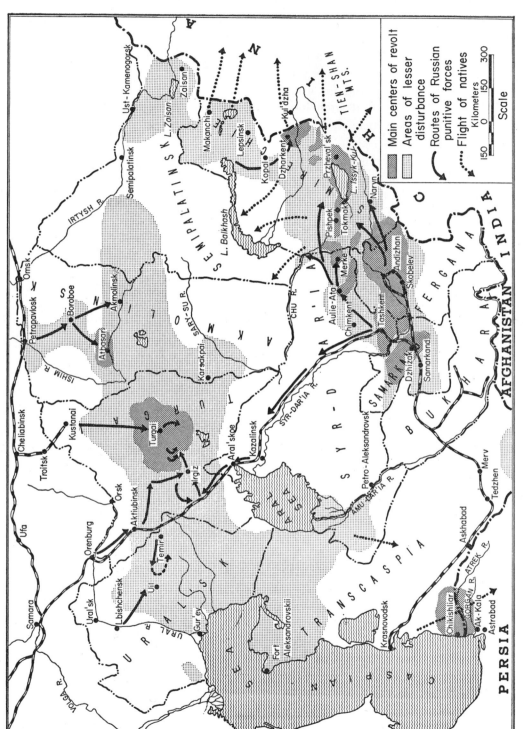

MAP 2. THE NATIVE REVOLTS OF 1916 IN CENTRAL ASIA.

region.[83] There are no figures regarding punishments in any of the Steppe oblasts except Ural'sk, where nineteen alleged ringleaders in disturbances were tried by a military court and put to death in December, 1916.[84]

Some rebels joined the Bolsheviks (e.g., Amangeldy Imanov) in order to continue the fight against those they supposed would continue the old order; others joined the anti-Soviet Basmachi movement in order to prevent establishment of a new order which they considered inimical to their entire way of life. To an important degree, however, the uprisings retain significance even today, for Soviet historians have never been able satisfactorily to answer the questions involved in the native rising, directed not merely against the Imperial regime, but frequently against the Russian people.

Some earlier writers made naïve assertions that, in Semirechie at least, the uprisings were deliberately provoked by Imperial officials so that an excuse could be found to exterminate the natives and to seize their land.[85] Others rejected these views, but tried to give a blanket characterization to the uprisings as "national-liberation, antitsarist, and antifeudal." Still others, with an eye on its anti-Russian manifestations, condemned the whole movement.[86]

Modern Soviet writers still favor the idea of external provocation as a cause of the uprisings, accepting uncritically the rumors of the time concerning Imperial officials of German ancestry (e.g., Follbaum and Martson), and reports of the machinations of Austrian prisoners or of German and Turkish agents.[87] However, no shred of reliable evidence has ever been produced to support allegations regarding disloyal officials or war prisoners, which seem based purely upon wartime spy mania and Germanophobia. The presence of enemy agents seems likely, in view of German activities in adjacent regions and the ease with which Turkish nationals or local hirelings could move undetected among the native population, but there is virtually no concrete evidence of this either.[88] The causes must be sought in local conditions.

On the other hand the modern writers have abandoned earlier explanations of the nature of the uprisings for a more reasoned view that they differed in various areas, although in general they were (if we translate the Soviet terminology) spontaneous in origin, involved mainly the poorer classes, had no central leadership, and were directed against the government, military service, and the more well-to-do native elements in a struggle for national liberation (more generally referred to now as *popular* liberation).[89]

This seems fairly well borne out, but complications arise from attempts to explain why the rebelling natives frequently struck at Russian peasants and workers as well as officials, and from the introduction of value judgments. Attempts are made to distinguish between "progressive" and "reactionary" elements in the uprisings, the first evidently having been those natives who rose against "tsarist" troops and officials and well-to-do natives, and the second those who attacked ordinary Russians, destroyed property, and began to entertain ideas of a Holy War and independence. A handful of instances—not enough to be significant— are selected to show that there was actually a great bond of sympathy between poor Russian peasants and the rebelling natives.[90] Excesses on the Russian side are blamed on "tsarist authorities" and "punitive expeditions" [91] whereas excesses on the native side, such as at Dzhizak and in Semirechie, are blamed on instigation by "feudal-bai elements, bourgeois nationalists, and foreign agents" who "used the ignorance of the remainder of the population to provoke anti-Russian, reactionary outbreaks." [92]

Specious reasoning of this sort merely evades reality. The evidence shows that regardless of the material benefits accruing from Russian rule, most of the natives apparently continued to regard the Russians as interlopers. Consequently, the government's sudden departure from one of the fundamental tenets of its colonial rule—the exemption of the natives from military service—led to panic and the expression of pent-up hatreds by natives throughout the region, followed by bloody retaliation on the part of Russians either equally panic-stricken or eager for plunder. Desirable though it might be from the Soviet standpoint to explain the uprisings of 1916 away, they indicate clearly the failure not only of the Imperial government but of the Russian people to win the friendship and trust of the peoples of Central Asia.

THE COLLAPSE OF THE IMPERIAL REGIME

XIX

HAVING weathered the storm of native revolt, the Imperial administration in Central Asia entered upon the fateful year of 1917. There was ample cause for concern. The war in Europe continued to sap the empire's manpower and economic strength as well as the morale of its people. Locally there were the problems of restoring normal relations between Russian and native, of continuing to meet the heavy economic demands made on the region by the war effort, of coping with rapidly rising living costs and shortages of food and essential goods, and of supplying native labor to aid the fighting forces.

In all, between 150,000 and 180,000 Central Asian natives were mobilized in Turkestan and the Steppe as a result of the decree of June 25, 1916. Sent by the trainload to European Russia and put at the disposition of military commands throughout Russia, the native laborers worked at a variety of tasks. Some were assigned to the *Zemgorsoiuz* (a contraction of *Zemskii gorodskoi soiuz*, Union of Zemstvos and Towns), a wartime organization which managed many business enterprises related to the war effort; others worked under various ministries and other agencies, a hundred men in one place, a thousand in another, replacing Russians needed at the front. Few actually worked in the zone of military operations; most worked in Central Russia and Siberia.[1]

On February 1, 1917, Kuropatkin sent a comprehensive report to the tsar regarding his administration of the region, its condition at that time, and his recommendations concerning future policy. The native resistance was at an end in all oblasts, he wrote, but he warned that because some of the reasons for the revolt still existed it could be expected to be resumed in the spring, with the appearance of new pasture.[2] By February 1, he stated, a total of 110,000 workers had been sent from Turkestan, 10,000 others had been put to work within Turkestan on the railroads, and 80,000 more workers would be available by the end of May, 1917. Enumerating the great quantities of raw materials which had been sent from Turkestan to the army, he urged the dispatch of grain, because of the shortage resulting from the large acreage devoted to cotton.[3]

Leaving immediate problems, Kuropatkin then went farther afield, into matters involving Imperial military and foreign policy. "For the guarantee of the internal peace of the region, and the securing of its frontiers," he cited point by point the direction he thought Russian policy should take with regard to the empire's Asiatic neighbors. Concerning Persia, he advocated "the return to Russia of the holdings of Peter the Great—the provinces of Astrabad, Gilian, and Mazanderan, and besides that, by agreement with England, the establishment of a Russian protectorate over the northern part of Persia, with Tabriz, Teheran, and Meshed." From Afghanistan he advocated the acquisition by Russia of full control over the headwaters of the Amu-Daria, the Murgab, and the Tedzhen Rivers. He urged the opening of Afghanistan to Russian trade and, again "by agreement with England," the construction of a railroad through Afghanistan to India.

Regarding China his ambitions were equaled by his fears:

As far as China is concerned, the future danger for Russia from this empire of 400,000,000 people is beyond all doubt. The most vulnerable part of the Russian frontier, as 800 years ago, remains that great gateway of peoples through which the hordes of Ghengis Khan poured into Europe.

So long as Kuldzha rests in the hands of the Chinese, the protection of Turkestan from China will remain very difficult, or will demand a great number of troops.

This gateway must not be left in the hands of the Chinese. A change in our border with China is urgently necessary. By drawing the border line from the Khan-Tengri range and the Tien Shan in a direct line to Vladivostok it will be shortened by 4,000 versts, and Kuldzha, northern Mongolia, and northern Manchuria will become a part of the Russian Empire.[4]

These recommendations make curious reading, written as they were on the very eve of the collapse of the empire which they were designed to raise to new heights of power. Their originator had been one of the major figures of his time. But that time was past. He was more a man of the nineteenth century than of the twentieth, more of the time of Von Kaufman and Skobelev. The old empire-builder's world, though he did not know it, had come to an end in 1914. Like the quick vision of a lifetime passing through the mind of a dying man, his fantastic program summarized all the unrealized goals of the past and dreams for the future of an empire and a way of life. But for both the state structure and the way of life of Imperial Russia the drama was nearly over.

On February 27, 1917, the tsar abdicated. The news reached Tashkent late on the night of February 28. Kuropatkin delayed his official proclamation pending clarification of the situation,[5] but word of the change leaked out almost at once.

As soon as the news from Petrograd spread, the revolutionary spirit of 1905 revived quickly. On March 2 the workers in the Tashkent railroad workshops met and voted to form a Soviet of Workers' Deputies, which soon became affiliated with the Petrograd Soviet. The Tashkent Soviet called on all the railroad workers in Turkestan to organize soviets and send representatives to Tashkent, and urged similar action upon the military units in the vicinity. On March 4 a Soviet of Soldiers' Deputies was formed in the Tashkent garrison. A Soviet of Peasant Deputies appeared next, composed mainly of Russians, and occupied with the land and water problem. Soviets were set up in the peasant villages, and the peasants prepared to seize land from the natives.

The moderate and conservative classes also organized, hastening to protect their interests and to help fill the sudden power vacuum. There were societies of doctors, lawyers, engineers and other professional people, officials, and even a "Society of Sales Clerks," and a "Society of Employees in the Governor-General's Office." On March 2 a "special committee of the local business and professional classes formed "to direct the social and economic life of the city and to comply with the directives of the Provisional Government." Out of this group grew a more permanent organization, formed at a meeting of the Tashkent City Duma on March 5–6, 1917—an "Executive Committee of the Provisional Government." This body, composed of nineteen members, took on itself the task of governing the region until the Provisional Government in Petrograd could send a committee to take over control. The Tashkent Executive Committee sponsored the election of local executive committees elsewhere in the region, and planned the election of oblast, uezd, and volost commissars.

The native population was also caught up in the fever of organization. A Congress of Turkestan Moslems which met in Tashkent came out for a Russian democratic federative republic, territorial autonomy for Turkestan, and moved to form a Turkestan Moslem Central Council, of which Mustafa Chokaev was elected chairman. As soon as the congress was over, various of the Dzhadid groups, under the leadership of Munevver Kari, united in a Council of Islam (*Shura-i-Islamiia*), pledged to pursue reformist aims. In opposition to this, conservatives under Shir Ali Lapin, formerly an interpreter for the military governor of Samarkand oblast, and shortly before the February Revolution a lawyer at Ak-Mechet, formed a "Union of the Clergy" (*Ulema Dzhemiyeti*).[6]

Simultaneously, various Russian political parties became active, particularly the Constitutional Democrats, the Socialist Revolutionaries, and the Menshevik and Bolshevik wings of the Social Democrats. The emergence from the underground of a vociferous Left brought demands for a still more complete revolution that would secure a government not by the "bourgeoisie" but by the "toilers."

Kuropatkin, still the lawful head of the government, tried to retain control of this situation. On March 8, 1917, he issued a circular bestowing on the people of Tashkent the right of municipal self-government, the right to form trade unions, and proclaimed the end of the *Okhrana,* the secret police. At the same time he stated that officials then serving were all to remain at their posts until confirmed or replaced by the new government.

But the pace of events was too fast for the old regime to be preserved in republican guise. The Soviets tried to take over the authority of the regular organs of government, frequently countermanding official orders, so that a *dvoevlastie* (diarchy) resulted and no one knew where the power lay. As the pressure from the Left continued to mount, the representatives of the old regime who still held office were gradually replaced by new men.

Faced by this situation, Kuropatkin was all but helpless. He continued to make speeches and to issue orders, trying to hold back the growing political agitation until the Provisional Government could send aid. He warned of the danger of famine if the economic equilibrium of the region was upset, and of the possibility of new native uprisings. Finally he resorted to threats. At this point, on March 31, 1917, a joint meeting of the Executive Committee and the Soviets voted to remove Kuropatkin from office. He was placed under house arrest, and a few days later was sent out of the region, never to return.

With the decline of the central authority to a point where even the head of the region could be unseated, the old regime in Russian Central Asia was as good as over. Other vestiges of the past—both people and institutions—remained for a few more weeks or months, but gradually all gave way to the commissars, executive committees, and soviets of the new order. The Bolshevik triumph in Tashkent on October 31, 1917, and eventual seizure of control over the Kazakh Steppe and Transcaspia in the course of the Civil War of 1918–1920 merely made formal the end of an era.

CONCLUSION:

THE COLONIAL HERITAGE OF THE USSR

THE CLOSE in 1917 of the half century of Imperial Russian colonial rule in Central Asia poses the question of what was accomplished to the benefit or detriment of the region, and how much may have been carried over from that period into our own time. There is no need of any apologia today for the Russian intrusion into Central Asia a century ago. The drive for national security and economic advantage, and the intangibles of glory and a share in the task of bringing the fruits of Western civilization to backward lands, although not valid today, were adequate enough reasons at that time.

Neither can there be any question, from a Western point of view, of the over-all beneficial changes wrought following the conquest. One need only cite the extension of peace and order and of Russia's newly reformed legal and administrative system to the region; the expansion of trade; the improvement of agriculture; the beginning of mining and manufacturing; the construction of railroads and irrigation works; the building of modern cities; and the establishment of modern schools, and of newspapers, libraries, and scientific organizations. These were all net gains of which any Russian could be proud. So, too, could any Westerner, for this was not merely a Russian affair but a facet of the entire Western colonial tradition, traceable to the days when Rome brought water, roads, and bridges and her pax to the ends of the known world, including some of the very lands which in modern times built their own empires around the globe.

The innovations necessarily were based on national self-interest, but they also included a conviction that good was being done the conquered regions. Much was undertaken which went beyond mere exploitation. The abolition of slavery and cruel punishments, for example, served no practical end for Russia, but expressed humanitarianism and consciousness of the responsibility to be borne.

Present-day Soviet historians acknowledge readily enough what was achieved in Central Asia during the Imperial period. But, as spokesmen for a revolutionary regime, they still feel called upon to justify the seizure of power. Therefore, rather than give any credit to the regime they overthrew, they ascribe the good works to "the Russian people," and the errors and omissions to "tsarism." This is falsification. Examination of the record shows that the benefits which came from the period of Russian colonial rule were synonymous with the very figures and institutions associated with "tsarism." Von Kaufman, Kolpakovskii, Korol'kov, Komarov, Grodekov, and many another paladin of "tsarism" were the initiators of the best that was done during the period of Imperial rule. The distinction drawn between the "good works" of the "progressive Russian people" and the alleged enslavement of the natives and suppression of native culture ascribed to "tsarism" creates a duality in the description of this period which is simply pseudo-historical nonsense. There can be no disputing the fact that most of the "progressive people" of this era wore officers' epaulettes and were inspired in what they did by the very ideology and ideals abjured by their Soviet successors.

Certainly more could have been done. The low status of women, persistence of the veil, child marriage, and nearly universal illiteracy cried out for change. The lack of effort in these sectors was not due to indifference but rather to observance of a principle of Western "colonialism" requiring persuasion and a good example rather than coercion. It was a reflection of a society governed by the Christian ethic, which observed certain bounds in dealings with other peoples that were not to be passed.

There was, of course, the aspiration to draw the natives closer and to remake them in the image of the occupying power. This was the purpose of the bilingual schools for natives, and Von

Kaufman's policy of intentional neglect which he hoped would cause the Moslem religious influence to wither away or become modified. However the total effort of this kind was comparatively small. Unlike the British in India, for example, the Russians in Central Asia did not train a political, technological, and administrative elite; they never risked training a large body of native troops; and they undertook nothing comparable to the vast educational work undertaken in India by British missionaries. Nevertheless, even the small number of Central Asians trained in the Russian schools and exposed to Western influence through association formed a basis for native change.

But along with the hoped-for "drawing closer" there arose a national consciousness among the natives. Those who drew closer sought and obtained not just Russian culture but modern culture. Thus, while benefiting Russia, the occupation served also as a period of tutelage for the natives, setting them on a new course and starting new trends which paradoxically were directed toward the end of foreign rule.

When the Soviets seized power in Central Asia, existing trends were halted abruptly. The administrative and economic forms of the previous regime were scrapped and replaced by a more highly centralized and inflexible system, able to mobilize labor and capital as never before. The intentions and spirit of the Imperial regime were supplanted by a new ethic valuing the group more than the individual, and impelled by a Messianic zeal.

Using 1917 as a point of departure, Soviet writers cite an impressive string of achievements to justify their regime in Central Asia. Production of coal, steel, oil, and other minerals has reached high levels; large hydroelectric plants and factories have been built. In the Kazakh Steppe the sown area, and consequently the output of grain and other agricultural products, has been expanded greatly through the application of modern techniques and the utilization of virgin lands. The zone of cultivation in the Steppe has been pushed farther south than was dreamed possible in 1914. Large irrigation projects and planned allocation of crops have made the USSR almost self-sufficient in cotton. New railroads facilitate the exploitation of the region's resources. In the realm of culture there has been a vast enlargement of the school network. Illiteracy has practically been conquered and there are many native as well as Russian specialists. Women are now emancipated and take their places with men in schools, in factories, on farms, and in the professions.

These achievements are real enough, but there is another side to the coin. First of all, much of this development would probably have taken place even without the Soviet regime. Had Central Asia become an independent republic in 1917, or even a mandate of another power, the Central Asians would also have experienced much of the same advance during the past forty years. For the world moves forward, and progress is not the monopoly of any one system.

Secondly, the purposeful acceleration of certain "progressive trends" already under way before 1917 has taken a great toll. Indeed, the Kazakhs are now a settled people, but the collectivization which accomplished this set off a famine costing nearly a million lives. Certainly the Steppe has been won for cultivation, but Russian colonization has continued until the Kazakhs are now a minority in their own land. The Kazakh SSR, which in 1939 had a population of 6,146,000, with 47 per cent Russians, had in 1956 an estimated 8,500,000, so far in excess of the normal increase that the proportion of Russians is now probably over 60 per cent. Continued industrialization and the completion of great new irrigation projects will undoubtedly increase the number of Russians correspondingly throughout the other Central Asian republics. Self-sufficiency in cotton has been achieved through ruthless collectivization of the farms of the native peasants. Those who resisted these changes were exterminated or sent to join slave labor gangs building the giant industrial complexes in the Urals or in the Steppe.

Much of the cultural development and change during this time has also been brought about by compulsion. The practice of religion is discouraged, and the vaunted educational system furthers sovietization. Artificial boundaries and the fostering of linguistic differences hinder unification of the native peoples. Native literature and leadership have repeatedly been purged of elements considered nationalistic and hence inimical to the Soviet regime. "Fraternal aid" notwithstanding, the "elder brother" has indeed become a domineering and oppressive brother.

Heir of military rulers like Von Kaufman and Skobelev, holder of a land taken by bayonet, which has not had a free election in forty years, the USSR continues many of the trends started under its Imperial forerunner. At a time when one after another of the dependencies of the capitalist powers are being given self-government, the peoples of Central Asia are still under the tutelage begun a century ago. The worst time of collectivization, famine, and purge is probably over and the people can now begin to enjoy some of the benefits from what they have been made to build. But, at present, they can serve as an eloquent example for peoples in other parts of the world who remain under colonial rule, or for those newly freed and considering the direction they may take. The peoples of Central Asia have the prospect of everything but the right to decide their own fate, to travel, or to speak, vote, and worship as they please. In fact, they have the prospect of everything but freedom.

APPENDIX

List of the Governor-Generals of Turkestan

	b. d.	Period in office
Adj. Gen. K. P. Von Kaufman	(1818–1882)	(July 14, 1867–May 3, 1882)
Lt. Gen. M. G. Cherniaev	(1828–1898)	(May 25, 1882–Feb. 21, 1884)
Adj. Gen. N. O. Rosenbach	(1836–1901)	(Feb. 21, 1884–Oct. 28, 1889)
Lt. Gen. Baron A. B. Vrevskii	(1834–1910)	(Oct. 28, 1889–Mar. 17, 1898)
Lt. Gen. S. M. Dukhovskoi	(1838–1901)	(Mar. 28, 1898–Jan. 1, 1901)
Lt. Gen. N. A. Ivanov	(1842–1904)	(Jan. 23, 1901–May. 18, 1904)
Cav. Gen. N. N. Teviashov	(1841–1905)	(June 22, 1904–Nov. 24, 1905)
Lt. Gen. D. I. Subotich	(1851– ?)	(Nov. 28, 1905–Aug. 15, 1906)
Inf. Gen. N. I. Grodekov	(1843–1913)	(Dec. 15, 1906–Mar. 8, 1908)
Adj. Gen. P. I. Mishchenko	(1853–1919)	(May 2, 1908–Mar. 17, 1909)
Inf. Gen. A. V. Samsonov	(1859–1914)	(Mar. 17, 1909–Aug. 1914)
Adj. Gen. A. N. Kuropatkin	(1848–1925)	(July 21, 1916–Mar. 31, 1917)

In addition to the above, various figures served as acting governor-general for considerable periods. For example, General G. A. Kolpakovskii served in that capacity during the last year of Von Kaufman's regime, and until the appointment of Cherniaev. General F. V. Von Martson served from August, 1914, until June, 1916.

List of the Governor-Generals of the Steppe

Inf. Gen. G. A. Kolpakovskii	(1882–1889)
Lt. Gen. Baron M. A. Taube	(1889–1901)
Gen. N. N. Sukhotin	(1901–1906)
Lt. Gen. Sakharov	(1906–1907)
Lt. Gen. Nadarov	(1907–1909)
Cav. Gen. E. O. Shmitt	(1909–1914)
Lt. Gen. N. A. Sukhomlinov	(1914–1917?)

The data for Turkestan are derived chiefly from K. K. Palen, *Kraevoe upravlenie*, and A. I. Dobrosmyslov, *Tashkent v proshlom i nastoiashchem*. Precise data concerning personnel of the Steppe governor-generalship are lacking, and this list had to be made up from the *Almanach de Gotha*, obituaries, and passing references in other works.

TABLE A-1

TOTAL AREA, AREA UNDER CULTIVATION, AND POPULATION OF THE STEPPE OBLASTS

Areas and population	Ural'sk	Turgai	Akmolinsk	Semipalatinsk	Total
No. of square versts	277,990	400,470	497,190	449,850	1,625,500
Millions of desiatines	29.0	41.7	51.8	46.8	169.3
Desiatines farmed by Russian settlers and Kazakhs (Jan. 1, 1913)	5,280,000		6,514,000	2,307,000	14,101,000
Population (Jan. 1, 1911)	804,245	712,615	1,443,721	873,760	3,834,341
Russians	297,711	235,480	835,441	174,873	1,543,505
Kazakhs	485,863	426,669	550,187	675,240	2,137,959

SOURCE: *Aziatskaia Rossiia,* Atlas, pls. 34, 35.

TABLE A-2

TOTAL AREA, AREAS UNDER IRRIGATION AND CULTIVATION, AND POPULATION OF TURKESTAN OBLASTS

Areas and population	Syr-Daria	Fergana	Samarkand	Semirechie	Transcaspia	Total
No. of square versts	429,890	125,470	76,940	335,250	525,540	1,493,090
Millions of desiatines	44.8	13.1	8.0	34.9	54.8	155.6
Desiatines under irrigation	635,000	840,000	480,000	703,000	150,000	2,808,000
Desiatines under cultivation (Jan. 1, 1913)	...	...	541,000	2,503,000	...	3,054,000
Population (Jan. 1, 1911)	1,816,000	2,041,900	960,202	1,201,540	472,500	6,492,692
Russians	103,500	34,200	22,929	204,307	41,671	406,607
Natives	1,713,050	2,007,700	937,273	997,233	430,829	6,086,085

SOURCE: *Aziatskaia Rossiia,* Atlas, pls. 34, 35, except for area under irrigation, *ibid.,* II, 244.

List of Equivalents

1 verst	500	sazhen	1.067	kilometers	0.6629	miles
1 kilometer	1,000	meters	.938	versts	.621	miles
1 mile	5,280	feet	1.6093	km.	1.509	versts
1 sq. verst	104.17	desiatines	1.138	sq. km.	.439	sq. miles
1 desiatine	2,400	sq. sazhens	1.0925	hectares	2.70	acres
1 hectare	10,000	sq. meters	.914	desiatines	2.471	acres
1 acre	0.370	desiatines	.405	hectares		
1 pood	40	Russian pounds	16.38	kilograms	36.113	pounds (avoirdupois)
1 ruble (1914)	2.16	marks	2 s. 1⅜d.			$0.515

ABBREVIATIONS

Alektorov: A. E. Alektorov, *Ukazatel' knig, zhurnal'nykh i gazetnykh statei i zametok o kirgizakh.*
BEES: Entsiklopedicheskii slovar'. (Brockhaus-Efron.)
BENES: Novyi entsiklopedicheskii slovar'. (Brockhaus-Efron.)
CDSP: Current Digest of the Soviet Press.
GDSO: Gosudarstvennaia Duma. Stenograficheskii otchet.
IIRGO: Izvestiia Imperatorskogo Russkogo Geograficheskogo obshchestva.
IKS: Istoriia Kazakhskoi SSR.
INU: Istoriia narodov Uzbekistana.
IUS: Istoriia Uzbekskoi SSR.
KNO: Korrespondenzblatt der Nachrichtenstelle für den Orient.
POA: Polozhenie ob upravlenie oblastei Akmolinskoi, Semipalatinskoi, Semirechenskoi, Ural'skoi i Turgaiskoi.
PUT: Polozhenie ob upravlenii Turkestanskim kraiem.
PSZ: Polnoe sobranie zakonov Rossiiskoi imperii. . . .
SAGU: Sredneaziatskii gosudarstvennyi universitet.
SZRI: Svod zakonov Rossiiskoi imperii.
TUGU: Trudy Uzbekskogo Gosudarstvennogo Universiteta.
TV: Turkestanskie Vedomosti.
ZhMNP: Zhurnal Ministerstva narodnogo prosveshcheniia.

NOTES

NOTES TO CHAPTER I

[1] See, e.g., "Kirgizskaia SSR," *Bol'shaia sovetskaia entsiklopediia*, 1st ed., XXXII (1936), col. 377; "Kazakhskaia SSR," *ibid.*, XXX (1937), cols. 591–595.

[2] Nechkina, "K voprosu o formule 'naimen' shee zlo' (pis'mo v redaktsiiu)," *Voprosy Istorii*, April, 1951, pp. 44–47; an English translation in *CDSP*, III:31 (1951); later discussion in each.

[3] *IKS* (1943), 308.

[4] A. S. Shcherbakov, speech, *Izvestiia*, Jan. 22, 1942.

[5] J. V. Stalin, toast, *Izvestiia*, May 25, 1945.

[6] Pankratova, *Istoriia SSR*, II, 258.

[7] Nechkina, *loc. cit.*

[8] Sokol, *The Revolt of 1916 in Russian Central Asia*, pp. 172 ff.; "Central Asia and the Russian people," *Central Asian Review*, I:3 (1953), 1–8.

[9] *Pravda Vostoka*, Feb. 12, 1954 and *CDSP*, VI:7 (1954), 7; *Central Asian Review*, II:4 (1954), 308–313.

[10] *Pravda*, Mar. 25, 1954 and *CDSP*, VI:12 (1954), 35.

[11] *IUS*, I (part 2), 392; Radzhabov, *Rol' velikogo russkogo naroda v istoricheskikh sud'bakh narodov Srednei Azii*, p. 83; *IKS*, I (1957), 573.

[12] Cf. *Istoriia SSSR*, II, 573 ff., and II (2d ed.), 531 ff.; *IKS* (1943), 242 ff., and *IKS* I (1957), 337 ff.

[13] *IKS*, I (1957), 355; Gafurov, *Istoriia tadzhikskogo naroda . . .* , I (2d ed.), 424; *IUS*, I (part 2), 106; Radzhabov, *op. cit.*, p. 30; Lutskii, *Istoriia SSSR, 1861–1917*, p. 81; Kary-Niiazov, *Ocherki istorii kul'tury sovetskogo Uzbekistana*, p. 48; Taimanov, *Razvitie sovetskoi gosudarstvennosti v Kazakhstane*, p. 3; *Istoriia Kirgizii* (2 vols.) and review in *Voprosy Istorii*, Aug., 1957, p. 202.

[14] Émigrés from this region generally refer to it as "Turkestan" (The land of the Turks). See, e.g., Togan, *Bugünkü Türkili (Turkistan) ve yakın tarihi;* and Hayit, *Turkestan im XX Jahrhundert*. However, as Russian usage of this term excludes the Kazakh Steppe it has seemed advisable in the present work to use the more explicit though less convenient "Russian Central Asia."

[15] Cressey, *Asia's Lands and Peoples*, p. 343.

[16] *Ibid.*, p. 350.

[17] *Ibid.*, p. 343.

[18] *Ibid.*, p. 347; Mirov, *Geography of Russia*, pp. 150–151.

[19] *Cressey, loc. cit.;* cf. Suslov *Fizicheskaia geografiia SSSR, Aziatskaia chast'*, 2d ed., p. 547.

[20] Reinhard Junge, *Das Problem der Europäisierung orientalischer Wirtschaft dargestellt an den Verhältnissen der Sozialwirtschaft von Russisch-Turkestan*, p. 55. Junge postulated that the widespread incidence of despotism throughout the Orient arose from the need of centralism to overcome tendencies toward individualism detrimental to an economy based on irrigation, and even ascribed aspects of personality to natural influences in arid lands. Olzscha and Cleinow, *Turkestan, die politisch-historischen und wirtschaftlichen Probleme Zentralasiens*, p. 268, linked progress with water management and decline with resurgence of nomad power. This field of inquiry has been carried still further by Karl Wittfogel, *Oriental Despotism: A Comparative Study of Total Power* (New Haven: Yale Univ. Press, 1957) p. 557.

[21] See Kostenko, *Sredniaia Aziia i vodvorenie v nei russkoi grazhdanstvennosti*, p. 88.

[22] Bartol'd, *Istoriia kul'turnoi zhizni Turkestana*, p. 160.

[23] Von Schwarz, *Turkestan, die Wiege der indogermanischen Völker*, p. 134. Von Schwarz goes so far as to state that during the course of several centuries not less than a million Persians were supplied to the Central Asian slave markets by raiding Turkmen. Persians, who were members of the Shiite sect of the Moslem religion, were regarded as heretics by the Sunnites of Central Asia, and hence eligible for enslavement. The Kazakhs supplied occasional Russian slaves, taken in border raids on the peasant settlements or Cossack outposts in the north, or in attacks on unwary fishermen on the Caspian shore.

NOTES TO CHAPTER II

[1] Terent'ev, *Istoriia zavoevaniia Srednei Azii*, I, 294. Hereafter cited as Terent'ev.

[2] *Loc. cit.;* Maksheev, *Istoricheskii obzor Turkestana i nastupatel'nogo dvizheniia v nego russkikh*, p. 225. Hereafter cited as Maksheev.

[3] As quoted in Schuyler, *Turkistan*, II, 261. Hereafter cited as Schuyler. For complete text see "An Indian Officer," *Russia's March Towards India*, II, 307. See also Olzscha and Cleinow, *Turkestan*, pp. 46 ff.

[4] Maksheev, p. 227; Terent'ev, I, 298 ff.; A. I. Dobrosmyslov, *Tashkent v proshlom i nastoiashchem*, p. 51, hereafter cited as Dobrosmyslov.

[5] Schuyler, II, 210.

[6] Maksheev, p. 231; Terent'ev, I, 308.

[7] Maksheev, p. 232.

[8] Dobrosmyslov, pp. 54–58.

[9] Terent'ev, I, 335.

[10] Maksheev, p. 243; *Voennaia entsiklopediia,* St. Petersburg, XI, 23; Terent'ev, I, 347.

[11] Terent'ev, I, 354.

[12] *Ibid.,* pp. 355–356.

[13] From Lt. Col. Glukhovskoi, *Zapiska o znachenii Bukharskogo khanstva dlia Rossii i neobkhodimosti priniatiia reshitel'nykh mer dlia prochnogo vodvoreniia nashego vliianiia v Srednei Azii,* St. Petersburg, 1867, pp. 34–38; as quoted in extract in *Khrestomatiia po istorii SSSR,* III (2d ed., Moscow, 1952), 316–317.

[14] Maksheev, p. 246; Terent'ev, I, 371.

[15] Maksheev, p. 251.

[16] *Ibid.,* p. 268; *Voennaia entsiklopediia,* X, 476, 517–518.

[17] Maksheev, p. 268; also Simonov, "Vosstanie protiv tsarizma v Samarkande v 1868 godu," *TUGU,* n.s., no. 1 (1940), 10–16.

[18] Von Kaufman, *Proekt vsepoddaneishago otcheta . . . ,* p. 75. Hereafter cited as Von Kaufman.

[19] Maksheev, p. 280.

[20] For a detailed discussion of this matter see Warren M. Engstrand, "The Kuldja Affair and Its Significance in Sino-Russian Relations," University of California M.A. thesis (unpublished), Berkeley, California, 1933. See also H. Manzooruddin Ahmed, *Kampf um leere Raume, Turan, Turkestan, Tibet,* pp. 88–110, and Olzscha and Cleinow, *op. cit.,* pp. 112–118 concerning the career of Yakub Beg.

[21] Schuyler, II, 334.

[22] *Ibid.,* pp. 336–337.

[23] *Loc. cit.*

[24] MacGahan, *Campaigning on the Oxus and the Fall of Khiva,* pp. 226–227.

[25] Schuyler, II, 351.

[26] MacGahan, *op. cit.,* pp. 278–279, 309–312.

[27] Schuyler, II, 357; Terent'ev, II, 266 ff.

[28] Maksheev, p. 325; MacGahan, *op. cit.,* p. 390; Schuyler, II, 354–363.

[29] MacGahan, *op. cit.,* p. 413; Schuyler, II, 359.

[30] Maksheev, p. 325. See complete treaty text in MacGahan, *op. cit.,* pp. 416–420.

[31] Von Kaufman, p. 76.

[32] Schuyler, II, 370–377.

[33] *Ibid.,* p. 288; Terent'ev, I, 357–358; *Times* (London) Oct. 22, 1875.

[34] *Times* (London), Oct. 14, 1875.

[35] Schuyler, II, 294.

[36] *Ibid.,* p. 296; *Voennaia entsiklopediia,* II, 543; Terent'ev, I, 376.

[37] Schuyler, II, 298.

[38] *Ibid.,* p. 299; *Voennaia entsiklopediia,* II, 544.

[39] Schuyler, II, 300.

[40] *Ibid.;* Maksheev, p. 344. Still hoping to return to power, Khudoiar Khan escaped from Orenburg in December, 1877, with the aid of Kazakhs and made his way to Herat. He visited Mecca, and died in Afghanistan in 1886 at the age of eighty. *TV,* Jan. 26, 1916. After a short residence in Orenburg Abdurakhman-avtobachi was allowed to return on parole to Kokand, where he died. *Niva* (1888), 290.

[41] Schuyler, II, 378.

[42] Terent'ev, III, 3.

[43] Terent'ev, II, 434–435; Marvin, *The Russians at Merv and Herat and Their Power of Invading India,* pp. 392 ff.

[44] Marvin, *The Eye-Witnesses' Account of the Disastrous Russian Campaign Against the Akhal Tekke Turcomans . . . ,* p. 266. Cf. Maksheev, p. 355; Terent'ev, III, 22.

[45] Maksheev, p. 358.

[46] Curzon, *Russia in Central Asia . . . ,* pp. 82–83.

[47] Maksheev, pp. 370–372. Cf. Terent'ev, III, 220.

[48] James G. Allen, "Anglo-Russian Rivalry in Central Asia, 1865–1885," University of California Ph.D. dissertation (unpublished), Berkeley, California, 1934. This work traces the diplomatic history of the imperial rivalries in Central Asia which came to a crisis with the actual drafting by England of a declaration of war. Only hasty action by the Russian ambassador in London averted the conflict.

[49] Maksheev, p. 292.

[50] Curzon, *op. cit.,* pp. 85–86.

[51] *Ibid.,* p. 86.

NOTES TO CHAPTER III

[1] The other members of the Commission were Major General Gutkovskii, Colonel A. K. Geins, and Lieutenant Colonel A. P. Protsenko. Geins' diaries, *Dnevnik 1865 goda: Puteshestviia vo Kirgizskim stepiam* and *Dnevnik 1866 goda: Puteshestviia v Turkestan,* are valuable sources on the work of this commission.

[2] The Special Committee included the minister of war (presiding); Adjutant General N. A. Kryzhanovskii, governor-general of Orenburg; Adjutant General Geiden, chief of the General Staff; Privy Counsellor Stremoukhov, director of the Asiatic Department of the General Staff; Actual Counsellor of State Mansurov, director of the Department of General Affairs of the Ministry of the Interior; Major General M. G. Cherniaev; Major General D. I. Romanovskii; Major General Graf Vorontsov-Dashkov; State Counsellor Galkin, chief of Section of the Committee of Ministers; and the four members of the Steppe Commission (Palen, *Kraevoe upravlenie,* p. 7).

[3] *Ibid.*

[4] Schuyler, II, 204; Bartol'd, *Istoriia kul'turnoi zhizni Turkestana,* p. 182.

[5] Schuyler, *loc. cit.;* Demetrius C. Boulger, *England and Russia in Central Asia,* p. 68.

[6] *PSZ,* XLII:1 (ser. 2, no. 44831).

[7] These plenipotentiary powers were set forth in a letter of July 17, 1867, from the director of the Asiatic Department, Privy Counsellor Stremoukhov. The text is given in Palen, *op. cit.,* pp. 11–12.

[8] N. Frideriks, "Turkestan i ego reformy. Iz zapisok ochevidtsa," *Vestnik Evropy,* VII:3 (1869), 692.

[9] *Ibid.,* p. 710.

[10] *Syn otechestva,* no. 80 (1868), as quoted in Palen, *op. cit.,* pp. 13–18, and Dobrosmyslov, pp. 61–67.

[11] Von Kaufman, p. 47–50.

[12] *IKS* I (1957), 394.

[13] *IKS* (1943), 271; *IKS* I (1957), 395.

[14] *IKS* I (1957), 397–398.

[15] *IKS* (1943), 274.

[16] Terent'ev, II, 69.

[17] Maksheev, p. 298. Cf. *IKS* (1943), 276, and *IKS* I (1957), 398–399.

[18] *IKS* (1943), 275–276; *IKS* I (1957), 398–399; Maksheev, p. 298. Cf. Terent'ev, II, 69–70, who states that Rukin, eager to negotiate with the Kazakhs, acceded to their request that his men first stack arms as a sign of good faith. As soon as this was done, the natives overwhelmed the small force.

[19] Maksheev, p. 298; *IKS* (1943), 276, 278; *IKS* I (1957), 399.

[20] *IKS* (1943), 279; *IKS* I (1957), 400.

[21] Von Kaufman, p. 75.

[22] *Ibid.,* p. 78.

[23] Fedorov, "Moia sluzhba v Turkestanskom krae (1870–1906 g.)," *Istoricheskii Vestnik,* CXXXIV (1913), 465–466.

[24] Palen, "Erinnerungen," p. 108.

[25] Gafurov, *Istoriia tadzhikskogo naroda* . . . , I (2d ed.), 455; Ishanov, *Sozdanie Bukharskoi narodnoi sovetskoi respubliki (1920–1924 gg.),* pp. 34–37.

[26] *IKS* (1943), 269.

[27] *Istoriia SSSR,* II, 592; *Istoriia SSSR,* II (2d ed.), 550.

[28] See, e.g., Coates and Coates, *Soviets in Central Asia,* p. 61; Olscha and Cleinow, *Turkestan,* p. 61; Mandel, *The Soviet Far East and Central Asia,* pp. 100–101; Sokol, *The Revolt of 1916 in Russian Central Asia,* pp. 52–53.

[29] Bartol'd, *op. cit.,* p. 120; Terent'ev, III, 343.

[30] *IKS* I (1957), 387.

[31] *IUS,* I (part 2), 101.

[32] Von Kaufman, p. 76.

[33] *Ibid.,* pp. 78–80.

[34] Ignat'ev, *Komissiia . . . Protokol zasedanii 23, 24 i 28 fevral'ia, 3 i 6 marta 1884 goda*, pp. 2–5.

[35] Alektorov, p. 294.

[36] See, e.g., Anichkov, "Eshche o proekte novoi gubernii," *Okraina*, no. 68 (1896), and his *Ocherk narodnoi zhizni severnago Turkestana. Sbornik*, pp. 47–52.

NOTES TO CHAPTER IV

[1] *SZRI, Obshchee uchrezhdenie gubernskoe*, sec. 208.

[2] *Ibid.*, secs. 441, 442.

[3] Schuyler, II, 227.

[4] *Ibid.*, pp. 221–223.

[5] Von Schwarz, *Turkestan*, p. 493.

[6] Dobrosmyslov, p. 445.

[7] Fedorov, "Moia sluzhba v Turkestanskom krae (1870–1906 g.)," *Istoricheskii Vestnik*, CXXXIII (1913), 786; Dobrosmyslov, p. 109 n.

[8] Dobrosmyslov, pp. 453–454; Schuyler, II, 250.

[9] Dobrosmyslov, p. 457.

[10] Von Schwarz, *op. cit.*, 494.

[11] *Loc. cit.;* Terent'ev, II, 415.

[12] Dobrosmyslov, p. 61.

[13] *Ibid.*, p. 113.

[14] *Ibid.*, p. 461.

[15] Terent'ev, III, 318.

[16] *Loc. cit.*

[17] *Dobrosmyslov*, p. 476.

[18] Iushkov, *Istoriia gosudarstva i prava SSSR*, part 1, 3d ed., p. 559.

[19] Dobrosmyslov, p. 107; Schuyler, II, 238.

[20] Dobrosmyslov, p. 108.

[21] Schuyler, II, 246–247 n., quoting article by N. Petrovskii in *Vestnik Evropy*, Oct., 1875.

NOTES TO CHAPTER V

[1] Burnaby, *A Ride to Khiva*, p. 393, quoting an official report made by Eugene Schuyler.

[2] Schuyler, II, 251 ff.

[3] Fedorov, "Moia sluzhba v Turkestanskom krae (1870–1906 g.)," *Istoricheskii Vestnik*, CXXXIII (1913), 786 ff.; *Kaufmanskii sbornik*, p. lxxxiii.

[4] Dobrosmyslov, p. 117.

[5] Terent'ev, I, 315–316; Girs, *Otchet revizuiushchago, po Vysochaishemu poveleniiu, Turkestanskii krai.*

[6] Terent'ev, I, 316; Fedorov, *loc. cit.*, CXXXIV (1913), 438–439; Girs, *loc. cit.*

[7] Terent'ev, *loc. cit.*

[8] *Ibid.*

[9] Ignat'ev, *Komissiia . . . Protokol zasedanii 23, 24 i 28 fevralia, 3 i 6 marta 1884 goda*, p. 1.

[10] *Ibid.*, pp. 11–12.

[11] Fedorov, *loc. cit.*, CXXXIV (1913), 444.

[12] Terent'ev, III, 343–345.

[13] *Ibid.*, p. 369.

[14] SZRI, *Vremennoe polozhenie ob upravlenii Zakaspiiskoi oblasti*, secs. 13–24.

[15] Fedorov, *loc. cit.*, CXXXIV (1913), 872–873.

[16] Palen, "Erinnerungen," p. 215.

[17] *Ibid.*, p. 310.

[18] *INU*, II, 256.

[19] Krivoshein, *Zapiski . . .* , pp. 78–79.

NOTES TO CHAPTER VI

[1] Schuyler, I, 76.

[2] *Ibid.*, p. 78.

[3] *Ibid.*, p. 83.

[4] Von Schwarz, *Turkestan*, pp. 514–515.

[5] Schuyler, I, 84.

[6] Majerczak, "Kaufmanskii Sbornik," *Revue du Monde Musulman*, XXVI (1914), 194. The collection was prepared by General M. A. Terent'ev and A. L. Kun in seven sets, including one for Tsar Alexander II, one for Von Kaufman, one for the Rumiantsev Museum Library in Moscow, and one for the Tashkent Library. One incomplete set of this extremely interesting collection has found its way to the Library of Congress, in Washington, D. C.

[7] Von Schwarz, *op. cit.*, p. 507; N. A. Burov, "Istoricheskaia spravka o vremeni osnovaniia Tashkentskoi Publichnoi (nyne Sredne-Aziatskogo Gosudarstvennogo) Biblioteki," in *V. V. Bartol'du*, pp. 122–124.

[8] Palen, *Gorodskoe upravlenie*, p. 215; Vetter, "Rospis' stat'iam i zametkam po istorii i arkheologii Srednei Azii, pomeshchennym v gazete 'Turkestanskie Vedomosti' za vremia ee sushchestvovanii (28 aprelia 1870—15 dekabria 1917)," in *V. V. Bartol'du*, pp. 479–531.

[9] Ostroumov, *Sarty. Etnograficheskie materialy*, 2d ed., p. 170; Palen, *op. cit.*, p. 218; Bartol'd, *Istoriia kul'turnoi zhizni Turkestana*, p. 139.

[10] Ostroumov, *Konstantin Petrovich fon-Kaufman, ustroitel' Turkestanskago kraia. Lichnyia vospominaniia . . .* , p. 4; Fedorov, "Moia sluzhba . . . ," *Istoricheskii Vestnik*, CXXXIV (1913), 55.

[11] Curzon, *Russia in Central Asia*, p. 240.

[12] *Ibid.*, pp. 241–242.

[13] Palen, *op. cit.*, p. 44.

[14] *Aziatskaia Rossiia,* I, 331.

[15] Graham, *Through Russian Central Asia,* pp. 57–58.

[16] Palen, *op. cit.,* p. 4.

[17] Bartol'd, *op. cit.,* p. 163.

[18] *Ibid.,* pp. 161–162.

[19] *Ibid.,* p. 168.

[20] *Ibid.,* p. 169.

[21] *Aziatskaia Rossiia,* I, 348–354, Atlas, plate 61.

NOTES TO CHAPTER VII

[1] Von Kaufman, p. 150.

[2] *Ibid.,* p. 149.

[3] *Ibid.,* p. 150.

[4] *Ibid.,* p. 160.

[5] *Ibid.*

[6] *Ibid.,* p. 151.

[7] *PSZ,* XLII:1, ser. 2, no. 44845; *BEES,* XIII:2 (1894), col. 891.

[8] Von Kaufman, p. 174.

[9] *Aziatskaia Rossiia,* I, 449–451.

[10] Von Kaufman, p. 174; *IKS* (1943), 289.

[11] Von Kaufman, p. 184.

[12] Ignat'ev, *Komissiia* . . . , "Protokol zasedanii . . . , April 3–May 3," p. 19.

[13] Von Kaufman, p. 199.

[14] *IKS* (1943), 289.

[15] Von Kaufman, p. 199; A. Zhakmon, "K voprosu o kolonizatsii Kirgizskikh stepei," *Moskovskiia Vedomosti,* nos. 159, 162 (1892), quoted in Alektorov, p. 329.

[16] Ignat'ev, *Komissiia* . . . , "Ob'iasnitel'naia zapiska . . . ," p. 95.

[17] Von Kaufman, pp. 17, 125, 136, 139–141.

[18] *Ibid.,* p. 204.

[19] Almost 70 years after Kuropatkin's warning, official estimates of April, 1956, placed the population of the USSR at 200,200,000. No figures on ethnic distribution have been published since 1939, but the number of Russians now in Siberia and Central Asia is doubtless close to Kuropatkin's minimal goal of 25 million which he believed necessary for Russian dominance.

[20] Ignat'ev, *Komissiia* . . . , "Protokoly (April 3–May 3)," p. 19.

[21] Ignat'ev, *Komissiia* . . . , "Ob'iasnitel'naia zapiska . . . ," p. 95.

[22] *Loc. cit.*

[23] Ignat'ev, *Komissiia* . . . , "Protokoly (April 3–May 3)," pp. 19–20, "Polozhenie ob upravlenii Turkestanskim kraem," pp. 30–31, "Ob'iasnitel'naia zapiska . . . ," pp. 95–96.

[24] A. A. Isaev, "Pereselentsy v Srednei Azii," *Russkiia Vedomosti*, no. 61 (1890), quoted in Alektorov, p. 382; E. Shmurlo, "Pereselencheskie i Kirgizskie voprosy v Akmolinskoi stepi," *S.-Peterburgskiia Vedomosti*, nos. 188, 200 (1898), (Alektorov, p. 937). Isaev praised policy in the western United States, where "the building of roads . . . precedes the settlement of the western states, and attracts it. These roads are built for economic and not administrative ends." But in Asiatic Russia ". . . roads are put through for administrative reasons, to connect towns, and to provide the shortest communication with European Russia, without taking settlement into account."

[25] Shmurlo, *op. cit.* (Alektorov, p. 939).

[26] *Loc. cit.*

[27] *Loc. cit.*

[28] Shmurlo, *op. cit.* (Alektorov, p. 940); *PSZ*, ser. 3, IX, no. 6198; A. A. Kaufman, *Pereselenie i kolonizatsiia* (St. Petersburg, 1905), p. 78; *Aziatskaia Rossiia*, I, 455. See also Treadgold, *The Great Siberian Migration*, pp. 73 ff.

[29] Shmurlo, *op. cit.* (Alektorov, 942).

[30] *Loc. cit.*

[31] *PSZ*, ser. 3, XII, no. 9140; ser. 3, XIII, no. 9354. See also Treadgold, *op. cit.*, pp. 108–111.

[32] Kaufman, *op. cit.*, p. 44; *Aziatskaia Rossiia*, I, 461–462.

[33] *BEES*, XXIII:1 (1898), col. 272.

[34] Shmurlo, *op. cit.* (Alektorov, p. 947); *Aziatskaia Rossiia*, I, 541.

[35] Alektorov, p. 714.

[36] *Narod*, St. Petersburg, no. 188 (1897), (Alektorov, p. 547); *S.-Peterburgskiia Vedomosti*, no. 307 (1898), (Alektorov, p. 807); *Stepnoi Krai*, no. 119 (1897), (Alektorov, p. 823); *Turgaiskaia Gazeta*, no. 3 (1898), (Alektorov, p. 872).

[37] *Aziatskaia Rossiia*, I, 542.

[38] *Ibid.*, p. 543.

[39] *Ibid.*, p. 461; *PSZ*, ser. 3, XVI:1, no. 13464. See also Treadgold, *op. cit.*, pp. 120–121 ff.

[40] Shkapskii, "Nekotoryia dannyia dlia osveshcheniia kirgizkogo voprosa," *Russkaia Mysl'*, no. 6 (1897).

[41] Shkapskii, "Kirgizy-krest'iane (iz zhizni Semirech'ia)," *IIRGO*, XLI (1905), 778.

[42] Kaufman, *op. cit.*, p. iii.

[43] *PSZ*, ser. 3, XXV:1, nos. 26172, 26369; *Aziatskaia Rossiia*, I, 464.

[44] *Smeta dokhodov, raskhodov i spetsial'nykh sredstv Pereselencheskago upravleniia . . . na 1912 god*, p. 46, and map facing p. 30.

[45] *Aziatskaiia Rossiia*, I, 543. Italics in original.

[46] *Loc. cit.*

[47] *Ibid.*, p. 546.

[48] Fedorov, "Moia sluzhba v Turkestanskom krae (1870–1906 g.)," *Istoricheskii Vestnik,* CXXXIV (1913), 456.

[49] M. Mustafin, "Nikolai Ivanovich Grodekov, 1883–1913. Vospominaniia i zametki," *Istoricheskii Vestnik,* CXII (1915), 145.

[50] Bartol'd, *Istoriia kul'turnoi zhizni Turkestana,* p. 152.

[51] *Ibid.*, p. 157.

[52] *Loc. cit.*

[53] Sharova, "Pereselencheskaia politika tsarizma v Srednei Azii," *Istoricheskie Zapiski,* VIII (1940), 25.

[54] *Ibid.*, p. 15.

[55] *GDSO,* 2d Session, 36th sitting, May 10, 1907, col. 445.

[56] *Aziatskaia Rossiia,* I, facing p. 493.

[57] *Ibid.*, p. 474.

[58] *Ibid.*, facing p. 492.

[59] *GDSO,* 2d Session, 36th sitting, May 10, 1907, col. 442.

[60] *GDSO,* 2d Session, 46th sitting, May 24, 1907, cols. 1113–1133; Sharova, *op. cit.,* p. 27.

[61] *IUS* I (part 2), 111–112.

[62] *Okrainy Rossii,* no. 35–36 (1909), 511.

[63] *Smeta dokhodov* . . . , p. 28.

[64] Stolypin, *Poezdka v Sibir' i Povolzh'e,* p. 39.

[65] *Ibid.*, p. 83. By 1913 Slavgorod had 7,000 inhabitants. *Aziatskaia Rossiia,* I, 485. See also Treadgold, *op. cit.,* pp. 158–159.

[66] Stolypin, *op. cit.,* p. 90.

[67] *Ibid.*, p. 92.

[68] *Ibid.*, p. 129. See also correspondence between Stolypin and Nicholas II (September 26, 1910), *Krasnyi Arkhiv,* XXX (1928), 82; Sharova, *op. cit.,* p. 22.

[69] *POA,* sec. 119–120; *PSZ,* ser. 3, XI, no. 7574.

[70] *PUT,* sec. 270; *PSZ,* ser. 3, XXX:1, no. 34501, sec. 3; Sharova, *op. cit.,* p. 24.

[71] Sharova, *op. cit.,* 26–27.

[72] Krivoshein, *Zapiska o poezdke v Turkestanskii krai v 1912 godu,* p. 80.

[73] *Aziatskaia Rossiia,* I, 67–68; Lorimer, *The Population of the Soviet Union: History and Prospects,* p. 27.

[74] *Aziatskaia Rossiia,* I, 87.

NOTES TO CHAPTER VIII

[1] Von Kaufman, p. 223; Hudson, *Kazak Social Structure,* pp. 31–35; Liashchenko, *History of the National Economy of Russia to the 1917 Revolution,* p. 577.

[2] Semenov, "Ocherk pozmel'no-podatnogo i nalogovogo ustroistva b.

Bukharskogo khanstva," *SAGU, Trudy,* ser. 2, Orientalia, Fasc. 1 (1929), 5.

[3] Schuyler, I, 298–300; Semenov, *op. cit.,* pp. 5–6.

[4] Iushkov, *Istoriia gosudarstva i prava SSSR,* p. 448.

[5] Von Kaufman, pp. 236–237.

[6] *Ibid.,* pp. 399–400.

[7] Schuyler, I, 173.

[8] To circumvent Moslem prohibitions against the public dancing of women, it was an established institution in Central Asia from early times to train boys to impersonate female dancers. Treated with great esteem, they were hired to perform before guests on special occasions or retained by the wealthy. Sometimes they were used for homosexual purposes. For an early reference by Maqdisī see R. Frye, *History of Bukhara* (Cambridge, Mass., 1954), p. 147 n. 265. See also Schuyler, I, 132–136; Lansdell, *Russian Central Asia* . . . , I, 210; Von Schwarz, *Turkestan* . . . , pp. 175, 296–298.

[9] Von Kaufman, p. 228.

[10] Middendorf, *Einblikke in das Fergana-Thal,* pp. 412–414; Hoetzsch, "Russisch-Turkestan und die Tendenzen der heutigen russischen Kolonialpolitik," *Schmoller's Jahrbuch,* XXXVII:1 (1913), 401–403; *Aziatskaia Rossiia,* I, 550.

[11] *INU,* II, 259.

[12] Liashchenko, *op. cit.,* p. 607.

[13] *INU,* II, 259.

[14] Von Kaufman, p. 402.

[15] *Ibid.,* p. 405; Schuyler, I, 305.

[16] Dobrosmyslov, p. 104.

[17] G. K. Gins, "Vakuf," in *BENES,* X, col. 321.

[18] Von Kaufman, p. 247.

[19] Gins, *loc. cit.,* col. 322.

[20] *PSZ,* ser. 3, VI, no. 3814, secs. 265–267; Gins, *loc. cit.,* col. 322; "Enquetes sur les vakoufs du Turkestan," *Revue du Monde Musulman,* XIII:2 (1911), 278, 311.

NOTES TO CHAPTER IX

[1] Hudson, *Kazak Social Structure,* pp. 24–26.

[2] Alektorov, p. 461.

[3] V. O., "Iz Turgaiskoi oblasti," *Russkaia Zhizn',* no. 5 (1893), quoted in Alektorov, p. 190; *Orenburgskii Krai,* no. 3 (1892), (Alektorov, p. 604).

[4] *St. Peterburgskie Vedomosti,* no. 357 (1898), (Alektorov, p. 808).

[5] Hudson, *op. cit.,* p. 29.

[6] *Orenburgskii Krai,* no. 13 (1893), (Alektorov, pp. 606–607).

[7] V. I. Kovalevskii, *Proizvoditel'nyia sily Rossii. Kharakteristiki razlich-*

nykh otraslei narodnogo truda (Alektorov, p. 461); Masal'skii, *Turkestanskii krai*, p. 467.

[8] *Aziatskaia Rossiia*, II, 314.

[9] Kovalevskii, *op. cit.* (Alektorov, p. 461).

[10] *Loc. cit.; Aziatskaia Rossiia*, II, 307.

[11] *Orenburgskii Krai*, no. 34 (1893), *St. Peterburgskie Vedomosti*, nos. 22, 27, 58 (1899), (Alektorov, pp. 609, 679, 810, 816).

[12] Dobrosmyslov, p. 305.

[13] M. A. Levanevskii, "Ocherki Kirgizskikh stepei," *Zemlevedenie*, no. 4 (1894), (Alektorov, p. 493).

[14] The Russian officials had to rely on figures supplied by the natives, but the latter, fearing higher taxation, usually falsified the number of their livestock. Lansdell, *Russian Central Asia . . . ,* I, 101–102 n., tells how in 1881 officials in Semipalatinsk oblast deemed it necessary to revise figures on livestock, based on native returns, by multiplying them two and three times. The *Encyclopaedia Brittanica*, XXVII (1911), 421, in describing the steppe region, merely stated: "Livestock breeding is extensively pursued. The flocks of sheep on the Kirghiz Steppe are so large that the proprietors themselves do not know their exact numbers."

[15] *Aziatskaia Rossiia*, II, 318.

[16] *Ibid.,* I, 309.

[17] *Ibid.,* II, 300–301, 318.

[18] *Ibid.,* I, 309.

NOTES TO CHAPTER X

[1] Liashchenko, *History of the National Economy of Russia to the 1917 Revolution*, p. 355.

[2] *Loc. cit.; Zakaspiiskoe obozrenie*, no. 72, June 28, 1896; *IUS*, I (part 2), 86.

[3] Liashchenko, *op. cit.,* p. 610.

[4] Brodovskii, "Ocherk proizvodstva khlopka v Srednei Azii," *Sredniaia Aziia, Almanakh . . . ,* Feb. (1910), 156.

[5] *Aziatskaia Rossiia*, II, 276; Fedorov, "Moia sluzhba . . . ," *Istoricheskii Vestnik*, CXXXIV (1913), 40.

[6] *Zakaspiiskoe Obozrenie*, no. 72, June 28, 1896. Cf. Liashchenko, *op. cit.,* p. 611; Olscha and Cleinow, *Turkestan*, p. 283; and Schakir, *Baumwollwirtschaft Turkestans*, p. 22.

[7] Liashchenko, *op. cit.,* p. 610.

[8] *Aziatskaia Rossiia*, II, 278; Liashchenko, *op. cit.,* p. 611.

[9] *Zakaspiiskoe Obozrenie*, no. 72, June 28, 1896.

[10] *Aziatskaia Rossiia*, II, 277.

[11] *Ibid.,* p. 244; *IUS*, I (part 2), 215.

[12] *Aziatskaia Rossiia*, II, 278.

[13] *Russian Yearbook,* (1916), 142; *IUS,* I (part 2), 209 states that the Russian demand for cotton in 1910 was 25,870,000 poods.

[14] Liashchenko, *op. cit.,* p. 615.

[15] Voeikov, *Le Turkestan Russe,* p. 256.

[16] *INU,* II, 273.

[17] *Zakaspiiskoe Obozrenie,* no. 72, June 28, 1896.

[18] Liashchenko, *op. cit.,* 610.

[19] *Zakaspiiskoe Obozrenie,* no. 72, June 28, 1896.

[20] Voeikov, *op. cit.,* p. 258.

[21] Safarov, *Kolonial'naia revoliutsiia: opyt Turkestana,* p. 34.

[22] *Zakaspiiskoe Obozrenie,* no. 72, June 28, 1896.

[23] Preliminary report on Cotton Situation, U. S. Consulate, Tashkent, State Department file 102.733/61, May 11, 1918, U. S. National Archives.

[24] Report on the Area and Condition of the Cotton Crop in Russia at the beginning of June, 1912. U. S. Consulate General, Moscow, State Department file 102.733/61, U. S. National Archives.

[25] *IUS,* I (part 2), 219.

[26] Liashchenko, *op. cit.,* p. 614; Voeikov, *op. cit.,* p. 145; Safarov, *op. cit.,* p. 36; *INU,* II, 277.

[27] *INU,* II, 279–281.

[28] From information supplied by an informant who helped organize such credit institutions.

[29] Liashchenko, *op. cit.,* p. 614.

[30] *Zakaspiiskoe Obozrenie,* no. 20, Feb. 18, 1896.

[31] Bartol'd, *Istoriia kul'turnoi zhizni Turkestana,* p. 160.

[32] *Zakaspiiskoe Obozrenie,* no. 20, Feb. 18, 1896.

[33] Voeikov, *op. cit.,* p. 230.

[34] *Russian Yearbook* (1916), 167.

[35] Voeikov, *op. cit.,* p. 276.

[36] Masal'skii, "Rural industries and forestry of Turkestan," *The Industries of Russia,* III, 444.

[37] Fedorov, *loc. cit.*

[38] Masal'skii, *op. cit.,* p. 463; *Zakaspiiskoe Obozrenie,* no. 76, July 7, 1896.

[39] Liashchenko, *op. cit.,* p. 613.

[40] *Russian Yearbook* (1916), 148.

[41] Fedorov, *loc. cit.*

[42] Voeikov, *op. cit.,* p. 272.

[43] Masal'skii, *op. cit.,* p. 469.

[44] Shcheglov, *Khronologicheskii perechen' vazhneishikh dannykh iz istorii Sibiri, 1032–1882 gg.,* p. 314.

[45] Russian Yearbook (1916), 166.

[46] According to the *Encyclopaedia Brittanica,* XVII (1911), p. 55, the

principal producers of the world's commercial cotton crop in 1906 ranked as follows (500-pound bales):

United States	13,016,000
British India	3,708,000
Egypt	1,400,000
Russia	675,000
China	418,000
Others	725,000
	19,942,000

NOTES TO CHAPTER XI

[1] *Aziatskaia Rossiia*, II, 247; Fedorov, "Moia sluzhba . . . ," *Istoricheskii Vestnik*, CXXXIV (1913), 41.

[2] Ostroumov, *Konstantin Petrovich fon-Kaufman, ustroitel' Turkestanskago kraia*, p. 40.

[3] *Aziatskaia Rossiia*, II, 248; Bartol'd, *Istoriia kul'turnoi zhizni Turkestana*, p. 151.

[4] Bartol'd, *op. cit.*, p. 142; *Aziatskaia Rossiia*, II, 249, Atlas, map 45; Sharova, "Pereselencheskaia politika tsarizma v Srednei Azii," *Istoricheskie Zapiski*, VIII (1940), 30; Alektorov, p. 695.

[5] Bartol'd, *op. cit.*, p. 154.

[6] *Russian Yearbook* (1916), 146; Sharova, *op. cit.*, p. 30.

[7] *PSZ*, ser. 3, VII, no. 4670; Auhagen, *Die Landwirtschaft in Transkaukasien*, pp. 48–49; Voeikov, *Le Turkestan Russe*, p. 178; Liashchenko, *History of the National Economy of Russia to the 1917 Revolution*, p. 607.

[8] *Aziatskaia Rossiia*, II, 251.

[9] Masal'skii, *Turkestanskii krai*, p. 648; Bartol'd, *op. cit.*, p. 154; Voeikov, *op. cit.*, p. 179; *BEES*, XX:1, 207; *Aziatskaia Rossiia*, Atlas, map 40.

[10] *Aziatskaia Rossiia*, II, 250; Bartol'd, *op. cit.*, p. 155.

[11] James, *Faraway Campaign*, p. 227; *Aziatskaia Rossiia*, II, 251.

[12] Lebed' and Iakovlev, *Transportnoe znachenie gidrotekhnicheskikh sooruzhenii SSSR*, p. 133; Curzon, *Russia in Central Asia . . .* , p. 404. *Times* (London), Dec. 3, 1873, p. 10.

[13] Kolarz, *Russia and Her Colonies*, p. 290; Barrett, *Russia's New Era*, pp. 268–277.

[14] *Okrainy Rossii*, no. 15–16 (1911), 239.

[15] *Ibid.*, no. 51–52 (1912), 725; Kastal'skii, "Istoriko-geograficheskii obzor Surkhanskoi i Shirabadskoi dolin," *Vestnik Irrigatsii*, no. 4 (1930), 21.

[16] Krivoshein, *Zapiski . . .* , pp. 80–82.

[17] *TV*, no. 13, Jan. (1906).

[18] Alektorov, p. 777.

[19] Von Kaufman, pp. 419–420, 426–427.

20 *Times* (London), June 2, 1873, p. 9; June 14, 1873, p. 5.

21 Curzon, *op. cit.*, p. 36; Terent'ev, III, 230–231.

22 Curzon, *op. cit.*, pp. 53–54; Biddulph, *Four Months in Persia and a Visit to Transcaspia*, p. 113.

23 Curzon, *op. cit.*, p. 49.

24 *Aziatskaia Rossiia*, II, 545–547; Voeikov, *op. cit.*, p. 50; Curzon, *op. cit.*, p. 51.

25 Dobson, *Russia's Railway Advance into Central Asia*, p. 19.

26 Curzon, *op. cit.*, p. 146; *Aziatskaia Rossiia*, II, 547; *Zakaspiiskoe Obozrenie*, no. 137, Nov. 27, 1896, no. 8, Jan. 17, 1897; Dmitriev-Mamonov, *Putevoditel' po Turkestanu* . . . , p. 296; Hoetzsch, "Russisch-Turkestan und die Tendenzen der heutigen russischen Kolonialpolitik," *Schmollers Jahrbuch*, XXXVII (1913), 344; Charykov, *Glimpses of High Politics*, p. 211.

27 *Aziatskaia Rossiia*, II, 548.

28 *Loc. cit.; Zakaspiiskoe Obozrenie*, no. 137, Nov. 27, 1896, no. 8, Jan. 17, 1897.

29 In November, 1896, the Russian government commissioned J. B. Pangborn, an American railway expert, to make a special study of the Trans-Caspian Railroad with the object of speeding up service. *Zakaspiiskoe Obozrenie*, no. 134, Nov. 20, 1896.

30 Dmitriev-Mamonov, *op. cit.*, pp. 400 ff.; *Aziatskaia Rossiia*, II, 549; Olscha and Cleinow, *Turkestan*, p. 239.

31 *Aziatskaia Rossiia*, II, 560; Fedorov, "Moia sluzhba . . . ," *Istoricheskii Vestnik*, CXXXIV (1913), 455; Voeikov, *op. cit.*, p. 285. See also Chirkin, "Proektiruemyia sibirskie zheleznyie dorogi i ikh kolonizatsionnoe znachenie," *Voprosy Kolonizatsii*, no. 6 (1910), 27–45.

32 Dmitriev-Mamonov, *op. cit.*, p. 380.

33 Karl Stählin, *Russisch Turkestan gestern und heute*, p. 16; Graham, *Through Russian Central Asia*, p. 226; Olscha and Cleinow, *op. cit.*, p. 241.

34 *Aziatskaia Rossiia*, II, 550 ff., Atlas, map 58; *Smeta dokhodov* . . . , map, facing p. 22.

NOTES TO CHAPTER XII

1 *IKS* (1943), 303.

2 Barrett, *Russia's New Era*, pp. 182–183.

3 *IKS* (1943), 565.

4 Drage, *Russian Affairs*, p. 431; *IKS* (1943), 303; Barrett, *op. cit.*, pp. 183–185, 189.

5 Iakunin, "Revoliutsiia 1905–1907 gg. v Kazakhstane," in *Revoliutsiia 1905–1907 gg. v natsional'nykh raionakh Rossii*, pp. 674–675; *IKS* (1943), 342–343.

6 *IKS* (1943), 342–343.

7 *Ibid.*, p. 356.

[8] Schuyler, I, 323.

[9] Palen, *Gornoe delo,* pp. 62–65. In recent times the drop in the level of the Caspian has caused Cheleken Island to become a peninsula.

[10] *Ibid.,* p. 63; Palen, "Erinnerungen," p. 207.

[11] Palen, *op. cit.,* pp. 171–176.

[12] Palen, *Gornoe delo,* p. 62.

[13] Schuyler, I, 320.

[14] Liashchenko, *History of the National Economy of Russia to the 1917 Revolution,* p. 316.

[15] Palen, *Gornoe delo,* pp. 143–144.

[16] *Ibid.,* p. 128; Voeikov, *Le Turkestan Russe,* p. 16.

[17] Palen, *op. cit.,* pp. 133, 145–146; Schuyler, I, 322.

[18] Voeikov, *op. cit.,* p. 17.

[19] Alektorov, p. 819.

[20] Palen, *op. cit.,* p. 102; Voeikov, *op. cit.,* p. 19.

[21] Voeikov, *op. cit.,* pp. 69–70.

[22] Alektorov, p. 603; *TV,* Mar. 1, 1906.

[23] Voeikov, *op. cit.,* p. 73.

[24] *Zakaspiiskoe Obozrenie,* no. 32, Mar. 17, 1896.

[25] Iakunin, *op. cit.,* p. 674.

[26] Liashchenko, *op. cit.,* p. 615.

[27] *IKS* (1943), 356; Iakunin, *op. cit.,* p. 674.

[28] Piaskovskii, "Revoliutsiia 1905–1907 gg. v Turkestane," in *Revoliutsiia 1905–1907 gg. v natsional'nykh raionakh Rossii,* p. 568.

[29] Iakunin, *op. cit.,* p. 675.

[30] Piaskovskii, *op. cit.,* p. 570.

[31] Iakunin, *op. cit.,* p. 676.

[32] Palen, "Erinnerungen," p. 199.

[33] *Aziatskaia Rossiia,* II, 413.

[34] *Ibid.,* p. 419; *IKS,* I (1957), 528.

[35] *Aziatskaia Rossiia,* II, 425–426.

NOTES TO CHAPTER XIII

[1] Von Mende, *Der nationale Kampf der Russlandtürken,* p. 25; Alektorov, p. 749; *BEES,* XIX:1 (1896), 446–448.

[2] Afanas'ev, "N. I. Il'minskii i ego sistema shkol'nago prosveshcheniia inorodtsev Kazanskago kraia," *ZhMNP,* LII (1914), 66–68.

[3] *Ibid.,* p. 143.

[4] *Turgaiskaia Gazeta,* no. 37 (1895), quoted in Alektorov, p. 862; *Novoe Vremia,* no. 5813 (1892), (Alektorov, p. 583).

[5] *Kirgizskaia Stepnaia Gazeta,* no. 45 (1895), (Alektorov, p. 439); *S.-Peterburgskiia Vedomosti,* no. 284 (1898), (Alektorov, p. 801).

[6] S. Rybakov, "Nuzhdy narodnogo prosveshcheniia," *Narodnoe obrazovanie,* 1:4 (1899), (Alektorov, p. 732).

[7] *Russkii nachal'nyi uchitel'*, no. 5 (1899), (Alektorov, p. 725).

[8] "Narodnoe obrazovanie v Ural'skoi oblasti," *Obrazovanie*, no. 5–6 (1891), (Alektorov, p. 955).

[9] *Glasnost'*, no. 107 (1898), (Alektorov, p. 271).

[10] *Volzhskii Vestnik*, no. 83 (1898), (Alektorov, p. 244); *Gorodskoi i sel'skii uchitel'*, 1 (1899), (Alektorov, p. 659).

[11] *Turgaiskaia Gazeta*, no. 16 (1895), (Alektorov, p. 860).

[12] *S.-Peterburgskiia Vedomosti*, no. 304 (1896), (Alektorov, p. 98); *Kirgizskaia Stepnaia Gazeta*, no. 17 (1897), (Alektorov, p. 444).

[13] A. I. Stepnoi, "Sredi kirgizov," *Kamsko-Volzhskii Krai*, no. 174 (1896), no. 320 (1897), (Alektorov, p. 821); *Russkii nachal'nyi uchitel'*, no. 5 (1899), (Alektorov, p. 725); *S.-Peterburgskie Vedomosti*, no. 284 (1898), (Alektorov, p. 802).

[14] *Kirgizskaia Stepnaia Gazeta*, no. 34 (1897), (Alektorov, p. 446).

[15] Alektorov, "Iz istorii razvitiia obrazovaniia sredi kirgizov Akmolinskoi i Semipalatinskoi oblastei," *ZhMNP*, CCCLXII (Dec., 1905), 178.

[16] *Ibid.*, p. 179.

[17] K. A. Belavin, "Kratkii istoricheskii ocherk Orenburgskoi muzhskoi gimnazii za 1868–1893 goda," *Orenburgskii Krai*, no. 140 (1893), (Alektorov, p. 185).

[18] *S.-Peterburgskie Vedomosti*, no. 284 (1898), (Alektorov, pp. 803–804).

[19] *Okraina*, no. 49 (1892), (Alektorov, p. 602); *Sibirskii Vestnik*, no. 232 (1898), (Alektorov, pp. 764–765).

[20] Masal'skii, *Turkestanskii krai*, p. 335.

[21] *Ibid.*

[22] *Ibid.*, p. 336.

[23] Von Kaufman, p. 438.

[24] *Ibid.*, p. 439.

[25] *Loc. cit.*; Gramenitskii, *Polozhenie inorodcheskago obrazovaniia v Syr-Dar'inskoi oblasti*, p. 4.

[26] Gramenitskii, *op. cit.*, p. 5; Ostroumov, *Konstantin Petrovich fon-Kaufman . . .* , pp. 43, 107.

[27] Gramenitskii, *op. cit.*, p. 11.

[28] *Ibid.*, p. 12.

[29] *INU*, II, 329; *IUS*, I (part 2), 162–163, 165.

[30] Bartol'd, *Istoriia kul'turnoi zhizni Turkestana*, pp. 131–133.

[31] Quoted by Bobrovnikov, "Russko-tuzemnaia uchilishcha, mekteby i medresy Srednei Azii," *ZhMNP*, XLV (1913), 197. Italics in original.

[32] *Loc. cit.*

[33] Gramenitskii, *op. cit.*, p. 15.

[34] *Ibid.*, pp. 17, 19; *IUS*, I (part 2), 163.

[35] Gramenitskii, *op. cit.*, p. 22.

[36] Alektorov, p. 732; Masal'skii, *op. cit.*, p. 338; Bartol'd, *op. cit.*, p. 137. Cf. Bobrovnikov, *op. cit.*, p. 227; Zenkovsky, "*Kulturkampf* in Pre-Revolu-

tionary Central Asia," *American Slavic and East European Review,* XIV (1955), 25.

[37] Gramenitskii, *op. cit.,* p. 79.

[38] *Ibid.,* p. 80.

[39] *Ibid.,* p. 82.

[40] Kary-Niiazov, *Ocherki istorii kul'tury sovetskogo Uzbekistana,* p. 40.

[41] *Bol'shaia sovetskaia entsiklopediia,* SSSR volume (1948), col. 1928.

[42] Zhmuida, *Ashkhabad,* p. 28.

[43] *Bol'shaia sovetskaia entsiklopediia,* SSSR volume (1948), col. 1851.

[44] *IKS,* I (1957), 545.

[45] *Ibid.,* p. 546.

[46] *Loc. cit.*

[47] *Loc. cit.*

NOTES TO CHAPTER XIV

[1] Girs, *Otchet revizuiushchago, po Vysochaishemu poveleniiu, Turkestanskii krai . . . ,* p. 414.

[2] Terent'ev, III, 325–327; T-ov, "Andizhanskoe vozstanie i ego prichiny," *Istoricheskii Vestnik,* CXII (1908), 661; Seng-zade, "K 30 letiiu vosstanie 1898 goda," in *Revoliutsiia v Srednei Azii. Sbornik,* no. 1 (1928), 41; *IUS,* I (part 2), 99; Togan, *Bugünkü Türkili (Türkistan) ve yakīn tarihi,* p. 332; Hayit, *Turkestan im XX Jahrhundert,* p. 28. Details of these uprisings are still exceedingly scant; no detailed study based on archival materials has been published.

[3] Terent'ev, III, 372–375.

[4] *Ibid.,* pp. 376–378; *IUS,* I (part 2), 131.

[5] *INU,* II, 361.

[6] *Zakaspiiskoe Obozrenie,* Feb. 18, 1896.

[7] Terent'ev, III, 473.

[8] *Ibid.,* pp. 477–479.

[9] *Ibid.,* p. 431.

[10] *Ibid.,* pp. 447–449.

[11] *Ibid.,* pp. 430–434.

[12] *Ibid.,* pp. 449–452.

[13] *Ibid.,* pp. 435–436.

[14] *Ibid.,* pp. 463–464.

[15] Cobbold, *Innermost Asia. Travel and Sport in the Pamirs,* p. 214, tells of the excitement and fantastic rumors that spread among the Kirgiz on the Chinese border concerning the events at Andizhan.

[16] Terent'ev, III, 471–472.

[17] Palen, "Erinnerungen," p. 88.

[18] Terent'ev, III, 483; Iuvachev, "Kurban-Dzhan-datkha, Kara-kirgizskaia tsaritsa Alaia," *Istoricheskii Vestnik,* CX (1907), 977; Bartol'd, *Istoriia kul'turnoi zhizni Turkestana,* p. 156; Fedorov, "Moia sluzhba . . . ,"

Istoricheskii Vestnik, CXXXIV (1913), 862–863. See also Kuropatkin, "Vosstanie 1916 g. v Srednei Azii," *Krasnyi Arkhiv,* XXXIV (1929), 86; *Niva,* XXVIII (1898), 514–516; T-ov, *op. cit.,* p. 661; Tolqun, "Madali Eschan (1856–1898)," *Millij Turkestan,* no. 80–81 B (Aug.–Nov., 1952), 25–28; Togan, *op. cit.,* pp. 332–334; and Caroe, *Soviet Empire,* pp. 88–89. Gafurov, in the first edition of *Istoriia tadzhikskogo* . . . , pp. 443–444, attaches great significance to the uprising as a school for later revolts, but in the second edition, pp. 457–458 he accedes to criticism and characterizes it as a "reactionary movement" which would have led to a slaughter of the Russian population and "the annihilation of all the progressive elements in Middle Asia."

[19] T-ov, *op. cit.,* p. 666.
[20] Terent'ev, III, 485–486.

NOTES TO CHAPTER XV

[1] Iakunin, "Revoliutsiia 1905–1907 gg. v Kazakhstane," in *Revoliutsiia 1905–1907 gg. v natsional'nykh raionakh Rossii,* p. 680.

[2] *INU,* II, 374. Cf. *IUS,* I (part 2), 247. See also Piaskovskii, "Revoliutsiia 1905–1907 gg. v Turkestane," in *Revoliutsiia 1905–1907 gg. v natsional'nykh raionakh Rossii,* p. 602.

[3] Piaskovskii, *op. cit.,* p. 602.

[4] *Ibid.,* pp. 602, 605.

[5] *Ibid.,* p. 588.

[6] *Ibid.,* pp. 593–594.

[7] *Ibid.,* p. 595.

[8] *Ibid.,* p. 593; Dobrosmyslov, pp. 491–492.

[9] Dobrosmyslov, p. 493; Piaskovskii, *op. cit.,* p. 596.

[10] Dobrosmyslov, *loc. cit.;* cf. Piaskovskii, *loc. cit.*

[11] Dobrosmyslov, p. 494; Piaskovskii, *op. cit.,* p. 597.

[12] *Voina v peskakh,* p. 24.

[13] Mel'kumov, *Materialy revoliutsionnogo dvizheniia v Turkmenii v 1904–1919 g.,* p. 46.

[14] Dobrosmyslov, p. 495.

[15] *Loc. cit.;* Piaskovskii, *op. cit.,* p. 598; Maksimovich, [Report to Tsar Nicholas II . . .], in *Revoliutsiia 1905 g. i samoderzhavie,* p. 122; *INU,* II, 386.

[16] Piaskovskii, *op. cit.,* p. 600.

[17] *TV,* Jan. 13, 1906.

[18] *TV,* Jan. 24, 1906; Maksimovich, *op. cit.,* p. 118.

[19] *TV,* Jan. 31, 1906.

[20] *TV,* Jan. 18, 1906.

[21] *TV,* Feb. 8, 1906; Piaskovskii, *op. cit.,* pp. 650–651.

[22] *TV,* May 28, June 29, July 12, 1906; Piaskovskii, *op. cit.,* p. 614. *INU,* II, 388; *IUS,* I (part 2), 271–272.

²³ Maksimovich, *op. cit.*, pp. 119, 125–126; Piaskovskii, *op. cit.*, p. 617.

²⁴ Maksimovich, *op. cit.*, pp. 119, 127; *TV*, July 5, 1906; *INU*, II, 388–389; Piaskovskii, *op. cit.*, pp. 617–618.

²⁵ Piaskovskii, *op. cit.*, pp. 615, 624–625.

²⁶ Maksimovich, *op. cit.*, pp. 128–131.

²⁷ *Ibid.*, p. 121; *PSZ*, XXVI:1 (1906), nos. 28350, 28367.

NOTES TO CHAPTER XVI

¹ Togan, *Bugünkü Türkili (Türkestan) i yakīn tarihi*, pp. 544 ff.; Caroe, *Soviet Empire*, pp. 225–226. *IKS* (1943), 316–321, describes Valikhanov's anger at the Russian atrocities he witnessed while serving with Cherniaev's forces in 1864, and his decision to forsake all "civilized" society. *IKS*, I (1957), 443–449, describes his acceptance of Russian culture and his achievements, but omits the final painful chapter of his life.

² *Niva*, XXIII (1891), 258–260; Togan, *op. cit.*, p. 550.

³ Schuyler, I, 166; Bartol'd, *Istoriia kul'turnoi zhizni Turkestana*, I, 184–185.

⁴ Schuyler, I, 98; Bartol'd, *op. cit.*, p. 186.

⁵ Ostroumov, *Sarty*, p. 111.

⁶ *IUS*, I (part 2), 171–173; Gafurov, *Istoriia tadzhikskogo . . .* , I (1949), 430–432.

⁷ Von Mende, *Der nationale Kampf der Russland Türken*, pp. 44 ff.; Tokan, *op. cit.*, pp. 551 ff.; Caroe, *op. cit.*, pp. 226–227.

⁸ Hayit, *op. cit.*, p. 38.

⁹ Zenkovsky, *"Kulturkampf* in Pre-revolutionary Central Asia," *American Slavic and East European Review*, XIV (1955), 29.

¹⁰ *GDSO*, Ukazatel'.

¹¹ Alisov, "Musul'manskii vopros v Rossii," *Russkaia Mysl'*, VII (1909), 34.

¹² *Loc. cit.*

¹³ Bobrovnikov, "Russko-tuzemnaia uchilishcha, mekteby i medresy Srednei Azii," *ZhMNP*, XLVI (1913), 65.

¹⁴ *GDSO*, Ukazatel'.

¹⁵ Alisov, *op. cit.*, p. 47.

¹⁶ *Ibid.*, p. 49.

¹⁷ Oktay, "O molodykh godakh i o politicheskoi deiatel'nosti Mustafa Beia Chokai ogly," *Türkeli*, no. 4 (1951), 14; Hayit, *Die nationalen Regierungen von Kokand (Choqand) und der Alasch Orda*, p. 75.

¹⁸ Zenkovsky, *op. cit.*, p. 31.

¹⁹ Oktay, "Turkistan'da Cedid Matbuati," *Turkistan*, I:5 (Aug., 1953), 19–24, I:6 (Sept., 1953), 15–18; Hayit, *Turkestan im XX Jahrhundert*, pp. 38–39; Kary-Niiazov, *Ocherki istorii kul'tury sovetskogo Uzbekistana*, p. 89 n.; Zenkovsky, *op. cit.*, pp. 30–31, 33, 38; Benzing, "Das turkestanische

Volk im Kampf um seine Selbstandigkeit," *Die Welt des Islams*, XIX (Dec., 1937), 113–114.

[20] Hayit, *op. cit.*, pp. 44–45; Benzing, *op. cit.*, pp. 111–112; Olscha and Cleinow, *Turkestan*, pp. 385–386; *IKS* (1943), 368–369; *IKS*, I (1957), 556–557.

[21] Benzing, *op. cit.*, p. 112.

[22] Sokol, *The Revolt of 1916 in Russian Central Asia*, p. 70.

[23] Hayit, *op. cit.*, p. 45.

NOTES TO CHAPTER XVII

[1] *SZRI*, vol. IV, Ustav o voinskoi povinnosti, secs. 42, 60.

[2] Von Mende, *Studien zur Kolonisation in der Sovetunion*, Ost-Europa Institut (Quellen und Studien, Abteilung Wirtschaft, n.s., no. 11), pp. 21–22. Cf. *Rech'*, no. 190, July 17, 1914, which states that 176,873 crossed the Urals eastward in the first half of 1914, and 17,944 returned, but this probably refers to those of male sex only.

[3] Brändstrom, *Bland krigsfångar i Ryssland och Sibirien: 1919–1920*, pp. 63–64; Brun, *Troublous Times*, p. 48.

[4] Krist, *Prisoner in the Forbidden Land*, p. 113; Blond, *Ein unbekannter Krieg*, p. 49.

[5] *TV*, Mar. 20, Apr. 24, Apr. 27, May 12, July 2, 1916; *KNO*, II, no. 41, Aug. 4, 1916, p. 260.

[6] Asfendiarov, *Natsional'no osvoboditel'noe vosstanie 1916 goda v Kazakhstana*, pp. 75–76.

[7] *Loc. cit.*

[8] Togan, *Bugünkü Türkili (Turkistan) ve yakın tarihi*, p. 337; Ryskulov, *Vosstanie 1916 goda v Kirgizstane*, p. 141.

[9] *INU*, p. 417; *IUS*, I (part 2), 328.

[10] *INU*, pp. 449–451; Shteinberg, *Ocherki istorii Turkmenii*, p. 62.

[11] A. N. Kuropatkin, "Iz dnevnika A. N. Kuropatkina," *Krasnyi Arkhiv*, XX (1927), 62. Here Kuropatkin says that 18,000 rifles were called in, but on p. 50 he states 7,500.

[12] *KNO*, II, no. 12, Dec. 11, 1915, p. 70.

[13] M. Tynyshpaev, Deposition of February 1917, presented in Ryskulov, *op. cit.*, p. 141.

[14] *IKS* (1943), 371; Asfendiarov, *op. cit.*, p. 76. I have failed to find any reference to a "blood price" in the *GDSO* for this period. The term may have been used during one of the closed sessions, the debates of which were not published.

[15] Kuropatkin, Diary, July 1916–February 1917, in "Vosstanie 1916 g. v Srednei Azii," *Krasnyi Arkhiv*, XXXIV (1929), 48.

[16] For text, see *Sobranie uzakonenii i rasporiazhenii pravitel'stva, izdavaemoe pri pravitel'stvuiushchem senate*, sec. 1, no. 182, July 6, 1916.

This would normally have appeared in *PSZ*, but the publication of the annual compilations of Imperial legislation was suspended because of the War.

NOTES TO CHAPTER XVIII

[1] Ryskulov, *Vosstanie 1916 goda v Kirgizstane*, p. 16.

[2] *Ibid.*, pp. 24–27.

[3] *Ibid.*, p. 23.

[4] *Ibid.*, p. 17.

[5] *Ibid.*, pp. 17–18.

[6] Uel's, "K voprosu o vosstanii 1916 g. v Khodzhente," *Revoliutsionnyi Vostok*, no. 4 (1936), 82; Ryskulov, "Vosstanie v Srednei Azii v 1916 g.," *Bor'ba Klassov*, VI:6 (1936), 2; *INU*, p. 431; *IUS*, I (part 2), 383; Kovalev, "Narodnye volneniia v vosstaniia v uzbekskikh i tadzhikskikh raionakh Turkestana (v iiule-avguste 1916 goda)," *SAGU, Trudy*, n.s., vypusk 78, Istoricheskie nauki, no. 11 (1956), 73; *Materialy nauchnoi sessii, posviashchennoi istorii Srednei Azii i Kazakhstana v dooktiabr'skii period*, pp. 339–340.

[7] *IUS*, I (part 2), 384; Kovalev, *op. cit.*, pp. 74–76.

[8] *IUS*, I (part 2), 386; Kovalev, *op. cit.*, pp. 77–78; Kuropatkin, "Vosstanie 1916 g. v Srednei Azii," *Krasnyi Arkhiv*, XXXIV (1929), 68; *KNO*, II, no. 48–49, Sept. 27, 1916, p. 300.

[9] Kovalev, *op. cit.*, pp. 78–79; *IUS*, I (part 2), 386–387.

[10] Kovalev, *op. cit.*, p. 79.

[11] *Loc. cit.*; *IUS*, I (part 2), 387.

[12] Kovalev, *op. cit.*, p. 83.

[13] *IUS*, I (part 2), 391; Ryskulov, *op. cit.*, pp. 2–3; *KNO*, II, no. 48–49, Sept. 27, 1916, pp. 299–300.

[14] Ryskulov, *op. cit.*, p. 3; *INU*, p. 433.

[15] Willfort, *Turkestanisches Tagebuch; sechs Jahre in Russisch-Zentralasien*, p. 81.

[16] Kuropatkin, *op. cit.*, p. 67; Shestakov, "Vosstanie v Srednei Azii v 1916 g. (k desiati-letiiu sobytii)," *Istorik-Marksist*, II (1926), 95; "Dzhizakskoe vosstanie 1916 g.," *Krasnyi Arkhiv*, LX (1933), 62.

[17] "Dzhizakskoe vosstanie 1916 g.," *ibid.*, p. 63; Sokol, *The Revolt of 1916 in Russian Central Asia*, p. 93.

[18] Willfort, *op. cit.*, p. 81. But Hayit, *Turkestan im XX Jahrhundert*, p. 58, states that 4,000 natives were slain.

[19] *INU*, p. 434.

[20] *IUS*, I (part 2), 393.

[21] *Ibid.*

[22] "Gubernator v roli propovednika Korana," *Krasnyi Arkhiv*, LXXV (1936), 189; Kovalev, *op. cit.*, p. 88.

[23] *IUS*, I (part 2), 394.

[24] *TV*, Aug. 17, 1916; Kuropatkin, *op. cit.*, pp. 45–46.

[25] Ryskulov, *Vosstanie 1916 goda* . . . , pp. 154–155.

[26] M. Tynyshpaev, Deposition of February, 1917, in Ryskulov, *op. cit.*, pp. 144–147.

[27] *Ibid.*, p. 148.

[28] Ryskulov, *Kirgizstan*, p. 55; Ryskulov, *Vosstanie 1916 goda* . . . , p. 164; Anson, "Vosstanie kazakhov (kirgiz) v 1916," *Sibirskaia Sovetskaia Entsiklopediia*, I (1929), 530; Belotskii, *Kirgizskaia respublika; popularnyi ocherk*, p. 27.

[29] Ryskulov, *Vosstanie 1916 goda* . . . , pp. 162–163.

[30] *Ibid.*, p. 50.

[31] *Ibid.*, pp. 37, 45.

[32] *Ibid.*, pp. 37, 43, 53.

[33] *Ibid.*, p. 44.

[34] *Ibid.*, pp. 38, 50.

[35] *Ibid.*, p. 39; Ryskulov, *Kirgizstan*, p. 55.

[36] Ryskulov, *Vosstanie 1916 goda* . . . , p. 50.

[37] Ryskulov, *Kirgizstan*, p. 56.

[38] *Ibid.*, p. 56; Ryskulov, *Vosstanie 1916 goda* . . . , pp. 51, 52.

[39] *Ibid.*, p. 166; Ryskulov, *Kirgizstan*, pp. 56–57; Kuropatkin, *op. cit.*, pp. 69–70.

[40] Tynyshpaev in Ryskulov, *Vosstanie 1916 goda* . . . , p. 147; *ibid.*, 78–81.

[41] *IKS* (1943), 378; Brainin, *Vosstanie kazakhov Semirech'ia v 1916 godu*, p. 61.

[42] Ryskulov, *op. cit.*, p. 81.

[43] *Ibid.*, p. 51; Kuropatkin, *op. cit.*, p. 50.

[44] Ryskulov, *op. cit.*, p. 81.

[45] *Ibid.*, pp. 80, 83.

[46] *Ibid.*, p. 10; Belotskii, *op. cit.*, p. 25.

[47] "Dzhizakskoe vosstanie . . . ," p. 63; Sokol, *op. cit.*, p. 94.

[48] *TV*, Aug. 26, 1916.

[49] *KNO*, III, no. 3, Nov. 4, 1916, p. 89; no. 4, Nov. 20, 1916, p. 126; no. 10, Feb. 22, 1917, p. 425.

[50] In an interview on April 13, 1959, at the Hoover Library, Stanford, California, A. F. Kerensky has stated that he made the tour at his own initiative in order to obtain first-hand knowledge of the uprisings. He visited Dzhizak, Samarkand, and the main centers of Fergana. At Tashkent he had a long and amicable conversation with Kuropatkin. (The account of a dinner at which he refused to shake Kuropatkin's hand, accusing the latter of undue harshness in the suppression of the disturbances, is apocryphal.) On September 10, 1917, he reported his findings before a secret session of the Duma, which approved unanimously his proposed interpellation of cabinet members to establish responsibility fcr initiation

of the labor draft. Upon his recommendation an amnesty for both Russians and natives involved in the uprisings was decreed soon after the Provisional Government took power in 1917. In September, 1917, an indemnity of 11,150,000 rubles was appropriated in an effort to satisfy the demands of the Russian peasants of Semirechie for compensation.

[51] Kuropatkin, *op. cit.*, p. 62.

[52] *Ibid.*, p. 43.

[53] *TV*, Sept. 20, 1916.

[54] *TV*, Sept. 29, 1916.

[55] *TV*, Oct. 5, 1916.

[56] Kuropatkin, *op. cit.*, pp. 45–46, 71

[57] *Ibid.*, pp. 51, 71.

[58] *Ibid.*, p. 51.

[59] *Ibid.*, p. 56.

[60] *Ibid.*, p. 52; cf. Brainin, *op. cit.*, p. 62.

[61] *Ibid.*, p. 59.

[62] *Ibid.*, p. 60. Such a transfer would have been a hopeless blunder because of geographic factors alone. The Naryn area is a desolate, stone-covered locality, of high elevation, with little pasture and sowing area and no possibilities for irrigation. It is sparsely populated even today.

[63] *Loc. cit.*

[64] Shestakov, "20-letie vosstanie v Srednei Azii (1916–1936)," *Revoliutsiia i natsional'nosti,* no. 9 (1936), 42; Filippov, "Karatel'naia ekspeditsiia generala Madridova," *Turkmenovedenie,* IV:6–7 (1930), 17–20; Filippov, "Bezzastenchivyi grabezh (Po sledam karatel'noi ekspeditsii generala Madridova)," *Turkmenovedenie,* IV:11 (1930), 19–21. Togan, *Bugünkü Türkili . . .* , p. 343, states that when Madritov was arrested after the revolution of February, 1917, in his home were found seventeen poods of silver jewelry taken from Turkmen women, and over sixty fine Turkmen carpets.

[65] Sokol, *op. cit.*, p. 70; Tynyshpaev in 142.

[66] S. D. Asfendiarov, *Natsional'no-osvoboditel'noe vosstanie 1916 goda v Kazakhstane,* p. 78.

[67] Sokol, *op. cit.*, p. 111.

[68] *IKS,* I (1956), 574.

[69] Sokol, *op. cit.*, p. 106.

[70] Asfendiarov, *op. cit.*, p. 82; Shestakov, *op. cit.*, p. 41; *IKS* (1943), 391–392.

[71] Asfendiarov, *op. cit.*, p. 85.

[72] Hayit, *op. cit.*, p. 67.

[73] Kuropatkin, *op. cit.*, p. 74.

[74] Sokol, *op. cit.*, pp. 109–111.

[75] Kuropatkin, *op. cit.*, p. 83.

[76] *Ibid.,* p. 90; Shestakov, *op. cit.,* p. 42.

[77] Kuropatkin, *op. cit.,* p. 68.

[78] *Ibid.,* pp. 69, 85; Sokol, *op. cit.,* p. 159.

[79] Ryskulov, *Vosstanie 1916 goda . . . ,* p. 11.

[80] *Loc. cit.*

[81] E.g., Sharova, "Pereselencheskaia politika tsarizma v Srednei Azii," *Istoricheskii Zapiski,* VIII (1940), 36, states: "300,000 Kazakhs . . ."; Brainin, *op. cit.,* p. 67, ". . . more than 300,000 fugitives . . ."; *Bol'shaia Entsiklopediia* (Granat), "SSSR," col. 595, ". . . 300,000 Kazakhs and Kirgiz . . ."; *IKS* (1943), 378, ". . . 300,000 families of Kazakhs, Kirgiz and Dungans . . ."

[82] Lorimer, *The Population of the Soviet Union,* p. 30.

[83] Kuropatkin, *op. cit.,* pp. 87–88.

[84] *IKS* (1943), 383.

[85] Sokol, *op. cit.,* p. 168.

[86] *Materialy nauchnoi sessii . . . ,* p. 279.

[87] Cf. Kuropatkin, *op. cit.,* p. 75, mentioning "the work of German and Turkish prisoners and agents"; Nazarov, *Hunted Through Central Asia,* "Von Martsohn provoked the rising . . . ," (p. 150), and "The Kirghiz detachments were under the command of Turkish officers, prisoners of war escaped from Siberia" (p. 167); and V. A. Purishkevich, in a speech before the Duma on November 19, 1916, "To this outlying territory, which is so important and so necessary to us in a military sense, there were sent veritable mobs of Germans, who, as instructors of the natives, stirred up social unrest." *GDSO,* 4th Sitting, Session 5, November 19, 1916, col. 275. All of these ideas are still to be found in Soviet works, e.g., *Materialy nauchnoi sessii . . . ,* pp. 298, 309, 317, 346–347, 395–396.

[88] Togan, *op. cit.,* p. 341 states that five Turkish officers fought on the side of the Kazakhs during the uprising in Semirechie oblast.

[89] As examples of this newer approach see the majority of reports on the nature of the uprisings of 1916 in *Materialy nauchnoi sessii . . . ,* pp. 277–409.

[90] *IKS,* I (1956), 577.

[91] *IKS,* I (1956), 585.

[92] *IKS,* I (1956), 577–578.

NOTES TO CHAPTER XIX

[1] Zorin, "Iz istorii vosstaniia kirgizov i kazakhov v 1916 g.," *Bor'ba Klassov,* II:7–8 (1932), 138–139.

[2] Kuropatkin, "Vosstanie 1916 g. v Srednei Azii," *Krasnyi Arkhiv,* XXXIV (1929), 74.

[3] *Ibid.,* p. 80.

[4] *Ibid.,* pp. 81–82.

[5] *TV*, Mar. 5, 1917; Kuropatkin, "Iz dnevnika A. N. Kuropatkina," *Krasnyi Arkhiv*, XX (1927), 59.

[6] Hayit, *Turkestan im XX Jahrhundert*, pp. 49–50. Cf. *IUS*, I (part 2), 411.

GLOSSARY

aksakal—a native elder, literally "white beard."

ataman—the head of a Cossack group.

adat—Moslem customary law.

aul—a nomad patriarchal family group comprising up to about 1,000 people. Equivalent to a village.

baranta—retaliatory raids by Kazakh individuals whose grievances were not satisfied by recourse to customary law.

bek (or *beg*)—a provincial governor in a native state.

bii—a judge among the Central Asian nomadic population, deciding cases on the basis of the adat. See kazi.

buran—a blizzard on the Kazakh Steppe.

Dzhadid—an adherent and propounder of the "new method," a reformed system of Moslem education.

gazavat—a Moslem Holy War.

gubernia—a Russian province, headed by a Governor.

imam—prior of a mosque.

internat—dormitory at a Russian school.

ishan—a leader of the Moslem Sufi sect.

kazi—a judge among the native settled population of Turkestan, deciding cases on the basis of the Shariat. See bii.

kibitka—a native yurt or dome-shaped felt dwelling supported by a portable wooden framework. Also used by the Russian administration in the sense of a household, for taxation and administrative purposes.

kishlak—a settled native village, corresponding to the nomad aul.

medressa—a Moslem higher school of secondary or college level.

mekteb—a Moslem primary school.

mulla—a teacher of the laws and dogmas of Islam.

nachal'nik—a Russian commandant of an uezd or other administrative unit.

oblast—a Russian province, but with less self-government than a gubernia, usually because of location in a frontier region. Headed by a Governor or Military Governor.

okrug—district.

pristav—Police Officer, head of a pristavstvo or uchastok, directing a small police and administrative force.

pristavstvo—a subdivision of an uezd; see also uchastok.

Shariat—Moslem law; see adat.

sotnia—a troop of 100 Cossacks.

uchastok—a subdivision of an uezd, headed by a Pristav.

uezd—a subdivision of a gubernia or oblast, similar to a county; headed by a Commandant.

vakf—a tax-free grant given by an individual to be held in trust by a Moslem state or institution, the income to be devoted to charitable or pious purposes.

voisko—a cossack host, occupying a large, officially designated region.

volost—a subdivision of an uezd, comprising several kishlaks, auls, or Russian peasant villages, governed locally.

zemstvo—an elective local administrative assembly introduced in many parts of Russia after 1864.

BIBLIOGRAPHY

This bibliography includes only those works cited in this book. A more extensive list, arranged topically, may be found in the author's *Russian Central Asia, 1867–1917: A Selected Bibliography*, issued by the Institute of Slavic Studies, University of California, Berkeley, California, in 1953.

Afanas'ev, P. O. "N. I. Il'minskii i ego sistema shkol'nago prosveshcheniia inorodtsev Kazanskago kraia," *ZhMNP*, n.s., LII (1914).

Alektorov, A. E., "Iz istorii razvitiia obrazovaniia sredi kirgizov Akmolinskoi i Semipalatinskoi oblastei," *ZhMNP*, CCCLXII (Dec., 1905), 154–191.

———. *Ukazatel' knig, zhurnal'nykh i gazetnykh statei i zametok o kirgizakh.* Kazan, 1900. Also in Kazan University, *Obshchestvo arkheologii, istorii i etnografii, Izvestiia*, vols. XVI–XX, prilozhenie, 1900.

Alisov, G. "Musul'manskii vopros v Rossii," *Russkaia Mysl'*, VII (1909).

Anichkov, I. V. "Eshche o proekte novoi gubernii," *Okraina*, no. 68 (1896).

———. *Ocherk narodnoi zhizni severnago Turkestana.* Sbornik. Tashkent, 1889.

"An Indian Officer." *Russia's March Towards India.* London, 1894. 2 vols.

Anson, A. A. "Vosstanie kazakhov (kirgiz) v 1916," in *Sibirskaia Sovetskaia Entsiklopediia*, I (1929), 530.

Asfendiarov, S. D. *Natsional'no-osvoboditel'noe vosstanie 1916 goda v Kazakhstane.* Alma-Ata, 1936. Bibliography, pp. 143–149.

Auhagen, Otto. *Die Landwirtschaft in Transkaspien.* Berlin, 1905.

Aziatskaia Rossiia. St. Petersburg, 1914. 3 vols. and atlas.

Barrett, R. J. *Russia's New Era.* London, 1908.

Bartol'd, V. V. *Istoriia kul'turnoi zhizni Turkestana.* Leningrad, 1927.

Belotskii, M. *Kirgizskaia respublika; populyarnyi ocherk.* Moscow, 1936.

Benzing, Johannes. "Das turkestanische volk im Kampf um seine Selbständigkeit. I. Von der russischen Eroberung bis zum Sturz des Zarentums," *Die Welt des Islams*, XIX (Dec., 1937), 94–137.

Biddulph, C. E. *Four Months in Persia and a Visit to Transcaspia.* London, 1892.

Blond, Kasper. *Ein unbekannter Krieg. Erlebnisse eines Arztes wahrend des Weltkrieges.* Vienna-Leipzig, 1931.

Bobrovnikov, N. A. "Russko-tuzemnaia uchilishcha, mekteby i medresy Srednei Azii," *ZhMNP*, XLV (1913), 189–241; XLVI (1913), 49–84.

Boulger, Demetrius C. *England and Russia in Central Asia*. London, 1879. 2 vols.

Brainin, S. *Vosstanie kazakhov Semirech'ia v 1916 godu*. Alma-Ata, 1936.

Brändstrom, Elsa. *Bland krigsfångar i Ryssland och Sibirien; 1919–1920*. Stockholm, 1921. An English translation: *Among Prisoners of War in Russia and Siberia*. London, 1929.

Brodovskii, M. I. "Ocherk proizvodstva khlopka v Srednei Azii," *Sredniaia Aziia, Almanakh, Tashkent*, Feb., 1910.

Brun, Alf H. *Troublous Times; Experiences in Bolshevik Russia and Turkestan*. London, 1931.

Burnaby, Frederick G. *A Ride to Khiva; Travels and Adventures in Central Asia*. London, 1877.

Burov, N. A. "Istoricheskaia spravka o vremeni osnovaniia Tashkentskoi Publichnoi (nyne Sredne-Az. Gosud.) Biblioteki," in *V. V. Bartol'du*, Tashkent, 1927. Pp. 122–124.

Caroe, Olaf. *Soviet Empire; The Turks of Central Asia and Stalinism*. London, 1953.

Charykov, N. V. *Glimpses of High Politics; Through War and Peace, 1855–1929*. New York, 1931.

Chirkin, G. F. "Proektiruemyia sibirskie zheleznyie dorogi i ikh kolonizatsionnoe znachenie," *Voprosy Kolonizatsii*, no. 6 (1910), 27–45.

Coates, W. P., and Zelda K. Coates. *Soviets in Central Asia*. London, 1955.

Cobbold, Ralph P. *Innermost Asia; Travel and Sport in the Pamirs*. London, 1900.

Curzon, George N. *Russia in Central Asia in 1889; and the Anglo-Russian Question*. London, 1889.

Cressey, George B. *Asia's Lands and Peoples*. New York, 1944.

Dmitriev-Mamonov, A. I. *Putevoditel' po Turkestanu i Sredne-Aziatskoi zheleznoi dorogi*. . . . St. Petersburg, 1903.

Dobrosmyslov, A. I. *Tashkent v proshlom i nastoiashchem. Istoricheskii ocherk*. Tashkent, 1911–1912.

Dobson, George. *Russia's Railway Advance into Central Asia; Notes of a Journey from St. Petersburg to Samarkand*. London, 1890.

Drage, Geoffrey. *Russian Affairs*. London, 1904.

"Dzhizakskoe vosstanie 1916 g.," *Krasnyi Arkhiv*, LX (1933), 60–91.

"Enquêtes sur les vakoufs du Turkestan," *Revue du Monde Musulman*, XIII:2 (1911), 276–311.

Fedorov, G. P. "Moia sluzhba v Turkestanskom krae (1870–1906 g.)," *Istoricheskii Vestnik*, CXXXIII (1913), 786–812; CXXXIV (1913), 33–55, 437–467, 860–893.

Filippov, S. T. "Bezzastenchivyi grabezh (po sledam karatel'noi ekspeditsii generala Madridova)," *Turkmenovedenie*, IV:11 (1930), 19–21.

———. "Karatel'naia ekspeditsiia generala Madridova," *Turkmenovedenie*, IV:6–7 (1930), 17–20.

Frideriks, N. "Turkestan i ego reformy. Iz zapisok ochevidtsa," *Vestnik Evropy,* VII:6 (1869), 691–712.
Gafurov, B. G. *Istoriia tadzhikskogo naroda v kratkom izlozhenii.* Vol. I. Moscow, 1949; 2d ed., 1955.
Geins, A. K. *Sobranie literaturnykh trudov.* St. Petersburg, 1897–1898. 3 vols. Includes his *Dnevnik 1865 goda: Puteshestviia vo Kirgizskim stepiam* and his *Dnevnik 1866 goda: Puteshestviia v Turkestan.*
Girs (Giers), F. K. *Otchet revizuiushchago, po Vysochaishemu poveleniiu, Turkestansii krai, Tainago Sovetnika Girsa.* [St. Petersburg, 1883.]
Graham, Stephen. *Through Russian Central Asia.* New York, 1916.
Gramenitskii, S. M. *Polozhenie inorodcheskago obrazovaniia v Syr-Dar'inskoi oblasti.* Tashkent, 1916.
"Gubernator v roli propovednika Korana," *Krasnyi Arkhiv,* LXXV (1936), 188–191.
Hayit, Baymirza. *Die nationalen Regierungen von Kokand (Choquand) und der Alasch Orda.* Münster, 1950.
——. *Turkestan im XX Jahrhundert.* Darmstadt, 1956.
Hoetzsch, Otto. "Russisch-Turkestan und die Tendenzen der heutigen russischen Kolonialpolitik," *Schmollers Jahrbuch,* XXXVII (1913), 903–941, 1427–1473.
Hudson, Alfred E. *Kazak Social Structure.* Yale University Publications in Anthropology, New Haven, Conn., no. 20 (1938), 109.
Iakunin, A. F. "Revoliutsiia 1905–1907 gg. v Kazakhstane," in *Revoliutsiia 1905–1907 gg. v natsional'nykh raionakh Rossii. Sbornik statei.* Moscow, 1955. Pp. 661–714.
Ignat'ev, N. P. *Komissiia dlia razsmotreniia predstavlennago revizovavshim Turkestanskii krai, Tainym Sovetnikom Girsom, proekta polozheniia ob ustroistve upravleniia v oznachennom krae. . . . Protokol zasedanii. . . .* [St. Petersburg, 1884.]
Ishanov, A. I. *Sozdanie Bukharskoi narodnoi sovetskoi respubliki (1920–1924 gg.).* Tashkent, 1955.
Istoriia Kazakhskoi SSR s drevneishikh vremen do nashikh dnei. Edited by M. Abdykalykov and A. Pankratova. Alma-Ata, 1943.
Istoriia Kazakhskoi SSR. Vol. I. Alma-Ata, 1957. From early times to 1917.
Istoriia narodov Uzbekistana. . . . Vol. I. Tashkent, 1950. Vol. II. Tashkent, 1947. From early times to 1917.
Istoriia Uzbekskoi SSR. Vol. I, part 1. Tashkent, 1955. Vol. I, part 2. Tashkent, 1956.
Istoriia SSSR. Edited by M. V. Nechkina. Vol. II. Moscow, 1949; 2d ed., 1954.
Iushkov, S. V. *Istoriia gosudarstva i prava SSSR.* Part 1. 3d ed. Moscow, 1950.
Iuvachev, I. P. "Kurban-Dzhan-datkha, Kara-kirgizskaia tsaritsa Alaia," *Istoricheskii Vestnik,* CX (1907), 954–980.

James, F. *Faraway Campaign*. London, 1934.

Junge, Reinhard. *Das Problem der Europäisierung orientalischer Wirtschaft dargestellt an den Verhältnissen der Sozialwirtschaft von Russisch-Turkestan*. Weimar, 1915.

Kary-Niiazov, T. N. *Ocherki istorii kul'tury sovetskogo Uzbekistana*. Moscow, 1955.

Kastal'skii, B. N. "Istoriko-geograficheskii obzor Surkhanskoi i Shirabadskoi dolin," *Vestnik Irrigatsii*, Tashkent (1930), no. 2, pp. 64–88; no. 3, pp. 3–19; no. 4, pp. 3–21.

Kaufmanskii sbornik. Edited by N. P. Ostroumov. Moscow, 1910. A collection of articles commemorating the twenty-fifth anniversary of Von Kaufman's death.

Kolarz, Walter. *Russia and her Colonies*. London, 1953.

Kostenko, L. F. *Sredniaia Aziia i vodvorenie v nei russkoi grazhdanstvennosti*. St. Petersburg, 1871.

Kovalev, P. A. "Narodnye volneniia i vosstaniia v uzbekskikh i tadzhikskikh raionakh Turkestana (v iiule-avguste 1916 goda)," *SAGU, Trudy*, n.s., 11(78), Istoricheskie nauki (1956), 71–104.

Krist, Gustav. *Pascholl plenny!* Vienna, 1936. An English translation: *Prisoner in the Forbidden Land*. London, 1938.

Krivoshein, A. V. *Zapiska glavnoupravliaiushchago zemledeliem i zemleustroistvom o poezdke v Turkestanskii krai v 1912 godu*. St. Petersburg, 1912.

Kuropatkin, A. N. "Vosstanie 1916 g. v Srednei Azii," *Krasnyi Arkhiv*, XXXIV (1929), 39–94. Diary, August, 1916–February, 1917.

———. "Iz dnevnika A. N. Kuropatkina s 6 marta–15 maia 1917 g.," *Krasnyi Arkhiv*, XX (1927), 56–77.

Lansdell, Henry. *Russian Central Asia, Including Kuldja, Bukhara, Khiva, and Merv*. London–New York, 1885. 2 vols.

Lebed', A., and B. Iakovlev. *Transportnoe znachenie gidrotekhnicheskikh sooruzhenii SSSR*. Munich: Institut po izucheniiu istorii i kul'tury SSSR (Issledovaniia i materialy, ser. 1, no. 14), 1954.

Liashchenko, Peter. *History of the National Economy of Russia to the 1917 Revolution*. New York, 1949.

Lorimer, Frank. *The Population of the Soviet Union; History and Prospects*. Geneva, 1946.

Lutskii, E. A. *Istoriia SSSR, 1861–1917*. Moscow, 1956.

MacGahan, Januarius A. *Campaigning on the Oxus and the Fall of Khiva*. New York, 1874.

Majerczak, R. "Kaufmanskii Sbornik," *Revue du Monde Musulman*, XXVI (1914), 162–196.

Maksheev, A. I. *Istoricheskii obzor Turkestana i nastupatel'nogo dvizheniia v nego russkikh*. St. Petersburg, 1890.

Maksimovich, K. K. [Report to Tsar Nicholas II concerning revolutionary disturbances in Turkestan], in *Revoliutsiia 1905 g. i samoderzhavie.* Moscow-Leningrad, 1928.

Mandel, William. *The Soviet Far East and Central Asia.* New York, 1944.

Marvin, Charles. *The Eye-witnesses' Account of the Disastrous Russian Campaign against the Akhal Tekke Turcomans, Describing the March Across the Burning Desert, the Storming of Dengeel Tepe, and the Disastrous Retreat to the Caspian.* London, 1880.

———. *The Russians at Merv and Herat and Their Power of Invading India.* London, 1883.

Masal'skii, V. I. "Rural Industries and Forestry of Turkestan," in *The Industries of Russia.* St. Petersburg, 1893. Pp. 444–471.

———. *Turkestanskii krai.* St. Petersburg, 1913. In *Rossiia, polnoe geograficheskoe opisanie nashego otechestva.* Edited by V. P. Semenov-Tian-Shanskii. Vol. XIX.

Materialy ob'edinennoi nauchnoi sessii, posviashchennoi istorii Srednei Azii i Kazakhstana v dooktiabr'skii period. Tashkent: Akademiia nauk Uzbekskoi SSR, 1955.

Mel'kumov, A. *Materialy revoliutsionnogo dvizheniia v Turkmenii v 1904–1919 gg.* Tashkent, 1924.

Middendorf, A. T. *Einblikke in das Fergana-Thal.* St. Petersburg, 1881.

Mirov, N. T. *Geography of Russia.* New York, 1951.

Mustafin, M. "Nikolai Ivanovich Grodekov, 1883–1913 gg. Vospominaniia i zametki," *Istoricheskii Vestnik,* CXLII (1915), 141–166.

Nazarov, P. S. *Hunted Through Central Asia.* London, 1932.

Nechkina, M. V. "K voprosu o formule 'naimen'shee zlo' (pis'mo v redaktsiiu)," *Voprosy Istorii,* April, 1951, pp. 44–47.

Oktay, A. "O molodykh godakh i o politicheskoi deiatel'nosti Mustafa Beia Chokai ogly," *Türkeli* (Munich), no. 4 (1951), 11–16.

———. "Turkistan'da Cedid Matbuati," *Türkistan* (Istanbul), I:5 (Aug., 1953), 19–24; I:6 (Sept., 1953), 15–18.

Olzscha, Reiner and Georg Cleinow. *Turkestan, die politisch-historischen und wirtschaftlichen Probleme Zentralasiens.* Leipzig, 19

Ostroumov, N. P. *Konstantin Petrovich fon-Kaufman, ustroitel' Turkestanskago kraia. Lichnyia vospominaniia. K istorii narodnago obrazovaniia Turkestanskom krae.* Tashkent, 1899.

———. *Sarty. Etnograficheskie materialy.* 2d ed. Tashkent, 1896.

Palen (Pahlen), K. K. "Erinnerungen." [Reminiscences of senatorial inspection in Turkestan 1908–1909.] Written abroad in 1920. Unpublished.

———. *Otchet po revizii Turkestanskogo kraia, proizvedennoi po Vysochaishemu poveleniiu. . . .* St. Petersburg, 1909–1910. 19 vols. Official report of Palen's inspection in Turkestan. The following volumes have been consulted: *Gornoe delo; Gorodskoe upravlenie; Kraevoe upravlenie.*

Pankratova, A. M. *Istoriia SSSR.* Vol. II. Moscow, 1948.

Piaskovskii, A. V. "Revoliutsiia 1905–1907 gg. v Turkestane," in *Revoliutsiia 1905–1907 gg. v natsional'nykh raionakh Rossii. Sbornik statei.* Moscow, 1955. Pp. 557–660.

Radzhabov, S. A. *Rol' velikogo russkogo naroda v istoricheskikh sud'bakh narodov Srednei Azii.* Tashkent, 1955.

Ryskulov, T. R. *Kirgizstan.* Moscow, 1929.

———. *Vosstanie 1916 goda v Kirgizstane. Dokumenty i materialy.* Moscow, 1937.

———. "Vosstanie v Srednei Azii v 1916 g.," *Bor'ba Klassov,* VI:6 (1936), 1–15.

Safarov, G. *Kolonial'naia revoliutsiia: opyt Turkestana.* Moscow, 1921.

Schakir (Çagatay), Tahir. *Baumwollwirtschaft Turkestans.* Berlin, 1934.

Schuyler, Eugene. *Turkistan. Notes of a journey in Russian Turkistan, Khokand, Bukhara and Kuldja.* London, 1876. 2 vols.

Semenov, A. A. "Ocherk pozemel'no-podatnogo i nalogovogo ustroistva b. Bukharskogo khanstva," *SAGU, Trudy,* ser. 2, Orientalia, Fasc. 1 (1929).

Seng-zade, "K 30 letiiu vosstanie 1898 goda," in *Revoliutsiia v Srednei Azii, Sbornik.* Tashkent, 1928. Vol. I, pp. 41–58.

Sharova, P. N. "Pereselencheskaia politika tsarizma v Srednei Azii," *Istoricheskie Zapiski,* VIII (1940), 3–36.

———. "Pereselencheskaia politika tsarizma v Srednei Azii v 1906–1916 gg.," *Istorik-Marksist,* LXXXII (1940), 90–102.

Shcheglov, I. V. *Khronologicheskii perechen' vazhneishikh dannykh iz istorii Sibiri, 1032–1882 gg.* Irkutsk, 1883.

Shestakov, A. V. "20-letie vosstanie v Srednei Azii (1916–1936)," *Revoliutsiia i natsional'nosti,* no. 9 (1936), 38–44.

———. "Vosstanie v Srednei Azii v 1916 g. (k desiati-letiiu sobytii)," *Istorik-Marksist,* II (1926), 84–114.

Shkapskii, O. A. "Kirgizy-krest'iane (iz zhizni Semirech'ia)," *IIRGO,* XLI (1905), 765–778.

———. "Nekotoryia dannyia dlia osveshcheniia kirgizkogo voprosa," *Russkaia Mysl',* XVIII (1897), no. 6, pp. 44–58; no. 7, pp. 31–48.

Shteinberg, E. L. *Ocherki istorii Turkmenii.* Moscow, 1934.

Simonov, A. V. "Vosstanie protiv tsarizma v Samarkande v 1868 godu," *TUGU,* n.s., no. 1 (1940), 10–16.

Smeta dokhodov, raskhodov i spetsial'nykh sredstv Pereselencheskago upravleniia Glavnago upravleniia zeml. i zeml. na god 1912. St. Petersburg, 1911.

Sokol, Edward D. *The Revolt of 1916 in Russian Central Asia.* Baltimore, 1954.

Stählin, Karl. *Russisch Turkestan gestern und heute.* Königsberg-Berlin, 1935.

Stolypin, P. A. *Poezdka v Sibir' i Povolzh'e (Zapiska. P. A. Stolypina i A. V. Krivosheina).* St. Petersburg, 1911. A German translation: *Die Kolonisation Sibiriens. Eine Denkschrift.* Berlin, 1912. Omits part concerning Volga region.

Suslov, S. P. *Fizicheskaia geografiia SSSR. Aziatskaia chast'.* 2d ed. Moscow, 1954.

Taimanov, G. T. *Razvitie sovetskoi gosudarstvennosti v Kazakhstane.* Moscow, 1956.

Terent'ev, M. A. *Istoriia zavoevaniia Srednei Azii.* St. Petersburg, 1906. 4 vols.

Togan, A. Zeki Velidi. *Bugünkü Türkili (Turkistan) ve yakın tarihi.* Cilt I, Bati ve Kuzey Turkistan. Istanbul, 1942–1947. A German translation, unpublished, by Wolfram Eberhard.

Tolqun, I. "Madali Eschan (1856–1898)," *Millij Turkestan* (Munich), no. 80–81 B (Aug.–Nov., 1952), 25–28.

T-ov, S. "Andizhanskoe vozstanie i ego prichiny," *Istoricheskii Vestnik,* CXII (1908), 659–670.

Treadgold, Donald W. *The Great Siberian Migration; Government and Peasant in Resettlement from Emancipation to the First World War.* Princeton, N. J., 1957.

Uel's, A. "K voprosu o vosstanii 1916 g. v Khodzhente," *Revoliutsionnyi Vostok,* no. 4 (1936), 78–84.

Vetter, E. K. "Rospis' stat'iam i zametkam po istorii i arkheologii Srednei Azii, pomeshchennym v gazete Turkestanskie Vedomosti za vremia ee sushchestvovanii (28 aprelia 1870–15 dekabria 1917)," in *V. V. Bartol'du,* Tashkent, 1927. Pp. 479–531.

Voeikov (Woeikoff), A. I. *Le Turkestan Russe.* Paris, 1914.

Voina v peskakh; materialy po istorii grazhdanskoi voiny k XII tomu Grazhdanskaia voina v Srednei Azii. Leningrad, 1935.

Von Kaufman, K. P. *Proekt vsepoddaneishago otcheta general-ad'iutanta K. P. fon-Kaufman 1-go po grazhdanskomu upravleniiu i ustroistvu v oblastiakh Turkestanskogo general-gubernatorstva, 7 noiabria 1867–25 marta 1881 gg.* St. Petersburg, 1885.

Von Mende, Gerhard. *Der nationale Kampf der Russland-türken. Ein Beitrag zur nationalen Frage in der Sovetunion.* Berlin, 1936.

———. *Studien zur Kolonisation in der Sovetunion.* Ost-Europa Institut (Quellen und Studien, Abteilung Wirtschaft, n.s., no. 11), 1933.

Von Schwarz, Franz Xaver. *Turkestan, die Wiege der indogermanischen Völker. Nach fünfzehnjahrigen Aufenthalt in Turkestan. . . .* Freiburg, 1900.

V. V. Bartol'du. Turkestanskiia druz'ia, ucheniki i pochitateli. SAGU, Vostochnyi fakul'tet. Tashkent, 1927.

Willfort, Fritz. *Turkestanisches Tagebuch; sechs Jahre in Russisch-Zen-tralasien.* Vienna, 1930.

Zenkovsky, *"Kulturkampf* in Pre-revolutionary Central Asia," *American Slavic and East European Review,* XIV (1955), 15–41.

Zhmuida, V. B. *Ashkhabad.* Moscow, 1957.

Zorin, A. "Iz istorii vosstaniia kirgizov i kazakhov v 1916 g.," *Bor'ba Klassov,* II:7–8 (1932), 128–139.

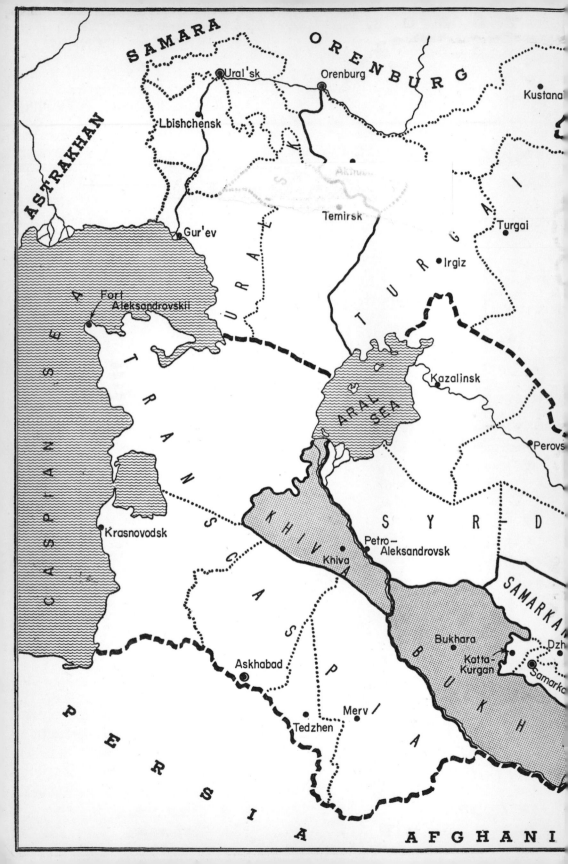